SECOND EDIT

NOW WITH "VALUES ELICITA
"THE SIX SITUATIONS OF FEEDBACK

CHIEF OF ANY THING

~~WHY~~ WHEREFORE RELAXED-PRODUCTIVE
LEADERSHIP MAKES A BETTER WORLD

MICHAEL PORTZ & CHRISTIAN KOHLHOF

FOREWORD BY MARK WEINBERG

★ ★ ★ ★ ★ **From the practice for the practice**

The title CoA may be somewhat confusing, but somehow each of us is the boss of something. And that's what makes this book so interesting. The two authors draw on their professional and private experience in a very entertaining and appealing way. I can recommend this book to any prospective or practicing boss. "Management is about People," and "When it comes to leadership, the focus is on people." Conclusion: great!

RENE SCHRADER-BOELSCHE

★ ★ ★ ★ ★ **Take you further ...**

Coming from an industry that traditionally DOES NOT deal with such topics (a medical background), this book has exceeded my expectations. Learning mechanisms and strategies without needing prior experience, yet identifying with the authors. The presentation is personal and the whole book is entertaining. I haven't read anything that was so much fun, yet enriching in a long time.

JOST KAUFMANN

★ **Kindergarten book**

Title interesting, topics even more interesting according to the table of contents ... but then written in a substance-free dialogue style. Zero added value.

MARK PFEFFER

For Hella, Magdalena, Charlotte, and for all the other teachers
I have and have been allowed to have in my life.
Thank you very much.

Christian Kohlhof

Our special thanks go to the following wonderful people:

Leonie Schulze Bölling in Germany: We think it's fabulous how you've brought the transcripts of our casual podcast conversations up to the literary level of writing. Without you, this book would not be what it is.

Mark Weinberg in the USA: Thank you for generously sharing your 'presidential' English writing expertise with us.

Catherine Anabel White in Texas, USA, Deniz Aksu in Turkey and Germany, and Mick Swiney in the USA: Thank you for your great support with the German-English translation and for doing a glorious job editing.

Andy Haines and Leon Cayford of the Origami agency in New Zealand, and Jade Robertson: Thank you for the magic of your designs and illustrations that keep making us shine.

Karthigeyan Vijayakumar and Zakira Vijayakumar in India: Thank you for the excellent typesetting with which you brought us to the finish line, both for the German and the English editions.

Michael Asshauer and Paula Lotte Thurm: Thank you for your inspiration and your tips for our podcast.

Sally Jackson, and everyone involved in Vodafone's Global Leadership Program, where I was introduced to many of the concepts included in this book.

We thank you all from the bottom of our heart for making this book a reality.

Michael & Christian

English edition first printed February 2021.
German edition first printed October 2020.
All rights reserved. Copyright © 2020 by Michael Portz & Christian Kohlhof
Website: coa.academy

CoA
ACADEMY™

In order to achieve even more in a relaxed way, we will send you all insights and tools from this book and beyond summarized as a regular newsletter. **Subscribe now on https://CoA.Academy or with the QR code on the right.**

PREFACE FROM AN ENGLISH EDITOR

When Michael and Christian first told me about this book and asked if I might be willing to help with the English edition, I was leery. Even though I learned some important skills during my more than 10 years at the side of Ronald Reagan, who was rightly known as "The Great Communicator," and even as a published author myself, I was intimidated by the prospect of getting involved with what I thought was a book about how to run a successful business and make money. To the eternal regret of my wife, that is not an area in which I have shown any expertise at all!

Michael and Christian said I was wrong to think of their book in such terms, and, to their credit, pressed me to read the first chapter. I did, and that's all it took. I quickly realized this book is not about schemes for profitability, but rather about how to lead and manage people Purposefully in a work environment. While ultimately the Purpose of doing so in a business is to maximize profitability—after all, businesses that do not make money cannot exist for long—the lessons Michael and Christian seek to impart here are much more important and intriguing. Indeed, what can be learned from this book goes well beyond a mere profit and loss statement.

This book comes from a remarkable series of podcasts Michael and Christian conducted over the span of a year, during which they exchanged interesting, often amusing, personal anecdotes that give a glimpse into who they are. And, more importantly, they share views, experiences, and practical advice on how one builds and develops a team of women and men who can work successfully to achieve a goal. Simply put, this is a book about people, not profits. Because, as Michael and Christian show us, at the end of the day, people are what make an enterprise succeed.

Intentionally, this book follows the format of a conversation. Indeed, it is based on a computer-generated translation of Michael and Christian's podcast conversations from German to English. My mission was to give that translation a human touch, taking it from a technically accurate artificial intelligence product to something that could be read, understood, and appreciated by an English-speaking audience, while maintaining the tone and tenor of the original conversations. My goal was to maintain the authenticity of Michael and Christian's voices, while removing anything "clunky" from the translation.

Whether I succeeded is up to you, the reader. If you're looking for a book to give you a shortcut to getting rich, this is not the book for you. Rather, the authors and I hope you will find this an insightful, candid, and practically applicable guide to how to create, manage, and motivate teams to achieve maximum success from the perspective of two men who have "been there and done that" in the real world.

Mark Weinberg
November 2020
Former special advisor and press secretary to President Ronald Reagan

CONTENTS

FOREWORD

When Michael, Christian and I crossed paths, I thought it was a happy coincidence. The two of them told me about their book project on relaxed productivity and Purpose-driven leadership. I told them that I was also writing a book and that, as an innovation consultant, I was very familiar with their topics. Far too many people complain about a lack of motivation on the job, a lack of leadership skills on the part of their superiors, and, as a result, a declining willingness to perform, right up to dismissal. Many simply lack Purpose in what they do.

I started listening to the *Chief of Anything* podcast and understood that it was not just a coincidence. Since the end of 2019, I have been following my own Purpose, my own personal Vision. The more episodes that I listened to from Christian and Michael, the clearer it became to me that our encounter was the logical consequence of our striving to fulfill our every Purpose.

When they asked me if I wanted to support them in their book project, I immediately agreed. "Of course," I thought. There could hardly be a better opportunity to pursue my passion for writing and coaching-related topics. Besides, I could learn a lot more with regard to business leadership. The NLP toolbox is new to me as well, and the experience of two such successful leaders is worth its weight in gold. I really enjoyed working with them and the discussions we shared.

Maybe you'll feel the same way as I do when reading this book. Some of my thoughts, as an unbiased reader and listener, I have summarized at the end of each chapter. It serves to bring out the quintessence of what Michael and Christian convey and to take a broader perspective. I hope it will give you food for thought so you can digest and process the concepts discussed.

I wish you lots of fun and a relaxed learning experience.

Leonie Schulze Bölling

INTRODUCTION

Imagine you are standing at the gates of Heaven. Many of your friends are waiting there for you. "Well, finally, there you are," they say excitedly when they first see you, and ask almost in unison, "How was your vacation?" You're confused and reply, "What do you think? What vacation are you talking about?" They say, "Well, you were just on Earth. You really earned that vacation. Now you have to play the harp with us up here for another thousand years, until you are allowed to go back to the world for a human life. And before we start playing the harp right away, tell us, How was it? How did you live your life?"

What is your answer to this question? How have you led your life?

We are Christian Kohlhof and Michael Portz, and our Purpose is to help you find a simple and satisfying answer to this question. We have both experienced a lot and learned a lot — including that we will never stop learning.

Some would call us successful managers or entrepreneurs, maybe even successful people. If this is true, one reason may be that we have studied the qualities of great leadership over the past 20 years. On our journey, we have taken many severe hits, learning a lot of humility and gratitude. We have had many companions along the way. Some made it easier for us, some more difficult. Each one helped us to get to the point where we are today. For this we express our deep gratitude to all of them.

To remind ourselves of our Purpose in life and what we want to achieve, we have compiled this collection of methods, experience, knowledge, and ignorance. What we have learned, some of it the hard way, we gladly share with everyone who is interested and who can take it further.

Please understand this book as the personal empirical science of two entrepreneurs who have experienced, learned, and been through quite a bit and are happy to share their insights (and not as a scientific treatise on employee management).

The leadership methods and techniques we present have proven to be of Value to us. Not only do we hope they will make your life easier, we hope they will make it more fulfilling for you personally, professionally, and everywhere in between, so you can become a really good boss in life, in your team and in your company.

After many years of unnecessary stress, we both prefer to follow the principle of relaxed productivity today. We still have big goals and ambitions and intend to achieve them easily and happily. In this book we will explain how we make that happen.

The Purpose of our collaboration is to make the working world easier and better for everyone involved. We want to contribute in turning even more companies into positive places where people enjoy working together to achieve common goals, and a happy and successful life for all parties. If we can make your journey a little bit more relaxed and productive and help you to take a step forward in your life, then we have fulfilled our Purpose.

For us, this book is a great project of the heart, for which we have tremendous respect. To create this project in a relaxed way, we did what we do best: telling each other about our experiences. Over the last year, we have recorded and published 60 podcasts on the topic of leadership, and used them to produce *Chief of Anything* as a book. Since we didn't want to write the ten thousandth uptight and exhausting hunk of a guidebook, we kept the dialogue format to keep things light, effective, and most importantly, refreshing. We hope you like it, too, and that it will perhaps bring a smile to your face every now and then.

For us, all people are of equal Value, regardless of gender, age, ethnic origin, and all other differences. That's why we like to alternate between the masculine, feminine, and neuter gender instead of listing all grammatical genders every time. With this form of writing, we emphasize how important diversity is to us, regardless of grammatical correctness.

We welcome honest feedback. Just let us know via your preferred channel. We can be reached on most digital or analog channels.

We ourselves have come to understand the game-changing secret about leadership quite late. We wish you to internalize it sooner so that everything else will be even easier for you. That is why we start the first section with *guiding myself*. Once I comprehend who I am, how I function, and how unique I am, I understand the benefits of adjusting my behavior and charisma to match any kind of situation and interaction. This way, I can be a positive influence on others and lead them more successfully, whether that be as an entrepreneur, as a boss, as a partner, as a friend, or as a father or mother. The realization that happiness and success begin with ourselves was a mind-blowing moment for both of us. My head and what happens inside of it is the linchpin for success or failure in life.

The second section is devoted to the challenge of *leading others*. Here, we show the Value and importance behind the diversity of people and their personalities and how differently we all think, feel, see and hear. There are very cool methods that dive into understanding these differences and dealing with them better in everyday life. These tools help me to appreciate other people and their strengths, in particular those that are complementary to my own.

In the third section we talk about how to *lead a team*. Whether a group of people becomes a successful team or not is determined by trust, a common Vision, and the alignment of Values. Only when the 'wherefore' is clear and everyone has agreed on it can we achieve great things. We will, therefore, talk a lot about Purpose and the motives behind companies and individuals.

In the fourth and last section, we come to the supreme discipline of *leading companies and organizations*. We look at the importance of culture and how to consciously design, establish, and maintain a corporate culture. We also discuss how making money is Purposeful.

Since we know what successful leadership means, we find it easier to follow, especially when we are being led well. This also helps us on the way to relaxed productivity.

We wrote this book in 2020, just as the Coronavirus pandemic was pushing us all to change our world and ourselves differently and faster than we had anticipated.

We are often asked what impact and influence these changes have on leadership. Our hypothesis is that the principles of successful leadership will continue to exist in the world of *remote work.* Only the channels in which we live and exercise leadership are changing and becoming digitalized faster than we thought. In this new world, we operate with a lot of curiosity and willingness to experiment. We continue to learn and confidently face the challenge of mastering this situation with relaxed productivity.

One more thing: each of us has a unique path through life and each of us has a unique experience of life. We are not only to read about life, we are free to try it out.

What we have learned and shared here may work for you or it may not. The responsibility for you, your life, your company and your team lies with just one person: you!

We are happy about this book and grateful to all of our companions, fellow travelers, mentors, and shadow figures from whom we learned all of this.

Have fun reading and doing!

Christian Kohlhof and Michael Portz

1.

LEADING MYSELF

"KNOW THYSELF"

— SUN TZU, 500 B.C.

SELF-FULFILLING PROPHECIES

STORIES THAT I TELL MYSELF

Christian: Let's talk about stories.

Michael: Oh, beautiful.

Christian: About stories that we tell ourselves. I remember a story from my youth very well. At school, I was quite good at math. That's why many teachers and my parents said to me, "Since you're good at math, you must be bad at sports and languages. Because you are either good at one or the other." But never in both disciplines at the same time. I actually believed that and made that into my own story. So, I was the one who studied physics, even theoretical physics. Because I didn't need to be good at sports and it was enough to speak English. Other languages were not required. At some point, I eventually realized that I'm quite good at languages and, once I found the right sport for me, that I'm quite good at sports, too. In other words, I told myself a story about myself that influenced my life very much and wasn't right at all. The story was not true.

Michael: How do I know if a story is true?

Christian: It is true when I believe it to be true.

Michael: Ah, right.

Christian: It was like that in my case. If I tell myself all the time, "Wow, I'm so bad at sports," then it becomes a *self–fulfilling prophecy*.[1] If, on the other hand, I say to myself, "Hey, I'm good at languages, I just haven't learned enough in the last few years," then maybe I can really step on the gas and become a great language speaker.

Michael: That brings to mind the concept of *self-limiting belief*, or *self-limiting decision*. This is the decision that creates such a limitation in our lives. It

---

1   A self-fulfilling prophecy is a prediction that causes its fulfillment. More about this: https://www.britannica.com/topic/self-fulfilling-prophecy.

means that at an earlier point in your life, perhaps even unconsciously, you actively chose not to be so good at languages or sports.

Christian: Yes. Because there are the children who are good at languages, the children who are good at sports, and those who are good at math. It is part of history that there are only these categories. So it's either-or. I am either good at one or the other. Now I know that I can be as good as I want to be at anything.

Michael: You know what comes to my mind? The definition of *or* and *xor* from computer science. *Or* allows both, the command before and after. *Xor* is exclusive, meaning that a decision is automatically made, an *exclusive or*. Both cannot exist at the same time.

Christian: So I am either good at sports and in languages *xor* at math.

Michael: Well, that's not necessarily so bad. How did you deal with it? How has that expressed itself in your life?

Christian: It actually expressed itself quite well. I studied physics and theoretical physics, because this was as far away from languages and sports as I could get. I was convinced of that; I believed that. It was quite exhausting at times, because I couldn't shake the feeling, and would think to myself, "Hey, there's something else in me that I would like to try, something that appeals to me."

Michael: What happened then?

Christian: Then I distanced myself more and more from pure mathematics and pure physics and sought more intensive contact with people and language. I have been doing a lot more sports and I really enjoy it.

Michael: That means you made a different decision at some point. You made the decision to not let this earlier childhood belief stop you?

Christian: Right. I started to tell myself a different story about myself. Namely, the story that I can create everything I want.

Michael: Yeah, very cool. There you were again *at cause*, at the origin and not in the effect. You were not a victim, you were a creator.

Christian: That's the way it is. It is probably relatively well known that people tell themselves stories, isn't it?

Michael: Sure, I've got a few of those.

Christian: Why don't you tell a story that you have told yourself?

Michael: I liked to tell myself the story that I can't sing well.

Christian: Oh!

Michael: Yes. I was always the boy in the choir who played the piano and didn't sing. So I never sang. That became my story: "I can't sing. Instead, I can play the piano."

Christian: Yes. Because you can either play piano *or* sing.

Michael: Exactly. It had manifested itself in me. I didn't get much feedback on my singing for four years. Then I made a decision. I said to myself, "Michael, you can sing well." I started to get more involved with my singing. I thought about what I had to do to become a good singer. I'm not going to say that I've already arrived there. I've started to do some things differently and have gotten more into it. And at some point, I actually got positive feedback. Someone said to me in astonishment, "You can sing really well." *Move your mind and your body will follow*. That's how it really was with me. It took some time, and I still haven't reached my goal. But I have become much better. I have dissolved this limiting belief system I had. It also only took 20 years [*laughs*]. But what the heck? These are all nice examples about us. In your case, the analytical, like mathematics and physics versus languages and sports. With me, the piano competed against singing. So what does that mean for me as a boss? How can I take advantage of that?

Christian: Now, even as a boss, I can figure out what stories I'm telling myself about myself. You, for example, started telling yourself the this story: "I can sing well." The feedback you got from others might have strengthened that. You also didn't know why people had given you less positive feedback before. Maybe it wasn't because of you, but because of the others. Or because the listeners also had the limiting belief that Michael can either play the piano well or sing well.

Michael: Am I *at cause* or *at effect*? *At cause* means, I take the world as it is. So I take the feedback of others as it is and think about what I do with it, what I radiate, and how I behave. That would be the conclusion of *cause and effect*. I am *at cause* of everything that happens in my life. That means that I am also *at cause* of my ability to sing well. I am also *at cause* of being a good boss. I am *at cause* of being able to lead well. Even though it may take a little more practice, I can and I want to. I am *at cause* and make the decision to be a good boss. This is a decision that I can make as a boss: "I am a good boss."

Christian: Okay, let's take a closer look. The first decision is about wanting to be the boss in the first place. I know many entrepreneurs who say to themselves, "We are all a team and we are all at eye level. I don't want to be the boss at all. Because then things are demanded of me that I do not even want to do. Things that do not fit into my story of myself."

Michael: Yes. I know that from myself in the past and from some of my clients.

Christian: The second decision is to be a good boss. When am I a good boss?

Michael: Good question.

Christian: I am a good boss when I achieve results and retain my employees.

Michael: I knew you were going to say that.

Christian: Did I ever mention that before?

Michael: That's your famous saying inspired by Peter Drucker: "The task of management and leadership is to achieve results and retain employees."

Christian: So when I decide to be a good boss, I decide to get results and to achieve them in such a way that makes employees happy to stay with me.

Michael: And now back to our current topic, the stories I tell myself. [*grins*] I have these stories going on all the time. My auditory-digital channel, my inner voice, is something that I experience very acutely. I actually talk to myself a lot. Please don't tell anyone.

Christian: What do you hear? What happens there?

Michael: I hear many voices. No, actually they're not voices, not different voices. It's just my inner voice that often criticizes me. It's like a constant subtext for everything that happens. Like a subtitle. A separate monologue that goes something like this: "You could have done better" or, "I guess it didn't work out so well." There's a lot of criticism in my head. It's not good. It's exhausting. That's why I've learned how to change my inner voice's tune, to make it positive and actively encourage and support myself. I have learned to affirm myself, that is, to confirm and strengthen myself through my inner voice. I still practice this. Some years ago, I learned that everything starts with the inner voice. The root of evil is in my head. It is that inner voice that is causing me to choose to feel down from time to time. All the crap I often tell myself with my inner voice. Since realizing that, I'm getting ahead much faster in life. If I talk myself into it and confirm to myself that I can and will learn, it is much easier to do so. Of course, I can do some things even better, although every now and then I still get angry with myself when I am not doing something so well. I really feel how I am more and more relaxed with myself over time and accept myself as I am. When I make mistakes, I give myself the positive assurance that I can do even better. *Leading myself*— this is exactly what this first chapter is about.

Christian: Okay, so I say to myself that I want to be a good boss. But I am not a good boss, at least not yet. Not according to my criteria. The voice in my head still says, "You can still get better, you can still work on this." One approach would be to pretend that I'm already a good boss: *Fake it till you make it*.

Michael: I love it.

Christian: Just say, "I am a good boss. And that's why I do this or that now. Let's see what happens." Then I will get feedback. And no matter how this feedback turns out, I have already made the decision to tell myself this story about myself. Because "I am the cause," I tell myself this story about myself. "I am a good boss and I believe in it." Then I will learn the tools that will help me to become what I believe in, because I am attentive and open to improvement.

Michael: There's something else that fascinates me. Let's say that I now make the decision to be a good boss. I also know now that I can be an even better boss. Even better than *good*, which I already am. That means I can learn, develop and improve my boss skills even further. How do I do that now?

Christian: I direct my attention and my senses exactly to being a good boss and to what happens around me. I observe and find out who is a good boss. How does a good boss behave? I continuously tinker with my story, taking certain parts out while adding new parts in. A good boss has weekly meetings with all employees or with each employee individually. A good boss has team meetings, perhaps incorporating a *daily huddle*.[2] In this way, I let my story develop piece by piece. It's easy for me because I know that I want to tell this story.

Michael: What is the best way to start this journey? After I have made the decision that "I am a good boss and I will continue to develop myself in order to be a good boss later on," how can I approach this development? So let's assume that I want to consciously develop as a boss.

Christian: There are people who say to themselves in front of the mirror 20 times every morning, "I am a good boss." That would be one approach.

Michael: Okay. Are there any other methods? I'm thinking of something like 360-degree tools, for example. I mean, where people give each other feedback and then the whole thing is analyzed. Or the one-on-one conversation. I could simply ask my employees, "Tell me, how do you see me as a boss? What do I do well as a boss and what can I do even better?" What other similar methods are there? It took me a long time to become aware of my strengths. My weaknesses were clear to me relatively quickly. It took me longer until I realized which strengths I have. So how can I accelerate this?

Christian: To find your own strengths?

Michael: Yes.

Christian: I once participated in a seminar where each of us wrote down 50 things we are really good at.

Michael: Cool.

---

2   Daily Huddles are daily, often morning, short and pointed meetings on the project status.

Christian: The next day, we continued with fifty things that we enjoyed. When we compared the two lists, we saw that everyone is often really good at the things they enjoy.

Michael: That's clever.

Christian: That has directed my focus to the things I am really good at. I suddenly had a much more positive mindset. Instead of constantly looking at what I'm not so good at, what I'm doing wrong, I suddenly became aware of what I'm really good at. Fifty things that I have been successful with so far and that I can stick with.

Michael: Do I have to be able to do everything well as a boss? That's a rhetorical question, of course. I'm still curious about your answer [*smiles*].

Christian: As a conductor, do I have to master every instrument?

Michael: Good answer, I'll remember that.

Christian: Of course it helps to have some idea. As a conductor, it can't hurt to know how a bassoon or an oboe works or to be able to estimate what a violin can play. In order to really master each instrument, I need to have professionals on my team.

Michael: That means that, in my role as boss, I don't need to be able to play every instrument that I might need?

Christian: Maybe that's true. A conductor is the master of the baton.

Michael: Okay, I see. There are also different specialists among conductors. One is good at conducting Wagner, the other is known for Beethoven.

Christian: Three-four time or four-four time. [*laughs*]

Michael: Applied to the boss thing, for example, I think I'm more the snappy type. I like to get ahead quickly. Sometimes it gets me into trouble. I'm not necessarily the super sensitive type. As a boss, do I have to master the whole range of behavior patterns? Does that help me?

Christian: A certain flexibility in behavior definitely helps. I have also learned a lot about this in the last few years. For example, I have learned a lot about your red energy and how to handle it during our collaboration. As you said, sometimes we clash [*grins*]. At times I wonder, "What's wrong with him now? Where has the harmony suddenly gone?"

Michael: Yes, exactly. We'll talk more about colors and energies later.

Christian: I have learned to deal with it. I am getting better every time. In those moments I also tell myself the story, "I'm good at being flexible."

Michael: *Ultimate behavioral flexibility* — I learned this expression once in a seminar. My first thought was, "What is this bullshit? Another buzzword?" *Ultimate behavioral flexibility.* Now it's becoming increasingly clear to me what that means. To internalize this is damn helpful in a leadership role. It means being able to adapt to other people in a flexible way and to radiate this to the outside world. As a manager, it is important to understand what each and every one of my employees needs so that we can all work well together and ultimately achieve our goals and results. It can be very stressful for me, because it also means sometimes being or behaving differently than I would normally do. It means eliminating carelessness. On the other hand, some things are also easier for me because of it. This whole empathy thing used to be very difficult for me. Now I can do it better. [*pauses*] A nice story we told each other today.

Christian: And that was just a story. Most likely there are thousands of other stories we're telling ourselves, not even including those around us.

Michael: Yes, that's true. There are 7.7 billion people in the world and all of them have their very own story in their head.

The realization of being the cause of everything that happens in my life feels to me like a liberation, a bit like Pippi Longstocking. If what you say is true and I have this power over myself to be able to do anything I want to be able to do and all I have to do is tell myself the right story about myself, it sounds like music to my ears. "I make the world as I like it."[3] At the same time, I also feel an insane weight on my shoulders. Checking if all the stories in my head—all the words and sayings of my inner voice are really true—could be exhausting. If everything I thought I knew until now is not true—it is just a story I took over from my childhood, from my parents or my teachers—does this mean that I have to make a new decision about everything I think and do? I may always question everything I think and do myself. Do I want this or do I not want this?

---

3   Theme Song of TV-series "Pippi Longstocking."

LEADER (NOT VICTIM)

CAUSE AND EFFECT

Christian: We talked about the fact that I can achieve everything I want if I just tell myself the right story. I can simply decide to be a good boss. Now that sounds like I'm *at cause* for the goals I can achieve.

Michael: Yeah, great. So it is. I fully agree. That makes this chapter complete.

Christian: Do you think we can still get some intellectual meat on these bones?

Michael: Phew, that's a lot of red energy. So the question is, who is responsible when I achieve, right?

Christian: Yes. Of course, It's me. I am responsible.

Michael: What if something goes wrong? What if the goal is not achieved? Who is to blame then?

Christian: Others, of course.

Michael: Right! Because the dog ate my homework.

Christian: And then there was this earthquake. The train broke down.

Michael: There was a traffic jam on the highway.

Christian: If I achieve something good, I have done it. If it doesn't work, others are to blame.

Michael: If only I could see it that way. No, I can't see it like that. I might have seen it that way before.

Christian: That means, no matter what happens, I am the cause.

Michael: Yes. I am the cause of everything that happens in my universe. I have a saying about that too: *It appears in life that you either achieve the results that you want or you get the excuses that you make.*

Christian: Either I arrive at my destination or I have an excuse like, "Such a hassle, there were so many things I had to do. I urgently had to create the table of contents, I had to record so many podcasts, and... and... and. And after that, I didn't feel like it anymore."

Michael: Look what happens when I cross out "either" and "the excuses I make" from the sentence. What's left is an absolute killer phrase. Then it just says, *In life I achieve the results I want.* Period. Little mindfuck. [*smiles*]

Christian: So when I write this book and I'm constantly thinking about how much work that means, I get a lot of work.

Michael: Right.

Christian: Then it also feels like a lot of work.

Michael: And if you simply cross out the thought about all the work, then you only get the result that you want: the book.

Christian: And there is no work in between, which I didn't want anyway.

Michael: You don't have it in your head anymore.

Christian: I have not even thought about it.

Michael: Right.

Christian: Now that sounds like relaxed productivity.

Michael: Absolutely. Looks that way, too.

Michael: Cause and effect. I am the cause of everything that happens in my life. Everything is in my hands. This is a basic state of mind.

Christian: We're talking about mindset!

Michael: That's right. What is my basic attitude toward what is happening? Do I choose to be the Michael who blames the dog that ate his homework or the one who blames the traffic jam on the highway? Or, do I choose to be the Michael who achieves his goals? I like the latter version better.

Christian: Will you stop running into traffic jams on the highway?

Michael: Probably not. I just handle it differently. It's nothing new that there are traffic jams. So I leave early. I make sure I reach my destination. If my goal is to be on time and I want to reach that goal, then I know how to take care of it.

Christian: Because you are the expert for yourself. You know how Michael does it, that he gets stuck in traffic jams.

Michael: It's basically just that voice in my head again, explaining to me what my excuse could be. I tell myself, "There was a traffic jam," or "The kids poured cocoa on my pants at breakfast." Blah, blah, blah. I make up the excuses in my head so that I can make them credible later on. Basically I know it's bullshit, total bullshit. I just didn't leave early enough. I could have taken care of it if I had wanted to. That's the truth.

Christian: Do you admit that to yourself?

Michael: More and more often. Let's just say that as I grow older and supposedly wiser, I admit to myself that I take full responsibility for everything that happens in my life. This makes me feel better. Then I know that only I am to blame. As in the agreement I made with my wife about who is at fault. With everything that happens and everything that goes wrong, I know that this year it's my fault. Next year it's all her fault, or it's me again, it doesn't matter. The main thing is that the question of guilt has already been clarified. From there on it's all about the results we achieve together.

Christian: Now there is something that feels negative about *being guilty.* Basically, it is actually simple and non-judgmental. You get what you want. It appears in your life. Is that guilt or your achievement? Actually, it is completely irrelevant. It just is. I have adopted this way of thinking for myself.

Michael: The word *responsible* means *I have the ability to respond*. So when I say, "I am responsible," I am aware that I have the ability to respond to something. So I can do something to achieve a different result. I am *response-able, responsible*. If I am not *response-able*, then I am only a subject, a victim, of something that happens in the world, something that is someone else's fault. Then I have no control, no response-ability. My friends would then all be stupid, because, after all, they treat me like this and that. At work, everything would be unfair because here, too, the others do something wrong. Where does that get me in life? Nowhere. From the moment I recognize my response-ability and make the decision to transform the situation and to change something, then I move forward. If I take it upon myself, I can get anywhere. Then I'm the leader of my life. I'm the *chief* of my life.

Christian: The world around us often mirrors our behavior. When I walk through the streets and think, "All the drivers who honk at me are dumb bastards," it has much more to do with me than with the drivers. After all, all these drivers most likely drive every day exactly as they are driving when I see them. Some in this direction, others in the opposite direction. If now, suddenly, the whole world is full of car-driving morons, it is very likely that I am the only moron.

Michael: The dangerous thing is that I radiate what I think and how I feel, consciously and unconsciously. Let's assume that I consider all those motorists to be dumbasses and then find myself in the situation of talking to them. If I then still think, "Wow, what a bunch of morons they are," then I radiate that too, maybe unconsciously. That means that the other person notices this—consciously or unconsciously— and might actually start behaving like a dumbass. Then I have helped him to be a dumbass, even though I don't want dumbasses around me. We have already talked about self-fulfilling prophecies. When I believe in something, I cause something to happen and can make something come true that actually wasn't true at the time. Through my behavior and my charisma, I am back at the cause of what is happening, namely that the other person behaves exactly as I was previously afraid he would. So when I go into a meeting and think, "Wow, there's this one employee who is so stupid. She's totally getting on my nerves," I prepare a mindset beforehand. I will hide everything else and only perceive the statements of the employee that confirm my image. I will totally miss all her clever statements. My charisma and thus my effect on her will make it easy for her to say only stupid things. On the other hand, if I have a positive image of her in advance, I might go into the meeting smiling and acting accordingly. I will be quite surprised at how extremely clever this employee suddenly behaves. See, my behavior also changes that of others. If I enter a room and smile, I will also be smiled at. We reap what we sow. Okay, okay. I'm getting a penalty for over-using clichés. Here's a euro for the proverb-pot [*laughs*].

Christian: [*laughs*] And it is true: *perception is projection*. In the end it's all about my behavior. With my behavior, I always trigger something in the people I am dealing with. Their behavior is dependent on my behavior and so another behavior comes out of it, to which I can react again. In addition, it is not only my behavior via the five sensory channels that influences how the other person behaves, but also my expectations of her. What I expect from another will most likely happen.

Michael: *Cause and effect.* I can be the cause of everything. I can well be the cause of other people's behavior.

Christian: In my world.

Michael: In mine, too. So there are two of us already.

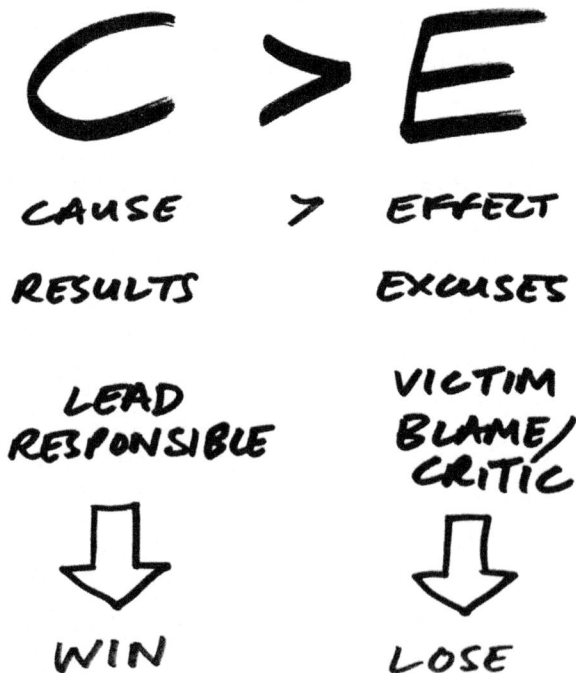

$$C > E$$

CAUSE > EFFECT

RESULTS EXCUSES

LEAD RESPONSIBLE VICTIM BLAME/ CRITIC

⇩ ⇩

WIN LOSE

Illustration: Cause> Effect
It appears in life that I get either the results I want or the excuses I make.

Christian: Do you know the song by Lassie Singers, *Everyone is in His Own World, But Mine is the Right One*? Fabulous.

Michael: Too bad there are over seven billion worlds. If we think they are all right, then goodnight.

Christian: *Cause and effect*. I am the cause of everything that happens in my life.

Michael: And I have everything in my hands. I had a mentor once. Have I told you about that?

Christian: Which one? What exactly?

Michael: This mentor was the chairman of a really big company. He was about seventy years old and gray-haired. Before he became my mentor, I had the opportunity to present something to him. He had been the CEO of a very big international bank before he became chairman of the company I was working for at that time. He was a big deal. So he was sitting there with another board member he had brought along. Both were extremely successful and very rich. They sat there with us, in a far corner of the world in Qatar, and I presented the progress of the venture we had started. One of them suddenly said, "You know, you can do anything in life that you want to. That is what life is all about." That caused a lot of noise in my head. At first I thought they were just joking around, which they did quite a lot. But it wasn't a joke; it was their absolute conviction. "You can do anything that you want in life. That is what life is all about." That was their mindset. And they were super successful with it. Everything they could dream of, they achieved. It was their mindset that led them there. Since then, I have internalized the truth: it's the attitude—*my* mindset—that makes me able to achieve anything I want to achieve. I am *at cause*. I have it in my hands. I can make something of it. Sometimes it might take a while. For some of my goals, it took me 10, 12, 15 years or more to get there. Since then, I have achieved everything I wanted to achieve. Now, in retrospect, I have started to see a caveat in this subject of "achieving goals." The question I sometimes ask myself is whether the goals I set for myself back then were actually the right ones.

Christian: I understand that. It has to be learned. What goals do I actually set for myself?

Michael: *Be careful what you wish for 'cause you just might get it.*[4] At least if I am at the cause, then I get it. Then I have to deal with it.

Christian: Great Michael, thank you very much. I am at the cause of this chapter and I want us to come to the end now.

---

4   From the song "When I Grow Up" by the band The Pussycat Dolls, 2008.

Once again you talk about responsibility. I bear responsibility for everything that happens around me. That's quite powerful. I understand that my attitude is the foundation of my success, regardless of what I define as success. If only it wasn't so difficult to change my own mindset. Saying something to myself that feels good is not enough. In order to be really successful, I have to be able to convince myself of it.

SELF-RESPONSIBILITY

WHY OR WHEREFORE?

Michael: Let's talk about *why* and why *wherefore* can be much better than *why*.

Christian: Tell me, why are you always late for our podcast recording sessions?

Michael: Excuse me?!

Christian: Yes, I am interested in that. Why?

Michael: Because the dog ate my homework.

Christian: Should I take care of your dog?!

Michael: The cab was late.

Christian: Then take an Uber.

Michael: It was very foggy this morning.

Christian: Then leave earlier.

Michael: The subway was late, there was a problem with the track. Okay, okay, so I didn't leave early enough.

Christian: So you are to blame for that?

Michael: Sure, I'm to blame for that. This year it's all my fault.

Christian: Really? That's excellent.

Michael: I made that agreement with my wife.

Christian: That you are basically to blame for everything now?

Michael: Yes. We've found that the whole *blame* game doesn't help at all. That's why we decided early last year that my wife was to blame for everything that year and I was to blame for everything this year. So we have already clarified the question of guilt and do not need to argue about it. We can immediately dedicate ourselves to finding a solution.

Christian: That means you start directly with the question of *why*? Why didn't you unload the dishwasher?

Michael: Why do you ask that? Why do you keep asking *why* questions?

Christian: I don't want to answer that yet. Let's see what is happening here right now. You are late for the podcast and I ask you, "Why?" After that, I get a lot of excuses from you. Of course, that doesn't help me. Because what should I as your manager do now? Should I make sure that you call a cab earlier? Should I set up your Uber App? Or unload the dishwasher for you? Although it would be nice for you, it is not my job. So when I ask you or one of my employees *why*, I get a lot of answers that I don't know what to do with and honestly don't want to hear.

Michael: That's right. I'm immediately defensive and I try to protect myself. I'm looking for a justification to explain myself. "Why?" is a difficult question.

Christian: What might a better question be?

Michael: What can you do differently to always be on time in the future?

Christian: So the responsibility would be yours.

Michael: That's right. I just arrived too late. Just to be clear, of course, I wasn't late.

Christian: We are only pretending.

Michael: Thanks, and yet I do feel so guilty.

Christian: [*seriously*] Why are you doing this?

Michael: I feel guilty right away. I immediately feel the need to defend and justify myself. And, even though this was a made-up scenario for the chapter, I still felt the need to clarify that I wasn't actually late.

Christian: When I ask you, "What will you do differently in the future?" it sounds a bit better, doesn't it?

Michael: Yes, absolutely. You're still addressing the problem, while my thoughts are now turning directly to the solution: "Okay, I see. Maybe next time I'll do it better this way or that. The past doesn't feel so gloomy and I don't need to feel so guilty; I just think about what I can do differently next time. It's very solution oriented.

Christian: Because you are the expert for yourself. You yourself know how it happened that you arrived late.

Michael: Well said. I am the expert for myself. Of course I know why I was late.

Christian: You also know what you could do differently. For example, you could set your alarm clock earlier, get up earlier, take a shorter shower, eat breakfast faster, be more organized. These are all accusations that I don't mean seriously.

Michael: That's okay; that's what we're here for.

Christian: What would be even better?

Michael: The best thing, of course, is to take full responsibility from the start and to make sure I'm on time. So I think about what I can do to achieve the result that I want to have. The best thing would be for each of us to do that.

Christian: Then the directions from my side would only be: "Michael, please be on time for the podcast."

Michael: Yes, exactly. Ideally, such a request wouldn't even be necessary because, thanks to my mindset, I have already accepted that everything starts with me. I am the cause of everything that happens in my life. Also, our example highlights that "I am aware from the beginning that I am the cause of being punctual or unpunctual." In the NLP[5] world, this concept is called *cause and effect*.

Christian: What does that mean?

---

[5] Neuro-Linguistic Programming - motivation and communication model, https://en.wikipedia.org/wiki/Neuro-linguistic_programming.

Michael: I was about to ask you the same thing. Basically, it's an old concept that Immanuel Kant addressed in his philosophy several hundred years ago. *Cause and effect* means that there is a cause for everything that happens in the world. This is the insight of Kant, an old hand. For our mindset, this means that I can either be at the cause or at the effect.

Christian: In our previous example where you were late, the reason was that you got up too late.

Michael: Let's start with the effect. When I'm *at effect,* I say, "The train was late, the cab didn't come, it was foggy, the dog ate my homework." In these cases, I am exposed to the effects that happen in the world. I am the victim rather than the cause of these effects. *To be at effect* means to *be in the victim role*. I am not to blame, but rather the circumstances are. The world is to blame for what happens around me.

Christian: And the alternative is that you are a creator rather than a victim of your reality?

Michael: Right. I am *at cause* for everything that happens in my life. That's the point. This thought has totally helped me to be freer and in control of my life. In the beginning I found it hard to accept it because there seem to be a lot of things that I'm not the cause of or don't want to be the cause of. I realized that this is nonsense. I am the cause of everything that happens in my life.

Christian: You are also the reason why the train is late. You are also to blame for that.

Michael: In a way, that's my fault, too, because I didn't take into account that the train might be late. Unfortunately, it's not unusual for a train to be late. I can take that into account. To be sure to be on time, I'll take an earlier train. Or I'll choose another mode of transport. Or I'll arrive the evening before in order to be able to walk the next morning without having to rely on the train.

Christian: Planning buffer time makes everything much more relaxed.

Michael: If I am the cause, *at cause* for everything that happens in my life, then I factor that in. I, and nobody else, am responsible. *It appears in life that* *you either achieve the results that you want or you get the excuses that you make.* I always get one of the two, results or excuses.

Christian: So you mean that if you prepare yourself for the fact that the train will be late, then it will be late? *Law of attraction*—you direct your energy towards it?

Michael: Bingo, *law of attraction, cause and effect, results and excuses*—they are all the same concept. I take responsibility for myself.

Christian: "Why are you late?" When I ask you *why*, you dump all your excuses on me. Of course, I don't want that as a manager. I don't want to know all that. It's much easier to tell you what I expect from you: "I want you to be on time."

Michael: Otherwise, I have it right at the top of my head that the dog ate my homework, the train was late, it was foggy, and the cab didn't come either.

Christian: Also the tank was empty, the car was stolen, and then there was this earthquake.

Michael: As a bad manager, I then start looking for solutions. I explain how to use the cab app and what you can do about the fog. I start solving everyone else's problems!

Christian: I can literally see it in front of me. In the past I would have done the same. I would certainly have installed the cab app on my employee's smartphone and explained to him how to use it.

Michael: You have a problem? Let me solve it for you!

Christian: Right. Then I'm the big shot who does everything. It really doesn't help anyone. I make my life as a manager much easier by simply saying what I want instead of saying what I don't want: "I want you to be on time."

Michael: I am *at cause*. Thus, I influence the result that I want to get. Namely, that an employee solves his tasks and problems independently.

Christian: Successful managers also build good relationships with their employees. This includes understanding how their employees are doing and what challenges they face. How does that fit together now?

Michael: Good question. So far, we have talked about what it means to take responsibility for myself. That is my job as a boss. At the same time, as a boss, I expect my employees to take responsibility for themselves. The key is empathy. Of course I am allowed to empathize and to be understanding of my employees' situation. Suppose an employee apologizes and says, "I'm sorry I was late. I drove my mother to the hospital. She is seriously ill and it is important to me to be there for her." In this case, of course, I will empathize and might answer, "I am sorry to hear that. I hope your mother will get better soon." Nevertheless, I still expect the employee to take responsibility for himself in the context of his self-chosen priorities, of course. We all decide for ourselves what is important in life. This does not mean, of course, that I should act ignorantly and tell the employee, "I don't care about all that; please come on time." Also, that would not help to achieve the result I want to achieve. Here again, as the boss, I am *at cause* and I have the opportunity to shape my communication in such a way that in the end I reach the goal I want to achieve: a happy employee AND results for the company.

Christian: As the boss, for example, I can suggest starting the next meeting at 10:00 instead of 9:00. I could say something like, "I understand your situation. It will certainly help you if we set the meeting an hour later. Please be here tomorrow at 10:00 sharp so we can start on time."

Michael: So we make a different plan. We're *at cause* and we can adapt and do things differently.

Christian: So *why* is a bad question. Although some people strongly recommend to always start with *why*, we are now saying that *why* is not a good question.

Michael: Simon Sinek surely has a point. *Start with Why* is a great book about Purpose. That's exactly what the question of *why* refers to. What do I exist for? What difference do I make in the world? What difference does my company make? These are great questions to ask. In our case, it has become clear to ask: *wherefore?* or, *for what Purpose?* These questions get to the heart of what we are talking about much more so than *why*. It is not a question of guilt. It's a question of what Purpose I or my company fulfills in the world. It is about what good we do in the world. Therefore, I do not feel that I contribute anything to this by defending myself.

Christian: This is a strategic question, so to speak. Whereas in our example of being late, it is about the behavior of an employee. After all, I don't want to know from him *wherefore* he is late in the sense of: *Surely you want to annoy me.* If that is the case, I have a different problem altogether.

Michael: Maybe we should invite Simon Sinek and explain to him that instead of *why*, *wherefore* is an even better question.

Christian: [*laughs*] Thanks a lot.

Michael: Wherefore?

Christian: For your contribution.

So before I ask my employees or fellow human beings a question, it helps me to put myself in their shoes. I ask myself the question and think about what I would answer. I will then certainly be able to save myself some of my questions. So I don't try to get rid of my displeasure about the misconduct of an employee by asking him a stupid question like, "Why are you doing this?" I first assume that he himself is responsible for his actions and that there is a valid reason for his own behavior. So I try to work with him in a more objective way to find a solution, while showing understanding. "Can I help you to be on time next time? Your presence is important for us." The same applies to myself, of course. I, too, may ask myself whether my answer to a question is an excuse or whether it's really me who bears the responsibility for my actions.

WHO AM I?
PREFERENCE, COMPETENCE, AND VALUES

Christian: Who is this Christian you always talk about?

Michael: Well, you.

Christian: Me? Who am I then?

Michael: Who am I? Where do I go? What are we doing all this for?

Christian: What, if not? Who am I?

Michael: Well, you are Christian.

Christian: My name is clear. I also know my date of birth, I know some of my vital statistics like my blood pressure, my height, my weight. I know where I live and I know all the demographic information about me.

Michael: I'm glad you remember.

Christian: I remember. I have the feeling that this could be important for me as a manager.

Michael: So, where does this feeling come from?

Christian: I remember that a Chinese general once said, "Know thyself. If you know yourself and know your enemy, you need not fear any battle." That's why I'm interested in knowing who I actually am. How can you help me find out?

Michael: Let's see. You just mentioned some information about yourself. You know your name, your date of birth, and your blood pressure. You obviously remember these things. So could I say that a part of who you are is your memories?

Christian: Yes, I think so.

Michael: Good. So there are memories within you. What else makes you unique?

Christian: Hmm, let's see. My Purpose in life. My motivation for why I am in this world. Also my Values, my interests, my skills, and my preferences.

Michael: Those are a lot of things that define you. What else?

Christian: What I do all day. My actions.

Michael: Let me summarize again: Things that describe who you are include your Values, interests, skills, preferences, and your actions. Let's start with Values. Which Values distinguish you?

Christian: Good question. *Knowledge* is one of my Values. I want to understand a lot and learn a lot in my life. *Happiness* is also one of my Values. I make the decision to be happy, or at least to keep trying until I really am. *Productivity* is another important Value, implemented through knowledge and resulting in happiness. Is anything missing? I can certainly think of more Values.

Michael: Where do these Values come from? It is nice to hear what is important to you in life. Because that is what Values are, things that are important to you. How did you get to these Values?

Christian: These Values have emerged over the years. I estimate that about 30% are genetic and 70% are the result of experience.

Michael: So you're saying that some simply come out of your DNA. Some are virtually predetermined by your genetic structure, while others you've experienced. Do you think you can change these Values?

Christian: It's difficult to change them. I don't want that at all. I think they are so firmly anchored in me that I don't want to change them at all.

Michael: Suppose you would like to change them. Could you perhaps change them using psychological methods?

Christian: I think so. Definitely.

Michael: Okay. What else do you think?

Christian: I think that I am good at math. Are we now on the subject of beliefs?

Michael: Sounds like it. Where does this belief that you're good at math come from? What makes you choose to think that?

Christian: I used to get good grades in school. Many people used to say, "The boy is good at math" [pauses], "... and he is bad at languages and sports."

Michael: Did you believe that then?

Christian: Yeah, sure. I believed that, too. Then I studied theoretical elementary particle physics. There I did a lot of calculations. As I recall, I believed I was pretty good at that.

Michael: You used the word *believe* again. What else do you choose to believe?

Christian: Now I believe that I can also learn to be good at languages. I also believe that I can learn anything I want to learn—sailing, flying, playing musical instruments—everything I want to learn, I can learn.

Michael: When I think of beliefs, I always think of faith, that is, religion. What do you believe in religiously?

Christian: Phew, I am still looking for that. I took some kind of test in the past. It was about finding out which religion and philosophy of life suits me best. The result was Buddhism.

Michael: There's a test for that?

Christian: Yes. In the test, I ticked off which of the beliefs of different religions and philosophies shared Values, beliefs, and morals similar to those that I hold. I had the most similarities with Buddhism and its European variant, Stoicism.

Michael: So you do have faith. You believe that there's something else besides us — you and me — in the here and now?

Christian: Yes, I am convinced that there is something else. I experience and feel it every day.

Michael: So we've already gotten to know two of the facets that make you who you are. We know more about your Values and your beliefs. Let's go back to your memories. What do you remember particularly well from your life?

Christian: Frankly, I am glad that there are some things I don't remember. This is also one of my beliefs. I often hear my mother saying to me, "Christian, do you remember when...?" "No, I don't remember," I often think in response. And that's just as well. I'm sure I could bring back these memories with psychological methods, and I'm convinced that I can do without some of my memories. It is not necessary to remember everything.

Michael: [*smiles*] Well, we've got that cleared up. Basically, we live in the here and now, so who needs memories? We talked about Values, about beliefs, about religion, and about memories. What remains are preferences and skills. What about your preferences? Do you have any?

Christian: Absolutely. I've gotten to know my preferences, thanks to you. Through you, I realized that I am full of creative, yellow energy. So I like to have fun and talk to people. Until then, I had always believed that my preference was mainly mathematics and more precise work, skills I had acquired over many years. Even now, I can still sit down and solve mathematical problems. I still enjoy doing that for a certain amount of time. It is just not my preference; it's not something I'd like to do for my entire life.

Michael: Where do you think your preferences come from? You know, the things that come easily to you, what you like to do, and what flows effortlessly. Your so-called *comfort zone*.

Christian: In terms of preferences, I would say that the proportion of genetics is higher, perhaps 70%. The remaining 30% come from my environment, i.e., my early childhood imprint. Childhood is always partly to blame.

Michael: You mean like your performance in the high jump? You once told me how easy it was for you to get a certificate in high jumping because you are so tall. You said to me, "I just walked up to that bar, jumped up, and turned my body in the air. And someone gave me a certificate." That was easy for you because your physique made it possible.

Christian: [*laughs*] I also used to think that Olympic swimmers develop a wide back and short legs because of all their training. Now I think it is the other way around. They are good swimmers because they have a wide back and short legs.

Michael: You mean because their physique makes swimming easier.

Christian: Yes. Of course, they also train hard to swim well and build up their performance to a very high level of competence. What I want to say is, my legs are simply too long for me to become a world champion swimmer. Besides, it would also be too boring for me.

Michael: You've probably heard of strength-based management. It's about identifying and managing your strengths. Strengths are related to my preferences. If I discover my natural preferences, or what comes easily to me, then I can easily develop preferences into strong competences—strengths at which I excel. This is how I can become a world champion.

Christian: At least in the area of a preference that I am good at.

Michael: So let's get back to our initial question. This was, "Who is Christian?" Or in general, "Who am I?" We've learned a lot about you. Admittedly, we didn't learn much about your memories. However, we do know that you have some imbedded and coded memories. Everything you perceived on the five *VAKOG channels* in the past: visual, auditory, kinesthetic, olfactory, and gustatory.

V A K O G + Ad.

VISUAL AUDITORY KINASTHETIC OLFACTORY GUSTATORY AUDITORY DIGITAL = THE INNER VOICE

Illustration: VAKOG
Each of us perceives a multitude of sensory impressions through these channels every day, every second even. The computing power and storage capacity per channel is different for each individual. We all prefer our own channel mix.

It would certainly be exciting to hear on another occasion what memories you have stored. We have also learned something about your Values, about what is deeply rooted and important for you. You said something about it like, "My Values are fun, learning, and productivity. I don't want to change these. I'm fine with keeping these." After that we talked about beliefs. You used to believe that you were good at math and not at languages. Later, you realized that you are also good with people and languages. So you believe that you can learn everything you choose to. I can control and choose what I believe. Even in terms of religion. Then we considered the topic of preferences, things that come easily to me by nature. Competences are the skills I acquire, even if I have long legs and short arms and still want to be a world champion swimmer.

Christian: Then it might be a lot harder for you to become a world champion.

Michael: So who do you think you are now? Who is Christian?

Christian: I am Christian. With all these facets, memories, Values, beliefs, skills, and preferences. I know that now. How does that help me to lead myself? First and foremost, leadership begins with myself. It means leading myself, then leading others, and finally "not having to fear battle" anymore.

Michael: So you know the first part: yourself. The quote you mentioned from Sun Tzu, the Chinese military strategist and philosopher, comes down to this: *Know thyself and know your enemy, and you will win 100% of all battles.* So now you know who you are in the dimensions of Values, beliefs, preferences, memories, and skills. Now, you can find out who the people that you lead are and how they differ from you. Let's assume that you still have the belief that "I am good at math and I am good at languages." Someone else on your team who has different beliefs from yours is now facing a mathematical or language task. How do you deal with this?

Christian: Knowing your own beliefs is an important step, I can work with that. Let me give you an example from the time of my coffee bar company, *chicco di caffe*. Because I was the physicist in the company and knew how to deal with numbers, I was, of course, initially responsible for the company's bookkeeping. I took over this area from the tax consultant and built up the financial department. At some point, I realized that someone else was much better at it than I was. I enjoyed building up the department and also getting into the cash book. I found that totally exciting. However, I only had fun doing something like that until I knew how to do it and it became routine. From that moment on, it was better to hand it over to someone else. If I know which activities are easy for me and which require less energy to achieve a good result, I can take on these tasks. On the other hand, if I know that an activity tends to cost me a lot of energy while someone else finds the same task much easier, I should hand it over, ideally to a person who says, "I can do the bookkeeping for hours every day, it's easy for me."

Michael: So, if I understand you correctly, for me as a manager, if I know where my own abilities lie, and those of my colleagues, I can delegate tasks in a way that everyone does what he or she does best and where he or she achieves the best results. This way, the overall performance of the team would be higher, and the result better.

Christian: It does not necessarily have to be delegated. The tasks can also simply be distributed together, so that we can talk about them together and learn even more about each other's skills.

Michael: Just like you and I work together?

Christian: "You'd better do that, you are better at this than I am." Great. Thanks for letting me do this.

Michael: I think this way of working is great. A part of *who you are* is very auditory. You like to listen and you like to talk. You clearly have a preference for the auditory channel. That's why you came up with the idea for our podcast. It simply suits you and is easy for you. I am more of the visual type. I like to get a flipchart and start painting or typing something on my keyboard so I can see it. If I can't see it, I can't think. So I take care of our videos and the visuals. This is a great arrangement, aligned with our different sets of strengths. It's also much more fun when I can do the things that I find easy and that I'm good at, while the things I don't like to do are taken care of by someone else who loves doing those things someone who is really good at them. That way the whole team feels great and delivers great results.

Christian: We once did an exercise on this. Everybody wrote down which tasks they do all day, which ones they enjoyed and which ones they didn't.

In the end, we had five sheets full of tasks. We then put them together and distributed the tasks so that everyone got mainly tasks that they enjoyed. The team's productivity increased enormously, and it was much easier on everyone.

Michael: That's a great idea. It means that I sit down with my team, each one writes down 10 tasks they are working on, categorizing task enjoyment into: little, medium, and a lot. Then we put it all together and everyone picks out what they enjoy the most. "Oh, you enjoy that? I didn't know that, well then there you go. The job is yours." That's a wonderful way of distributing work. Then everyone is much happier and the results are better.

Christian: Exactly. And this is basically how you and I work together.

Michael: Now I have only one question at the end: You are Christian. Who am I?

Christian: You are Michael.

The exercise of understanding who I really am, what preferences and competencies I really have, is a great idea for the whole team. It creates understanding and draws attention much more consciously to the strengths of each individual. It builds appreciation. I immediately know who I can turn to for which topic. However, I am afraid that in many companies, tasks and projects of employees and managers are still often chosen based on visibility and prestige rather than on their own skills. So how honest can I be with myself and the team? What happens if my preferences and skills do not meet the expectations of my role? Especially as a boss, the expectations others have of me are very high. Am I allowed to be who I am? Does the answer to this question indicate a possible conflict of Values?

I AM WHO I WANT TO BE
I HAVE THE POWER TO CHANGE

Christian: Tell me, what was your IQ when you were little?

Michael: I did have the opportunity to take an IQ test as a child. The result was 115 or 125. Or maybe it was 105. Anyways, something with a 5, maybe just 5.

Christian: *[grins]* I got a 240.

Michael: I knew it.

Christian: In any case, that's the story I like to tell myself.

Michael: So what are you doing here?

Christian: Good question, that is what I am trying to find out.

Michael: A 240 is an insane number for an IQ.

Christian: No, no. I have never taken an official IQ test, I have just practiced tests from time to time. I got bored very quickly. Oftentimes, I found solutions weren't technically the "official" solution. That's why I think I'm either too intelligent for these tests, or I don't concentrate enough while taking them.

Michael: I think it's quite good that you never did an official test.

Christian: Because otherwise I would know how overly intelligent I am?

Michael: Well, imagine if the result was really 240? If I imagine I had an IQ of 240, I would feel under constant pressure. I'd feel like I had to be the greatest genius on earth all the time.

Christian: Definitely.

Michael: So, what do I do when I don't know or can't do something?

Christian: You would get into trouble with yourself and your stories. There would be an incongruence between what you experience and the stories you tell yourself.

Michael: What does the story sound like in my head as it plays out?

Christian: It could be different stories that you hear. One could sound like this: "I am the greatest genius and the others don't even realize it. They behave so strangely, maybe they are just too stupid."

Michael: Do you think you could extrapolate what would have happened in your social environment?

Christian: You mean if I had actually taken an IQ test and a genius result like that had come out? I probably would have become insufferable.

Michael: [*laughs*] Good to know.

Christian: That's why I'm really glad that I never did it. I quickly realized that these intelligence test tasks are something I will probably never learn. You need a lot of concentration to do them. It is also a matter of practice to concentrate on them. That was not for me.

Michael: Isn't the point of these tests that you can't practice them? I thought I couldn't fake these tests because they're supposed to test how intelligent I really am.

Christian: I think I can influence the result through practice.

Michael: You're probably right. Back when I took this test, there were actually people who scored with an IQ of 130 or 160. That's very close to genius level. My score wasn't bad, and not really great either. I didn't feel pressured afterwards. My story was more like this: "Well, if I'm not naturally as intelligent as others, I will just compensate with something else. I will learn more, work harder and educate myself." That's what motivated me. It pushed me.

Christian: That's not bad, is it?

Michael: Yeah, I think it was actually very helpful. The result of an IQ of 240 I can well imagine as a mental fuck-up. It might not be that easy to deal with.

Christian: Let's turn the whole thing around. Imagine you have a bad day when you take the test. Your result is 80 points total. An IQ of 80 is below average. How would your life have been then? What would your story sound like?

Michael: Wow. That could have turned into a *self-fulfilling prophecy.* When someone tells me as a child, "You have an IQ of 80. That's below the norm," the stories in my head sound more like, "The other kids are smarter than me," and, "I'm not as good as others." Perhaps then that story will eventually become true and I will end up a failure. Simply because I told this to myself and did that stupid test at the wrong time.

Christian: I don't necessarily have to take an IQ test to certify that my children have a low IQ. If I keep telling my children, "Well, silly you. What stupid thing did you do again today?" Or, "I know you don't understand. You're too little," I may be leading them to a narrow mindset. They then start telling themselves the following story: "I don't understand it because I'm a silly girl. I'm just too slow."

Michael: It was the same with you. You were told that you were super intelligent and therefore good at math, but bad at sports.

Christian: Right. I was good at math. That's why everyone thought I was bad at sports. At school, I actually was.

Michael: *Self-fulfilling prophecy.* That's the way it was until you decided otherwise.

Christian: Yes, doing the high jump made me realize that I wasn't bad at sports at all. I was tall and could just walk over to the bar, jump over it, and get a good score.

Michael: A lot has happened on this topic in science in the last 10 years. There is the concept of neuroplasticity. What is that?

Christian: I don't think I'll ever understand what that is.

Michael: Clever. [*grins*] I better watch what you say. So, *neuro* to me means *nerves* and *brain*, the mass inside my head and its extensions. *Plasticity* means that it's shapeable. In the past, it was assumed—and this is what I learned in school—that this mass is more intelligent for some people and less intelligent for others. That's the way it is and that's the way it would always be. That was the story I was told. The world assumed that the brain, once it is fully grown, is the way it is. It is structured and interconnected with certain talents, language, and so on. Now, science has realized that this belief was bullshit. It turned out that the brain is indeed malleable, and up to old age. So there are indeed methods to train intelligence. Today, the story that I believe sounds like this: "I have an IQ of 80. And if I want to, I can get to an IQ of 160."

Christian: That's big. I can suddenly decide for myself which story I believe and tell myself. Of course, it's easy to say, "I have an IQ of 80. That's the way it is, that's the way it stays. So I don't have to make any effort at all. It's easier for me, for the teachers, for the parents, and for my boss. I am just a silly person. There's nothing I can do about it." If I decide to believe the other story, it means I can learn to be intelligent. That's naturally more strenuous than remaining stupid.

Michael: And we're back at *cause and effect*. In the first story, or mindset, I am the victim *at effect*. The circumstances, the world, nature, the others are to blame for everything. In the other story, I am at *cause*. When I'm in that state of mind, then I have the opportunity to change things. My mindset tells me that I will use these possibilities and work on my result, if I want to. I can make something of the situation. I can change it. Then, I will also achieve a different result next time.

Christian: Previously I said, "It is exhausting. Of course this is again a decision I made."

Michael: Yes, exactly. If you want, it feels exhausting.

Christian: It is my decision. To say, "This offers me many chances," or "This makes it easier for me" is a decision. Everything becomes much easier when I can suddenly decide for myself who I want to be, who I am, and which stories I believe. That is great.

Michael: That's the genius of it. I can choose all that myself. I can choose how I see things, what I feel, what state I'm in, and what feelings I have. If a client says to me, "This feels exhausting for me," I ask, "How would it feel if you imagine it is easy for you?" I ask clients to remember something that felt easy in their lives and help them transfer that feeling. There is a *copy and paste* command for feelings. I can just transfer that feeling from one context to another, and suddenly something that was previously exhausting feels light. I can choose my feelings. This is one of the biggest lessons I have learned in my life so far. How does it work for you?

Christian: *Copy and paste,* that sounds good. At first, I asked myself the question of how to do it. Once I'm convinced that it works, it becomes very easy. Then I just do it: *copy and paste.* It's so simple.

Michael: There are good NLP methods for that.

Christian: Yes, it is totally easy.

Michael: How does all this help me as a manager? This is *Chief of Anything.* So what?

Christian: Who do I lead as a manager? First and foremost, I lead myself. Then I lead my employees, and then I lead everyone around me with whom I communicate. Leadership is the ability to communicate. So if I am convinced that it is easy to change myself and to control my emotions, I can easily start doing so. I tell myself, "I can easily adapt and change."

Michael: Then I can also choose how I feel in situations where I may have felt uncomfortable before, perhaps in circumstances where I had previously felt uncomfortable in dealing with other people. Let's take a staff meeting that didn't go so well. I am totally annoyed. The first step is to realize that I am annoyed, because after I have observed this, I can make a choice. I can either decide to continue having this feeling and allow the feeling to control me. Or, I can decide to use the *copy and paste* command and replace the feeling with another feeling that has a more positive impact on the outcome. I decide to be above feelings, to have superiority in situations. I can rise above a feeling and simply choose another one. I suddenly deal with an employee in a completely different way and am able to communicate with him or her in a new context than I do when I am annoyed. The result is much better, all because I decided not to feel the way I was programmed, but to choose a more Purposeful feeling. The whole thing is a concept that can be expressed in a simple formula: E + R = O.

$$E + R = O$$

$$EVENT + RESPONSE = OUTCOME$$

$$\downarrow$$

$$CHOICE$$
$$FREEDOM$$
$$POWER$$

Illustration: E + R = O
I can always choose my reaction and thus have the power to influence the outcome, regardless of the event which is merely a trigger.

Christian: I know that. That is Einstein's.

Michael: Yeah, something like that. The letters stand for *E = Event*. The *R* stands for *Response:* my response to this event. The *O* stands for *Outcome*, or the result I get from my response. There is a very famous insight shared by Viktor Frankl,[6] who wrote about prisoners in Nazi concentration camps who held the belief that no matter what happens —no matter what event occurs—they always have a choice of response. In a superior mindset, I know that I always have a choice of *R*. I always have the ability to choose my response. I have *response-ability* with which I determine the outcome. It is not the circumstance that determines the outcome, it is the response that I choose which determines the outcome. Unbelievably powerful! From a philosophical point of view, I think we are along the subject lines of *free will*.

Christian: Crazy.

6   Viktor Emil Frankl, Austrian neurologist and psychiatrist, https://de.wikipedia.org/wiki/Viktor_Frankl.

Michael: Everyone has trigger buttons like this. My wife, my parents, and my children know them very well. They have an impressive gift for pushing them very specifically.

Christian: There is always one who pushes the buttons and one who is allowing for them to be pushed.

Michael: I gladly admit that. When that happens, it's a special challenge for me to choose the *R* myself instead of surrendering to everything. Then I always think of the formula E + R = O. There is an event that happens, completely triggering me. I would love to freak out. Instead, I choose my R to get the result I want to have. Because if I don't do that, I get a result that is influenced from outside of myself. Then I'm back *at effect* and resign to circumstances, thus becoming a victim. I do not want that. I choose to be the leader in my life and to get the results that I want, so I consciously decide for an *R* of my choice, an R that serves the Purpose of what I want to achieve. Because I am *at cause* of every O in my life.

Christian: If I look at this formula mathematically, I realize that for every *E*, i.e. for every event, there is an *R*, or an answer from me. From this follows that every event and every answer of mine results in an *O*, an outcome, which I influence. So every *O* is determined by me.

Michael: That's right.

Christian: This means that the result is completely independent of the outer world.

Michael: That's right.

Christian: My favorite saying is: *happiness is a decision*. I decide to be happy, regardless of the external circumstances.

Michael: Buddhist monks are the absolute world champions in this. They just sit there and meditate day in, day out, for twenty years and just feel happy and content. Simply because they choose to do so.

Christian: Well, I don't really need to sit and meditate like that. I can also get in contact with the outside world. The important thing is that I make myself aware that the world and my emotional state are linearly independent.

Michael: I don't understand that, yet.

Christian: This is difficult.

Michael: I'll choose to understand it in a moment.

Christian: I ask again, how can I use this as a leader?

Michael: Basically, in any situation where something or someone is getting on my nerves. For me, that's the essence of the subject. I can decide in every situation how I feel and thus skillfully influence the result in my favor. This is always better than someone else determining the result.

Christian: I can choose from a large pool of reactions. You know the saying: *If the only tool I have is a hammer, then everything looks like a nail.* If the only reaction I have as a boss is to verbally scream or shout, then I don't get very far with that. If, on the other hand, I simply keep quiet, smile, and realize that I can get a better outcome with flexibly choosing a behavior that is expedient for the outcome I want, then I can go much farther. I've had a team member suddenly say to me, "All right, I get it," merely because of me smiling at him, without saying a word. Doing so was uncomfortable at first, but it did create a better outcome for both of us.

Michael: I just try a different R in the equation of $E + R = O$. I try new R's to find out how my outcome changes.

Christian: Right. That's a lot of fun.

Michael: What do we choose now?

Christian: We choose now to be super happy and to move on.

Michael: Leading myself!

I'm beginning to understand why there's so much talk about the responsibility and true capabilities of managers. You might think that being a boss is quite easy. I simply delegate all tasks and enjoy the good life. The real challenge is to constantly maintain mental superiority. Leadership means self-reflection, sensitivity, and self-control. It is my job to constantly deal with myself and the people I lead, to exercise response-ability at all times, and to behave Purposefully. It is a very rational task that also requires dealing with many emotions. This is the real challenge as a people leader, a task much more difficult than just managing a full desk.

STORY OF MY LIFE

"WE ARE WHAT WE PRETEND TO BE, SO WE MUST BE CAREFUL WHAT WE PRETEND TO BE." - KURT VONNEGUT

Christian: We are now going to do a little exercise, the lifeline exercise. It serves to get to know oneself and others better and to build trust in the team. In this exercise, everyone shares ten minutes from their life. We'll start with you. You tell me about the ups and downs you have experienced, what you have learned from them, and how you have managed. The more openly and honestly you deal with your weaknesses and emotions in particular, the more understanding each team member will have for you and your behavior, deepening group trust as a whole. Trust is the basis for good, productive cooperation.

Michael: Absolutely. I know this exercise very well. Both of us have done it many times, especially with clients and groups that we coach. We first learned about the lifeline exercise a few years ago at EO.[7] And we have done this many times together with other entrepreneurs. I love observing what highlights each person shares and how they behave when sharing. The quotation of Kurt Vonnegut[8] proves to be true again and again. He said, more or less, that we must be careful what we pretend to be, because what we pretend to be, we become. When I tell my life story right away, I tell it in the awareness of how and what I want to tell. Consciously or unconsciously, I pursue an intention to present myself in the way I want to be perceived by others. Vonnegut warns against this. Be careful how you present yourself, because it will come true. Whoever you pretend to be, you will become.

Christian: Okay. Here we go. Do you start with your lifeline, Michael?

Michael: Yes, gladly. How much time do I have?

Christian: I set the timer for 10 minutes.

---

7   EO, the Entrepreneurs' Organization is a worldwide association of entrepreneurs - www.eonetwork.org.

8   US-American writer with German roots.

Michael: Okay. So I'll tell you my life story, my highs, my lows, and what I've learned so that you and the readers get to know me better and our relationship is strengthened. Here we go.

LIFELINE MICHAEL

My story begins in 1946. In 1946 my mother was five years old. She was born in Hungary. My family emigrated from Germany to Hungary in the 1700s and had lived in Hungary ever since. At the end of the Second World War, they were expelled from Hungary because of their German descent. This flight, which lasted for about ten years with many twists and turns, had a strong impact on my mother, and later on me. Through my mother I understood that "home" is not necessarily something for eternity. Even as a child, my family's experiences created deep emotion in me. I wanted people to treat each other peacefully, so that the world would become a better place and something like this would not happen again in the future. This was important to me.

My father, on the other hand, gave me the entrepreneurial spirit. He comes from the Rhineland, near the Dutch border. I grew up there as well. He was a tax consultant and entrepreneur and is now retired. All four grandparents were active in agriculture, which I still notice in some of my parents' and also my own behavior.

I was born successfully in 1970, so I am 50 years old now. I deliberately say I was born "successfully" because my mother had already experienced two unsuccessful pregnancies before I was born. I would actually have had two brothers. Medicine was not advanced enough at the time. Today, they certainly could have been saved, unfortunately not back then. So I grew up visiting the child graves of my brothers on Sundays. Growing up, life and death played a big role for me. When I was 12 years old, my grandfather died of stomach cancer. One year later, my grandmother took her own life. The death of my grandparents had a great impact on the whole family, especially on my mother and, therefore, on me as well. Given the terrible impact the war had on my mother's family, I decided to do community service. Military service was out of the question for me. I never wanted to be involved in any acts of war. I worked as a paramedic with the Red Cross and again was often confronted with death.

I learned a lot about life and death. My cousin died after years of being in a coma caused by a car accident. My other grandmother slowly died of cancer and I never met the other grandfather who died from lung cancer caused by smoking. Then my mother fell ill with breast cancer. She recovered, thank God. This sort of fate ran through my life like a red thread. A school friend of mine was killed in a traffic accident, a colleague at work died of a heart attack in his early 30s. When I was 40, my mentor and boss suddenly died. I do take death very seriously and have learned that it can come at any time.

Three great Values or passions have always played a major role in my life. The first is the big, wide world. My second passion is music. The third is progress, meaning technical progress in the world, and also personal development.

The big, wide world has led to many beautiful things in my life. My motto is: *Life is colorful.* I grew up in a very small town and I always had a great wanderlust. I am sure this has something to do with the Hungarian refugee history of my mother's side of the family. I never really felt quite at home as a child. When I was 16, I was an exchange student in the USA. For the first time, I experienced how different life can be in different places. At 35, I went to South Africa for two years to live and work there. It was only later that I realized that I had basically emigrated. I cut all ties to the German system: no more health insurance, no more pension. I signed off everywhere. It felt very liberating. In South Africa, I managed several call centers for a corporate subsidiary. I was entrusted with building an organization from zero to 200 employees. After that we achieved a turnaround with well over 2,000 employees. I felt very successful back then. It was a very great time. Life in Cape Town was wonderful. I liked the lifestyle so much that I could have stayed forever. But I had other goals in life. I wanted to see more of the world. I then went on to Qatar when I was 38. There I set up a corporate start-up for the mobile network operator Vodafone. My role was that of the CMO, Chief Marketing Officer, part of the founding team. After two years, we made an IPO[9] worth 2.2 billion dollars. Harvard Business School even wrote a case study about us.[10] It was an incredible time. I traveled a lot back then—all over the world. It was not until I was about 46 years old that I returned to Germany.

9   IPO, short for Initial Public Offering, a first-time offering of shares on the stock exchange.
10   Alcacer, Goodman: Vodafone Qatar: Building a Telco in the Gulf - HBR 2010.

I spent more than 10 years abroad. In the meantime, I have had children and am happily married. Since then, I have sought closeness to my family and friends, feeling more at home in my hometown than ever before.

The second great influence in my life was music. It still is and always will be. Since I was five or six years old, I have been fascinated by the sound when technology and music meet, especially synthesizers and electric organs. As a child, I found that incredibly fascinating. I took piano lessons very early, and later on took up the organ. I played in bands, and worked as a music teacher for piano, organ, and later guitar starting at 14 years old. I played in the big band at school, in various student bands, and even co-founded my own band. I always did that on the side. After I started to study computer science, I got the offer to play in a professional band. That was awesome. I played bass and sang, especially the rock genre. We also did a lot of dance music, which wasn't really my thing. It was a very cool time. I did that for four years. We got around, playing 50 to 60 gigs a year. I was the bass player of Drafi Deutscher[11] and Andrea Berg used to often sing in our band back then. She has since become very well known in the German music scene. It was a really nice time in which I made very good money and learned a lot. Music was always very important to me. At some point, though, I realized that it was a means to an end and not my life's Purpose. That was a conscious decision I made at that time.

The third major theme is *progress*. Technical and entrepreneurial progress, and also my own further education. I experienced some ups and downs. As a child, I was active in the Catholic Church as an altar boy, as a pianist accompanying the choir, as a lector, and as an organ player during Mass. I even went to Rome once and saw the Pope up close. After graduating from high school, I left the Church. I learned a lot about philosophy and made some conclusions for myself that did not fit in with the convictions of the Church. Values are still hugely important for me. I think that the Church represents very good Values, but I no longer agree with its delivery mechanism, form, and institution as such.

I studied computer science, with medicine as a minor subject. The first degree was pretty hard. It was a lot of mathematics that I didn't really enjoy.

---

11 Drafi Deutscher (1946-2006) was a German singer, composer and music producer.

At some point, I realized that computer science doesn't have as much to do with technology as I had imagined. I took some time off and worked as a professional musician for four years. When I came back after that, I still finished my studies, earned my degree and was able to pick and choose jobs. In order to learn as much as possible and gain practical experience, I went to a management consultancy. The plan worked out. I learned a lot and worked a lot; I was always out of town, always on the road. My first marriage suffered a lot from this. Finally, I changed jobs. I accepted an offer from a client. It was a company where I received incredible support. I was given the opportunity to pursue my Master of Business Administration (MBA) while employed there and traveled all over the world again. I was exposed to incredible people and great mentors. It was then that I made my first exit from the start-up we had built for the corporation. I made good money and was able to save a lot. I had no shares in the company, but very good bonuses and a great leaving package. It was a new start for me, which became a recurring theme. I became an entrepreneur and "business angel," invested in various companies and again got around a lot. I built up a strong network and was very active, including through EO, the Entrepreneurs' Organization. I founded a company. We developed, patented, produced, and sold water pipe capsules, inspired by what Keurig and Nespresso did so successfully with coffee. Unfortunately, the company didn't make it and we ran out of money. Harvard Business School published a case study on this as well.[12] I continued to invest in different companies and lost a lot of money in the process. Many investments went wrong. Luckily, one or two investments were very profitable in the end. This is what led me to start a new project a few years ago. I was curious about what I wanted to do next. I quickly realized that I wanted to become an Executive Coach. I wanted to coach people in leadership roles and help them to achieve their goals. So, I got trained and certified as a coach. I learned a lot and exchanged ideas with others. Now I have arrived at what I consider to be the destination of my professional career, and have already achieved many of the goals I set myself.

I have become aware that besides the three big themes in my life—the big, wide world, music, and progress—there is a fourth theme which has become extremely important to me only in the last few years: family and

---

12 Kerr, Yucaoglu: MISHA: Modernizing the World of Shisha - HBR 2018.

close friendships. In the first part of my lifeline, unfortunately, a lot of things went wrong in this department. I have been divorced twice, and am now happily married. Many unpleasant things happened back then because I made a number of poor decisions. Things went back and forth. I hurt myself and other people in the process.

Fortunately, from these dark low points, a great feeling of freedom eventually emerged. I savored this freedom and finally broke free from a number of limiting beliefs. I went to Qatar and met my great mentor, Graham, who sadly died much too soon, less than three years later. I learned a lot from him, from both his successes and his failures. At the same time, I ventured into my second marriage and, soon after, slid into the second divorce. My boss's death, my business exit, and my divorce all came together within less than a year and turned into a real shit story. Although I considered myself rich, in my personal life I was poor and lonely in the Middle East. So I decided to start all over again. I decided to be prudent not to jump into any quick relationships again. I traveled around the world, visited old companions, and spent a little time on a retreat in India. I tried a lot of things until I realized that family and close friends are very important to me. I wanted to have a relaxed, loving relationship with a significant other.

That's when I met my third current and final wife, Patrizia. We are still very happy. Of course, we also have the occasional challenge, yet it works out great. We have two wonderful daughters together. The older one is now six years old and is an absolute sunshine. The little one is almost three years old and totally cuddly and sweet. Patrizia is a violinist. We share many things that are very important to both of us. She plays the violin beautifully, we make music together, and sometimes we give concerts. I play the piano and sing. Patrizia is half Peruvian and half German and also lived in Qatar playing for the Qatar Philharmonic Orchestra. I came back to Germany with her and our oldest daughter five years ago. I was 46 years old and moved back into a house with my parents, a great new building. It was originally intended as a temporary solution, but we have been living together for four years now. We still haven't moved to Berlin or Munich, as we actually intended to. We've arrived in a three-generation situation and are totally happy. A life in the countryside with my parents in one house. If you had told me that 10 years ago, I would have said you were crazy. Now I find it totally awesome.

My friends are also very important to me. I turned 50 this year. Despite the corona crisis, my friends gave me a birthday party. It was a "drive-through party" where I was driven through the village on a tractor and my dear friends cheered me on from their parked cars at the side of the road as I drove by. It was an absolute highlight for me amidst a challenging year, and a confirmation that family and old friends are very important to me.

Well, the 10 minutes are up. That was my lifeline exercise. It was interesting for me to tell it again. Every time the story is a little different. How was it for you? I'm also interested in what it was like for the readers. You can leave me a comment or send me your lifeline. I will listen to it or read it with pleasure to get to know you better as well.

Christian: Many thanks, Michael. I have heard your lifeline a few times already. Nevertheless, your two sides are always remarkable to me. When we met again four years ago, you were this globetrotter from South Africa and Qatar, at home in the world. In addition to your traveling experiences, your family has shaped you a lot. These two facets of *home* and the *world*, which make you up, amaze me again and again.

Michael: I have only realized these big themes and how important they are to me, who I am, and how it's all connected, in the last few years. Only then did my Purpose statement become clear to me: helping people to have an easier life and bridging differences. This again serves the Purpose of making the world more peaceful so that life becomes easier for all people. It has a lot to do with memories and experiences from my childhood, even with experiences of my parents and grandparents. To recognize this is a cool and valuable realization for me.

Christian: Thanks for sharing, Michael.

LIFELINE CHRISTIAN

Michael: We're still on the lifeline exercise and we maintain that this exercise is designed to build a deeper relationship and more rapport[13] with other

---

13 Rapport refers to a relationship that is currently based on trust and mutual empathic attention, i.e. "good contact" between two people. More about this under: https://de.wikipedia.org/wiki/Rapport_(Psychology).

people. It works very well in a 1:1 conversation like we are doing right now or in a group to strengthen the team feeling. Both of us have been doing this again and again for many years. It is also a kind of discipline, a recurring mechanism. So now, in the next 10 minutes, I would like to learn more about your lifeline, ups, downs, and lessons from your life.

Christian: Okay, let's go. I am an Autobahn child. I was born in Karlsruhe and was taken to Neu-Ulm by my parents immediately after my birth, more precisely to Neu-Ulm-Pfuhl. It is a small town near the Danube. I had a great childhood. I played and romped around a lot. I was a wild boy and was well-protected. My father worked a lot and in different cities. For a while he worked in Dusseldorf, then in Hamburg, and finally in Munich. He kept his home base so that we could continue to live in Neu-Ulm. My mother took very loving care of me and my brother, who is four years younger than me. Because I was older, I was allowed to try out a lot of new things. I tested many different kinds of sports. First I started with judo, then I played field hockey and soccer in the garage yard. I once broke a big toe when I kicked a curb.

I also played different instruments, first the recorder, then the flute, then the violin, later the guitar, and even a little bit of the piano. We often went on vacation as a family. That was great. My grandparents had a cabin in the Black Forest. We often all went together to our vacation home in the Eifel. From time to time, we made a special trip, for example to Italy, London, or even to America. So even as a child I traveled a lot and saw a lot of the world. I am very grateful for that. It was certainly a highlight in my lifeline. It became a bit more difficult when I developed into an absolute nerd during puberty. I didn't want that at all, I was simply interested in different things than other teenagers my age. I read a lot. Back then we still had a Brockhaus encyclopedia. I checked that out and read it, too. I had these Tessloff knowledge books called *What is What*. In one of them I even wrote on the first page, "This book belongs to the astronomer Christian Kohlhof." I was 12 or 13 years old. The book was called *Our Stars* or something like that. Only in retrospect did I realize that this was probably the first visualization of my life.

I had one really good friend back then. His name was Reinhard and we did everything together. The older I got, the stranger it felt to be the intellectual loner. Then something great happened. My father suddenly said to us that he was going to work in Munich for a longer period of time and suggested that we move to Bavaria. I thought the idea was great, it was just before my 18th birthday. I entered the 12th grade of the Gymnasium Unterhaching and was the new kid. The one with the John Lennon glasses, about whom you didn't know that he, too, had once gone through puberty. Little fun fact: It's the high school from the German movie *Fack ju Göhte* and our high school graduation prank was showcased a few times in the movie.

From then on things went uphill again. I played in a band, had many friends, and even a girlfriend. I decided to do community service in Taufkirchen because I liked life there so much that I didn't want to leave. Funnily enough, I was mainly babysitting. I spent a lot of time on playgrounds and had a lot of time for music, parties, and girls. Music still plays a big role in my life today. I almost studied music. I was about to take the entrance examination and took a lot of piano lessons. Then I realized that music alone is not for me. It is a nice hobby, but being a professional flute or piano player, and maybe if I was lucky, a music teacher, that was not what I wanted. Therefore, my first important lesson was: *It will not only be one thing.* I started to study physics. The career counselor at my high school said to me, "If you want to become an astronomer, you have to study physics." I even deselected physics in school and decided to take the advanced chemistry and math courses because I knew that I would learn physics in detail later. I took the intermediate diploma also in Munich. Basically, it went on just as it did during community service: studying, parties, music, girls.

After the intermediate diploma, I moved to Aachen with my girlfriend at that time. I wanted to be as far away from home as possible so that I wouldn't be tempted to bring my laundry home on the weekends. Somehow I ended up in Aachen. I met some exchange students from England, we had a lot of fun. Eventually the exchange students left and my girlfriend broke up with me. I was suddenly sitting all alone in a strange city. To make matters worse, there was a first health warning. It manifested itself as rheumatoid arthritis, most likely due to too little sports and an unhealthy lifestyle. The Aachen canteen simply offered far too many fries and sweets. I managed to get out of the loneliness and even fight the arthritis.

I met my first only and current wife, Hella. We have been together for 25 years. That's a really long time. The nice thing is that we have always pushed and supported each other in our relationship over the years. When I met her, she was working as a medical-technical assistant. I was studying. Then I started working while she studied. I earned money as she wrote her doctoral thesis. Then the children came, I started a company, and she worked in a company. She's had her own company for four years now. I think that's great. She is very successful. They are real rock stars in their industry. It's so much fun to watch her and see what's going on. It's a great feeling to fly through life together. We have two amazing daughters, Charlotte and Magdalena. Charlotte is 13 years old and recently was in France for a six month exchange program. Magdalena will graduate this year. Family is just great. What is really nice is that we travel together a lot as a family. We have been to Kenya, Cambodia, and Costa Rica, among other places. Everyone enjoys these trips. The fact that the two girls at 17 and 13 years of age are keen on it and don't say to us, "You old folks, you do it without us," I find very gratifying, of course.

After my physics studies I worked in two companies. That was relatively boring. The best part of the day was actually drinking coffee. Then I was lucky. At the bank, Ralf was the personnel manager. We got along pretty well and always thought how cool it would be if there was a real coffee bar here in the company. We then went through with it together and founded *chicco di caffe.* That was a tough time in the beginning. We had no mentors or coaches. I didn't even have the right literature. Up to this point, I had not been involved in any entrepreneurial thing and I just hoped that my additional business studies would help me somehow. Of course, it looked good on my CV and I was competent in accounting. We got off to a rather poor start, but we kept going and tried to open more bars with limited financing and leasing.

In 2011, we almost went broke. The cash flow was negative, we opened too many branches. During this time, I slept pretty badly. A local savings bank was our main financier and from one day to the next they cut off our credit line. They said to us, "We will now first see if you have a positive prognosis to continue, otherwise it's over." That was a violent experience. I was young, we had two children, and suddenly there was no money coming out of the ATM. The second health warning came. I went to the doctor and told him about my constant tiredness and so on. He said, "That sounds like the beginning of a burnout. You need to take care of yourself, eat healthier food, sleep more, get more rest, and exercise more." I listened, pulled myself together and *chicco di caffe* began to be profitable. Soon thereafter, the Sparkasse advisors proudly patted each other on the back about how much they helped us out. I was grateful for the clarity with which they communicated, "Guys, enough," and also for the determination with which they then helped us. *Chicco di caffe* has continued to grow.

Today, I believe we have over 160 coffee bars. What I am also very grateful for is the last project with *chicco di caffe*, our roasting plant. From the beginning, we had the dream of roasting our own coffee. We wanted to produce the 100 tons we consumed per year ourselves. It was a great project for me to build a roasting plant from scratch. Buying coffee and creating roasting profiles — that was exactly my thing!

We held many Strategy discussions about how to best structure our financing. Those led to me selling part of my shares and leaving as managing director. Since then, I have been financially, temporally, and spatially independent. I now enjoy my life to the fullest. I am happy to pass on my know-how and management skills, both as a coach and as a mentor. I enjoy the relaxed productivity with which we work on our podcasts and our books. And I am looking forward to traveling again with my family. That's where I stand right now. Until a year ago, I would have said, "I'm healthier than ever." Then came the third warning: My rheumatoid arthritis was back. I will now get rid of that, too. I can do it. As I said before, "It is not only music, and it is not only physics." The freedom I currently have in terms of time and money I use more for music, physics, and other things. This is extremely important to me: always trying out and learning something new. I take singing lessons, am learning Italian, and greatly enjoying time with my family.

Michael: Great, thank you, Christian. We've done this exercise a few times together. So in terms of content, I know your lifeline. And, I keep noticing that every time I listen to you, I still get to know you a little bit better. The story is a little bit different every time. Every time I learn a little bit more. I appreciate it very much to get to know you this way. Funnily enough, we've met again and again in the past decade. It's always nice to take those 10 to 15 minutes and hear the story again. Every time I take something new out of it. Today, I have become particularly aware of the commonalities that unite us, especially in our Values. Music is very important to both of us, though we both decided that it is not music alone that fulfills our Purpose in life. Distance, travel, and different cultures are very important to both of us. We both delight in educating ourselves, containing an insatiable thirst for knowledge. And we both enjoy sharing and passing on our knowledge to support others on their journey. This is what I have taken away in this iteration of our mutual lifeline exercise. I thank you very much for it. I am also grateful to have you as a partner in the CoA Academy and to publish our podcast and book together. I am looking forward to all the steps we take together in this lifelong journey.

Christian: Thank you very much, Michael.

Wow. It is impressive how close I feel to you when you talk so openly about your experiences, weaknesses, and emotions. Just reading about it helps me to understand you better and to get to know you better. You show me respect and appreciation by opening up to me like this. This is nothing like just dully reciting your own CV. To present yourself as a boss so "naked" in front of your team requires a lot of courage and strength. It pays off. Whoever has this strength, I gladly follow. Suddenly I understand why this person takes a certain attitude or reacts in certain situations. As a boss, it is important to be understood and respected by your team. Real leaders are courageous, forward-thinking, and strong enough to show weakness.

"IT'S MY LIFE"

— DR. ALBAN, 1992

ACHIEVABLE LIFE GOALS

THE POWER OF IMAGINATION

Christian: We do have a common goal. We want to write this book.

Michael: That's right. *Chief of Anything* will be the title.

Christian: When we talked about it, we realized that there is a lot to do. First of all, we'll record some episodes of our podcast, we'll construct a table of contents, and develop a structure. How do you feel about that right now?

Michael: Overwhelmed. There's a lot of stuff for us to do, seemingly without end.

Christian: Tell me, what are you working on right now?

Michael: I'm thinking about what content to put in the book. Then I write a table of contents. I collect key points, sub points, sub points for the sub points. Then, of course, I worry about the cover. What could the cover for our book look like? I have sleepless nights thinking about what we want to write about on hundreds of pages. And I don't like writing and typing, at least not that much. The thought constantly crosses my mind as to how we are going to do this in the first place. How do we find the time for it? A thousand worries.

Christian: Well, we decided to just record our podcasts and transfer them into a book. Does that help you?

Michael: We'll see how we can convert our dialogues. That's a lot of dillydallying, too. A lot of work.

Christian: It means sitting in front of the computer and recording a lot. Then I do the whole post-production. It really is so much work. When I say it like that, I don't enjoy it anymore.

Michael: Yeah, a giant, mega project.

Christian: How do we get out of this downward spiral of thoughts? It's really no fun that way. We are totally caught up in this process: this has to be done, that has to be done. This is the decision that has to be made. That sounds incredibly exhausting, after months of work.

Michael: I have a to-do list that's a mile long and it doesn't even begin to list all the things I have in my head. There's at least ten times as much to do. I have no idea how I am going to do it. Do you have an idea?

Christian: Let's take a time-out at this point and think again about what exactly we want. We want to write a book.

Michael: Yes, exactly. Actually, we don't want to *write* a book, we want to *have* a book.

Christian: And when it is finished, we will have the book in our hands. How does it feel?

Michael: I imagine a hardcover, medium thickness yet not too thick, otherwise I panic. Then it is too much to read. It should be of high quality and have a nice cover. It's solid, not super fancy.

Christian: What do you see exactly?

Michael: I see the cover of the book. I'm not quite sure what it looks like yet. It has our typical colors: blue, purple, pink—quite colorful. Our CoA design is recognizable. I see the title in bold letters. I don't really see photos of the two of us. I see a cool tagline, maybe something like *IN YOUR FACE*— to the point.

Christian: Do you hear something?

Michael: I hear the paper rustling as I flip through the book. I can feel the pages, they are a bit rough and thicker than normal, standard paper, high quality. I can feel this quality.

Christian: I hear a loud thump when the book falls over onto the desk. That shows me that there is consistency behind it, physical and intellectual mass.

Michael: It feels good to just dream.

Christian: I can smell the freshly printed book.

Michael: Oh yes, it smells like ink. And when you open the book for the first time, the hardcover binding creaks.

Christian: What have we done now? We have a goal. If we are constantly thinking about the process on the way to the goal, we can think of a thousand things that need to be done between now and then. We can think of many little things, more little things, and even more little things. The path to the goal seems eternal. At the end, I also have to correct all the spelling mistakes in the book. At some point, that really isn't fun anymore.

Michael: I stopped listening while you enumerated all this.

Christian: It sounds like a universal sound, which I then hear in the back of my head: "Woooaahh." When I hear that, I don't really want it anymore. I hardly have the energy to get started.

Michael: It sounds like too much work. Shit, now I feel bad again. I just felt so good when we talked about the finished book.

Christian: Exactly, when I imagine the finished book with a super cool cover, the many valuable pages, the smell of fresh ink, the creaking, the flipping pages, it is an experience I can feel. I can make the book even bigger in my imagination.

Michael: Really?

Christian: Sure, I can see it from the outside, from a distance. For example, I can see how the book stands on a bookshelf. I can see the spine of the book, how it stands out from the mass of books. Then I can zoom into the picture of our book. I can zoom into every single page, even down to every letter, and imagine what it will look like, how it will feel, and what I will smell.

Michael: I think that's great. We're going to stick with that Vision for now. With all the finished letters on the thick, high-quality paper. What are we doing here right now?

Christian: We are just now making it clear what we want. Because when I am clear about what I want and I can visualize it, and it even feels haptically pleasant, then all the things I have to do along the way might feel pleasant, too. They are just to be done on the way there. No more and no less. My focus is the goal, and I can almost feel that.

Michael: You know what I'm thinking about right now? The saying, *move your mind and your body will follow.* Or, as a street musician once said, "Move your legs and your body will follow." We have visualized our goal. We have imagined it on all channels. We could see, hear, feel, and smell our book. We did not taste it. I am not sure if this would help, anyway. For me, the book suddenly became tangible, real. It was totally fun and felt really good. I was suddenly incredibly motivated. This was very different from before, when we were just looking at the process and all the things that still needed to be done.

Christian: I felt the same way. It's like ordering a pizza to pick up from my favorite Italian restaurant. I don't think about the lengthy drive ahead or the difficulty in getting dressed. I think about the delicious pizza, the crispy base, and how I'll shove a big piece of it into my mouth. The way to the restaurant is not important to me. It is not difficult for me. I just think about pizza.

Michael: Okay, stop. Move your mind and your body will drive us to the pizza place.

Christian: A book or a pizza can of course be visualized quite well. Is that also possible in a business environment?

Michael: Sure, you can do that with anything. Did you ever arrive at a destination and only then realize, "Oops, I'm already here?" Like in the book *The Secret.*[14]

Christian: Yes, that often works for me with parking spaces. I went to a party with my wife the other day. Shortly before we got there, she said, "Look, why don't you take the parking spot here on the right? It will be difficult to find a free space right by our destination." I was so convinced that I would get a parking space right in at the front door that I drove right up to it. And lo and behold, there were two parking spaces available. I didn't even need to maneuver, I just drove in.

---

14   https://de.wikipedia.org/wiki/The_Secret.

Michael: This universe is a great thing.

Christian: I have another similar example. I once saw a photo on the internet with a sailing boat in front of a beautiful background. It was anchored at an archipelago in Sweden. I really wanted to sail to this place. Three years later, I decided to take a picture while sailing. When I looked at it, I realized that it looked almost exactly like the picture from the internet, a photo I hadn't thought about for a long time. This works the same way in a business context. I used to have the romantic idea of my own coffee bar. I saw myself entering the small café, the sun shining lightly into it, and catching whiffs of warm, fresh croissants and coffee. *[gushes]* I imagined the wooden floor, the foaming milk, and two baristas behind the counter. They looked at me and said, "Good morning, Mr. President, what'll it be today?" [*pause*] And indeed, three years later, the time had come. I had my own coffee bar, walked inside, and had a total *déjà vu* moment. The only thing they didn't say was, "Mr. President." They just said, "Hello Christian." [*disappointed*]

Michael: As of now, that's our synonym for *Mr. President*.

Christian: Maybe I should have corrected that. I should have just said to the baristas, "I want you to call me Mr. President." [*thinking*] Better not.

Michael: There is a matching story from the book, *The Secret*. It was also made into a movie. I thought it was very American and a bit kitschy. Anyway, there is a scene with a man in California. After many years, he decides to clean out his basement and finds something called a *Vision board* that he once made. With this collage, he has portrayed his personal Vision of life and how he imagines his future. For example, he cut out a house from newspapers, which he liked at the time. He thought that he might want to live in such a house one day. In the book's scene, when the man finds the collage, he says, "My blood was freezing in my veins. The house I cut out of a magazine 15 years ago I had recently bought and now I live in it." He couldn't remember the Vision board at all. He had just cut out a few things somewhere, looked at the Vision board for a while, and unconsciously worked on it, even when it was out of sight. As time passed by, he became successful in his job, got married, had a family, and even moved a few times. Years later, he cleans up his basement and finds the picture of the house he had bought on this collage. It still gives me goosebumps. It is supposedly a true story.

Christian: And it is the same with our book. If we imagine it that way, it is actually already finished.

Michael: Great!

Christian: I can see it in front of me at this moment. In my little world, the book is finished. I am only allowed to rework a few small things.

Michael: *Tell your conscious mind exactly what you want to have, how and by when, and then your unconscious mind will get it for you.* I like this sentence very much. The more precise and detailed, the better. I feel right into it. *Move your mind and your body will follow.*

Christian: There is certainly an esoteric explanation for this. I believe in the simple explanation that I always do exactly the things that lead me to my goal, because these things are not difficult for me, because I can do them simply, and because I know what I am doing them for.

Michael: I try to figure out in detail what I really want and then feed my brain with this information. Then, when my brain knows what it's about and what the goal is, it starts looking for clues. Tracks that lead to my goal. My brain extrapolates these tracks and unconsciously leads me directly to the goal. It helps me to notice the tracks and follow them. So it happens that I take exactly the steps in my life that lead me to the goal I visualized. There are studies about what percentage of our brain capacity happens in the unconscious. Our consciousness is only a marginal part of the computing power that we carry around on our shoulders every day.

Christian: I was not aware of that at all.

Michael: Maybe it's better that way. [*laughs*] What do we do now? What does all this mean for our readers now?

Christian: Well, when I have a goal, I think very carefully about how it feels, looks, sounds, or smells when I reach the goal. What is it like when I hold the book in my hand? I choose not to think at all about what I have to do, not until I can imagine it exactly as if it were already reality.

Michael: Is there a method or a kind of question set I can use?

Christian: Of course. Let's try the following. Michael, you address yourself directly to our readers and name the whole set, question by question. Our readers can pause briefly after each question and think about it.

Michael: Okay, great. Here we go...the magic questions. Dear reader, please think of a goal in your life that you would like to achieve. Write it down, be as specific as you can and get a good feel of your goal, the idea of it all. I will now ask you a series of questions that will help you to actually get where you want to go. With these questions, you simply let your mind wander and answer them in your head. You are welcome to write down your answers on paper if you like.

The first question is: "**How is it possible that I have not yet reached this goal?**" [*pause*]

The second question is: "**What exactly do I want to achieve? Describe it precisely in detail.**" [*pause*]

Continue: "**Where do I stand now in relation to the goal I want to achieve? What is already behind me? How much is still ahead of me?**" [*pause*]

"**What will I see, hear, feel, smell, and taste when I have reached my goal?**" [*pause*]

"**How will I know that I have reached the goal? How can I factually measure that?**" [*pause*]

"**What will reaching this goal allow me to do afterwards?**" [*pause*]

"**Do I really want to achieve this goal for myself?**" If the answer to this question is, "No, it's for someone else," please start again from the beginning and choose a goal that you really want to achieve for yourself. [*pause*]

"**Where, when, how, and with whom will I achieve this goal?**" [*pause*]

"**Have I ever achieved such or similar goals before?**" [*pause*]

"**Do I know anyone who has already achieved this or a similar goal?**" [*pause*]

Now comes my favorite question: "**Can I act as if I have already reached the goal?**" [*pause*]

"**For what Purpose do I want to achieve the goal?**" [*pause*]

"**What will I gain and what will I lose when I reach the goal?**" [*pause*]

"**What happens when I get there?**" [*pause*]

"**What won't happen when I get there?**" [*pause*]

"**What will happen if I don't reach my destination?**" [*pause*]

"**What won't happen if I don't reach my destination?**" [*pause*]

Now the last question: "**How has my goal changed through these questions?**"

That's it.

Christian: Thank you very much, Michael.

Michael: Good luck to you all and have fun achieving your goals. Choose them wisely, and be careful what you wish for...

I have had a similar experience to this. I, too, have already achieved goals unconsciously. Up until now, I have never thought about why I have actually achieved them. It feels really good to feel into your own goal, your own Vision, and to imagine everything vividly. It motivates me. Even if the way to get there seems endless, it is easier for me when I have the goal in mind. It feels closer, more tangible. It makes it easier for me to complete the tasks that lie ahead. As Immanuel Kant (allegedly) said, "I can do what I have to because I want to."

PURPOSE

WHEREFORE AM I IN THIS WORLD?

Michael: Christian, what is your Purpose in life, what are you in this world for?

Christian: Hmmm, I haven't really formulated that for me yet. The formulation that perhaps comes closest is that I'm the best possible Christian I can be, like the world's best Karlsson,[15] just the best Christian. That means the best coach, the best family man, and the best person I can be.

Michael: [*laughs*] I just imagine you with a propeller on your head.

Christian: [*grins*] He actually has the propeller on his back.

Michael: Right. On my back. Okay, I understand that you want to be the best Christian in the world that you can be. And what is that good for? How does it make the world a better place?

Christian: For allowing me to develop my full potential. So I can make the greatest possible contribution to a better world. If I can do that, it will be better for all the people around me. The world becomes a better place for everyone who works with me and for those who live together with me, like my family.

Michael: So it serves the Purpose of making the world better or more beautiful for the people in your life. Can you define more beautiful and even better?

Christian: By that I mean above all, it makes the world more pleasant, more amiable, more comfortable. Probably *amiable* is *the* best word. My Purpose in life is for the people around me to make life a little bit more lovable.

Michael: That sounds nice, I think. That is, if one day, in the distant future, you lie on your deathbed and look back on a fulfilled, happy life, and then

---

15   According to Astrid Lindgren's book "Karlsson from the roof.

this thought comes to mind: "Gee, I'm glad I made a contribution to a more amiable world, now I can go in peace." Would that work for you?

Christian: Yes, that fits. There I would say "thank you." What is a *Purpose* anyway? How would you define it?

Michael: In English, *Purpose* or the *deeper Purpose*. We have identified that for you personally right now. That helps a lot in coaching situations. It helps clients to focus on what is really most important to them. That's why we do this *frame-up*. Imagine that you have arrived at the day of your death—in the distant future, of course—and look back on your life with a feeling of gratefulness and completeness. What is the one thing that makes you think, "Gee, I'm glad I did that?"

Christian: I do not necessarily need this deathbed perspective. I also like to look back on my life now and think, "Yes, I have made it more amiable."

Michael: This death-bed frame-up works well for many because it has something final. It creates this feeling of, "Oh shit, now I don't have time to take care of what's really important to me." The frame-up helps to tickle that feeling out a little bit. I'd like to confess at this point that it was not so clear to me for a long time and I spent a lot of time doing things that didn't necessarily contribute to what was really important to me. This became clearer and clearer to me over time. Here is a nice anecdote. Earlier you said, "It's not quite clear to me yet," although it was then quite clear to you.

Christian: [*grins*] I was buying myself some time. I didn't know before what you were going to ask. So I could rummage a little bit.

Michael: If you're asking yourself, "Hmm, what's the one thing I care about?" In Cologne we say, *Et kütt, wie et kütt*— it comes as it comes. I was first asked the question about my Purpose when I was 35 years old. I was in a leadership role that was quite big for me at that time. That was in South Africa. I had an executive coach at that time. She seemed to me like a wise, old, gray-haired lady. Her name was Bev. Bev and I met for one of our monthly sessions. She brought me a A4-sized piece of paper to read, which had a small article on it about Purpose. She then asked me with a big smile, "Michael, what is your Purpose in life?" Of course, I had no answer. In the next session, I still didn't have a really clear answer either. And then she said something very beautiful. She said, "It's okay, Michael. My Purpose came to me when I was 55. It will come when it comes." So then I knew that I didn't have to stress myself about it. Just asking me the question helped a great deal. It set a process in motion that has been unfolding over many years. It has helped me to center myself better in my life and to live closer to my core.

Christian: Sounds exciting. Thanks for that. What does that have to do with management now?

Michael: Well, once again, people and organizations are similar. Companies also have a deeper Purpose.

Christian: Earn money.

Michael: Good point, making money is, of course, important. However, because of that, Purpose is often neglected. The definition of Purpose in a business context that I like best is: *Purpose is why we do, what we do, beyond making money.*

Christian: So why I do what I do, apart from earning money. And maybe also, apart from creating and securing jobs.

Michael: Right. This end in itself is not enough. It's more about the questions: *What does the world actually need this company for? What are we improving?* That can be something very small. Not every company has to save the planet or cure humanity from cancer.

Christian: There are others.

Michael: Yes. If we can contribute something to that, that's cool, of course. Somehow, everything is contributing in some way to the advancement of our world, the planet, or humanity. It's important to acknowledge that. Because contribution to a greater cause happens the moment we decide it and it becomes clear to us. Who gets up in the morning and jumps enthusiastically into the shower, just because he can hardly wait to get to the office, for the sole reason that he gets a paycheck the next first of the month? Well, maybe it depends a bit on the amount of the salary. Eventually, the motivation does stop, however, as people rarely find fulfillment in money alone, at least not for very long. If, on the other hand, I know I'm working on something here that makes a cool contribution, then my jumping-out-of-bed-morning is much more motivating, inspired, and Purposeful.

Christian: What could be such a Purpose in a company that everyone thinks is great?

Michael: There are many possibilities. What could they be? Let me think.

Christian: This is most likely dependent on the company and varies for each. Maybe one thing makes sense in one company and not in another.

Michael: It also depends on the founders. They bring their personal life Purpose into the company, even if they are not yet aware of it. Their Values and Vision also play a major role. We will talk about Values later. Purpose, Vision, and Values are the foundations of the corporate culture. For example a company could express these saying, "Our company exists to defeat cancer," or even better, "To cure mankind of cancer," put positively.

Christian: Or simply, "Cure cancer."

Michael: Or a cancer, exactly. That would be fantastic. Of course, a Purpose doesn't always have to be as life-saving as curing cancer. Disney, for example, has a wonderful Purpose: To make people happy.

Christian: Right. When I go to Disneyland or watch a Disney movie, I am happy. I have a good time for at least a few hours.

Michael: And when I'm an employee at Disney and I know that the Purpose of why we exist, is to *make people happy*, that gives me a good direction. I know what I am allowed to do, how I can behave, and what counts in the end. The result is *to make people happy*. I can even measure that.

Christian: Then maybe I'll have a phone call with a customer or a supplier in a completely different way.

Michael: The goal is that the person you are talking to is happy when he or she comes out of the phone call. If we all live out our Purpose, even with small things like a single phone call, they add up to something big. Something like Disney.

Christian: What other examples of Purpose are there?

Michael: Coca-Cola, for example, has a fancy Purpose statement. I like the first sentence best. The whole statement is a bit long. The first sentence is, "To refresh the world in mind, body, and spirit."

Christian: For whom may this make sense?

Michael: First and foremost for the people who work in the company. Purpose has nothing to do with marketing directly. It is all interconnected, however, its main Purpose is to make people understand why the company exists and what their work contributes to.

Christian: And what would that be for in the case of Coca-Cola?

Michael: According to the first part, "(...) to refresh the world," I am refreshed when I have a cold drink. For me personally, it would be even more refreshing if all the sugar wasn't in it. Then comes the second part: "In mind, body and spirit." *Body* is clear right away. I pour the drink into my body and feel refreshed. Then follows *mind* and *spirit*. So there is something else happening.

Christian: You can see that in the advertisements.

Michael: Right. We can feel that. If you go inside yourself and feel what Coca-Cola means to you—regardless of brand, big company or sugar water. Of course, I prefer to drink healthier beverages. Nevertheless, when we hear the Purpose statement, we have a feeling of, "Yes, they do leave an impression that goes beyond the purely functional drinking of a sugar-water drink."

Christian: Definitely.

Michael: There is also the good feeling of Christmas: "The holidays are coming." That's also refreshing in a way when the Christmas season kicks off. Or when I see the water droplets running down the outside of the bottle in the summer ads because it's so cold that the water in the sun is already beginning to condense. They do a great job in conveying this feeling in their marketing.

Christian: The examples of Purpose that we have talked about are actually only one step away from *improving the world.* Are all corporate Purposes formulated to be about improving the world, to make the world more beautiful, more amiable?

Michael: Yes, they should, I think. What is it all about? Why are we all on this planet? Why are there companies? Why are there companies beyond making money? A company has to make money, that's the definition of the thing. A company also brings with it jobs, perhaps also prosperity for the people who are involved in the company and who work for it. That is all well and good. Only, if all this serves no Purpose for the world we live in, the question arises whether such a company can be really successful in the long run.

Christian: But I could also imagine a company that has a negative Purpose.

Michael: For example?

Christian: Achieving world domination in the next five years, for example.

Michael: [*laughs*] Brian-International, yes. And then?

Christian: That does not sound particularly attractive to me, neither as an employee nor as a supplier.

Michael: Hard to imagine, indeed.

Christian: When I think about Purpose and a big project or enterprise, the moon landing comes directly to my mind. When the Americans flew to the moon, they had to expend an incredible amount of energy, resources, money, people, and material to make it happen. The way I understood it, their Purpose was to win against the Russians.

Michael: Yes, sure.

Christian: That is not a Purpose that really makes the world a better place. Nevertheless, it seems to have worked.

Michael: Yes, that's a good point, of course. I didn't exist back then, it was before my time. As I understand it, it was quite a political race and had something very competitive about it. Competition also has a positive effect. It has spurred the whole country to work towards this goal. And in the end, they actually did it. What was very clear at the time was the Vision of the whole thing, which Kennedy made clear in his statement. "We are gonna put a man on the moon this decade," is how he put it. They just about made it within ten years. Unfortunately, he himself did not live to see it. The ostensible Purpose was to win the race against the Russians. So similar to our conversation at the beginning when you said, "My Purpose is to optimize myself and to be the best version of myself," I ask the question, "Wherefore?" This is typical for a Purpose conversation. I keep asking the questions: *Wherefore? For what Purpose, actually?* Even if the answer from the Americans is "to beat the Russians." Then I say, "Yes, okay. And wherefore?" How does that make the world a better place? And it has actually improved the world, basically. The project has led to a lot of innovation. It has produced many technical achievements that have helped us humans a lot in the aftermath. This might not have been possible without this mega-funded space project. At least, it would have taken many years longer. So it has already served a good Purpose that has gone beyond the competitive. In the end, it has also led to the world becoming a more peaceful place, at least for a while. The *Pax Americana,* as I believe the ensuing period is called, was a very long period of peace and stability in the world, even though we may be beyond the peak now. The project did certainly change the world in a positive way. So perhaps there was a deeper Purpose behind the alleged space race after all.

Christian: What else is important when we talk about the Purpose of the company?

Michael: To get to the point, and if possible in one sentence. The Purpose statement is the heart of the culture, the heart of the company, and thus also what shines into the outside world. So it should be short and to the point. I like that anyway, to *the point*. That's particularly important for the Purpose. For example, when we do Purpose workshops, participants are tasked to formulate in 7±2 words *wherefore* the company exists. Then we polish that until those couple of words sink in so that everyone says, "Whoa, awesome, that's what I get up for in the morning."

Christian: What do you get up in the morning for, Michael? What is your Purpose?

Michael: My Purpose is "to help people make their lives easier."

At first, I find it hard to believe that every company follows a deeper, greater Purpose for society. I am thinking of entrepreneurs who have merely discovered a gap in the market and smelled big money, solely to make money. For a company to be successful, it must meet some kind of customer need. This is per se a good starting point for a good cause. The power of a strong Purpose statement is undoubtedly great—for companies and employees. However, it is not easy to unfold this power, to find one's own Purpose, to fulfill it, and thus to be convincing with it. I wonder how you manage to anchor this in your company's day-to-day business.

VISION

ONLY WHAT I SET MY MIND TO WILL COME TRUE

Michael: Imagine, starting today, everything in your life is running smoothly. You and your family are doing well, you are happy, your company is doing great. In five years, we'll run into each other by chance. I ask you how you are doing and you answer, "Hey Michael, good to see you. You can hardly imagine how great the last five years have gone for me. I'm doing really well. I think I've arrived."

Christian: You ask what my life would look like then? Where exactly would I have arrived, and what would I tell you?

Michael: Yes, exactly.

Christian: Hmm... [*thinking*] we start with CoA Academy. In five years, we will be the coaching platform for learning experiences in Germany, maybe even across Europe. We are known for being particularly entertaining and competent. I can work from anywhere and am totally flexible. I can even see myself realizing our Vision under palm trees. I can feel the sun, hear the rustle of the palm trees, the warm air. It even smells a bit exotic. While I am working on new learning experiences for our clients, I hear the sound of the sea in the background. We have made it, we are the best coaches we can be.

Michael: What would your inner voice say to you when you got there?

Christian: Congratulations, Christian. Welcome home. Maybe even, *What's next?*

Michael: How does it feel to have arrived in five years?

Christian: I feel relaxed. That is important for me. It is warm, it feels warm, and comfortable.

Michael: I can already see it in front of me and hear and smell it. I can feel what it will be like. A beautiful Vision.

Christian: I also taste fresh fruit, maybe a papaya or fresh coconut water. Then, I will have described my Vision in all five senses.

Michael: Okay, go on. Be really greedy. What else happens?

Christian: Well, if I may be really greedy, I hear my phone ringing. It's my bank calling to say, "Mr. Kohlhof, unfortunately your account is full. Please open another one." I actually asked how much money there would have to be in an account for that to happen. Nobody was able to answer this question, it probably has never happened before.

Michael: [*laughs*] I'll remember that. "Hello Mr. Portz, I'm afraid your account is full." What the hell are we doing?

Christian: But that would only happen if I was really greedy. That is not necessary at all. A half-full account is also enough. "Mr. Kohlhof, I inform you that your account is already half full." I don't want to hear *half-empty* from my bank consultant.

Michael: What did we just do?

Christian: I created a little film in my head. I have visualized pictures in my mind. I saw, heard, tasted, and felt something; it's a kind of target film in my head. This is the goal I want to reach. I am ready to do something to get there.

Michael: So we are on the subject of Vision.

Christian: Was that already a Vision?

Michael: Yeah, that was at least an approach. We can go even deeper and describe your Vision in more detail. You probably noticed the frame-up we used. I asked you to visualize what your future would look like if you had already reached your goal, your Vision, and looked back from there. Imagine we meet in five years and you tell me where you have arrived at that time. You changed your perspective and looked from the future into the past. What has happened? What has led you to arrive at your destination? You have described this very beautifully with all your sensory channels. You went through every channel and described what you saw, what you heard, what you felt, what you tasted and what you smelled. The sea air, the tropical paradise, the wind, and the air—I could literally feel all that. This is exactly what Vision is all about. So what do I need it for as a company? There are many concepts for it: *BHAG, 3HAG, 5HAG*. These approaches are all very similar.

Christian: Can I proceed in a similar way in a corporate context, i.e., along the sensory channels?

Michael: Sure, you can do that.

Christian: What are typical Visions that companies have? I often hear things like, "We will become the market leader in segment XY within the next three years."

Michael: Before we answer that question, I'll ask another one. What do companies need a Vision for anyway? What Purpose does a Vision serve?

Christian: I would say so that all employees know where it's going.

Michael: What is that important for?

Christian: So that the next steps that happen are obvious. I compare it to the ascent of Mount Everest. If I know that the goal is the summit of Mount Everest, I can plan appropriate steps. Everyone who is involved knows that uphill can't be wrong. Even if the first step does not bring me directly to my goal, and it can still take some time, I know that uphill is the right direction. Every step brings me closer to the goal.

Michael: You talk about a common direction. Even if the exact path is not yet clear, everyone knows the goal. Everyone knows the direction in which they should go.

Christian: Right. Because it can also happen that it is necessary to take a detour, run a curve, or even take a step back. I may also need to walk downhill on the way to the summit. This is much easier for me if I know the goal and I can orient myself accordingly. Kind of like a compass.

Michael: I was very impressed with Amazon's Vision statement. I often use it in workshops. It's now very well known, it says, "To be Earth's most customer-centric company, where customers can find and buy anything they might want to buy online." They have chosen every word very carefully.

Christian: The description of my Vision at the beginning was more about answering the question, "How do you know that you are there?" I look around, see the palm trees, see my laptop, and know that I can work flexibly from here. I have the awareness of having achieved what I want to achieve with the CoA Academy. How can you tell that Amazon has reached its Vision?

Michael: You mean, how do I measure the Earth's most customer-centric company?

Christian: Measuring or recognizing having arrived there.

Michael: Amazon could commission a survey and ask people around the world, "What are the most customer-oriented companies?," "Where do you like to shop, online and offline?," "Where do you get the best service and experience?," "At what retailer have you experienced a buying process that is so easy and convenient that you want to keep shopping there?" I think many people would answer, "I prefer to buy at Amazon." I would answer the same. I am totally satisfied and hardly ever shop anywhere else. It just flows with them. With an opinion poll, I can make a lot measurable. "Earth's most customer-centric company," i.e., wanting to be the world's most customer-centric company is, of course, an ambitious statement. The question is in how many countries do people have access to Amazon and can have something sent to them. Apart from Alibaba, I don't know of any other major shipper with a greater reach than Amazon. So the question arises whether Amazon's Vision has not already been fulfilled.

Christian: You have just mentioned several approaches to formulating a Vision: *BHAG, 3HAG, 5HAG.* So how do I approach the matter as an entrepreneur?

Michael: There are several possibilities. Some think in different time horizons. They think about what they want to achieve in one, three, or ten years. The further I look into the future, the more Visionary it becomes, of course. Personally, I think a horizon of five years is appropriate. In five years, a lot of unforeseeable things can happen; at the same time, it is still tangible and feels predictable. The ideal time horizon is a matter of opinion. I have had very good experiences with five years and achieved results. Whether it will be five, seven, or four years later is not decisive, in my opinion.

Christian: It makes no real difference.

Michael: The point is that I am arriving. Committing yourself to a specific date would be more like reading a crystal ball and missing the point. It's about setting the goal and a rough time horizon to have enough flexibility on the way there.

Christian: You talked about the Vision of Amazon. I suppose I can describe the Amazon statement as BHAG, can't I? As a *Big Hairy Audacious Goal.*

Michael: You're probably right. At the time Amazon was formulating the Vision statement, Jim Collins' book didn't exist. *Good to Great* is an awesome book in which he coins the term *BHAG*, the *Big Hairy Audacious Goal*. It for sure sounds more intriguing than *Vision*. The various terms all do it equally. Well, is the Amazon Vision now a BHAG? Good question. What does it feel like o be "Earth's most customer-centric company, where people can find and buy anything they might want to buy online?" Does it feel like a BHAG?

Christian: Sounds more like a fight against Alibaba.

Michael: Isn't AWS, Amazon Web Services, now much bigger and more exciting than selling goods?

Christian: Remember the example of the moon landing? When Kennedy said, "In the next decade, we're taking a man to the moon and back," that's a great example of a BHAG. What was so big, hairy, and audacious about it was that, at that time, Americans had only been in space for a maximum of 15 minutes. So they didn't have the technology, nor did they know if it would really work. They couldn't even guess what it would cost. They just had a BHAG and ran.

Michael: That was big and hairy, no question. That's what Kennedy set as the goal. It had a tremendous effect at the time. It inspired and motivated people, at least that's what I read about it. People probably thought, "Wow, we're going to do that? Send someone to the moon? I'd like to work on that." That made an impression.

Christian: I can literally hear how some people have certainly said, "... but we don't know how to do that! Is he crazy? What will it all cost!?"

Michael: But...

Christian: Right. Then people start coming with "but...". And still it worked.

Michael: Even in the time frame mentioned, within *this decade*. That just about worked out. Really impressive.

Christian: In which companies does a BHAG work? Surely there are also companies where it might not work. Perhaps because they are geared to a shorter horizon.

Michael: Even though for some it feels like shooting over the top, I find it very charming to have a grand Vision. Because you often find there is more to it than you thought. We said earlier that the Purpose of a Vision is to give the team direction. Other reasons for a Vision are to impress the employees and, above all, to get the right people on board. Anyone who can identify with the Vision is exactly in the right company. After all, the goal must be achieved. That is the crux of the matter for me. The topic of Vision is often smiled at. Some people say, "It's unrealistic to talk that big talk and set such big goals." That's where it gets interesting. When Amazon formulated its Vision to be Earth's most customer-centric company, some people smiled at it. That was in 1997, 23 years ago.

Christian: That means that Amazon also had neither the technology nor any idea whether it could work at all.

Michael: That's right, they were as brave as Kennedy. What they set out to do back then was very Visionary. On the horizon, they could just start to see that the world was moving into a future where it might work. That was enough for them to give it a try. They started writing this Vision on posters to recruit employees. And those who applied for it also believed in this Vision. It was exactly the alleged nutcases who turned the Vision into reality.

Christian: That means a Vision may also polarize?

Michael: Absolutely.

Christian: Some say, "Wow, just my thing" and others say, "You're crazy!"

Michael: Imagine you have a Vision and someone says to you, "That's a nice idea, but I don't think it's going to work." Would you like that person on your team then? No, I don't want him on my team. If he doesn't believe in the Vision, I can't use him. He might even want to prove to me that he is right. I would rather have the people who believe in it and want to prove that it is possible. Those are the ones who will make it come true in the end. Steve Jobs put it very nicely when he starts with, "Here is to the crazy ones," and later ends with "... because they will end up changing the world." And that's the way it is. The crazy ones who believe in a grand Vision are the ones who change the world and achieve incredible results.

Christian: What is your Vision?

Michael: Our company Purpose is "to help people achieve relaxed productivity." And the Vision-2023 of our company CoA Academy is "to be the #1 brand globally for remote leadership education with growth companies, operating in three time zones with NPS>50% and over 200,000 people managed by a CoA educated leader." Personally, my Vision is to be "Zen-Michael" with a perfectly balanced and happy life. My wife and two children tell me every day how much they love me and we continuously grow and learn together. I will enjoy total financial independence and will lead my life 100% on my own terms.

Christian: How would you know that it is perfect?

Michael: Feels perfect to me, just like that.

I find the idea of selecting one's own employees based on the Vision very appealing. In fact, most Visions are rarely expressed in the daily business life of a company, or they are simply written somewhere on the website. Hardly ever does a Vision really make a difference in the company. It is formulated by the marketing department to make a good impression. It only becomes effective, however, when the management really believes in it and sticks to it. A Vision must be lived, otherwise, its magic fizzles out.

VALUES

VALUES GUIDE BEHAVIOR

Christian: I once worked in a bank. Since then, I have had a rather ambivalent relationship with the topic of corporate Values. We went through a very long Values process back then. Corporate Values were developed and visualized together in a very complex way. We even produced a small booklet about it. It was really well done. After we had put all that behind us, however, the reaction of the employees was rather reserved. They said something like, "It's crazy how much this has cost." They were really upset about that. The expensive Value booklets quickly disappeared in the back drawer of the desk. So I asked myself, what is this all about? One of the Values that was written down and painted back then was *trust*. What do you imagine when you hear *trust*?

Michael: When I hear *trust* different thoughts come to my mind. For me, trust has something to do with a human, with individuals. I have images in my head of how two people shake hands and look each other in the eyes. *Trust* means reliability. When we agree on something, I rely on both of us keeping the agreement.

Christian: You see two people in your mind right now, VAKOG-style?

Michael: Actually, I only see one. I am the other one. I see someone across from me. I look into his eyes and see us shaking hands. I feel the handshake. I would describe the feeling that comes up in me in this situation as trust.

Christian: Interesting. When I think of *trust*, I see a climbing harness. A very stable harness with a new, unused rope. I see no people at all.

Michael: Seems to be more of a security thing for you.

Christian: With me it is rather the material, with you it is more about the people. [*smirks*] So let's stick to the example of *trust*. When a company defines a set of Values, then each of the 10 or 15 thousand employees has a different image of these Values in their heads.

Michael: Of course, it would be exciting to find out what image the reader has right now.

Christian: Dear reader, please think of *trust*. Which picture or which film comes to mind? Please write to us what you think when you hear the word *trust.*

Michael: Or what you feel.

Christian: Share it on any platform where we can read it and we would be glad to hear from you.

Michael: Or send us a message. We trust in you.

Christian: Man and material cost was really high. What are the reasons for such a Value process in a company? I had really bad experiences with it.

Michael: Many of us have had bad experiences with this, myself included. Fortunately for me, I also had another experience with Values. I was able to experience what great things can happen when the Value base in a company is strong. That was really cool. In the business context, Values have become one of the most powerful leadership instruments for me, because they make up each and every one of us and determine how we behave. You have Values in you, I have Values in me. Some of them may agree, some of them may not. They each control a large part of our behavior. Therefore, they have an enormous impact on how we work together.

Christian: So if I know how someone ticks and which Values he has, I also know how he will behave in different situations.

Michael: Yes.

Christian: Under stress or under normal circumstances?

Michael: Both. A Value is a Value if I maintain it even under pressure. Otherwise, it is just a word or an idea. That is crucial. Often during such a Value process, which you described well, companies think about how they want to be as a company and why they want to be that way. The point is that they are often not as they describe themselves. In the case of a bank, I can imagine exactly what they would like to be. Granted, I have all kinds of stereotypes in my head right now. A lot of prejudices about bank employees immediately come to mind. I can well imagine that in the process you went through, the Values, while sounding nice and certainly desirable, still do not reflect the actual behavior of the company, even though there are certainly some Values that give the company strength. My bank does a lot of good things. I am sure there are some qualities that make it strong in the Value base. If the formulated Values do not ultimately match the behavior in the company, the employees naturally shake their heads and think, "What bullshit."

Christian: Trust is a Value that everyone in the company can quickly agree on. There was also a Value at the bank that says that we comply with the legal requirements.

Michael: That's a Value that we all find difficult to get around, unless we risk going to prison.

Christian: Does it make sense for my company to define Values that make me different, maybe even special? Or Values that polarize?

Michael: Under certain circumstances, this can be useful. To really answer the question, it is necessary to understand which Values serve a company. It is not about deciding what is right or wrong in terms of ethics or morals. Values serve to give the company a certain strength. That is the point. They should help to achieve the goals set. They show which strengths the company has and through which behavior the goals can be achieved. In the end, something should come out like: *This is our common Value base. This is how we behave in the company in order to realize our goals.* A common sense of strength. That is the whole secret. Values serve a Purpose.

Christian: Let's stick to the example of *trust*. What can I do to ensure that this Value helps me achieve my goals in the company?

Michael: The question is whether trust is a characteristic that is very strongly anchored in the team and is at the core of cooperation. The literature often refers to core Values. It is about the core of the company. Is this Value so pronounced in the company that it makes the company strong? If so, trust is a core Value. What remains is the challenge of common understanding.

What does the word *trust* mean for the team? We have just seen that you have one idea about what trust means, I have another. We need a common understanding. So we need to define what exactly trust means in our company. What makes our behavior when we live the Value of trust on the team and in the company? How do we deal with each other? How does trust make us strong on the way to our goal? Only when this is clear and actually applies, i.e., is truthful, does it have Value. The emphasis is on *truthful*. To write in some booklet, "We need more trust, because that helps us to achieve our goals in the future," does not help. If the Value is not truly anchored in the team, it has no Value. Unless we assume a fundamental cultural transformation that a company is undergoing, then Values can also change. Unfortunately, that rarely works out.

Christian: Let's pick another company. I have heard of a company that defined *fun* as a corporate Value.

Michael: I like that.

Christian: Happy to hear. We have tested it in our Chief Seminars. At the beginning, the participants often think, "This is a strange Value." Especially since it is not an adjective. It just doesn't mean *funny*. Funny means something else. The Value is *fun*.

Michael: With this statement, you are already limiting the meaning. In your mind there is a difference between *fun* and *funny*. The question is, do the other employees in the company see it the same way? The others may not even know your explanation. And here we are again at the problem of common understanding. I am a Rhinelander. I come from near Cologne. Carnival is great fun for me. For others it is no fun at all. For some, a joke is fun. Others can't laugh about it at all. For some it is great fun to dash across the water with a surfboard or through the Eifel in a Porsche. Others consider it fun to jump out of an airplane.

Christian: From a functioning aircraft. With a parachute.

Michael: You see, the crux lies in the definition of the Value.

Christian: This company I heard about is ours. We, the CoA Academy, have defined *fun* as a corporate Value. And by that I don't mean that we have written the word down somewhere, but we have agreed together on a definition of the Value. So that the picture in everyone's mind is the same. That is important. It is completely irrelevant what image outsiders have of the Value fun. The important thing is that we have a unified picture of it.

Michael: It is also important that it reminds us which of our behaviors give us strength. In this way, we can make a clear selection based on our Values, who we want to work with and who we don't, who we want to hire, who we want to promote and who we want to let go because he or she doesn't fit.

Christian: Values, therefore, make a major contribution to employee leadership, employee development, and employee selection.

Michael: Absolutely. Values may have teeth. They have to have teeth. Values really make a difference in a company. If they are really lived out and not just hanging on some poster on the wall or lying in an expensive booklet in a drawer, then they determine who comes, who goes, and who stays in the company. Then we are clear about what behavior gives us strength as a company and how we can achieve our goals, so that we can cultivate this Value base.

Christian: How did we define *fun* again?

Michael: Carnival did not come up. Despite my Rhenish roots, I couldn't get that through. We defined fun like this: "We are entertaining, motivated, and productive. Working with us is fun."

Christian: It is a completely different definition than the one I had in mind at first.

Michael: It's also different from my first thoughts about it. I had carnival in my head. And suddenly it says, "We are entertaining." The sentence begins with "We are..." Some companies start in the first person singular *I am* to make it clear that the behavior is expected of each individual. I think *we* is good, too. It supports the team feeling. "We are entertaining, motivated, and productive." Something happens directly in my mind. When I only hear *fun*, I think of a fun club. Then comes *entertaining,* which gives the whole thing a different meaning. With *motivated and productive,* fun becomes something even more special.

Christian: Fun becomes efficiency or effectiveness. And results.

Michael: It's definitely getting more concrete. Then, *"...working with us is fun," follows.* This reminds everyone who works with us that it is important to have fun while working with us.

Christian: And if you don't like that, you might not be the right employee.

Michael: Right. So, in turn, we can make a choice that helps everyone achieve our goals. If someone doesn't fit in, it doesn't help anyone. That's the beauty of Values. They help us make the right decisions. We use our Values to support our decision-making.

Christian: These Values must mean something to us. Outside the company, they do not need to have any special meaning.

Michael: The more people profess to or against this meaning, the finer the separation and the clearer our decisions. Values create selectivity, then it works.

Christian: It was a lot of fun again with you. I am confident that we will also master the next chapters with a lot of joy, entertainment, and productivity.

Values make a difference in a company. That is what matters. I make business decisions based on these Values. That's the difference between a true Value base for my company and the marketing slogans on the website or the posters on the office walls. What I find exciting is the fact that Values do not represent a target image. So I don't think about which Values we want to represent in our company from now on. This is probably the most common mistake made with classic Value definitions. Values reflect what is already there. They represent the existing, emotional strengths of the company. Viewed in this light, everything slowly makes sense. Purpose, Vision, and Values are a powerful management tool when they actually make a difference in the company.

STRATEGIES

STRATEGY IS SO SIMPLE

Christian: Tell me, what is Strategy?

Michael: Hmm... [*thinking*] This is again one of those big issues in the business context. How do I best explain Strategy?

Christian: Well, I can look at Strategy from different angles. On the one hand, I ask myself, "Which Strategy do I pursue in my company?" I can also ask myself, "Which Strategy do I implement in my life?" or "Which Strategies make sense for me?" On the other hand, I may pose the question, "How do I come up with these Strategies? How do I decide on the right Strategy?"

Michael: "What is Strategy?" was your initial question. Now I have more questions, and still no answers.

Christian: In the past, I could never remember the difference between Vision, mission, Strategy, and Purpose. Since working together, I understand this better every day.

Michael: I find the word *Strategy* totally fascinating. I used to have a tremendous respect for it. I used to think of the smart consultants at McKinsey, or military strategists, or super brains. That instilled respect in me and that's what sparked my interest. At some point, I looked up the word *Strategy* in the dictionary. I recall the definition of *Strategy* being "a plan that serves to achieve a goal."

Christian: A strategic plan.

Michael: Later on I got to know a model, a framework with three circles and a heart. It explains each element's Purpose, Vision, Values, and Strategy. With the help of this model, I can lead a company. This model made me realize that Strategy is nothing more than what we do.

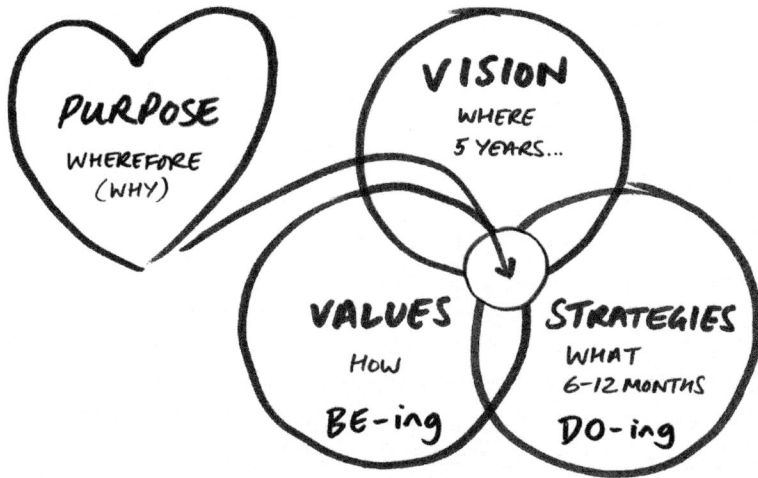

Illustration: Leadership Model with a heart and three circles.
For us, this is the greatest Strategy model ever.

Christian: *Strategy* sounds so daunting because it is often not clear what it is all about. The real question is, what exactly do you mean when you talk about Strategy? When we define it, we realize that we definitely have a Strategy within the company. What is important about Strategy?

Michael: We have already talked about Purpose, Vision, and Values. Once I have defined the Vision, I know where we want to go. I know the Purpose. The Strategy is nothing more than the plan for how we get there.

Christian: So the next steps?

Michael: Almost. The Vision shows where we want to be in three, five, or however many years. It's still relatively far away and we're not sure if the Vision can be realized. It is the Vision, a wish for the future, so to speak. We have defined Vision as the target image that we want to achieve if everything runs smoothly. For me, Strategy is what I can do in the next six to twelve months to get closer to the Vision. In my view, six to twelve months is a good period because I can still keep a good overview. I can assess what can realistically be achieved in this period and plan and define this in a concrete SMART goal. There are still a few imponderables. Nevertheless, on the whole, I am confident that I can take these things on and tackle them immediately. That is Strategy for me.

Christian: In this time horizon, we then tackle concrete projects as part of the Strategy to achieve the goal. I plan tasks and define who does what by when and who is responsible for what according to the RACI matrix.[16] This is where operational management begins.

Michael: Yes, exactly. Imagine you're at a New Year's Eve party and you're talking to a friend or business associate at the bar. He asks you, "Hey Christian, how did your year go?" You answer, "It was a great year for me. I came a lot closer to my Vision. Here's what I've achieved this year…" And then you enumerate the four or five highlights you have achieved this year. I also use this frame-up in workshops, both in a professional and private context. That works great. These four or five highlights describe my Strategies for me. I understand the term *Strategy* as something that can be counted up. That makes it more specific and concrete for me. *That is our Strategy,* sounds too vague for me. My Strategies for the coming year are: 1, 2, 3, 4, 5—all of these points are defined as a SMART Goal.

Christian: The picture that you like to paint, with the three circles and the heart, is a model that represents the entire corporate Strategy and shows the individual Strategies that are currently being worked on.

Michael: *This is how we are gonna run this company.* This title is the headline of the picture you are talking about. It is the leadership model that we will use to move the company through the universe, through life. It contains the deeper Purpose behind why this company exists. It contains the grand Vision, where we want to go. It shows our Values that drive our behavior and it describes the Strategies, including what we will implement in the coming months. This management model outlines the major strategic areas that we are working on.

Christian: Do you remember the deathbed perspective? We used this frame-up to formulate the Purpose.

---

16   RACI is a technique for the analysis and representation of responsibilities: https://de.wikipedia.org/wiki/RACI.

Michael: Yes, to see what it feels like when I leave the world satisfied one day.

Christian: So the Strategies are now the New Year's Eve perspective, a somewhat shorter look into the future. From a long-term perspective, I say, "I have achieved this Vision. I have fulfilled my Purpose." The New Year's Eve perspective describes the rather short-term things I have achieved from year to year or from quarter to quarter. We had a few good examples of corporate Visions. Are there also typical examples of corporate Strategies? What are typical Strategies that companies have?

Michael: A typical Strategy includes a specific implementation goal with one or two concrete metrics that show that I have achieved that goal. An example from the sales area would be, "Next year, we will expand our sales team with three additional employees. These are hired and trained by July 31, so that we can achieve an additional sales volume of 120,000 Euro by December 31."

Christian: Or, "We will close another financing round with a volume of five million euros by October 31."

Michael: Or, "By March 31, we will define our new brand positioning and carry out a brand relaunch by July 31. The relaunch includes the website, LinkedIn, Facebook, and newsletter communication channels. We will increase customer satisfaction and achieve an NPS[17] of at least 70% by the end of the year."

Christian: That no longer sounds as pompous as it did at the beginning.

Michael: No, that sounds simple. I can just make it happen now.

Christian: In our workshops we often start with the topics: Purpose, Vision, and Values. When we then come to the Strategies and ask, "What are we going to do in the next year or two to get closer to the Vision?" the participants already know what will happen.

Michael: Oh yes, that was a big learning experience for me too. In the past, I used to go about strategic planning all wrong. We spent days and weeks

---

17 The Net Promoter Score (NPS) is a key figure from marketing, which expresses customer satisfaction in the form of a recommendation rate.

in endless discussions about what we wanted to do, what we wanted to achieve in the first place, and how we should do it. It was incredibly tough and difficult to agree on a Strategy. Since I know and use the model, it has become much easier. First, we define our Purpose, then our Vision and our Values. Sure, it takes a few days to find and define this North Star. The great thing is that it is then very easy for the individual teams to decide on the four, five, six Strategies they want to work on. These become the easiest part of the whole management process. If the Purpose, Vision, and Values are clear, the teams simply write the Strategies down. In two hours, the annual Strategy is suddenly set and everyone looks at each other with a broad grin and is happy. "Cool, let's get going."

Christian: That is logical. If I know where I want to go and why I want to go there, the next steps are much easier to decide. If I have no idea whether I want to climb a mountain or become a deep-sea diver, it is also difficult to decide what I train for, what I pack in my suitcase, and which flight I book.

Michael: Everything looks easy in the rearview mirror.

Christian: What is the name of the song? *I don't know what I want, but I know how to get it*. If I don't know what I want and know exactly what I'm doing, it doesn't help much.

Michael: *Move your mind and your body will follow*. Once I have made up my mind (...), if I know what I really want, it also quickly becomes clear how I can get there.

Christian: The time I spend with my team, my employees, to determine the Vision and Purpose is well invested, right?

Michael: These one or two days are priceless. It saves so much time and brings an incredible amount of alignment, direction, and power to the organization. This is certainly the best time investment you can make in the history of the company.

Christian: When I have defined all this—the Vision, the Purpose statement, and the company Values—how do I tease these Strategies out of my team in a concrete way? Basically, my employees know best what needs to be done. How do I approach this exactly?

Michael: The first question that is often asked is, "Who will participate in the Strategy workshop?" Many answer, "We do it better in small groups."

Christian: How big is this small circle?

Michael: From my point of view, the ideal size is 7±2, and ten to twelve is still ok, but no more. Some founders or bosses would like to decide this among themselves, in twos or threes. The danger is that the effect, the identification, and the motivation can fizzle out. A feeling of loss of control arises. It is more skillful to involve the team from the very beginning. A collective is formed. The team gets a much better idea of all things. The discussions that arise in such workshops are very valuable. People become clear about where each individual stands and where everyone wants to go together. People come to an agreement and create commitment. When friction occurs, these issues become clear as does what needs to be clarified before the strategic goals can be achieved. All this would otherwise remain hidden. When the Strategies are defined, it is immediately clear to everyone what he or she is doing it for. *Start with why*. Everyone knows what we are doing it for. We do it to fulfill our Purpose and to realize our Vision. We're ready to move! The question, "Why on earth?" no longer comes up. The entire management team brings this to the company with full conviction, instead of secretly justifying it and telling their own employees, "Management decided so. They gave us these Strategies, and hopefully they will have thought of something."

Christian: Right. From there I can move in a good direction. We now know where we want to go and why we want to go there. How we work together to achieve this Vision is also clear. On the second day I like to ask, "What competencies and structures do we need to achieve this Vision?" "What competencies and structures are we building up in the coming year?" That way people quickly gain insights like, "Right, we need a structure for the investment rounds," or, "We need a structure for our sales." I have had very good experiences with these questions.

Michael: I can only confirm that. There is this saying by your good friend Peter Drucker, *Structure follows Strategy*. He was also the one who said, "Culture eats Strategy for breakfast." If I believe him, the order is important. First of all, the culture has to be clarified. To do this, we define the Purpose, our Values, and our Vision. When the culture is clear and stable, I consider the Strategies to achieve the Vision. Three, four, five things we will do in the coming months. Once these Strategies are in place, I ask myself about the structure. What structure is appropriate to implement the Strategy? Once this is clear, I can delegate tasks to my team and make a list of additional resources I might need from outside: employees, partners, service providers, suppliers, etc. *First culture, then Strategy, then structure.*

Christian: Every strategic project thus becomes a structural project. So it's not just about agreeing to make sales better. It's about agreeing on the sales structure with which we can make sales better and more powerful in order to achieve the goal and fulfill the Strategy.

Michael: Right. The Strategies imply that all by themselves, because I also determine how I can identify and measure the achievement of the strategic goals. I define the three, four, five biggest fields of action, which I want to tell my friend on New Year's Eve. I want to say, "Awesome, this is what we accomplished this year." Just like you say, the Strategies imply what has happened structurally. "We've increased our completion rate in sales by 20% by hiring a head of sales this year." The structure has implicitly emerged from that. "We want to achieve a wider range, so we're going to expand our brand communication to the following channels." It quickly becomes clear that structurally I need people who can fulfill this role.

Christian: Okay, I will ask our initial question again. What is Strategy?

Michael: Strategy is what we do, in line with our Values, to get closer towards our Vision while fulfilling our Purpose.

Slowly, the puzzle is completed and I am more and more convinced of the model with the circles and the heart. In fact, I know these tedious Strategy discussions rarely follow a clear structure. Together with the Purpose and the Vision, it all makes sense. Nevertheless, many roads often lead to Rome. Shouldn't we agree on one? How do we manage not to get lost between the definition of Strategies and the operational, rather tactical measures? The line seems blurry to me. I think there's certainly a lot of fire in it. To be successful for this type of business leadership (as I understand the model), top management, each and every one of them, must be convinced of the procedure. It's worth giving it a try. After all, the outdated Strategy models have had their day and they are not really a great source of inspiration anymore.

THE MIND IS EVERYTHING. WHAT I BELIEVE, I BECOME.

— AFTER BUDDHA, ABOUT 500 B.C.

INDIVIDUAL PERCEPTION
SELECTING FROM TRILLIONS OF SENSORY IMPRESSIONS

Christian: I thought again about the topic of leadership. We understand leadership as *the ability to influence*. We have also already talked about communication and behavior and about the fact that I can adapt both to achieve my goals. I would like to go a little bit deeper into this topic.

Michael: *Leadership is my ability to influence*, exactly. This influence happens holistically, through the whole body and all senses: body language, expression, pace of my speech, volume, tonality, posture, gestures, and facial expressions. All of these convey something. With this holistic communication I achieve an effect on my counterpart. No matter with whom and in which environment. I always have an effect on my team, on my boss, on my company's shareholders, on my wife, and on my children. With all the people around me I achieve something with what I radiate, consciously or unconsciously. According to Paul Watzlawick,[18] "I cannot *not* communicate." On the same token, I cannot *not* radiate. I am constantly radiating something. So I am also responsible at all times to consider what I am projecting, because I can make a difference in my environment at any time.

Christian: This is because I, as your counterpart, have five sensory channels through which I receive messages from you: I see you, hear you, feel you... well, maybe not with us right now, because of the distance. The two other senses, which play a rather minor role in this case, are smell and taste. These five sensory channels continuously resonate with me and have an effect on me. So this is a gigantic sweep of data that comes to me.

Michael: It's gigantic. The five senses that you just mentioned are the ones I remember most easily with the help of the abbreviation VAKOG: V = visual, the sense of seeing, A = auditory, the sense of hearing, K = kinesthetic, the sense of feeling.

Christian: All over the body. Even when I move, I can feel a gust of wind or the sun on my skin, for example.

---

18   Paul Watzlawick (1921-2007), Austrian communication scientist, psychotherapist, philosopher and author.

Michael: Right. Everything physical. Then there are the two other senses you've already mentioned. The sense of smell is the olfactory sense, the *O* in *VAKOG*. The *G* stands for gustatory, the sense of taste. So now we humans are walking through our own world with all our senses. Each of us sees, hears, feels, smells, and tastes all these impressions in his own world. By the way, there is also a sixth sense, the so-called auditory-digital channel. Strictly speaking, it is not a sense, but a channel through which I talk to myself. My inner voice.

Christian: For example, when I say to myself, "Christian, what are you doing right now? What kind of nonsense did you say in that video?" that is the auditory-digital channel.

Michael: Yes, or when I'm thinking, "Gee, Michael, does it really make sense to talk about the auditory-digital channel right now or could I have done that later?" We have these five senses, plus the sixth channel. With these five senses we record data all the time. You just named it aptly, it's a *gigantic sweep of data*. In computer language, we talk about bits and bytes to measure amounts of information. Converted into bits, that is about 11 million bits per second that we humans record.[19] Two million bits of information per second, which come at us through the five sensory channels. That is quite a large amount. Extrapolated to our day-to-day, that is about 950 billion bits of information every day—almost one trillion.

Christian: This corresponds to some DVDs.

Michael: Yeah, we could watch about 50 movies for that.

Christian: And my brain wants to process all this. I have to go crazy at some point, right?

Michael: That's a good question. When I now communicate something to my employee in my leadership role, I have to be aware that not only my message, but also more than 950 billion pieces of information will be sent to him on the same day.

Christian: And your message is just a small part of the total amount that comes at him. Almost negligible, so to speak.

---

19 see https://www.britannica.com/science/information-theory/Physiology.

Michael: Right. Unless, of course, I babble to him all day, for 24 hours. Then maybe I'll manage to occupy the majority of the bits.

Christian: [*laughs*] Hopefully you only do that in the auditory-digital channel and not in the auditory.

Michael: How do we deal with that now?

Christian: We need a reduction of data.

Michael: Absolutely. No one wants to have 950 billion bits of data in their head every day. If I calculate what that means in a year and in a lifetime, it becomes even clearer to me how huge this amount is. That means we need a solution to reduce the data. Deleting a large part of the information, or simply ignoring it is an option. A second option is to generalize. Let me give you an example. I watch a car, a blue 3-series BMW with big rims and spoilers, passing me. A dark haired man with sunglasses sits behind the wheel. When I tell you about it and generalize about what I observed, I say to you, "A dark car just drove past me."

Christian: Or, "There was just something there." Then I would have deleted some additional stuff.

Michael: Or I could say, "I perceived a shadow." Then I generalized intensely and reported only the last perception.

Christian: What about the distortion of information?

Michael: In our example, the distortion of information would be if I said, "There's a Mercedes E-Class driving past me." I saw a 3-series BMW, but I thought it was an E-Class.

Christian: Maybe I don't care at all what kind of car it was.

Michael: Right. Maybe I thought it was a bus, too. Or just a shadow. That's *distorting*. So there are three filters: *erase, distort,* and *generalize*. This happens pretty much all by itself in our minds because it's the only way our brain can cope with this flood of information.

Christian: Let's assume that a co-worker is facing you and you say something to her. What happens to her with these three filters? Deletion is clear. What you say goes in on one side and goes out the other. How does the distortion work?

Michael: Then a classic misunderstanding usually happens. You must know the phrase, "Oh, I understood that quite differently." That's distorting information. What we can do about it, I save for later.

Christian: And the generalized statement, "It's my boss again, he always says the same thing."

Michael: [*smiles*] Or, "I'm supposed to write a report again. I'll just use the same one as last time." Now I make it even more complicated. There is, in fact, something else that is crucial. Not only do the 11 million bits per second rain down on us and are deleted, distorted, and generalized when received, but we also have memories stored in our mind that are also incorporated into the processing.

Christian: Stories, beliefs, goals.

Michael: Faith, Values, ... that's a lot of stuff that's in our heads. And all of this is mixed together with every bit of additional information, so that in the end it all adds up to a nice potpourri. The technical term from NLP for this potpourri is *representation*. So I take all the input, distort, generalize, and delete some details, mixing what is left with my already stored beliefs, Values and memories. What comes out in the end is my personal view or perception of things, my representation. This representation is shaped by my five sensory channels. To this one, I have a picture in front of my eyes, a sound in my ear, and a feeling I feel. Perhaps I also perceive a smell and a taste.

Christian: This personal representation then most likely has nothing to do with the real world at all.

Michael: Well, it is influenced and shaped by the real world. *Influence* was the keyword of the whole thing. There's an appropriate saying: *Everybody has their own unique model of the world.*

Christian: Who actually decides what the *real world* is?

Michael: Hmm, the universe, the good Lord?

Christian: [*laughs*] So the *real world* does not exist in the model?

Michael: *Everybody has their own unique model of the world*. This phrase has a lot going on. Because the sensory impressions that I have accumulated over my life so far—my memories and Values and everything that I have perceived, filtered, distorted, and generalized through the five *VAKOG channels*—are unique to each person. Thus, the representation that I take out of my perception in every moment of life is also completely unique.

Christian: Well, I will summarize it all again. The idea was that *leadership is my ability to influence*. When influencing, I try to make sure that what I say is received by my counterpart in the way I want it to be. However, on the way there, a big muddle happens with each individual, triggered by five different sensory channels, through distortion, deletion and generalization. With all this, do I have any chance at all to reach anyone?

Michael: [*smiles*] Yeah, you're right. When I listen to you like that, it all actually sounds like tilting at windmills. And it gets worse because I can't control it. Everyone takes something different from the information they get. Let's look at the chain further, we will see that there are ways.

Christian: We are not finished yet?

Michael: [*laughs*] No, we're not finished yet. We are at about half time.

Christian: Crazy.

Michael: Now it gets really complicated [*laughs*]. No, no, don't worry. It's about to become smooth. [*concentrates*] So I have my representation of all the input and all the things that I already have in my head. That reminds me of another saying: *This is all we've got in the world*. The only thing we really have and possess in life is this representation of the world. This is really a cool saying.

Christian: This is the Buddhist approach. That's what I'm trying to find out while meditating. The question is: What is there really? There is my breath, there is what I hear. Everything else is the stories that I tell myself.

Michael: Yes, exactly. I'd like to try that, too. So far, I'm not very deep into this meditation stuff. I like doing breathing exercises very much. It helps a lot. Anyway, my sensory impressions are all I really possess as a human being. Some people say, "All we have is time." The only catch is that we don't know how much time we really have. What I do know, however, is that the impressions of the world, and the image I have of it, is really the only thing I possess. It is unique and nobody has exactly the same impression. So now we have pulled the representation out of all the clutter. This representation now makes a difference. It puts the person with whom I communicate into a state. This state in which the person is includes both the mental state, (that is, what is going on in the head), and the physical or biological state: pulse down, pulse up, beads of sweat or none, heart rate, and so on. Something changes in me physiologically and physically by what comes at me from the outside. So my holistic state changes. And from this state I decide how I react and what I do about it. As information comes in, I make my own picture or my own soundtrack, so I conceive the story I tell myself, feel my pulse go up, and then I make a decision about how I behave. And then we're finally at the result: what the input has done for me. Behavior is the result of the whole thing. This is what I cause in my counterpart when I influence him.

Christian: And that's all I can perceive in turn, i.e., their reaction, their behavior to my input. Everything else is a total black box for me. This means that I tip in some information from my employee, then something happens inside that black box. In the end the result is a certain behavior. Only then, can I think about how to deal with it.

Michael: Exactly. And the crazy thing is, of these 11 million bits per second, the result is 7±2, only seven plus/minus two impressions. That's because our processing power per second, that is, what our brain can consciously process, is 50 bits per second.

Christian: We have a pretty good program going on, though.

Michael: We have some pretty awesome hardware.

Christian: Well, I can only speak for myself [*smiles*].

Michael: The circuitry is ingenious. We have thousands of connections between our brain cells. And the number of interconnections between our brain cells is supposedly bigger than the number of atoms in the universe.

Here Christian has doubts, because any connection between brain cells would consist of at least one atom.

In the unconscious, major data processing is taking place. In the conscious, on the other hand, there is only a result set of 7±2. I now come back to the challenge as a manager. To lead a person, I try to influence him or her. In order to influence them, the challenge is to choose my *charisma* in such a way that my message over all these streams, over the 11 million bits per second, is at the end among the result volume of 7±2, so that the person's behavior is also what I expect of them. That is the challenge as a leader. That is what it is all about. There are many techniques for this, but it is still an art, I would say.

Christian: With all the input that the reader has received from us, what is the result now? What are the 7±2 that should reach the reader?

Michael: I can formulate it in different channels. Everyone has their own preferences, by the way. There are people like me who prefer the visual channel. What we want to achieve, expressed through the visual channel, is an image with the number *11 million* and the text *bits per second* and next to it an arrow pointing to the right. There you can see the result = *7±2*, and if you can see this in your mind's eye now, you have already taken our message with you. What is the preferred result for you? You have more of an auditory preference. What result can we give our readers on the auditory channel?

Christian: I hear a lot of information on the input side, a lot of sounds. Then I see a messy machine in front of me and at the same time, I feel how I react to the complexity. I hear how I say a sentence to myself that describes my behavior... *[waffles]*

Red energy...

Michael: *[interrupts]* Then there's the emotion channel. Of course it would be great if our readers could develop this feeling of, "Wow, I'd love to learn more about how I manage to get into this result set of 7±2." Maybe someone will feel curious about how to do that, because there are a lot of methods and techniques that I use as a leader to get through to my team. Yes, and those who prefer smelling may now smell an opportunity to get super ahead in life.

Christian: And that tastes like success. *[deliberates]* And what do the digital-auditory ones say?

Michael: They're wondering now whether what we are saying here is really as promising as it sounds. Digital-auditory types often have a relatively analytical way of thinking and like to determine correctness.

Christian: Yes, I can definitely reassure them. It is correct.

Well, that explains a lot. Deleting, distorting, filtering — I can tell you a thing or two about all of this at home and at work. I used to call it the relevance filter. I only hear what I want to hear, the rest is simply filtered out automatically. With my partner, I also have the impression that he is neutralized by Will Smith from time to time, like in the movie Men in Black. Now, I am curious about the methods I can use to influence these filters.

BELIEFS

I AM WHAT I BELIEVE

Christian: I don't think I can do that.

Michael: Aha, was that a decision you just made?

Christian: No. I just think this is all a bit too much. Besides, I'm not a trained podcaster, I'm not a trained anchor, and all this technology is too much for me.

Michael: What is it that is causing you to choose to believe that you can't do this?

Christian: I just don't believe it. I have the deep conviction that it doesn't work for me.

Michael: What would it feel like if you were convinced that you can do it?

Christian: I don't know. I can't just decide to suddenly feel it. I need this experience. To be a good podcaster, I need a podcaster diploma.

Michael: I feel for you. I am in a similar situation. Let's try it the other way around. Has there ever been a situation where you felt that you were good at something?

Christian: Yes, yes. From time to time.

Michael: What situation was that, as an example?

Christian: I can cook pretty well and open wine bottles. I am good at drinking coffee. At *chicco* we always said, "Everybody does what he can do best." We, the managers, are best at drinking coffee and talking rubbish.

Michael: And opening wine bottles and cooking?

Christian: No, actually just talking.

Michael: How does that feel?

Christian: It makes me feel in *flow*.[20] That feels really good.

Michael: Describe what you feel when you are in *flow*?

Christian: It feels warm, like on a sunny spring day. I feel a pleasant light wind. I have a clear head, not even a slight headache. My head is clear and free.

Michael: Spring, warm air, a clear head. Great, what else do you feel?

Christian: I see that it is relatively bright when things are going well. I recognize warm colors like orange and green.

Michael: What do you say to yourself? What does your inner voice say to you in these moments?

Christian: "Let's go. Hey, that's easy. One more time..."

Michael: Very good. Now can you imagine how it feels when you decide that podcasting feels the same?

Christian: Yes, then it would be easier. I would just say, "Come on, Michael. Let's just try it out. We'll sit down now and do the podcast until it's ready." Before I realize that we have started, it's already over. We hit *record, stop* and give ourselves a high five. That went great.

Michael: Great, then we've already accomplished that. Let's move on.

Christian: What have you done with me now?

Michael: You describe it.

Christian: I said to you that there is something I cannot do. There are certainly many things that I am convinced I cannot do.

Michael: Then I said something to you. Do you remember?

Christian: Unfortunately not. I was so busy with my thoughts and my beliefs that I honestly didn't listen to you at all.

Michael: The first thing I asked you was whether you made this decision.

---

20   https://en.wikipedia.org/wiki/Flow_(psychology).

Christian: I am *at cause*. There are many things I believe. This is perfectly fine in my world. I believe that I cannot fly. At least not without additional equipment. That doesn't limit me in my daily life. There are also some things that would be easier for me if I believed I could do them, like the podcast example. It would be easier for me if I believed that I could do it. Then I would just do it without having to rack my brain. Because that's what I always do when I believe that I can't do something or that something is impossibly difficult to do.

Michael: [*smiles*] It's funny to hear the words *I believe* from you so often.

Christian: That was not intentional.

Michael: What a coincidence.

Christian: We talk about beliefs.

Michael: What you said in the beginning was a *limiting belief*. It's also called a *limiting decision*.

Christian: I have expressed something that makes me smaller than I am. It prevents me from doing something, something that I want to do.

Michael: When you say, "I don't think I can do this," what does your inner voice reply? What comes to me and maybe to everyone else who has heard it from you?

Christian: Probably something like, "I think so, too."

Michael: Well, if Christian himself says that he can't do that, I guess it's true.

Christian: When I say to myself and repeat, "I can't do this, I can't do this, I'm too big, I'm too small, I'm too fat, I'm too thin, I'm bad at math..."

Michael: [*interrupts*] ...then it suddenly becomes true and everyone around you supports the statement.

Christian: The whole thing also works in the other direction: affirmation.

Michael: Exactly, then it is about positive affirmation.

Christian: I am an eagle, I can fly. I am the best and the greatest. I believe that if I tell myself that every day, I will be convinced of it at some point. Then I believe it.

Michael: I think so. Whether that is appropriate is questionable.

Christian: Can I determine which beliefs I have?

Michael: Well, I believe that I can believe anything in life that I want to believe.

Christian: So I can build up a portfolio of beliefs and make decisions: I believe in that, I don't believe in that. Just to be clear, we are not in the religious realm, but in the realm of *truths about me*.

Michael: That reminds me of a good saying from a mentor. Imagine you are in a new role and you have no idea how to do it. My mentor said, "Fake it till you make it."

Christian: Pretend that you can, until you can.

Michael: Right. *Act as if*, pretend. Act as if at first and then work to make it a reality. The first step is to act as if I already can. The following question is also in our script of goals, which we often use: Can you already pretend that you have reached the goal? How does it feel then?

Christian: Because if I can imagine it, I already believe that I can achieve it.

Michael: That's how it works. That's what I just asked you. "How would it feel if you could do podcasting as well as drinking coffee and talking rubbish? Then you started to imagine what it would feel like to be as good at podcasting as you are at drinking coffee. And suddenly you had something else on your mind. A different feeling, a different image, a different sound. Suddenly, it becomes true.

Christian: I can take existing beliefs and edit them, i.e. change them. What NLP techniques are there for this?

Michael: Deleting, restructuring, reframing.

Christian: Like putting the belief into a shredder?

Michael: Exactly. Just go to the cinema and let the film run backwards, in black and white.

Christian: If I complain, I can just click on the red x in the upper right corner and the belief disappears in the trash can.

Michael: A *swish*.[21]

Christian: I often think that you have no limiting beliefs in you at all. Is this true? Or do you have any?

Michael: Hmm... I'd like to respond starting with "I believe." [*thinking*] I firmly believe that you're right. Maybe it'll work out. I remember that I learned the concepts of *limiting beliefs* and *limiting decisions* from you. We all make these limiting decisions often. I, for one, made them often in the past. Now I take less and less limiting decisions.

Christian: The fact that we make them often is also a statement of faith.

Michael: I'm already thinking about one of my mentors again. He once said to me, "You can do anything you want in life. That's what life is all about." That's his mindset, and it's basically a belief, too. I believe what I want. I take what I want. I believe that I can achieve everything I want. In one of the many leadership courses I took, I learned about this concept for the first time. I had just been promoted and I was sent to a series of seminars. The trainer showed us what we can respond to employees when they express a limiting belief. If someone says to me, "I don't think I can make this decision," I answer, "What is it that is causing you to choose to feel that you cannot do this?" I have used this many times before, and each time I observe how the conversation turns completely around.

Christian: Until the employee has deconstructed and understood this sentence...

Michael: The smartest part of the question are the words, *you to choose, meaning, your* choice. What I believe is my choice. Where do beliefs live? Only in my head. I can choose what I believe. I can also choose what I no longer believe and thus remove limitations from myself.

---

21 An NLP technique to change behavior. The Swish Technique.

Christian: There are employees who always say the opposite of what I say. I got to know these *mismatchers* in the NLP training. What helps when talking to them is to simply prove them right. Imagine I answer your statement, "Christian, I can't do this" with, "True. I see it that way too. I guess there's nothing you can do." Often, a mismatcher will then quickly change course again and state, "Yes, yes. I can still do something about it."

Michael: I see, because she absolutely wants to disagree. So if someone from my team is constantly *against it* and often says, "That's not possible," I just play along, affirm what she says, and bet that she will prove me wrong.

Christian: I've done it like this many times before. It works.

Michael: I'm like this, I'm a mismatcher. I often take a stand against it and look for a contrary point of view. My brain needs a balance, another extreme, to ensure that the result is right in the end. That's where my mismatching comes from. If I say to someone, "That's not possible," and this person confirms my statement, I suddenly start looking for solutions. Probably to refute that he is right, or that I was right.

Christian: It's like the motto: *Who is she, that she simply agrees with me?*

Michael: Yes, exactly. There could be something wrong. What other types are there?

Christian: There are still those who like to think about it. Their voice says to them, "Can I really believe that? Is that correct?"

Michael: Yeah, right. If I'm someone like that, maybe I can just go for it and decide that it's true. If I want to change my mind later, I can still do that.

Christian: Let's face it, there are limiting beliefs that prevent me from doing what I want to do. There are beliefs that strengthen me in what I do. Then there are limiting beliefs that are not important because they prevent me from doing things that I don't want to do anyway.

Michael: We've talked about beliefs before. It was about the mindset. Like the example with the IQ. When kids are told they have a low IQ and they start thinking they're stupid. When others hear my beliefs, they believe that, too, and they reinforce my own beliefs. This reinforces the whole system until I end up really having a low IQ and being stupid. If I am told early on that I have a high IQ and that I am very intelligent, I might make others believe this too, and so this also becomes more likely to be true. And again, we have a *self-fulfilling prophecy*.

Christian: What other beliefs are there?

Michael: My favorite among the limiting beliefs is, *I can only be successful in life if I work hard.*

Christian: A nice example.

Michael: Conditional: I can only be successful if I work a lot.

Christian: And it must hurt.

Michael: If I believe in it, it will happen in life. Today I'd rather make a different decision: I can be very successful and conveniently work a lot or conveniently work a little. Or I can work only a bit.

Christian: Or maybe you even choose to see it as something else instead of work.

Michael: Exactly. What we do here is not work, but rather a pleasure.

Christian: It runs so wonderfully smoothly again, it is very easy. I think I have just turned a limiting belief into a positive affirmation.

Michael: Absolutely. Affirm it further.

Christian: Good idea. I had a lot of fun recording this podcast with you. It felt like a spring day with a light wind in a green, orange blaze of color. I was just in the flow.

Michael: I know you were.

And again I begin to question myself. Which beliefs do I have that strengthen me and which limiting beliefs come into my head? I actually hear quite a lot. The inner voice has a lot of power, yet it is the most difficult to convince. Or is that also just a limiting belief? Is it perhaps quite simple, only that I still had the wrong beliefs? If you are really right and I can actually change these beliefs, I am very curious to know how I can do it best. How do I convince myself?

AWARENESS AND MINDFULNESS
#MEFIRST

Christian: We have already talked about beliefs. Do you remember the belief: *I have to work hard to be successful*? I used to have a similar belief system. I believed that in order to be successful, I had to spend a lot of time in the office and could only take a few vacations.

Michael: You're talking about overtime.

Christian: Right. A lot of overtime with little sleep.

Michael: Short lunch breaks, if at all.

Christian: No lunch breaks at all, but quickly eating something in front of the computer. Every free second that I have in the in-between moments, I spent on my cell phone, talking to someone, or checking my emails.

Michael: You have to work evenings and weekends. Hard work comes first, instead of family.

Christian: Fortunately, I got rid of this belief. A few seminars and workshops on the topic of performance helped me to do so. I had a great coach who trained special forces and Olympic athletes. It was all about being prepared to deliver great performance to the point and at the very moment it's needed. He always stressed that there are several factors that play a role in this. He talked about the importance of breaks for recovery, sufficient sleep, and longer recovery phases such as vacations. A healthy diet also plays a role. It is important to take care of yourself and your body. He also recommended meditation.

Michael: That doesn't sound like hard work. Sleeping, vacation, recreation, meditation—that sounds good. I would like that, too.

Christian: It was amazing. When I started to implement the things that the trainer recommended one by one, I actually felt much better. Many things really became easier for me. There was a time, for example during the financial crisis, when things were not going so well at *chicco di caffe*. I was on the verge of a burnout. It was time to change something. So, I decided to make one small change after the next in my life. I did sports regularly and started to meditate. I took a vacation, which I had not done before. From that point on, I felt better and better. I suddenly had everything under control again. Especially as a manager, it is important to lead by example. As you know, I once worked in a bank with investment bankers. Our reputation was measured by how much overtime each individual worked. Years later, leading my own company, I chose to implement a completely different mindset. When leaving the office early, we would say "I'm going on vacation now," "I'm going home earlier now," and "We're having lunch together now." What experiences have you had with this?

Michael: When I hear that, it makes me think of a sentence that probably everyone knows: "I don't have time for this." How do I deal with that?

Christian: I once read, "If you don't have time to meditate for half an hour a day, then you need two hours of meditation immediately."

Michael: I certainly don't have time for that. [*laughs*] The key word is *limiting beliefs*. If I believe or say that I don't have time for something, that is my choice at that moment. Because who decides what I have time for and what I don't have time for? God? The others? The universe? The world? The customers? None of them can decide what I do with my time. Only I can decide that. We all have 24 hours a day. What I do within these 24 hours is decided only by me. For example, you decided to go home in the evenings, take a vacation, and dedicate yourself to your family. When you made these decisions, you realized how much more balanced you had become in your life and at work. What impact did this have on the results of your work?

Christian: I have become more effective. The result was impressive. I realized what I actually want. Meditating has helped me a lot. It is always a little time out and exciting to observe what happens to me and the thoughts in my head during this half hour. I sit there, concentrate, and can just let many of my thoughts run unfiltered. Prioritizing is much easier for me afterwards. I suddenly gained focus in my tinkering. Before, I was one of those who was always busy, always on fire, always occupied, and constantly doing things.

Michael: That's what it must be like to work hard. [*grins*]

Christian: Inefficient moving around. [*shakes his head*]

Michael: Maximum occupation, minimum output.

Christian: Right. We have found a term for it: *The manager-actor.*

Michael: Cool. [*laughs*]

Christian: I used to spend a lot of time on bringing the things I do and considered important out into the outside world. [*laughs and shakes his head*]

Michael: *Manager-Actor. [pause]* I think of bad actors. Do you know when actors in some movies can't find their way into the role and still try to play the character? Every viewer can clearly see that they can't. It looks more artificial than competent. It's almost embarrassing.

Christian: How can I tell if someone is a good manager? Does she write emails and make phone calls all the time? Is that what makes someone a good manager?

Michael: Sure, they are definitely very busy. They always have a lot to do. [*laughs*] I was once that stupid. I used to work 18-hour days regularly, including Saturdays and Sundays. I used to work so much on the weekends that I actually had nothing more to do. I really fell into a hole. I didn't know what to do with myself. "What do I do now?" I thought. Then I spent another two hours tinkering with some PowerPoint presentation. Here another dot, there another line. It didn't make any difference in terms of the result. But for me it did. I thought if I didn't do anything now, I wasn't working hard enough. I couldn't be successful if I didn't work hard enough. Nonsense.

Christian: Not only did you present yourself this way to others, but also to yourself.

Michael: Absolutely. I totally underestimated the impact it had on the others. Colleagues and employees received emails from me at 02:00 a.m. on Sunday mornings. For me, that was a normal working time. I only realized the consequences later. At that time, it was not clear to me what signals I was sending out and what expectations I had of others. To colleagues who couldn't or didn't want to work like that, for example, because they have families. I was single at the time. In retrospect, I realized how inconsiderate I was. For me there was only full-throttle work. I wanted —and got— the success. Today I'm looking for opportunities to have as much, perhaps even more, success with much less work. The book *The 4-Hour Workweek* has helped me along the way. A lot of people recommended the book to me back then. All of a sudden, everybody was talking about this book. At some point, I bought and read it. The author, Timothy Ferriss, describes how he manages to achieve great success with only four hours of work per week. The guy seems rather hyperactive, so I don't really believe he was literal about the four hours. Apart from him, I have seen other examples that have worked moderate hours and been successful. So it is absolutely feasible.

Christian: Ferriss once said that the idea of the four-hour week is rather meant as an image, a metaphor, so to speak. He was mainly interested in showing that money-making and working hours are to be separated from each other. It's about filling the day with meaningful and productive activities instead of just keeping busy. Whether that is four hours a week or four hours a day is not so important.

Michael: The cover shows a picture of someone lying relaxed in a hammock, stretched between two palm trees, working and succeeding at the same time. It's similar to what you described in your Vision. This picture made sure that it clicked for me. The subtitle of the book is "More time, more money, more life." I don't need this super stress of the past anymore. That is not healthy in the long run. I myself have felt the stress physically. I had little blackouts now and then, forgetting simple things. Today, I have a different idea of success. I want to achieve a lot and be relaxed.

Christian: How can I apply this in my daily life? We have already talked about beliefs. Our *manager-actor* has a lot of limiting beliefs. How can I apply this to my daily life and prevent it?

Michael: At first, it helps me to become aware of the state I'm in. I reflect on the situation and look at the abstraction of myself. I disassociate from myself— that's what psychologists call it. I look at my situation from above and ask myself, "What condition is this Michael in right now, sitting down there?" I am floating in a dissociated state. I sit in a helicopter and look down on the world. What is Michael like right now and how do I want him to be? What would help him to be different? In which mindset is the guy right now and is this mindset helpful to get ahead? Looking at myself from the outside in, not every situation is easy. To be honest, I don't always get it right either. Sometimes I'm in such a rage that I need a moment or two to sit in a helicopter and look down on my situation from above. It's about *awareness*, about becoming aware of my condition. This certainly requires a fair amount of practice and discipline.

Christian: Looking at yourself from the outside-in is one way. Another is to look inside yourself, to remain associated. To feel what I am feeling right now. Is what I am feeling right now also what I want to feel? I had reached this point when I realized that I no longer wanted to be in this state. Feeling like this is not what I want.

Michael: I don't want to feel that way.

Christian: My family doctor said to me at the time, "I don't know anyone who sleeps enough, does enough sports, eats a healthy diet, and suffers from burnout at the same time."

Michael: That I believe.

Christian: So let's say that I can reach my goals much easier through recovery, sufficient sleep, and consideration for body and mind with the help of meditation and sports. What has felt like hard work until now I approach in a completely different way through mindfulness, through this newfound awareness. With a healthy body and a healthy mind, I can reach my goals much more easily.

Michael: The statement from your doctor reminds me of a question we often ask about employee layoffs: "Has anyone in this room ever fired an employee too early?" The number of people who raise their hands is the same number that raise their hand in response to the question, "Do you know anybody who suffers from burnout and sleeps enough, eats a healthy diet, and exercises regularly?" No, I don't. I've witnessed the opposite, actually. These things seem to belong together. What other limiting beliefs are there on this topic?

Christian: If I now exercise regularly, go home on time, and take a vacation, my employees will certainly do the same. Who will then do the work? After all, my employees are supposed to work. The more, the better.

Michael: I see. The motto would then be: *I choose the easy way. My employees should make a different decision from my own. Let them get burned out.*

Christian: That would be possible. After all, not everyone can work less.

Michael: That's nonsense, of course. The same law applies to everyone. Consciously or unconsciously, what I exemplify as a manager also applies to the employees. That is exactly the point. If we all make this decision to lead a balanced life in order to make our lives and our work easier, uniting the two together, we will still achieve our goals. It simply makes it easier on us; we no longer need to torture ourselves. That is super. It's a win-win situation for managers and employees.

Christian: Yes, right. The results are even better and the work is much more relaxed, effective, and productive.

Michael: And that is what we want.

Christian: I have one more point: beliefs can also be cleverly packaged into commands. I have an example from my time at the bank. If someone went home at about three or four p.m., a colleague would often say, "So, did you take a half-day off?" This is another way to anchor beliefs and control behavior.

Michael: [*smiles*] Oh yes, I know these lines too well.

Christian: "Well, only a half-day today?"

Michael: "Nice of you to drop in."

Christian: With these stupid sayings —I really find them stupid—I can ruin a lot of relationships with people on my team.

Michael: This is also a *self-fulfilling prophecy*. With it I support a behavior, a culture, that I actually don't want at all.

Christian: That also works the other way round. My employees often said to me at that time, "Oh, so you're at the office again?"

Michael: How did you react to that?

Christian: I tried to turn the message around. I replied, "Yes, but I'm going back home right now to go back to bed." I'm sure you know that line, too. Then everyone smiled and it was all alright again.

Michael: I also want to go back to the hammock between the two palm trees. I like it there very much.

Christian: If I'm not in the office, I can't stop my employees from working.

Michael: That's right, I agree. Actually, I'm doing everybody a favor. What happens when everyone does that? Let's extrapolate that. Full induction, element n=1. We just proved that. Now we extend the whole with induction n=n+1 to the totality. If we really apply this to all companies, all employees, to all humanity, where will we end up?

Christian: I would say we will end up at relaxed productivity. That is our goal. There are more people who enjoy doing the things they do. More people are doing what they really want to do with a healthy body, a relaxed mind, and a rested self. Bill Clinton once said that the biggest mistakes he made during his presidency were made when he was sleep deprived.

Michael: I also read that in his biography. He probably slept very little, only about three hours a day.

Christian: It took him a while to realize that.

Michael: We have now talked about *awareness.* About being aware of my condition, as well as my feelings. I decide what state I want to be in and what feelings I want to feel, which means I can make better decisions that help me achieve my goals. When everyone does this, employees and managers alike, we enter a world of relaxed productivity. So what does this mean for me as a manager? What can I pay attention to on my team?

Christian: It is always about the same thing. *This is how we are gonna run this company.* I need a Vision, a Purpose, Values, and Strategies for my company and team. Where are we going? How do we work together? What do we do for it? And what are we doing it all for? When I have time, when I am relaxed and rested, and when I feel good because I eat a healthy diet and my body is fit, I can think more clearly and make better decisions.

Michael: *It's all about people.* With the framework I give my company through Vision, Purpose, Values, and Strategies, I enable every single person involved in my company—employees, customers, partners, service providers—to make sure that they are healthy, well rested, balanced, and have enough time for family and recreation.

Christian: Yes. This could lead to the elimination of many pointless activities.

Michael: That sounds great.

Christian: Brilliant. Then I'm going back to my hammock now.

Michael: Well, I'm going to lie down again, too.

Oh yes, I also know these beliefs and have heard these lines before. At the same time they show the crux of the matter. If only I get rid of these limiting beliefs, while my colleagues or even my boss still appreciate long working hours more, they will get the impression that I am not working hard enough. So I don't necessarily become a manager-actor out of my own conviction. Rather, I become one because I want people to appreciate me for my work and to see and reward my commitment. The same applies to my employees, of course. I also appreciate their extra mile efforts. So it is a dilemma from which I cannot get out on my own. Maybe as a manager I should just start there. If I manage to eliminate these beliefs and lines from my team, it might inspire other teams to follow suit. At the same time, I have to find other ways to reward my employees' commitment so that they remain motivated and do not take advantage of the situation. If they are intrinsically motivated to contribute to the company's goals, I can trust them to do so. In the end, it is the quality of the result that counts, not how long it took them to achieve it.

"WHERE FOCUS GOES, ENERGY FLOWS"

— TONY ROBBINS

ENERGY VAMPIRES
ENERGY FOLLOWS ATTENTION

Christian: We are what we pretend to be.

Michael: Who said that again?

Christian: Kurt Vonnegut said that.

Michael: We are what we pretend to be.

Christian: Or, "fake it till you make it."

Michael: The second part of Vonnegut's quote goes like this: "So we must be careful who we pretend to be."

Christian: Right. Therefore, we should pay attention to what we pretend to be, because that is how we will be.

Michael: The way I present myself is the way I become. It's just like with goals. When I set goals for myself, I achieve them. *Mind over matter.*

Christian: I can actually move things with pure mental power. Look, I raise my hand and let it sink again. This proves that with my mental imagination, with my pure will, I can influence things, even physical things, not only those in my head.

Michael: That's basically the core idea of everything we talk about.

Christian: We imagine where we want to go and we go there almost automatically.

Michael: Raise your right arm.

Christian: [*raises his right arm*]

Michael: Was that conscious or unconscious?

Christian: I think it was unconscious.

Michael: Somebody did that to me once. My answer was initially *conscious, or so I thought*. Because I had decided to lift my arm. I gave that command consciously. I wasn't consciously controlling the millions of muscle fibers, nerve cells, blood circulation, and whatever else is going on in there, which means 99.9999% actually happened completely unconsciously. I then changed my answer to *unconscious.*

Christian: All pictures, videos, sounds that are in my head have an influence on who I am, or who I become.

Michael: I think of something in my head and bang, it becomes reality.

Christian: Right. We had talked about beliefs before. If I believe in it myself and say it often enough to myself, for example, that I can't do something, then I won't be able to do it either.

Michael: You can do anything you want in life. That is what life is all about.

Christian: How do all these pictures get into my head?

Michael: That was my thought, too.

Christian: Through me or through others?

Michael: I choose the pictures much more carefully now. I used to let any stuff into my head. All the crap that was on TV, every book I read. I let it all go into my head. I don't do that anymore. I've become much more careful. Now I think very carefully about what, and above all who I want to let into my mind. In the past, when someone asked me if I wanted to watch a horror movie, I would say, "Yes, why not?" I just let it in. Today? No chance anymore. I don't want that nonsense in my head.

Christian: I hardly watch any news either.

Michael: Which is worse, horror movies or news?

Christian: At the moment, it is almost one and the same.

Michael: Newspapers are like diet books to me: I just read the headline on the first page.

Christian: I used to read a lot of newspapers. Eventually, I stopped. I did not miss out on much. Most topics don't influence my life anyway. What is important for me I find out in other ways. Take the Coronavirus, for example. To learn about it, to stay updated on it, I don't need to watch the news. Many people kept and still keep me informed.

Michael: I decide which topics I open the door to in my head. For example, if I want to educate myself further in a particular subject, I intentionally let that into my head. I'm even choosy about that. Unless for pure entertainment, now and then I also like to just sit in front of the TV and watch some junk for an hour. Then I just zap through and see what's going on. Sometimes I'm curious about what's being broadcast and what the others are watching. It's good to be informed about what might be going into other peoples' heads.

Christian: The question I am dealing with is: *Who do I let into my life?* I don't just mean the news, I mean which people. There are very different people. On the one hand, there are the people who give me energy. In their presence I feel comfortable. When I meet them, I come out with more energy. Then there are *energy vampires*. They literally suck the energy out of my body. You think to yourself, "Everything is so terrible, so much terrible news. Everything sucks."

Michael: I know exactly what you mean. I'm often torn. On the one hand, I would like to just turn around and not expose myself to any more of this. I actually do that a lot. On the other hand, I would like to help the person. As a coach, I know by now that everyone can decide for themselves to seek support in order to change or recognize which behavioral patterns limit them. If I want to decide this for someone else, I am the one who judges and influences what is happening around them. In such moments, I think of the well-known saying, *When I have a problem with someone else, I still have something to learn.*

Christian: Then the question arises: *Do I even want to learn anything from this problem that I have with someone else?*

Michael: That's my decision then.

Christian: If someone wants help, for example, in the form of coaching, they are free to express that. Because only he himself can decide that, no one else. "I want help" or "I want to be coached." There is the so-called *advice monster*. Giving unsolicited advice is an absolute relationship killer. Advice is a vice.

Michael: I once had a very bad experience with that. There was a company I wanted to work with. I liked what they did and I got along well with the CEO. I then offered to support them in leadership development as a coach. That went very wrong. I learned that being a coach is not a good idea to do business development like that. At first, I thought it could work. Then when we started working together, and, unfortunately, it didn't work out at all. From my point of view, it was mainly due to the mindset. The expectations were very different. They didn't have the attitude of, "I need a coach with an outside perspective to help me change in order to move forward." Rather, they had the feeling that a guy from the outside was imposing himself. That was no use. I have learned from my mistake and will never do that again.

Christian: Since we are already in the middle of the management topic, what happens if I expose employees in my company as energy vampires? How do I deal with this? Can I simply tell them, "You are an energy vampire, I want you to leave?"

Michael: That's a trick question. You tell me.

Christian: That was more of a rhetorical question. [*smiles*]

Michael: All right, what is the definition of an *energy vampire*? Let me try it another way. My experience is that if there is a common Purpose and Vision that everyone believes in, along with a set of Values everyone agrees with, then there are no energy vampires at all. Because then everyone is motivated and pulls in the same direction. Of course, there are different personality types and different types of people. So there is the risk that someone is an energy vampire for me because he marches to the beat of a different drum. To get involved with this person, I often lack the patience. Now you understand why I hesitated with your question. I would consider all this before I put the energy vampire stamp on someone.

Christian: Because it is a judgment.

Michael: Right. Only I consider him to be an energy vampire. It's possible that the behavior is great for others on the team and even provides them with energy and motivation.

Christian: Kind of like sitting in a meeting and hoping to be the dumbest person in the room.

Michael: That sounds exciting.

Christian: If I feel like the dumbest person in the room, the others are most likely no energy vampires.

Michael: I like that. Then nobody really needs me there and I can just leave again. I can take care of the things I want to do. Energy vampire or not.

Christian: Then let's do it like this.

Michael: Energy![22]

---

22 Captain Jean-Luc Picard in the series "Star Trek Next Generation" - https://www.youtube.com/watch?v=ws3G4lgFXBw.

There is a lot of truth in this. Every day I get advice, stories, and content from all sides. It's not always easy to distinguish between valuable input and energy-draining discussions. To reflect and select the input channels more consciously seems to me quite appropriate. The same applies to energy vampires. It requires effort and patience to accept them, and a portion of empathy to recognize to whom my energy vampires provide support. However, knowing that it might be up to me and that only I see the vampire as a vampire makes it easier for me to accept this and change something about it. If I realize that an energy vampire is also a power snatcher for everyone on the team, I should question the common basis of Values. Slowly, more and more substance is coming to the matter of Values, Vision, and Purpose.

PRIORITIZE. FOCUS.

ROCKS, PEBBLES, SAND

Christian: I would like to travel again. There is this game called *I'm packing my suitcase.* When I pack my suitcase, I always pack my hiking boots first.

Michael: Why the hiking boots first?

Christian: Well, then I can still use the space in the shoes and put in small things like socks.

Michael: Efficient.

Christian: Once I pack the clothes and the underwear, the shoes won't fit into the suitcase. I have already hung them over my shoulder. That's no fun and the people in the plane always look at me funny.

Michael: I also just hang the shoes around my neck when they don't fit in the suitcase anymore.

Christian: When I mix cocktails, I put the ice cubes in the glass first, then the rest. If I do it the other way round, the glass gets too full. Mixing drinks, I am always too generous. If I fill them into the glass first and the lemons after, the ice cubes will overflow and make a big mess. So I put the ice cubes in first. Now, what does this have to do with management?

Michael: That's what I was just wondering. In any case, I'm in the mood for vacation and cocktails now. Images like these work well for me. I can imagine the taste of an alcohol-free Piña Colada today.

Christian: I was just thinking that it's clever to pack the big things first. Then the small things will find their way to come along. For small stuff like pens, socks, and so on there is always room in the suitcase. If I transfer this to my everyday work, it is also better in terms of time. First, the big things have to be done; the small things I can still find a few more minutes for.

Michael: Yeah, right. Yes, that's true. If you first dump everything in, then probably unload everything again, still having to stow the big stuff, it's an endless back and forth. That surely takes longer and is much more inconvenient.

Christian: Whereas I can unpack the suitcase again and start all over again, I can't start my working day all over again.

Michael: So we're talking about focus, doing big things first.

Christian: Right. First pack the big hiking boots, then the little things.

Michael: Given the hiking boots are important for your vacation. If you go hiking in the mountains, the hiking boots are not only a big thing physically, but essential for the trip. There is one model that comes to mind. It is called *rock, pebbles, sand.*

Christian: There is a model for this? [*amazed*]

Michael: Yes of course. You already described it perfectly, as if we had discussed it beforehand. [*smiles*] *Stones* are the big, heavy chunks. The ones that really make a difference. *Pebbles* are the little stones. I can still identify them well. When I have pebbles in my hand, I recognize each one. *Sand* consists of thousands of small grains and is not really tangible anymore. Nevertheless, the sum of the grains of sand makes a difference. There are very good videos on YouTube about this model. In the videos you can see what happens when I put the sand in the glass first, then the pebbles, and at the end the rocks. Not everything will fit. If I turn the order around, it will fit. If I put the rocks in first, then the pebbles and finally the sand and shake the glass a little, everything will fit in. It's just like you say; the sand looks for a place in between, just like your socks and pencils.

Christian: Okay, so the glass is my everyday working life: eight hours a day or four days a week, respectively. The rocks are the things I really want to have done. I tackle them first, they are practically at the top of my to-do list. The other small tasks will find their place in my everyday work.

Michael: Personally, I do it like this: In the morning, when I start the day, I look at my to-do list and decide which are the rocks, the pebbles, and the sand. That helps me to prioritize. I admit, sometimes I do a bit of the pebbles first, simply because I feel like it. I realize that I am pushing the big rock just aside. I use an app where I manage and track all the tasks. I can use it on my cell phone as well as on my desktop PC and decide at what time I do which tasks. Before I had the app, I did this on a piece of paper. I drew two horizontal lines on an A4 sheet of paper and divided the tasks into rocks, pebbles, and sand. The rocks were at the top, the pebbles in the middle, and the sand in the lower third of the sheet. At first, I did this every day. Then I had another sheet for the whole week and another one for long-term topics. I couldn't keep up with all these sheets of paper anymore, so I digitalized it. With the app, it is much easier now. I have been doing it this way for three years. It works great.

Christian: The advantage of the slips of paper is that I can simply throw them away.

Michael: That's right. Writing it by hand is also a good feeling. It's different when I write something by hand than when I type on a machine. It stimulates many more neurons in the head, and that in turn means that what is written has greater impact. Mentally, handwriting is much better than typing. I myself am often torn between handwriting and digital portability. Both have their charms.

Christian: The big rocks are not necessarily the things that take up the most time. They are the things that are most important. So the question is how I recognize what is important. Spoiler alert: it's related to my Vision, my Purpose and my Values.

Michael: Right. [*laughs*] It fits the plan, it's important in the sense of the plan. *This is how we are gonna run this company*. It's important to the personal life plan, to the Purpose, to the Vision, to my Values, and to my Strategies. The three levels—rocks, pebbles, sand— sound similar to the Eisenhower Matrix. This is a 2x2 matrix with four priority levels, which result from the combination of *important* and *urgent*. Importance in the sense of achieving the goal and urgency in the sense of time. The model is super. There are four priority levels. Whether I need the fourth level, I do not know. Basically, the fourth level is more of a parking lot for a lot of unimportant stuff that I won't get to anyway. It makes me aware of what I am not getting done.

Christian: You could pour water over the whole thing at the end.

Michael: Sure.

Christian: If there are rocks, pebbles, and sand in the glass, you can fill it up with water if you want.

Michael: It's a mess.

Christian: A huge mess. I also don't want to jump up after every important task I have done and dump water and sand in between.

Michael: When we talk about the *stop-start-continue model*, we will talk about the decision not to do things. I used to put everything I could think of on my to-do list for years. I'd include every little thing, just so I wouldn't forget anything. I have never made a conscious decision not to do anything. I never decided that this or that task would not go on my list. Terrible.

Christian: You did things because you forgot to take them off the list? [*surprised*]

Michael: No, they were just on the list. Those lists killed me, they were a million miles long. I stressed myself out. There were so many things on them that I might as well have decided from the beginning never to do some of them. It didn't make any difference in my life at all.

Christian: The agile approach would be to simply throw the list away in the evening and create a new one the next day. The next morning, I decide again what is important and what I want to get done today. Priorities can also change.

Michael: For me, it's safer to keep the list so I can look at it the next morning and copy down the important things. Then I don't have to start all over again. I always panic that I forget things.

Christian: I am relaxed. Most of the time somebody comes up to me and reminds me that I have forgotten something. That happens all by itself. [*grins*]

Michael: [*laughs*] I did that once. But then I missed out on a really big thing and got totally upset. So with me it's the other way around. I'm much more relaxed when I know that I've got the things I want to do noted somewhere. I am a control freak. That helps me to relax. It gives me the feeling of being in control of my life. Even if a bit of sand or mud is on my list, I can differentiate between rocks, pebbles, sand, and water. I am aware that some of the things on the list I will probably never get done, yet it gives me a feeling of completeness and control. The decision of what to do and what not to do is not random because I have forgotten some things, rather I make the decision consciously. Otherwise, I risk forgetting even rocks. That much I have learned about myself.

Christian: That's right, it clears the mind for other things. There are many productivity techniques that convey just that. They recommend simply writing things down. If I can't sleep at night because my thoughts turn over, then I write down everything I don't want to forget. I keep a small writing pad and a pen next to my bed for times like this.

Michael: I do that, too. It reassures me to know that I've captured it somewhere, on paper or in an app— it doesn't matter.

Christian: Do you use other techniques? Something like, *Everything that I can do in two minutes, I do immediately* or, *Everything that someone else can do, I delegate*? This is my favorite: *Everything that takes longer than two minutes, I do later*. There are a lot of wise tips such as these.

Michael: Since I read the book *The 4-Hour Work Week*, I've been trying to delegate as much as possible and build a system in which I do only what is necessary and only the things I really enjoy. I used to do everything myself. Today I think to myself, why do I still do anything at all when there are people to whom I can delegate it and who can do it even better?

Christian: A friend of mine has changed his status on WhatsApp to say, "You have to have everything done yourself."[23]

Michael: Very nice, I like that.

Christian: Even so, I still have a few pebbles and a little sand left to get the whole thing going.

Michael: Yeah, sure, kick things off with a few pebbles and then spread the big rocks around it. That's a good idea.

---

23   Song of dike child - https://www.youtube.com/watch?v=dapqMeQCdcs.

Christian: Right. Someone else is doing something that is a big rock for me, and I just need a little sand and a few pebbles to get the rock rolling, right onto someone else's desk. Great.

Michael: Delegate. There is one more little miracle technique that I have been using for a long time. I'm a very visual guy and I take a lot of notes during a meeting, coaching, or even in very simple get-to-know-you conversations. This way I make sure that I don't forget anything. I internalize things better when I see them in front of me. Now it often happens that I take so many notes that I can no longer distinguish what is important and what is not. Therefore, I draw a capital *A* with a thick circle around it in front of every action or to-do that I note down. I write a capital *D* in a circle when I have noted down a decision. This way, when I go through my notes later, I can see directly what I have to do and what has been decided. I put a capital *I* in front of it if it is particularly important information that I want to remember. I don't even know what this method is called or where it comes from. I copied it from a colleague years ago and have been using it ever since. With several pages of notes, I keep track of everything and know exactly what to look for. For an *A, D* and *I* with a thick circle around it.

ACTION   DECISION   INFORMATION

Illustration: A - D - I
This is how I structure and prioritize my own notes while writing.

Christian: That works really well, I do that too. In my case, I use *A to* mean that I give someone this task; *D* is a to-do for me; *I* points out important information. With me there is still a question mark with a circle around it. That means I will google the topic again later or look it up.

Michael: And there is a light bulb. When I have a realization, I paint a small light bulb next to it. In our book we could also do it that way.

Christian: In the time it took to paint the light bulb, you will have already internalized it and never forget it. That is the amazing thing about handwritten notes. I usually don't even look at them anymore and still remember them.

Michael: Yeah, something does happen in the process. It goes much deeper into the head and is immediately internalized. The brain processes it with many more cells. Except for highlighted parts, I usually don't even look at the notes anymore. It is helpful with the to-dos. There I find little tasks like: *Buy the book XY* or *call XY*. Even if I don't use the remaining notes any more, I collect them all in a folder that I look into once in a blue moon. It is like a little treasure, super exciting. When I flip through the pages after 10 or 15 years, I can see how I've developed and what I've learned. Then I remember some of the topics and see what has become of them. It's really fun to reminisce about it all after all these years. I am happy about what has become of me and the topics. There are always suggestions that make me think, "Gee, I had already heard about that. Now I'm finally taking a closer look at it."

Christian: I still make handwritten packing lists for my vacation. From now on, to make sure I get everything in my suitcase, I will definitely always write the big things on it first.

Michael: What else do you pack for your hiking vacation? The shoes are included. What else is important?

Christian: The backpack.

Michael: The pickaxe and a hat.

Christian: The rock collection.

Michael: I can already see the sun shining on the mountain. I can feel the light breeze on a beautiful spring day. Have fun on vacation!

I just watched the video Michael suggested on YouTube. That is really crazy. It's a simple method that I can easily remember. I'm well aware of this, of course, but every now and then I tend to do the things that are easy for me first. Urgent or not. So thanks for these little tricks. It helps me to organize myself even more consciously.

LISTENING

"WILL YOU SHUT UP, MAN?" - JOE BIDEN, 2020

Christian: Tell me, Michael, what would you like to think about today?

Michael: Interesting phrasing of your question. You could have asked me, "What's on your mind right now?" I'm thinking about becoming an even better listener. I keep hearing that this is important, privately as well as professionally, also in our job and especially as a manager. It is important to be a good listener. How do I become a better listener?

Christian: How would you know that you are a good listener?

Michael: I would deduce this from the feedback I get. For example, when people come up to me and thank me for the conversation, praise me and confirm that I am a good, empathic listener. Maybe they would send me an email or leave a review on our blog or on social media, on Facebook or LinkedIn. Maybe it would say something like, "Michael is a great listener and coach." The more that people leave a review and confirm that I am a good listener, the better I become as a listener and support my clients and the people around me.

Christian: That sounds like a Vision that you are describing. How does it feel for you to be a good listener?

Michael: Rather quiet, relaxed, *Zen-like*. Like in a flow state, just listening.

Christian: What do you think while you listen?

Michael: If I'm a good listener, I don't think about anything.

Christian: Very good, that was a trick question.

Michael: I just listen. I may be repeating in my head what I'm hearing and putting my thoughts towards the conversation, so that I can help my counterpart even more with the issues he's sharing.

Christian: What are you doing so far to keep yourself from being a good listener? When someone tells you something, what do you do instead of listening properly?

Michael: Often thoughts come up in me or I feel the need to say something about it. I want to make a contribution, for example an idea that comes to mind or an experience that I have had. I often feel the need to tell my counterpart about it and let him or her participate. I think that might help him or her. Of course, I am aware that I am interrupting the other person's flow of speech. I am slowly becoming more aware of this and I choose carefully when I interrupt the flow of speech and for what Purpose I do so.

Christian: For what Purpose do you listen?

Michael: I listen in order to really understand the other person and to help them with their problem or to get ahead in their topic. At least that's what I want to do. It's not always easy for me.

Christian: Well, on the one hand, we listen consciously in order to understand our counterpart better. On the other hand, I do it in order to learn something about the world. If someone tells me something about the world, politics, science, or economy, I can learn something from him. I might even learn something about myself. It is like my Purpose. What do I listen to others for? I like the saying, *I can learn something from everyone*. Everyone is an expert in a field in which I am not an expert.

Michael: Yes, that's right. I'm realizing that more and more. When I listen to someone and suddenly have comments, remarks or experiences shooting into my head, I ask myself, "Why do I have these thoughts and what do they say about me?" I then try to hold back with my own words. I learn a lot about myself when I listen to someone else in peace and quiet and observe and reflect upon my own thoughts. I often notice that I see the world quite differently than others. So I can learn more in these moments if I listen to my counterpart and keep my mouth shut. If, in addition, I ask questions, I find out I can learn even more.

Christian: Asking is a technique. Another technique is to just shut up.

[*pause*]

Michael: Point understood. I'd like to know from our podcast listeners what they were thinking when it was quiet.

Christian: It was not quiet for long, two seconds at most. I know a good technique that I use from time to time. Singing the *Happy Birthday song* once in your mind takes about 15 seconds. If I just want to shut up for 15 seconds, I sing the song once in my head. As a listener, 15 seconds of silence feels like half an eternity. For someone who is thinking about an answer to a question, 15 seconds is not very long. For a client or an employee to whom I ask the question, "What would you do now?" 15 seconds fly by.

Michael: I just tried that. While you were talking, I was humming *Happy Birthday* in my head.

Christian: And what did I just say?

Michael: My hypothesis was that if I sing the song and keep quiet, I can listen to you well. And I actually realized that I can listen to you very well. No thoughts or comments of my own came up in my head. It was almost a kind of out-of-body experience.

Christian: Crazy. Silence is a very powerful instrument, especially after a question. I like to use it during negotiations on the phone. Just being quiet, it works wonders.

Michael: In mathematics and computer science, the empty set is also a set. The zero element is quite important. To make the decision not to say anything is a big decision, which often leads to a better result than saying something. I will try it even more often from now on.

Christian: How can you become a better listener?

Michael: I learned an ancient proverb in a seminar once. It was about personal effectiveness. It says that I should listen twice as much as I should speak. *I have two ears and one mouth. I should use both proportionally.*

Christian: Again, there are beliefs involved. If I talk more than I listen, I believe that I have more to say.

Michael: Or, I'm just insecure or extroverted and I talk a lot because of that. Maybe I have to talk out loud to be able to think.

Christian: How can I know what I am thinking before I hear what I am saying?

Michael: I could just think quietly in my head instead of talking out loud.

Christian: Especially as a manager, I think it is very important to listen to my employees in meetings. If I, as the boss, talk all the time, I won't learn anything about my employees. I don't know if they are going in the right direction, if there are problems, or if they have smart ideas to share. We once said, "Hopefully I'm the dumbest one in the room." My employees are the experts on the issues that must be tackled and the problems that should be solved. The only way to find out whether they have this under control and what these solutions look like is to shut up and listen to my employees.

Michael: What other techniques are there? I understood how to just shut up and hold out in silence. That seems to work well. When I consciously decide to say or ask something afterwards, what models or techniques have worked for you?

Christian: I have had good experience with follow-up questions. So I'm going back to "What exactly do you mean by that?" I stay in the flow of my counterpart's narrative stream and accelerate or guide it at the same time.

Michael: "How exactly does it work again?" is also a follow-up question.

Christian: Correct. This is a follow-up question. I have had good experiences with being honest and sincerely interested.

Michael: How do I do that best? Sometimes my mind drifts off, I think of something completely different, and even get a little impatient. I already have ten other things on my mind. How do I manage to keep my focus and stay honestly interested?

Christian: We have talked about meditation before. Meditation can help. Of course, not in direct conversation, but in taking time for it on a regular basis. You learn to observe thoughts and let them go again. Like this: "Hello, thought, nice to have you here. Thank you, please go on now."

Michael: Can't I just ask my counterpart to get to the point?

Christian: Of course you can. We began this chapter with the question, "How can you become a better listener?" Such requests are not necessarily wrong, they just don't make you a better listener. So the question is whether you always want to be a good listener.

Michael: Okay.

Christian: It is a behavior that I can consciously use. I can listen well, if I want to.

Michael: So, at the beginning of a conversation, I think about what the conversation is good for and whether I want to be a good listener or whether it's an exchange where we throw each other the balls.

Christian: Right. We can also just have fun, tell each other jokes, throw remarks at each other, and laugh.

Michael: That feels very good from time to time.

Christian: It is just a different approach, a different situation. In emergencies or in the military, clear directions often work best. Then it just goes, "You go over there and do exactly this. You go right there and do the following...."

Michael: I'm just imagining myself dialing the emergency number and the voice on the other side of the line asking me, "How come you are feeling this way?"

Christian: "What happened and why are you interested in it?"

Michael: The person on the emergency call listens based on what is called for by the situation.

Christian: They are usually not interested in observing you in the thinking process, as it can be useful in other circumstances like coaching or employee development. They want you to provide them with tangible information, as precisely and as quickly as possible. The five *W* questions: What happened? How many injured? Where are they? And so on.

Michael: So it all comes down to this. What do you think about introducing the model of situational listening?

Christian: That depends. I think this rule applies regardless of whether it matters or not.

Michael: Okay, good. And what else?

Christian: Different communication situations require different communication styles. I am allowed to have different styles.

Michael: That sounds like a lot of flexibility. So I am allowed to know, master, and apply different styles.

Christian: Right. It helps to approach things in a very relaxed way. When I am relaxed, I see many more choices. I take a relaxed look at everything in my toolbox for listening, communicating, managing, and simply choosing the right tool. The right tool at the right time.

Michael: Isn't empathy very important in conscious listening?

Christian: Yes. But now get out of the shower.

Michael: I speak more of empathy in the sense of being able to recognize and respond to the feelings of the person I'm talking to. I can relate to how others feel in their skin, reflect upon these feelings, acknowledge them, and address them specifically. Especially when I realize that my feelings on the subject or in the same situation are different from my counterpart's.

Christian: You are referring to non-violent communication. Something like, "I hear what you say. It is important to me that ..."

Michael: So empathy is the basis for being a good listener. Because this is how I can help my counterpart to discover something new, to learn something about himself or herself that hadn't been discovered before. It could be a new idea, a new point of view, or a new perspective. I listen to him and respond without saying, "The solution is obvious. It's like this..."

Christian: Right. Without feeling the same way myself.

Michael: Honestly, it all sounds like a real art I want to get even better at it.

Christian: You have already become much better. You will be amazed how good you have become after all our podcast episodes over the following days, weeks, and months.

Michael: That's right, I listened to you carefully.

Christian: I know that. Thank you very much for that.

As an executive, I often tend to have an answer, some wise advice, or an even better story for every question. My own proportion of talking says much more about me than what I actually say. Oftentimes, we think we know better than our counterpart and might think something like, "We can do it your way, even though it'll fail in the end." I can achieve a lot more by listening and asking questions. I can also come across as much more understanding than when I constantly impose myself through my own advice and stories. It just requires a lot of patience and self-reflection. Patience and self-reflection seem to run throughout the chapter. Is this perhaps what makes a true leader? Does this contradict, or is it in line with a can-do mentality and thirst for action?

HERE AND NOW

...I AM AT HOME

Michael: Please tell me the story of the guru and Satsang again.

Christian: With pleasure. I once attended a Hindu Satsang. In front is the guru whose disciples sit on the floor in front of him. Then one disciple after the other goes to the front and asks the guru a question. He is completely free in his choice of subject —God, the world, life, death— the disciple asks whatever moves him. The guru answers the disciple's question, the disciple goes back to his seat, and everyone thinks calmly about the guru's answer. Then the next disciple comes forward and asks his question. This question can be related to that of his predecessor, to the Guru's answer, or it can be a completely detached question, it doesn't matter. It always goes on like this. It is similar to an oracle, only a bit more spiritual.

Michael: Everyone can hear the questions that are asked and the guru's answer? Do the other students also say something about the topics or are they in pure listening mode?

Christian: Everyone is in pure listening mode, unless they are asking their question.

Michael: A kind of group mentoring.

Christian: Yes, exactly.

Michael: What questions were asked in the Satsang?

Christian: All kinds of questions, and completely random: about death, life, illness. It is interesting that all the questions that the disciples asked were usually of universal interest. The big questions in life, as well as in companies, often concern everyone: Where do we want to go? Why do we want to go? How do we get there? What I found most exciting was what the guru told me before it started. All the disciples were sitting there quietly, meditating and completely absorbed in themselves. The guru came, sat down in front, kept silent for a while and began to tell a story. He talked about another Satsang in Munich, where he put up pictures in the front. They were pictures of his teachers: Buddha, Jesus, Laozi. He said, "This is my family." One of the students asked him why he put up the pictures of his family here in this public space and not privately at his home. The guru replied, "I am at home here. Here and now." [*pause*]

I would like to talk to you about that. What does it mean to be in the here and now? How can I use this for myself and my company?

Michael: *To be present in this moment.* To live in the moment and be truly present in a holistic way.

Christian: I have a good counter-proposal. At *chicco di caffe* we had a nice office in Grünwald. We also held our management meetings there. We often had the window open for fresh air. Grünwald is a very busy area, and often a sports car would rush past the window. Every time the loud rattling of a car came closer, concentration was interrupted. Everyone immediately looked outside and thought, "Who was that? Do I know him?" Even when we were discussing an important topic and a loud engine suddenly roared outside, everyone immediately looked out the window again. A few minutes passed until everyone was back on task the next Porsche whizzed by.

Michael: Obviously, the energy went more towards the passing cars with broken exhausts.

Christian: I also don't know why the exhausts of these sports cars are always broken. Poor people ... How do I manage to keep my focus and direct awareness to where I want it to be? Because my energy follows the attention. To where my attention is, my energy flows. In the example of the CEO meetings, I would like the participants to direct 100% of their attention and energy to company topics. The meeting was about important questions that concern our employees, our goals, customers, etc. That's where the group's energy should flow, so that we can solve the issues quickly, within the deadlines. I don't want us to worry about the car exhausts sputtering outside the window.

Michael: The same happens when the cell phone is on the table and flashes with a notification, beckoning me to take a quick look at it. Or when the laptop is open, distracting me with every incoming email. Our world is full of distractions that affect my consciousness and my awareness, pulling me away from my desired focus.

Christian: Who decides where I direct my attention?

Michael: I am tempted to answer, "WhatsApp decides." [*laughs*] Of course I do, I decide everything in my life.

Christian: Then you would have decided to let WhatsApp make that decision.

Michael: I'm now making a very conscious decision as to when to turn off my cell phone and put it away or leave it on the table. The best thing to do is to take it completely out of my field of Vision. There is an interesting study you once shared with us about what happens in classrooms that are allowed to bring their cell phones. What was that again?

Christian: I've heard a story about the so-called *iPhone effect*. Apparently, when two people are talking and a smartphone is on the table, on the bench or anywhere within reach, the conversations are rated as less deep. It does not matter whether the cell phone is directly visible on the table or not. As soon as the other person knows that the person with whom he is speaking has it handy, he perceives him as less attentive. Because if it beeps, rings, vibrates, and he looks at it even for a short moment, he sends a clear signal: "This is more important to me than our conversation."

Michael: The phone becomes an anchor for all the things that might distract me.

Christian: Yes, this anchor has a shocking impact. Because as soon as the device is there, I signal, "No matter the reason this cell phone flashes up, it is more important to me. Therefore I put it here." While I'm talking to you, I'm showing you this device and everything that might happen with it is more important to me than my relationship with you. Not a nice feeling for you, is it?

Michael: No, absolutely not. It reminds me of something my father does. As soon as the phone rings at home, he drops everything and rushes straight to the phone. Even in the middle of really important conversations—it could be a matter of life or death—he leaves me standing and picks up the phone as soon as the phone rings.

Christian: Well, in the past it was certainly very important. At that time in the 70s, telephoning was not very common and long distance calls were very expensive. If the telephone rang at that time, it was probably quite important.

Michael: You're probably right. Today the world is different. I hardly answer the phone anymore. When it's important, I call back. Ninety-five percent of my communication is asynchronous.

Christian: I think a little bit differently. I am a big fan of synchronous communication. There are certainly topics that I can handle well asynchronously, such as making appointments and short votes. However, when it comes to relationship work such as employee meetings, negotiations with suppliers, meetings with customers or a chat with colleagues, I find it very important to communicate synchronously.

Michael: I invite you to try out what it is like to build a relationship asynchronously. Soon we will just record our podcast via voice message.

Christian: By my standards, we're already pretty much asynchronous. [*grins*]

Michael: The world is changing.

Christian: The difficulty is to choose the right one for the situation among all the many communication channels.

Michael: There is another study about school children and backpacks from last year that I find very interesting. It is clear that smartphones have long been on the scene in schools. To think that we can forbid students from bringing them is an illusion. At least, few schools believe that. So the question is, where will the kids' smartphones go? The study examined different classrooms. In one , the students were allowed to bring their cell phones into the classroom but they had to leave it in a backpack under the table. In the comparison class, the children were not permitted to bring their cell phones into the classroom. They either had to put it outside in their locker or leave it at home. The learning efficiency in the class where the students didn't bring the phone into the classroom was significantly higher than the learning efficiency in the other classes where the students kept them in their backpacks, about 20-25%. The explanation is the same as for the cell phone on the table. Whether it flashes or not, it does not matter. The cell phone becomes an anchor for all the other things that happen and that can distract me. The children in the classrooms with the cell phone in the backpack constantly looked under the table and thought, "My phone is in the backpack. A new message might have arrived." While the children whose cell phones were stored out of reach did not have these thoughts at all. The distraction rate is much lower.

Christian: That's why it's better not to bring the cell phones to the meeting in the first place.

Michael: In my workshops I do it very demonstratively. I tell this story, take the phone, put it in my backpack, and carry the backpack outside. It disappears completely from my field of Vision and I am maximally focused on the participants.

Christian: Often, people come to a meeting completely unprepared. When they bring up topics that need to be discussed, they quickly check their cell phone and choose the urgent topics first, because they might be at the top of their email inbox. They then don't distinguish between urgent and important, but improvise using their smartphones. Of course, it's better to prepare a meeting accordingly so that you are clear about what you want to achieve and how you want to achieve it in this conversation. This makes it easier to get through the meeting successfully.

Michael: It's easier to focus on the goal first and then implement it. This can also be defined together at the beginning of the meeting. I often ask the group, "What is today's goal or the Purpose of the meeting?" I then write this goal and an agenda on a flipchart, which we use to structure the meeting and go through it together.

Christian: Right. And the cell phones go away.

Michael: There is an argument that comes up that goes something like this: "I need information from my cell phone for the meeting or I need the laptop to take notes. Is that okay?"

Christian: I guess... kinda.

Michael: I agree. In the end, it's like everything else: who makes the decision to be focused?

Christian: Only I can make this decision for myself.

Michael: Every one for himself. By putting my phone in the backpack, this is my way of manifesting that decision. I can also decide not to put it away and still stay 100% focused in the meeting. There are also inner triggers that distract me. Suddenly, in the middle of a meeting, I think about the fact that I really want to buy some orange juice. When I realize this and notice that other thoughts are distracting me, I can actively decide against these distracting thoughts and concentrate on my actual focus again. "Bye thought, hello moment in the here and now." Active awareness.

Christian: What do you think of the following definition? "Focus is my ability to do the things I said I would do, as long as I want to do them."

Michael: I think it's good. Long, but good.

Christian: The crucial point is: I am doing what I intend to do and not what I do out of a random impulse. Moreover, I do it as long as I set out to do it, until it is finished or until I make another decision.

Michael: I decide where my energy goes. *Where focus goes, energy flows*, or, *where awareness goes, energy flows*. I constantly make the decision what I use my energy for. And what I use my energy for is ultimately what happens. It is exactly what becomes true in my world. I determine what becomes true.

Christian: That's the way it is. We have concentrated on this chapter for as long as we wanted, until it is finished. Here and now we are done with it.

Awareness of what I am focusing on and whether or not I am distracted is a skill that will become even more important in the future. Technological progress is exponential and our world is becoming ever faster. Smartwatches vibrate directly on your wrist with every incoming email. I have to be able to balance between focus and accessibility autonomously and consciously, otherwise I will lose myself in wild actionism and become overwhelmed. When this happens, I can only helplessly watch how I run out of time —my most valuable resource. Energy follows focus.

ATTENTION TO DETAIL

"IF IT'S WORTH DOING, IT'S WORTH DOING IT RIGHT"
- ENGLISH PROVERB

Christian: Do you know the saying, *The devil is in the detail?* A colleague used to say, "The devil is not in the detail, but in the little crack behind it."

Michael: Nice. I also know the same saying, but turned around: *God is in the detail*, more positive, so to speak.

Christian: So it makes sense that we concentrate on details.

Michael: Yes. Attention to detail used to be drilled into me.

Christian: We learn this at an early age in school. Every spelling mistake is corrected and every detail is noted. There is a lot of attention to detail.

Michael: Oh yeah, that was annoying. I remember a math test I took. My teacher gave me a D or an F for the class test because there was a sign error at one point in the whole calculation. He gave the entire assignment a zero score. I found that quite unfair at the time. He said to me, "Well, the bridge would have collapsed, everyone would be dead."

Christian: I also know this from my physics studies. The i is the imaginary unit. It happens very quickly to place an i or a $-i$ in a wrong place. $1 : i = -i$ It then quickly becomes very confusing. We have already talked about personality types and different color energies. My first thought was that the only types that are particularly detail-oriented are those with blue color energy. So I would immediately have a suitable excuse for why I sometimes don't want to deal with details. In fact, I love to deal with details, just not with every single one.

Michael: [*laughs*] That's fine. To people with a lot of blue energy, correctness is very important, with or without details. [*grins*] Maybe you prefer to deal with the details that you enjoy, right?

Christian: Definitely. If I enjoy something and I see sense in it, then I am also very detail oriented. That happens often. Just not in general and not in every detail.

Michael: For you, it's certainly about *competence* versus *preference*. I think you have learned to work in a detail-oriented manner. In your studies you were certainly very analytical and very precise. You wrote software...

Christian: ... later built up the accounting department.

Michael: You see?! Accuracy and detail are important here, too. What's most important to you is having fun and doing things with other people, having joy and being creative. In the Insights Model, which of course is just a model, these are opposite energies. At first glance it is clear that the blue energy is suspected of being responsible for details. To some extent this also fits, at least when it comes to analytics. Because it is important to get to the bottom of things. In fact, however, what is more indicative of detail orientation in preferences is a third axis. It lies between intuition on the one side and sensory analysis on the other. People who have a sensory preference tend to be more in the here and now and very much focused on the five sensory channels. They perceive all the details that are happening at that very moment: everything they see, hear, feel, taste, and smell. People with an intuitive preference also have all these perceptions, yet are not 100% focused on them at every instant. Rather, their mind interprets what meaning this might have for the future. Who is now more interested in detail, the sensory analyst or the intuitive? Opinions differ on this. For example, I am a very intuitive person. My thoughts quickly revolve around what this and that means for the future, what could happen tomorrow or the day after tomorrow, and so on. I find it rather difficult to be in the here and now and pay attention to details. Delivering 100% accurate results costs me a lot of energy.

Christian: I hear many beliefs from you. The danger of such a model is that it can produce many beliefs in your head, such as, "Details are not my thing. I have trouble with them." At the same time, we talked about the motto, *Fake it till you make it.* So I can just pretend that I am detail oriented and that detailed tasks like mathematical equations or accounting are absolutely my thing, until I am. I sit down and do it until I learn to pay attention to the details. So I can turn preference into competence. At some point, it feels easy. The Insights Model is suitable for an initial classification, and above all for an understanding about my preferences. At the same time, caution is required, because I can run the risk of adding new limiting beliefs.

Michael: As always, I can be the decider for everything. I decide who I want to be. Who I pretend to be, I will be. It may take me a while to get there. I can set out to become the most detail-oriented person I know. If I seriously do that, I will. I can decide on anything and make it happen. The length of the road to get there, how long it takes, and how hard it is for me compared to others is another question. I hear you say again, "This, too, is a belief and your own decision."

Christian: Another proverb comes to my mind: *As you do one thing, so you do all things*. It means if I don't take care of the details in one place, I don't take care of the details in another.

Michael: Is that true, or is that also a belief?

Christian: It is a proverb.

Michael: I know of at least one exception. A good friend of mine is an absolute specialist in his field. He is absolutely brilliant in his subject, knows every detail, and is highly focused on making everything perfect. That applies to him only with regard to this special field. In all other disciplines he is rather messy.

Christian: This is again a question of focus. Your good friend may have turned his preference for this topic into a competence and then, consciously or unconsciously, made the decision to focus only on this topic. All others seem not to be so important to him.

Michael: Yeah, it probably is. He is a virtuoso in his field. There's the term *nerd*, a genius who is absolutely outstanding in one field and fails in many other disciplines, even after 10,000 hours of practice. The term sounds rather negative. I read in a book that I have to spend 10,000 hours to master something really well. That's why I came up with 10,000 hours. So I can spend 10,000 hours on many things in my life to become really good at them.

Christian: I also read something exciting about it. Let's assume that I want to become a good pianist. Then I will need 10,000 hours as you said. If, on the other hand, I only want to play a single piece on the piano, it goes much faster. So if my goal is clear to me, I can reach it faster. How do I recognize a good pianist? A good pianist plays everything. He sees the notes of a song and can play it, he knows his way around, he knows all the literature. If I only want to play the intro of *Let it Be* on the piano, I can learn to do it in a few days or weeks, from scratch. So the question is, what do I actually want to learn?

Michael: So playing a piece from the Rachmaninov Piano Concerts will be pretty tough without the 10,000 hour time investment, I'd say.

Christian: We can give it a try. [*thinking*]

Michael: Well, good luck. We'll meet in a few years.

Christian: *Attention to detail.* So we said, details are important. What effect does this have in the company or for me as a boss?

Michael: Well, as the boss, it's my job to make sure that things are done properly. At least the ones that matter. I have another saying to go with it: *If it is worth doing, it is worth doing right.* If I invest my valuable time and energy in something, it is worth doing right. Otherwise, my precious time is wasted.

Christian: So when I define what is done, I can also define how I know that these things have been done properly.

Michael: Just like defining a goal or a quality standard.

Christian: When I assign tasks, I don't just ask my employees to do them, for example to take care of customer XY, but I define how I can tell that the employee has done a good job.

Michael: This inevitably brings us to the topics of KPIs[24] and measured Values. *You get what you measure.* Conversely, it would mean that, *What I don't measure, I don't get.* If I want a good result, I have to measure it. Otherwise, I might not recognize the result at all. I have experienced this very strikingly in a call center. The service was officially considered bad. However, it was not clear why or how bad the service really was. It was more a feeling or an

---

24 KPI stands for Key Performance Indicator and describes a measurable performance indicator.

impression. So we first of all thought about what good service means to us at all. Does it mean that we answer the phone within 10 seconds or that the solution is perfect every time? Or does it mean that customers say that we are nice and friendly? Maybe it also means that our customers recommend us to others. What exactly is a really good service? It was only after we realized this and started to make these matters measurable that we realized how bad the service we delivered really was, at least according to our criteria. We first had to realize this. Then we could understand where we actually stood. Only then did we know what we wanted to improve in order to provide good service. It worked. After one year, we had implemented a world-class service, and the customers were delighted. If we hadn't thought about what good service actually is and what I can measure in order to spot a good result, we would have basically just gone 'round in circles.

Christian: Right. If you don't know where you stand, what makes a good result, and how to measure it, you are too forced to optimize many things at once without knowing if it makes sense.

Michael: That's exactly how it is. First, we did a little bit of tweaking here, then we tried something new there, initially setting up a new call routing, then we introduced a new system. All these were certainly nice things to engage with, at the same time a total blind flight. We had no concrete idea of what the success factors were and what these changes would achieve.

Christian: For example, if you have optimized for immediate problem solving and for a quick phone pickup, it also means that customers who prefer friendly service to quick service are not quite as satisfied with your service, right?

Michael: Absolutely. Another saying for the phrase pig: *You can't please everybody.* That's okay, too. I don't have to be liked by everyone. We have defined a service level of eighty percent as our goal. For us, a world-class level meant maintaining a service level of 80% in our business. That was a conscious decision. From 80% on, we are satisfied. In a market comparison, that was a very good result. Of course, there are always cases in which the 80% cannot be achieved. It is difficult when it comes to the service level of a famous German transport company, for example, which says, "In 80% of all cases, we do not want to be more than five minutes late." That is rather unrealistic.

Christian: *Attention to detail* also helps here. Because, of course, this has to be captured very precisely.

Michael: This also involves the question of the right goal. What is the goal I want to achieve and how do I measure it? If my goal is not to be more than five minutes late, it is very likely that I will always be five minutes late in the future. That is what I have set for myself.

Christian: So I decide what is okay.

Michael: Yes.

Christian: Okay, then I decide that it's okay that we are done now.

I see. I can learn anything I want to learn. If I want to achieve good results, I pay attention to the details, to the quality. It is important that I define how I measure quality. Then I can learn how to achieve these quality metrics —me or my team —depending on preference and competence. Sounds logical. I have the feeling that the closer we get to the matter, the easier it gets.

2.

"LEADERSHIP IS MY ABILITY TO INFLUENCE"

— NACH ROBERT JOHNSON, CA. 1930

INFLUENCING PEOPLE

AUSSTRAHLUNG MEANS CHARISMA AND IT CAN BE LEARNED

Christian: In our work as coaches, we help people to achieve relaxed productivity, especially people in leadership roles like CEOs, founders, entrepreneurs, and people with families. We always help when they need to lead other people and push them to do something they want them to do. What exactly is leadership?

Michael: What is your definition?

Christian: First of all, I'd like to tell you what I understand by management: management means achieving results and retaining employees. How do I manage to get my employees to do what I expect them to do and at the same time, enjoy doing it? They should have so much fun that they like working for me and the company and stay with it. So what is your definition of leadership?

Michael: There are many definitions of leadership, that's for sure. Basically, we can say that leadership can do many things. Leadership can motivate, take people along, and inspire. I find the following definition very fitting: *Management is about doing things right. Leadership is about doing the right thing.* So there is a difference between management and leadership. *Doing the right thing* connects my actions with the Purpose, morals, ethics, and big picture. There is another definition that I like and that is also useful in everyday life: *Leadership is my ability to influence.* How does it feel when you hear that?

LEADERSHIP IS...
MY ABILITY TO INFLUENCE
↓
COMMUNICATE
↓
"AUSSTRAHLUNG" = CHARISMA

Illustration: Definition of Leadership
Leadership is my ability to influence.

Christian: I already feel directly influenced by you. [*grins*] The definition is very general. It explains one term with another term. It is not very concrete. The term *influence* also needs to be defined. It goes hand in hand with my initial description. The question is, how do I influence those I lead so that they do what I want them to do?

Michael: When we write the definition, *Leadership is the ability to influence*, on a flipchart in our workshops, we often generate interesting and quite strong reactions.

Christian: Yes, it sounds manipulative. What is the worst thing about manipulation?

Michael: Good question. I always think directly about *Star Wars*. The so-called *Force* is used by both Darth Vader for evil and Luke Skywalker for good. The Force always works for both sides. Everyone can use it and makes the decision to use it for something good or not so good.

Christian: It's like with any tool. With a hammer, I can hammer a nail into the wall and attach something useful to it, or I can use it to hit someone on their big toe.

Michael: Thanks for saying it like that. That's the way it is. That's why I find the definition so fitting. *Leadership is your ability to influence.* The ego-form of the definition is: *Leadership is my ability to influence.*

Christian: How do you do that now?

Michael: First of all, let's keep the following in mind. On the one hand I can influence people negatively, I can manipulate them. On the other hand, I can positively influence someone in the sense of inspiring and motivating them. The next question that arises is: *Who do I influence?*

Christian: Well, all the others.

Michael: Everyone?

Christian: Employees, family members, suppliers, service providers, colleagues...

Michael: You often say, "I can't *not* communicate."

Christian: Yes, you are right. No matter what I do, I influence through communication as well as through non-communication.

Michael: Absolutely. Communication and influencing go hand in hand. How do I actually influence someone?

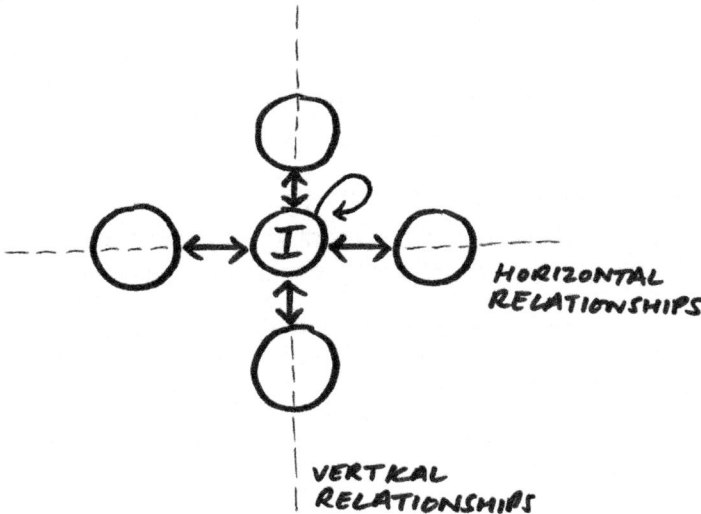

Illustration: Influence-360
I lead myself, my colleagues, my team, and my boss. In collaborative organizations, relationships are more horizontal while they are more vertical in hierarchical organizations.

Christian: In what you do and say. In how I speak, loudly or softly. I look angry or nice, I'm moving or I'm still, I'm looking at someone or I'm not. The way I dress and the way I perform is also a kind of influence.

Michael: So I influence through everything I communicate. I influence holistically through everything I radiate. I communicate through all my behavior and this communication always has an influence, whether I like it to or not. Every second I walk through the world, I am constantly influencing without realizing it. How do I lead? Who do I actually lead?

Christian: I want to ask another question first: Where am I leading to?

Michael: Good question. My answer: Purpose, Vision, Values, Strategies; I am leading to my great master plan. In the corporate context the following questions arise: How do we live our Purpose? How do we achieve our grand Vision? How do we bring all this in line with our Values? And what are the things we want to do, our short-term Strategies for this year in order to get closer to the big goal? Every influence I have serves the Purpose of implementing our grand master plan. I lead to the fulfillment of the grand master plan.

Christian: I will come back to the question of manipulation. So leadership can indeed be manipulative, except when used for a good Purpose?

Michael: *This is how we are gonna run this company.* If we run the company like this and have agreed on this master plan, consisting of Purpose, Vision, Values and Strategies, we have also agreed on the goal, the *where to lead.* As an employee, I commit to this plan, so the team can rely on me. Then it is no longer manipulation, but my contribution to the achievement of this common goal. All people in this company contribute to this plan through their influence, their communication, their mutual leadership. Mutually, I say consciously. It is a beautiful word. Leadership happens in all directions. The cliché of leadership is that I lead the people on my team more or less as subordinates. It's not like that at all. That is total bullshit.

Christian: The subordinates or the submitters.

Michael: [*laughs*] Exactly. I also guide my boss through my communication. Even if many people might not like that. I also lead my peers and my equals. Those who are hierarchically on the same level or in a similar role as I am Leadership works in all directions. I lead upwards, downwards, straight ahead, at eye level, and to the side. If I blur out hierarchies, I simply lead all people, in all directions, in all their roles. Then we collaborate and everyone takes on leadership where it is needed.

Christian: You just said, "I influence through my behavior." Behavior is all the things that I do and don't do, that I say and don't say. So that means that I am allowed to change my behavior if I want to achieve a different result?

Michael: Absolutely. That is exactly the point.

Christian: So if I am leading someone and they don't do what I want them to do, my behavior was probably not appropriate.

Michael: That's the way it is. For example, if someone on my team or someone I work with—hierarchically above, below, next to me, or in whatever direction—doesn't do what I think he should do, then I'm allowed to change my behavior. Until that person produces a different result, i.e., does what I would like him to do. And already I have changed my way of influencing him in such a way that we all achieve our common result.

Christian: The reaction I get from someone is feedback on my behavior. This is basically the core of the NLP idea.

Michael: Right. There's this fantastic saying about that: *The intention of every behavior is the result I get from the other person.* We have already talked about cause and effect. *I am at cause.* I am the cause of everything that happens in my life. I have influence on everything that happens in my world. If someone around me doesn't behave the way I want them to, for example as a leader, it means that I can start to change my own behavior. That was an important insight for me on the subject of leadership. It also includes how I influence myself. How I talk to myself is also an influencing factor. The stories I tell myself, how I talk myself into believing things, or how I make things look bad are all influencers. With this, I may sometimes stand in my own way. The communication with myself and how I influence myself is extremely powerful.

Christian: In addition, the only person I can change is myself. I can change my behavior and hope to indirectly receive feedback from others and create a different reaction. I can only influence the behavior of others by changing my own behavior. I can only change myself.

Michael: Wow. Imagine if all the people in the world had internalized that. Everyone is just changing their own behavior and not trying to change the behavior of others. Because one's own behavior is the only thing that anyone can really change. And that is in the sense that, in the end, he achieves exactly what he and the community he lives in want to achieve. There are 50 people in a company and everyone works on themselves, with their behavior contributing to the common result. Incredible.

Christian: Then the rule applies that *the greater the behavioral flexibility, the better the leadership.* The one who manages to adapt his behavior more easily is the one who can influence others better.

Michael: Maximum behavioral flexibility means maximum leadership.

Christian: If what I do does not lead to the desired result or reaction, I try something else. Then I behave differently.

Michael: Then the best managers are those who are the most flexible in their behavior.

Christian: We also talk about this when we talk about *situational leadership.* There are different situations that require different leadership styles. I can use different tools. You might remember the saying: *If the only tool I have is a hammer, everything looks like a nail.* Then I try to solve the problem by hitting it everywhere. With a screwdriver it's similar, in this case I try to turn everything.

Michael: I should actually do it differently.

Christian: That is true. There are different tools for every situation, for every person.

Michael: Firstly, there is situational leadership, where I adapt my behavior flexibly if I want to be successful as a manager. Secondly, there are different personality types, people with different preferences and competencies who can react differently. If leadership is the ability to influence and I want to be good at it, it means that I am constantly busy adapting my communication to different people and every situation.

Christian: Exactly. This is a full-time job.

Michael: I guess it is.

Wow. That is literally a mind-blowing thing you are saying. It sounds like all the people around me are little puppets and you tell me I have the power to be the puppet master—in a good way of course! It seems to me that the leadership task is moving further and further away from formal leadership and that the real competence for me as a leader is to reflect upon and manage my behavior and my communication in order to manage the behavior of the whole organization as a result. So a good leader is mainly in control of the interpersonal, of pulling the strings. I like that. Yet it also means that we should no longer select our leaders on the basis of formal competence or their years of service to the company, but on the basis of actual leadership competence. So the best chemist is not necessarily the best manager in a company producing chemicals.

POSITIVE LANGUAGE
LEADERSHIP LINGUISTICS

Christian: Hello Michael, how are you today?

Michael: Fantastic, preferably. It's a choice.

Christian: *[grins]* Happiness is a decision.

Michael: And I make this decision gladly.

Christian: Let's talk about language and linguistics, about leadership linguistics.

POSITIVE LANGUAGE

Michael: Positive language, one of my favorite topics!

Christian: Okay, let's start. Let me tell you what you shouldn't think about right now. Don't think about a blue elephant. [*pause*] And? Are you seeing a blue elephant?

Michael: Yeah, of course.

Christian: You are in fact a very *visual type*.

Michael: Yes, he looks a lot like the elephant in *The Show with the Mouse.*[25]

Christian: For the *auditory types*: Don't think about the noise of an ambulance in action. [*pause*] What did you hear?

Michael: Sirens.

Christian: With the next example I get almost everyone: Please do not think about the feeling when you scratch over a chalkboard with long fingernails.

Michael: Stop it, I have goosebumps.

---

25 Public TV program, "The show with the mouse."

Christian: Our brain is simply not made for *not* thinking. When I tell you not to think about a blue elephant, you cross out the 'don't' and think about a blue elephant. I can also use this technique when communicating with employees. We call this *leadership linguistics.*

Michael: Cool. How do I do that?

Christian: Let me show you. It is very simple. Just tell your counterpart what you want. I will give you an example. One of your employees is always late for a meeting. You are Michael, my boss. I am Christian. I'm always late for the meeting. Now give me a talk on this.

Michael: A real talk or a not-so-real talk?

Christian: A not-so-real talk, like you might have done before you knew this technique.

Michael: Based on the examples—elephant, sirens and chalkboard—I would say, "Hey Christian, you came late this morning. I noticed that you were also late last week. You are actually late very often. Why is that? Please don't be late!"

Christian: When you say, "I don't want you to be late," all my brain memorizes is "to be late." You have now said that I am late four times and that is exactly what I remember.

Michael: What will happen in the future?

Christian: I will most likely be late again. Instead of telling your employee what he did wrong, it's much easier to say what you expect. "Hello Michael, from now on I want you to be on time for the meeting, on time to the minute or even earlier." Suddenly, I made a positive statement. I said what I want to have and not what I don't want to have. This will make it easier for you to be on time. When I order something in a burger store, I say, "I want a burger." I don't say, "I'm not having salad today."

Michael: It would be better for my slim shape. Anyway, I got it.

Christian: I don't know what I will get when I say that I don't want salad. "I don't want a salad and I don't want a coke." That's nonsense.

Michael: The poor employee behind the counter. He will go crazy.

Christian: That's why I say, "I want a burger."

Michael: So a good way to order at the burger store is: "Hi, I'd like a burger without cheese with additional bacon, fries, a large diet coke, and two packets of ketchup."

Christian: Transferred to our example, this would go something like this: "Michael, I want you to arrive on time for the meeting, be there five minutes before, be prepared, and be in a good mood."

Michael: Why is it so easy for me in the burger store to make it clear what I want and so difficult to give directions to an employee?

Christian: I don't know why it is so difficult for you. Or rather, why it was so difficult for you in the past. [*pause*]

Christian skillfully shifts Michael's perceived difficulties into the past.

We can try some other things you can do with positive language, with leadership linguistics. Have you ever heard of modal operators?

Michael: Yes.

MODAL OPERATORS

Christian: Modal operators are very nice. So I say, "Michael, you must be on time for the meeting, please."

Michael: That "must" puts me right on the edge.

Christian: Ok, then I say, "You should come to the meeting on time, please."

Michael: That feels a little better, although still difficult.

Christian: How is this? "Michael, from now on you may be on time for the meeting?" How does that feel?

Michael: Very different. When I hear, "From now on, you may always come to the meeting on time," there is a lot in it. *From now on* and *always on time* is very clear. And I can almost smirk at this one little word "may." I can't take it seriously enough to get annoyed about it and at the same time I hear a very clear request. So I know exactly what I may do.

Christian: I could also say, "From now on you can always be on time for the meeting." If the employee repeats this sentence in his mind, it is like a little affirmation: "Hey, I can be on time." A lot happens in the subconscious. It's almost like a kind of hypnotic command that I give. The challenge is that every person reacts individually to the different modal operators. One modal operator can have a particularly positive effect on one person, while a co-worker may develop an aversion to it.

Michael: Again, for clarification: the words *must, may, shall,* and *can* are modal operators?

Christian: Right. And some others like *might* and *should*. The worst use is in "one should do…"

Michael: *One* more thing. Who is this one?

Christian: If you still use *one*, you have immediately dissociated yourself. That is, you have put yourself in the position of an outside observer. A completely wrong statement would be for example, "In our company, one should arrive on time for the meeting." That doesn't concern me personally, and the subjunctive makes it sound more like, "It would be quite nice if …" And if *shall* is not the modal operator the employee likes to hear, the statement falls flat completely.

Michael: I'm tempted to repeat that now and give you another statement with should, might, one, and so on. Instead, I'll refrain from doing so, because I don't want to put these examples into the reader's head. That is the big trick. In conversations with coaches and with people in leadership roles, this challenge is often the topic of discussion. In a leadership role, I only want to put into people's minds what I want them to have there. Put in other words, it's what I expect from them, not what I do not expect from them. I may have to repeat this more often, maybe it takes a little time to sink in. If, on the other hand, I repeat exactly what I *don't* expect from them, I help them very successfully to fail, and thus sabotage myself.

Christian: Definitely. Is this manipulation?

Michael: This is influencing. I get this question asked a lot. "Aren't these tricks manipulation?" I believe in freedom of will and that every person is free to make decisions. I believe that I can convince better with careful phrasing. Without careful phrasing, I can even end up achieving exactly the opposite of what I intended. The goal of management is to achieve results and retain employees. If I want to achieve these goals, it's actually necessary to choose the right phrasing. When asking about manipulation, I like to draw a comparison to *Star Wars*.[26] I apologize to those who are now rolling their eyes. Those famous phrases from the film when difficulties arise: *Use the Force, Luke,* and, *May the Force be with you*. So I can either use the Force, the skills I know and master, for the good side and be Luke Skywalker, who brings light into the world and saves the universe. Or, I use them for the *dark side* as Darth Vader and try to destroy everything. In the end, it is not the method that makes the manipulation, but the motivation of the person who uses it.

Christian: I'll again interject the quote from Watzlawick, who said, "I cannot *not* communicate." That is, even if I communicate badly and unconsciously, I communicate.

Michael: Then it is unconscious manipulation. That is, I unintentionally go wild with my way of communicating and get a random result.

Christian: This is really unfair to the employee, because he can't know where he is at.

Michael: "I cannot *not* communicate," positively rephrased, means that I always communicate.

Christian: Another quotation that fits well is: *Communication is what the listener does*. This means that I can carefully ensure that what the employee receives is what I want to express. It means that I can also adapt myself, my language, and my way of communicating to the employee. It is therefore important to find out which employees I can talk to and how to do so in a way that garners understanding. That brings us to the topic of personality types. I adapt to my counterpart. I go out of my comfort zone. And it's the same with modal operators.

---

26 US-American film series, in German: "Krieg der Sterne".

Michael: *The receiver is always right.* Even more blatant: *The result of any communication is its intention.* Learning this and accepting so much responsibility in my communication was a big challenge for me at the beginning. The saying suggests that the receiver of a message is always right. For me as a boss, this means that when I give direction or communicate something, what resonates with the other person in his universe is the deciding factor. So the recipient is always right. The entire responsibility for achieving my desired result lies with me. So if the recipient understands something other than what I intended, *I* am obliged to adapt. I then may express myself differently in order to achieve the result I want. This has helped me immensely. I have learned to refrain from statements such as, "I told you this yesterday," and, "We have already talked about that." You probably remember a few of these, too.

Christian: "I've told you that 10 times now."

Michael: Yes, exactly. I'm not getting anywhere with this. Except that the relationship gets worse. As a manager, I always have the opportunity to adjust my communication so that what reaches my counterpart is what should reach him.

Christian: And if I have said the same thing ten times and it still hasn't gotten through, then I just say it louder. Then the person will understand it at some point [*grins*]. Additionally, there are of course some hidden *nothings* in the language. Like *no blue elephant*. And there is the beautiful word *but*, which works like a "not-operator," or better yet, like a delete key.

Michael: *I don't even know the word but anymore;* I crossed it out at some point and completely banned it from my vocabulary.

Christian: Then, from now on, we'll remove it as well.

Michael: You mean that word that is spelled *b-u-t*. It was very difficult for me to omit this word and delete it from my vocabulary. I have been going through life much more pleasantly ever since.

Christian: I have noticed that my conversation partners often falter in the process. For example, when someone makes a thesis such as, "Michael, you always wear those nice white shirts and they look very good on you." This has a completely different effect and meaning than when I say, "Michael, you look good in those nice white shirts, but you always wear them." This word just erases everything that happened before that. The employee no longer even hears what was said before. "You did that very nicely and please do it maybe a little differently next time."

Michael: I was recently a participant in a training session with some coaching gurus. We also talked about this topic. It was fascinating. We all agreed that replacing *but* with *and* is the recipe for positivity. This has now also entered the mainstream. Do you know what they said about it then? They said, "We no longer just replace *but* with an *and;* instead of an *and*, we simply make a period and end the sentence."

Christian: That is also nice.

Michael: Wonderful. Then I just say, "Christian, you always wear such wonderful white shirts." Period.

Christian: Yes, thanks.

Michael: Now you can hear that I noticed that you always wear white shirts. You can draw your own conclusions and consider putting on your Hawaiian shirt for a change. For example, the one you wore last week. Meanwhile, this *and* story is known as a method by some people. This is a technique from the NLP trick box that has become quite popular. So they said, "We recommend our coaches to shut up more often." I thought that was very cool.

Christian: And it doesn't matter if the interviewer knows how I do it and knows my methodology. For example, sometimes I use tricks like this on my daughter, and she catches me and says, "Daddy, I know exactly what you're doing."

Michael: Now you again say *and*. Okay, I get it.

Christian: And it works. It's awesome.

It is a change and it works. Again, a lot of practice, patience, and reflection is required, yet it is worth it. Everyone knows these situations from everyday life: "Honey, on your way back, please bring a bouquet of flowers. It doesn't matter which flowers, as long as it's not gerberas." And in the end, you hold a bouquet full of gerberas in your hand because it is the only thing that stuck. It seems almost too easy: I can simply say what I do want, just like in the burger store. "I want tulips, honey. Tulips."

CHIEF REPEATING OFFICER

"THERE'S JOY IN REPETITION" - PRINCE

Christian: I thought I already knew all this and I just didn't listen.

Michael: [*laughs*] This is a nice start.

Christian: I just didn't listen the last few times, what was it all about again?

Michael: "I thought I already knew all this and I just wasn't listening." That's a nice line. There are people who think exactly that.

Christian: What do they think?

Michael: For example, they think, "I don't have to listen to the *Chief of Anything* podcast, I've heard it all before." Some people don't attend a seminar or training because they think, "I've heard it all before. So what?!" It's an erroneous pattern called *complex equivalence*, because I mistakenly consider two thoughts to be equivalent. In the example, I equate *I have already heard about this* with *I don't need to repeat this,* or with, *I am really good at this*. This can be a fatal error in thinking.

Christian: Besides, these two—Michael and Christian— are constantly repeating so much stuff. They always say the same thing. It's about ... what was the goal of management again?

Michael: Achieve results and retain employees.

Christian: We have certainly said this a thousand times before.

Michael: At least. I think by now it's gotten through to some people. Isn't this actually the point?!

Christian: Who in our company is actually the CRO, the Chief Repeating Officer?

Michael: Well, we are.

Christian: And who in your company is the Chief Repeating Officer? How often do you repeat things until your employees or team finally process the information? How often do you repeat something until you have the confidence that your employees have understood it?

Michael: The Google founders called themselves CRO's. They said, "We are not the CEOs, we are the CROs, the Chief Repeating Officers."

Christian: How often do you think I may repeat something until it sticks?

Michael: Very often. Basically all the time. I had a boss once, he was a little older. Vinyl records were very popular in his day. When records had a crack, they would skip and the same part would play over and over again. It is called *a broken record* when a record is scratched and always plays the same thing.[27] That was one of his management mantras. He used to say, "If people ever say to you, 'I can't stand hearing it again; you're like a broken record,' you know you've reached your goal." That's when the message has really gotten through. Only then.

Christian: I have a similar example. I repeat some things all the time. One day, my colleague in management told me that one of my employees already sounded exactly like me. "She constantly repeats the same things you do," he explained. I knew then that it had actually hit home. It can take different amounts of time until what I say actually catches on. Sometimes it takes a lot of time, sometimes it happens quickly. Why is that?

Michael: We are hit with a lot of sensory impressions all day long. Due to the variety of media and communication channels available, it is even more intense today than it used to be. According to science, about 11 million bits per second are coming at us. So when I open all five of my sensory channels—eyes, ears, mouth, nose, and kinesthetic cells all over my body—my receptors provide me with about 11 million bits of information per second.

Christian: That's about three rock songs, three minutes each.

Michael: That's almost one terabit per day. That's a number with 12 zeros. An insane flood of information that we process. It's gigantic. So now, when

---

27 Rappers and DJs use scratch records and create new sounds through repetition.

I say something to an employee as her boss, I expect her to memorize all of the thousand billion things that are thrown at her every day, the ones that come from me. To make this work, I may phrase them damn well, for example with a pattern interrupt.

Christian: Have you ever been to Ulm?

Michael: No, not yet.

Christian: Ha, as you see I've snuck in a pattern interrupt with my question about Ulm. It's similar to what happened to my colleague. For example, I say to him, "It would be nice if you were not late for the meeting."

Michael: Yes, that would be nice.

Christian: You see, it's another pattern interrupt. With the addition, *it would be nice*, I directly offered him a chance to filter this out of the amount of information, from the stream of consciousness without a guilty conscience. In the sense of "that's already nice, I don't need to do anything more now."

Michael: I see we are back on track now. And that's where we want to go, into that which is perceived in the stream of consciousness. The simplest method to achieve this is repetition: pure increase of the odds, so to speak. My message to the employee is in competition with the thousand billion others that rush at him every day. So the more often I send my message—two times, three times, four times, five times, six times—the higher my chances that it will get through to him. It's like playing the lottery. The chance of getting six right out of 49 is maybe one in 15 million. If I play two lottery tickets, my chance is at least twice as high as with just one ticket. If I play five, six, or nine times, my chance is always bigger. In the lottery, the business case is decreasing.

Christian: And besides, the lottery is a tax on poor math skills.

Michael: In management, however, it costs almost nothing to repeat things. So it makes sense to increase my chances immensely with each repetition. The principle is to repeat a message three times in order to convince my counterpart. Repeat three times to convince someone. Three times. Now, I have just repeated this three times.

Christian: Am I already convinced? Have I heard it now often enough to memorize it?

Michael: If not yet, my chances are going to increase right away, because I will repeat it three more times to get to six. The trick is to repeat it six times so I remember it the next day.

C.R.O.

CHIEF REPEATING OFFICER

3 X TO CONVINCE

6 X TO MEMORIZE

Illustration: Chief Repeating Officer
By repeating, I increase my chance of getting into the result set 7±2 of my counterpart within all the trillions of sensory impressions.

Christian: So I may hear the same thing six times until I memorize something?

Michael: Exactly. As a manager, I may say the same thing six times so that another person memorizes it. Six times.

Christian: Until the next day?

Michael: Yes, within 24 hours. Remember the broken record comparison that my dear old boss taught me back then. Repeat, repeat, repeat until my ears bleed. I can't repeat it often enough. I may repeat something at least six times in one day to help the recipient remember it the next day. Six times.

Christian: Do I not feel stupid at some point?

Michael: It is my own choice to decide how I feel about it.

Christian: So how I feel is my problem.

Michael: How I feel is my choice. This is an important thing I have learned in life. I can choose how I feel. It's not always easy, and yet it always works. Because ultimately, my feelings exist only in my head. I am the boss there. Therefore, I can choose how I feel. Since I decided that it is ok for me to repeat things all the time—because that is part of my job—I feel good about it.

Christian: And how do you feel when the employees roll their eyes at some point and say, "Now I really can't hear it anymore, boss?"

Michael: Then this is exactly what I say. It is my job. It's my job to repeat things until you can't hear it anymore. So if you roll your eyes because you've heard it a thousand times, then I've achieved my goal. I thank you, dear employee, for this measurement, this KPI. And maybe then the employee will realize that he can try it out with his team and his relationships as well. Maybe it works a lot better than the good old saying, "I told you that before." This line is totally unnecessary. So what if you've told me that before? If you've said it already, then just say it again.

Christian: Try it differently.

Michael: Just say it again. Repeat it six times. In one day.

Christian: The popular sentence, "I have already written you 10 emails and you still don't answer," is also very nice. I can change the communication channel if I realize that what I am doing is not leading to the goal. I can also try something else, for example calling, making personal contact, standing at her desk, or writing a postcard.

Michael: Emails are like water. They flow and flow. If I have time, I go into the river and take a bath. Then I read some of the emails and go back out again. If a couple of emails float by, I say, "Sorry, the river is hard to control." For some personality types, a clean inbox is important, to answer every email and check everything off conscientiously. Maybe they are people with a lot of blue energy or with a sensory preference.

Christian: I also know people with yellow energy who handle it that way.

Michael: Do you have a *clean inbox*?

Christian: I simply delete all emails. My inbox is totally clean.

Michael: Somebody told me that once before. He said that when he's on vacation, he writes in his *out-of-office notification*, "All emails will be deleted during my vacation. Please resend them when I return."

Christian: The things I repeat may well be consistent. So it is actually the same thing that I repeat over and over again. Or is it better to vary the statements?

Michael: What do you mean?

Christian: If I want my colleague to be on time, I always say the same thing "Please be on time for the meeting." Or do I vary and say, "Please be on time for the meeting every now and then," "Please be on time for the meeting on Wednesday," or, "It would be nice if you were on time." Is there any research on this?

Michael: Yes. NLP Achievable Outcomes, SMART Goals and OKRs[28] have a remarkable number of things in common. All state that the more specific, the better. The SMART method—**S**pecific, **M**easurable, **A**chievable, **R**elevant, **T**ime-bound—helps a lot. Goals can be specific; it is important to communicate them and give feedback. In your example, the best formulation would be, "Please be punctual for every team meeting from the next team meeting on, so please be present by 10:00 a.m. at the latest."

Christian: This is the right formulation, especially for someone with blue color energy, isn't it?

Michael: It's a precise statement: "By 10:00 a.m. at the latest," because the meeting starts at 10:00 a.m. What you are referring to is the adaptation of communication to different personality types. For someone with lots of red energy, clear directions work well. "Hey Michael, starting with the next team meeting, please be on time at 10:00 a.m. sharp." Period. Nothing more. With a lot of red energy, I answer, "Alright, got it. Thanks for the clear message." I

---

28 OKR, short for "Objectives and Key Results," is a framework for setting objectives and measuring key performance indicators

appreciate that. How would that be for you? You have a lot of yellow energy, you are creative, you have fun, what kind of feedback works well for you?

Christian: "Hey, Christian, please be on time for the team meeting so that we can move on with this together."

Michael: "Having fun together" would certainly work. What do you think of this? "Hey Christian, from the next team meeting on, please always be on time, because only together we can make progress and have real fun. If we're all on time, we are more likely to make the most of the meeting and make it really productive." It is important to emphasize the importance of community, having fun and sharing ideas. In green energy, the key is Value orientation. "We are a team and here the same rules apply to everyone. This helps us to work together, as a community we are stronger." Let's stick to our example, "In the future, always be on time for team meetings. If we are all there from the beginning, then we are respectful and in harmony as a group." We just had the blue energy. Here it's about a logical statement. "Please always be punctual in the meeting at 10:00 am. We need your intelligence to get 100% correct results."

Christian: Now we have intuitively repeated the color energies.

Michael: Funny, repeatedly repeated.

Christian: I would like to repeat something else at this point: the goal of management, which is to retain employees and to achieve results.

Michael: That theme certainly runs through everything we are talking about.

Christian: I will never forget that now.

Michael: I'm convinced and just remember that [*grins*].

Christian: Yeah, great. Thanks a lot [*laughs*].

Michael: Repeat three times to convince someone. Repeat six times to memorize it the next day. Accepting that as a boss, it is my job to repeat things very often, over several days or longer periods of time. It is very easy.

Christian: Because you mentioned the river of emails earlier, did you know that the Danube runs through Ulm?

Now some things become clear to me. Thank you very much for making it easier to internalize what I am reading through your repetitions. A great service that casually takes place on the side. After reading the book, I will certainly be a super leader. Great.

ICEBERG OF COMMUNICATION

"... IF YOU'LL JUST SMILE"
- CHARLIE CHAPLIN & NAT KING COLE, 1954

Christian: Hello James.

Michael: Hello John.

Christian: It's about behavioral flexibility. I'm glad you reacted to that. We have defined leadership as my ability to influence. We have already established that I influence others through my behavior. I behave in a certain way. My counterpart perceives this behavior through his five sensory channels—visual, auditory, kinesthetic, olfactory, and gustatory —in short: VAKOG. My counterpart processes this input. He or she deletes, distorts, and generalizes content and mixes it with their own beliefs, Values, Visions, and personal experiences. Based on the result, my counterpart chooses his or her behavior, which I in turn perceive through my five VAKOG channels. Of the millions of bits I receive through the five channels, the result set has only 7±2 elements. So it is a real black box. I basically have no idea what exactly is happening both with me and with my counterpart. You have a nice picture for it. It is not the black box. As far as I know, the Titanic did not have a black box. What picture do you have for it?

Michael: You mean the one where the Titanic crashed against the iceberg?

Christian: Right. The iceberg of communication.

Michael: That's the risk with an iceberg. If I'm not aware that it's an iceberg, I'll race full steam ahead, slam against what's under the surface and sink. It's a challenge to get through all those millions of bits per second that are coming at my interlocutor and be part of the 7±2 result set. As an executive, it's like playing pool and making a bank shot with a hundred balls.

Christian: And in the dark.

Michael: Yeah, it feels that way sometimes. Fortunately, there are methods that increase my chances of having my voice, my charisma, and my behavior become part of the 7±2 result set of my counterpart.

Christian: Well, I am very curious.

Michael: It works with the iceberg of communication. A large part of my communication is below the surface. There are three essential components of successful communication. First, the rapport. Second, how I communicate. Third, what I communicate. Leadership is influencing and influencing is done through holistic, whole-body communication, which we call charisma.

Christian: The most important thing is that I say very loudly what I want. [*grins*]

Michael: Absolutely, then you have already won. Good luck with that. [*laughs*] The *What* is probably clear to everyone. It's all about the message, about the actual content that I communicate. We don't need to go into this in detail here. *How* is the way I communicate, my charisma, my gestures, my facial expressions, my behavior, whole-body and holistic. *Rapport* is a term that I first learned through this model. In German, the word Rapport is only known in a quite old military context. In English, the word is rather common. In German—especially in the Rhineland—there is a term that comes close to the meaning of the report: *Chemistry.* As in, *the chemistry is right.* When the chemistry is right, everything flows.

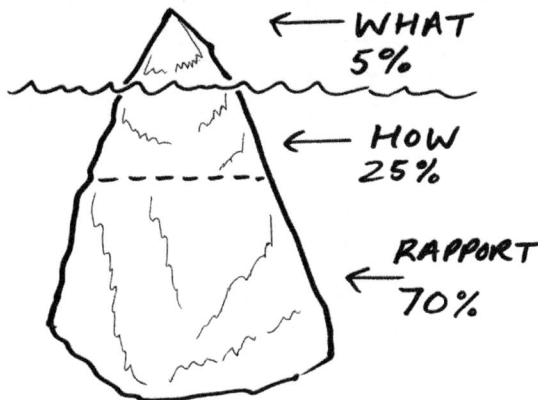

Illustration: Iceberg of Communication
The main part of communication takes place below the surface. If the chemistry is right (RAPPORT) and the right sound makes the music (HOW), then the content (WHAT) is easily communicated.

Christian: How can I tell that the chemistry is right?

Michael: Good question. How do we know that the chemistry is right?

Christian: The fact that we manage to talk about different things is one example. Chemistry goes something like this: you say something about your partner at home, I respond to it, and add something about my life. It's basically small talk. When we make small talk and talk about personal things, it helps us to build up rapport. We have a common theme, we talk about it, we have common experiences that we draw on. I am using all this to build up rapport with you.

Michael: We know each other a little bit and we didn't build the rapport in one conversation. Our relationship is a sum of all the moments and time we have spent together, the experiences we have shared. In the dictionary, there is a very simple description under "rapport." *Rapport is an interrelation or a connection.* Another definition is, *a good understanding of someone and an ability to communicate well with them.*[29]

Christian: People who were talking in the café and crossed their legs.

Michael: That's a nice analogy. There's the expression *dance in the moment*. If we get along well in that moment, then the chemistry between us is just right. If the relationship between two people is in the same rhythm, we think alike. Or when we don't even notice how time passes and we keep talking to each other, exchanging ideas. Now and then, someone draws a sketch for both of us and we are totally absorbed in the topic. We are in a flow state. All this is a sign that there is a rapport between us, a trusting mutual relationship, simply a good contact.

Christian: We deliberately build this rapport, for example, for our podcasts. If we arrange to record a podcast and we both sit in front of our computer, we don't start with the podcast directly and press the record button. We first tell each other how we are doing. "How are things at home?" We create a rapport, build a relationship, before moving on to do what we actually want to do. The actual result then flows much more easily because we have managed to bring ourselves into alignment.

---

29 https://dictionary.cambridge.org/de/worterbuch/englisch/rapport.

Michael: *Tuning-in* or *getting into the groove* are great expressions from the world of Music. It's about synchronization. With some people it is very easy for me, I get along with them right away. We just hit it off, we click, and then it just runs without much effort. With other people, I find it rather difficult. The first conversations are tough, and it takes quite a while before we get into some sort of common groove. With some people, it might not work at all.

Christian: You already said, *people like people who are like themselves.* So there is actually a pigeon-hole for people with whom you can probably build rapport relatively quickly. A pigeon hole in a positive sense.

Michael: There is actually a pigeon-hole distribution. Eighty-five percent of people are so-called *matchers*. That means they get along well with people who tick in a similar way to themselves. Matchers are people who like people who are similar to them. *People like people who are like themselves.*

Christian: *Cads' fighting when ended is soon mended.*

Michael: The phrase piggy bank is filling up! At the margin of the normal distribution are the remaining 15%. These are people who actually get along better with people who are different. These are so-called *mismatchers*. There are techniques for this as well. As a manager, I can tell whether my counterpart is a matcher or a mismatcher. If I have detected this, I can react accordingly. With a mismatcher, I behave differently, I transmit something different than with a matcher in order to respond to him. That is the rapport.

Christian: How do I do that exactly? With some people it comes easily to me. You and I are very likely both matchers. We get along very well with each other, it's not difficult for either of us. Now I'm standing opposite someone and I realize that the rapport is not right at all. That someone is one of my employees. What can I do to make the rapport right?

Michael: Do we want to go into that right now?

Christian: Yes, only briefly as a teaser.

Michael: All right, there's a whole range of techniques. For example, let's take one that we can remember well. I have a little anecdote about that. Can I briefly explain?

Christian: Absolutely.

Michael: I used to work for this corporation. I originally applied to work here because of an advanced training program for managers, which I really wanted to take part in. They had advertised the opportunity of becoming a future CEO of one of the subsidiaries once the program was completed. I thought at the time, "Future CEO? That's me. That's where I want to go." I actually started working for this company. I was not even promised a spot on the program at the beginning. Only as an employee did I have the opportunity to apply for this program. They told me right from the start that it was quite selective. Nevertheless, I quit my old job and started at this company. This program was pretty important for me. The requirement was that I pass the assessment center. I applied for it immediately. There were even several assessment centers where I was picked apart. There were different group situations in which we were observed. Then there were math tests, psychometric tests, and so on. The whole process lasted for months. The participation alone was a great experience. At the end, I had a meeting with the Group HR Director and two other HR managers. They told me the results. The HR Director took a writing pad and a thick black pen and just wrote "Yes" on the note and held it up in front of me. I really had goosebumps at that moment. I was really happy and totally relieved. The fact that I had actually managed to get into this program was completely insane for me, an incredible feeling. Then I got feedback on my results. After all, it was all about developing people into good leaders and training future CEOs. The training started right away. Of course, they did it super professionally and explained to me exactly what they observed and what I could do even better in the future. In the process, the HR Director taught me another lesson that I will never forget. He sat across from me, suddenly leaned over the entire table towards me and smiled at me with a huge grin. He grinned more and more and started to laugh. I also laughed along loudly. Suddenly he stopped abruptly and said, "You see? What just happened?" I said, "Yes, I laughed." He answers, "And how do you feel?" I said, "Good, laughing is nice." He said, "That's right. You should smile much more, because people feel better when they are smiled at, and as a manager, that's important."

Christian: You probably looked very serious because you took it seriously.

Michael: Yes. I was a relatively serious guy for a long time in my life, at least in a professional context. I took everything very seriously. In retrospect, maybe too serious, at least until I got that feedback. It was like the dragon in the book The Neverending Story.[30] Falkor with the smile who, like this guy, flies right at me. The guy had a similar broad grin as this friendly dragon. I will never forget how he hovered over the table with this broad smile, about 10 inches in front of my nose. Since then, I have always taken his advice to heart and noticed how much a smile can do for me. But the story goes on. That day we were in England, in Brighton. I flew back to Germany in the evening and thought to myself, "I'll just try this now." So I got on the plane and smiled broadly at the flight attendant who was standing in the doorway of the plane to greet me. I said smilingly and totally exaggerated, "Halloooo." Today this is not difficult for me anymore; back then it felt really strange. She looked at me baffled, then smiled back and we had a nice short conversation. Later I ordered a glass of wine from her, again with a smile, and this nice flight attendant poured more and more wine. Before landing, I praised the wine in all its glory, again with a big smile on my face. It became easier and easier for me. Admittedly, that day I was so happy about my triumph, I probably would have found anything tasty. And then the highlight of the story happened. When I got off in Düsseldorf, she handed me a bottle of the wine as a present in a bag, just like that.

Christian: Just because you smiled?

Michael: At least that's what I attribute to it. I didn't usually have that effect on people, I was totally baffled. I came out of the airport and thought, "This can't be true." The only thing that I consciously did differently was keep a constant smile. And it was really fun. The interaction with the stewardess was really nice and I even got a bottle of wine as a present. The wonderful Nick Holley, that was the name of the HR director, was actually right. It works! Smiling is a method I can use to create chemistry, a very rapport-enhancing thing.

Christian: Wow, thanks for the story.

Michael: Now we build a cliffhanger.

Christian: We make an iceberg hanger. So we talked about the iceberg. We realized that rapport is important. We talked about the *what* and the *how* of communication.

---

30 The Neverending Story is a novel from 1979 by Michael Ende. The book was later filmed.

Michael: Right. About the three important components of successful communication, especially, about the rapport. Now readers are probably asking themselves, "What is all this about?"

Christian: We will tell you about that in the next chapter. Just try to smile more. Look at the people you communicate with, smile at them, even if sometimes only via video call. It even works on the phone without seeing each other. Observe the feedback you get.

Michael: So far, we have talked about the three components of successful communication: The rapport, the *how* and the *what*. One question at the end of this chapter: How would you prioritize these components? If 100% success is to be distributed among these three components, what share does rapport have, what share does the *how* have and what share does the *what* have in the success of your communication?

A method that sounds very simple. It gets better and better. Just smile . I will try that! As a Rhinelander I certainly have an advantage here. Smiling also seems to be part of the mindset, part of the attitude toward life. Nobody wants to work for or with a grouch, obviously.

CREATING RAPPORT

ALL SOLUTIONS ARE INTERPERSONAL SOLUTIONS

Michael: It's nice how we smile at each other.

Christian: That's right, we have used the last 15 minutes to build up rapport. Rapport is one of the three most important components of successful communication. Communication is like an iceberg. Most of it is beneath the surface. The *what*, the content of communication, is what happens above the surface. The *how* and the rapport take place beneath the surface. You just shared that anecdote about how smiling helped you build up rapport. In what other way can I create rapport?

Michael: There are a number of methods for this. Do we first reveal how important these components are in relation to each other, and how it relates to the iceberg? We have set our readers a task.

Christian: Yes, good idea.

Michael: If I communicate 100% successfully, what percentage of that is my message, or *what* I say? What percentage is accounted for by my holistic and whole-body charisma, or *how* I get my message across? And what percentage represents rapport, the relationship between me and my counterpart? We have described rapport as the chemistry between people.

Christian: With my blue, analytical and factual energy, I say the content, i.e., the *what,* makes up about 95%. The content is most important. Whether or not I smile when writing an email doesn't matter.

Michael: [*laughs*] Good point. When we ask this question in our seminars, there are usually very different opinions about it. Some say, like you, that it's mainly the content that matters. The *how* and the relationship to each other is rubbish. Some also say that everything is equally important, one third each. This is more of a mathematical-democratic approach. Others swear by charisma as the most important component of successful communication. A few people have already read or heard something on the subject or their instinct tells them that the relationship, the rapport, is the decisive factor for success. In fact, the distribution for successful communication is in the order of 70-25-5. Seventy percent is accounted for by the rapport. We will get into this in more detail in a moment. Twenty-five percent is the *how, i.e.,* my choice of words, my expression, the communication channel, and so on. Only 5% of the success of my communication depends on the content. So basically, someone can sell me anything as long as they have a relationship with me and talk to me insistently. The 5% is then virtually just a veto that comes up when someone tells me total nonsense. So most of it takes place on the non-contextual level. It's remarkable, don't you think?

Christian: Absolutely. Somehow, also frightening. How can I use this knowledge to make my communication more successful? I immediately think of a presentation whose content I spent hours thinking about. I stand up front completely lost, and nothing of my content gets through to the listener. I may not even be taken seriously at all.

Michael: Yes, that's possible. Even in such situations there is a way to build rapport. It's a little different than in a 1:1 conversation, still with similar techniques. Your question was how I can use the 70-25-5 distribution key. The answer goes back to our insight: *Leadership is my ability to influence.* The question is, how do I influence people like Luke Skywalker versus abusing my power like Darth Vader? How do I influence my team to achieve our jointly agreed upon corporate goals? Our Purpose, and Vision to live in harmony with our Values? I have the challenge of getting past 11 million bits of information per second and mixing my message with the result of 7±2. We come back to the iceberg. As a manager, I want to influence through my behavior. Part of my behavior is my holistic and whole-body communication and charisma. I now know that 70% of my success as a manager depends on the chemistry between me and my employees. And that is exactly what it is all about.

Christian: That is what it is all about. With some people it is easy for me to build rapport because the chemistry is just right. With others it is difficult. All team members may have different preferences, one is totally detail-oriented, the other not at all. If I now try to impose rapport on everyone, no doubt some will wonder what it's all about. It must not seem ridiculous or manipulative. Most people have antennas for this and react exactly the way I don't want them to. They are right to become skeptical rather than to build up trust in me. So I am to pay very close attention to who is opposite me and how I behave towards this person.

Michael: That's how it looks.

Christian: How do I deal with it?

Michael: We have already talked about models of different personality types. Every person is an individual with different preferences. According to C.G. Jung,[31] for example, each person has a preference on the scale from *introverted* to *extroverted,* and each person has a preference on the scale from *task-oriented* to *people-oriented*. This already results in four different basic types with further distinguishing features. I can make use of these personality types. Another already known instrument is situational leadership. Here I determine which mode I am in at the moment. The bottom line is that I can say, "It depends." Shall we go through the different types and explain suitable methods?

Christian: It sounds like a big task. Let's get started.

Michael: We go through them step by step. *How do you eat an elephant? Bite by bite*. This elephant here is worth it. Let me start again. It's all about creating rapport, because successful communication depends 70% on rapport. So I increase my chances of ending up with the 11 million bits per second in the 7±2 result set of my counterpart. I have now repeated this about five times. Soon we have reached the six times that are necessary to remember it. We have already talked about the method of smiling and the effect on the flight attendant who gave me a bottle of wine. There is a second method other than smiling that helps me to build rapport. It is eye contact. Everyone feels something when they look into the eyes of another person. We feel this ourselves in video conferences, even if we can only look into each other's eyes indirectly. With eye contact, something happens in the mind, both in mine and in my counterpart's. However, the effect is very different depending on the personality type. What experience have you had in this regard?

---

31   Carl Gustav Jung was a Swiss psychiatrist and the founder of analytical psychology.

Christian: Eye contact is very important to me. There is only the danger of staring at someone. This is exaggerated and can lead to distortions. I was once at a conference where all the participants looked into the eyes of their immediate neighbors for a few minutes to practice. Some had murderous thoughts, others developed deep love. It is often difficult to find the right measure. Eye contact yes, though please do not stare. Chasing away my counterpart through eye contact is not the goal. It can be threatening too, like an animal that stares at me as though I'm prey.

Michael: Eye contact is perceived and interpreted differently depending on the personality type. For example, you and I are both rather extroverted types. You have primarily yellow and I have primarily red color energy. For extroverted types, eye contact is much more common and popular than for introverted personality types. For people with primarily green or blue energy, eye contact may be more interspersed. For these types, it is especially important that eye contact is authentic and appropriate to the situation. Especially in green energy, where people are harmonious and Value-oriented, I may perceive eye contact as a threat, especially when someone stares at me a little more intensely. So it is always important to find a good balance. When I talk to someone I don't know well, I try to read their preference in their own behavior to create rapport. I observe how my counterpart behaves. I observe how he or she handles eye contact with me and what the reaction is when I make eye contact. This is a good indicator of my counterpart's preference. During my stays abroad, I noticed that there are also cultural differences. In Africa, for example, direct eye contact is considered disrespectful, especially towards older people. For me, as a Western European, it feels rather submissive not to look people directly in the eye when I talk to them. Looking past my conversation partner to the right or left or even downwards was very unusual for me. Some Africans feel the exact opposite. In Arabia, it is considered impolite to look Muslim women in the eye. It is unwanted. I lived in Qatar for eight years and had real difficulties in the beginning. I simply did not know where to look. Fortunately, many of them already had some experience with our western culture, so most of them didn't feel quite so strongly about it. With rather conservative, traditional interlocutors, caution is indeed required in order to build rapport even without eye contact. In this case, it is more likely to succeed if I follow the rules. Eye contact is therefore a powerful tool for building rapport, though only in the right dose. It is important to adjust to my counterpart and recognize their preferences.

Christian: I find it thrilling that I create rapport by adapting to the behavior of my counterpart. If someone looks me in the eye, I can look her in the eye more intensively. If my conversation partner looks away, I also tend to look past the person to the right and left. I like to observe people in cafés when they sit there so comfortably, cross their legs and talk. It is like a kind of dance. I can almost see how the posture, the volume of the voice, even the rhythm of the breath is converging. All this happens subconsciously. When the behavior of my counterpart is in line with mine, I subconsciously think, "If he behaves exactly like me, he is thinking exactly like me." I find it super exciting to observe what happens. This is also part of the creating rapport.

Michael: *People like people who are like themselves*. At least for 85% of the people this is true, it is a normal distribution. These are so-called matches. Fifteen percent are mismatches who instead like people who are different from themselves. I can observe this in the café as well. Statistically, one out of eight people behaves differently than the others. When I observe groups of two, three, or more people in a café, it is often the case that they sit there talking, gradually adopting similar postures. They are often all leaning forward on the table or leaning back casually with arms crossed and legs crossed. One group always swings in somehow. In between, there is always someone sitting there differently than the rest. The probability is high that this is a mismatch. She feels most comfortable when she sits differently. It is important for this person to be different from the others. Exceptions confirm the rule.

Christian: So when I want to build rapport with a mismatch, I change my behavior, for example my sitting position.

Michael: Right. I'm literally doing something different.

Christian: It just must not seem unnatural. If I desperately try to match with my counterpart and consciously imitate him and his posture, he quickly thinks, "Are you imitating me?" Of course, that is not what I want.

Michael: That's right. I often try to respond to my counterpart two or three times to create rapport. If his posture changes again within 10 seconds, I stay in my posture and assume that it is a mismatch.

Christian: What other techniques are there besides smiling and eye contact to create rapport? What about shaking hands?

Michael: Shaking hands is also a method, definitely. The handshake is very common in our culture and has become a standard in our social behavior and business life. The handshake serves the kinesthetic sense, which is very important for people with kinesthetic preference. This is about 10% of the population. I can also observe this in language. When I have such a preference, I speak more frequently about feelings and am very focused on haptics. Images that I use in my language also tend to describe feelings, emotions, and haptics. I tend to remember how something felt or what I felt in a particular situation. I memorize things better when I have touched them. I often describe objects by gesturing. Therefore, people with kinesthetic preference tend to greet others with a connecting handshake rather than warm words. For them, the handshake is almost essential. As long as they have not touched the other person, they don't really exist for them.

Christian: Especially in times of Corona, this is of course really hard.

Michael: Absolutely. Right now many people are doing the elbow or fist bump, just a light physical contact. Even if it's only brief it's also an expression of us touching each other. Something happens in the mind, which is very important for some people. There are cultural differences about handshakes throughout the world. Even within Europe there are cultural differences in the firmness of the handshake. Men often press a little harder, it is an expression of strength. Women often press a little softer. It is a cultural grouping on the gender level. In Africa, soft handshakes are more common than a strong handshake. When I want to express special respect there, I take my second hand and put it under my forearm. With this I support the right, giving hand. A cultural researcher told me where this comes from. The hands have an important meaning in that they are visible. Visible hands build rapport. It has something to do with our basic instincts. If I have a hand behind my back, it is possible that I am holding a knife or a weapon in it, or that I am up to something else that is not transparent to the other person. Handshake, open palms, gestures, and posture all serve to build rapport.

Christian: All right. [*smiles*] [*eye contact*] Namaste, thank you very much.

Michael: Here's a hug through these pages, Christian.

Eye contact, shaking hands, posture—I often do many of these things very intuitively. It makes sense to me that these gestures are an expression of trust. We often do not pay much attention to the gestures and facial expressions of our counterpart or even to our own. It is good to know that I can consciously use them to establish a connection between myself and my conversation partner. So the wavelength between two people is actually less random than I thought. This can certainly be helpful in many situations. It gets interesting when both use these completely underestimated instruments consciously to improve communication.

BODY LANGUAGE

"SAY MY NAME, SAY MY NAME"
- BEYONCÉ WITH DESTINY'S CHILD

Christian: Hello Michael.

Michael: Hello Christian.

Christian: Michael, we are still talking about the iceberg of communication. About how I successfully communicate in order to influence. Because leadership, and that's what it's all about here, is the ability to influence. The success of my communication depends 70% on whether I manage to establish rapport with my counterpart or build a trusting interrelationship and make sure that the chemistry is right. So far, we have explained how I can achieve this by smiling, making eye contact, and shaking hands. Are there any other techniques for creating rapport, Michael?

NAMES

Michael: Hmm... [*thoughtfully*] Well, Christian. It helps to address people by their name to build up rapport. In the right dosage, of course. We may have just overdone it a little bit. Addressing people directly using their name is a sign of appreciation. It shows that I know who you are, that I know your name, and that it is worthy of pronouncing it. This is usually positively perceived. It also works in groups. If the members of a group don't all know each other, it helps if those who do address each other by name repeatedly in front of the others. These are rapport boosters that in turn improve the group's rapport thus making the team more effective. Suddenly, the participants learn each other's names, address each other by name as well, and a respectful relationship develops within the group. A rapport is created. It prevents embarrassing moments like, "Uh, what is your name again?" This is very unpleasant, I know this myself. I don't like to constantly struggle to remember someone's name, especially after the person has already introduced himself. It helps if everyone repeats the names more often. Repeat three times to convince and six times to memorize. Names help to build rapport.

Christian: That is why all participants in our seminars wear name badges. Everyone has a name tag and can add a little something to it. This is how we engage in conversation and repeat the name automatically. It draws attention to the name and gives it something special, something valuable.

Michael: The name tag with the drawing serves the visual channel. We already talked about the different VAKOG sensory channels and different preferences of people. Half of all people have primarily a visual preference, including me. Forty percent have mainly an auditory preference, including you. Ten percent have more of a kinesthetic preference, with feeling being very important. When I pronounce the name, I move in the auditory channel and target 40% of people. Another 50% I reach through a visual name tag. So I have a good chance to build rapport by pronouncing names and name tags. Therefore, this is often common practice in meetings or at conferences. It increases the chances of successful communication.

Christian: Smiling, eye contact, handshake, pronouncing names. What other techniques are there to create rapport?

MATCHING

Michael: There are still a few techniques on the physical, kinesthetic level. In the café situation, you mentioned body language. You described that adjusting your posture can seem unnatural. I can tell because my counterpart accuses me of imitating him. "Are you imitating me?" This reaction is a sign that your counterpart is a mismatch.

Christian: With me, I can definitely see this risk. I often don't notice how my attitude changes or that of my counterpart. I probably wouldn't notice it either if he imitated me. It happens unconsciously.

Michael: It is an unconscious competence. When we give our seminars and training sessions and dive deep into the NLP matter, I perceive this quite consciously. When I am back in my everyday life and my attention is focused on other things, all this happens unconsciously. What I do perceive quite consciously is when someone completely loses it with his body language. This can be damaging to the rapport. I once had a meeting and, to my understanding, I behaved quite normally. My interlocutor suddenly sat down sideways on his chair, put one leg over the armrest and crossed his right arm behind his head and his left arm behind the backrest. It looked totally strange.

Christian: Was that me? That happens to me sometimes. [*grins*]

Michael: [*laughs*] It's totally okay. Posture is individual and I have nothing against sitting comfortably. I just consciously noticed at that moment that I had difficulties concentrating on the conversation. My full attention was on this posture. I was totally distracted, it was a real rapport killer. Making my communication successful was difficult because the body language was not in sync and did not help me in the situation. Maybe it was comfortable and helpful for my counterpart. Maybe he took a lot out of the conversation. I couldn't tell.

Christian: Did you then sit down in the same way to produce rapport? [*grins*]

Michael: Let's put it this way, I learned about a new frontier. [*laughs*] If I had adapted to his posture, it wouldn't have felt natural. He definitely would have found that inappropriate. It was a funny situation, yet not exactly conducive to strengthening our relationship. When I meet new people, I like to use the adjustment of my posture in moderation to be able to deal with each other openly and quickly. I don't want my body language to get in the way, I rather want it to help me quickly establish a connection and create chemistry between my conversation partner and me. So I try to adjust my charisma so that it is helpful for my communication behavior.

Christian: Of course, it is also an interesting experience to realize that it is difficult to build a relationship with someone sitting across from you and to become aware that it is because of their posture. So the posture of the other person can also prevent you from establishing rapport.

Michael: Yes, exactly.

Christian: So I then take the intellectual detour and accept that she might be a mismatch, and still manage to communicate with her successfully in another way.

FIVE GESTURES

Michael: Right, good point. Even if someone else's posture irritates me, I can still make the decision to try to establish rapport. There's another technique that comes to mind, which is also physical: gestures. The way I use my hands. Here, too, I like to first observe how my counterpart behaves. This helps me to get into the groove and use my hands a little more or a little less, depending on what I observe in my counterpart. If my conversation partner gestures wildly and fiercely, I can also use my hands more strongly, even if it's not really my thing at first. I still remain natural and try to do it my own way. I just use my gestures a bit more than someone who sits there calmly with folded hands. In the international context, I have learned that there are very few gestures—in fact, five that I have identified— that are universal. That's why they are especially valuable and I use them as a kind of *safe base*. With these gestures, I know I can't do much wrong, no matter who sits in front of me or where they are from.

The Pointer

One of these gestures is the raised index finger in the sense of: *Here is a point that is very important*. This gesture is called the *Pointer*. Everyone understands it. It reminds me of a typical teacher's gesture, so I understand when some people don't like the raised index finger very much. At least it is not misunderstood and I can emphasize an important point with it. Of course, my index finger must not point at my counterpart, that is generally perceived as offensive. It typically looks like a weapon, a sword or a dagger. Pointing at someone is also internationally perceived as rude. In the past it was popular to point with five fingers at someone, and I did that too. It's much worse than pointing with the index finger, I practically draw five knives at the same time, which fly at a person. Everything that flies at me is threatening at first. The raised index finger in the sense of, *"That's an important point"* is okay. It's a universal gesture that works quite well.

Openness

Another international gesture is *Openness.* Here I show my open palms facing forward. Jesus was often depicted in this way, which is why some people call it the *Jesus pose*. In any case, it suggests openness, that I am open to the topics we are talking about and that I am not hiding anything. I let my hands hang down casually to the side of my body with the palms facing forward as in many depictions of Jesus.

The Thinker

Another gesture is the *Thinker*. I have one hand on my chin and pay full attention to the person opposite me. It seems as if I am thinking about everything that my conversation partner is telling me. It also has an important effect on me. If I notice that my thoughts drift a little bit during a conversation, I take my hand to my chin and am immediately focused on my counterpart again. This helps me to stay focused and direct myself into a state in which I listen better. By nature, I am not the best listener in the world. My wife will surely cheer when she reads or hears this. This gesture helps me to listen better.

Christian: So your body immediately understands your thinking pose as a signal that says, "Attention, here we go. Listen now." Do you mean it like that?

Michael: Yes, exactly. Let me come back to our understanding of leadership: *Leadership is my ability to influence.* We had established that I lead myself first and foremost, i.e., *influence myself by leading myself.* The thinker pose is a method to influence myself. It works great for me. It is important that the fingers are on the chin, not over the mouth. If the fingers are over the mouth, I give the impression that something bad has happened. "Oh, my God, something bad happened." [*puts his fingers in front of his mouth*] That's why I go into this typical thinker position with my fingers on my chin like in classical Greek sculptures or old drawings.

Christian: We perceive gestures visually and kinesthetically. There are also the so-called universal sounds, speech gestures so to speak.

Michael: What is your sensory preference again?

Christian: I have more of an auditory preference.

Michael: Oh, I see. I'm painting pictures and gesturing wildly in front of you and you're talking about sounds? [*laughs*]

Christian: I am talking about *ohh* or *hmmm*. I can use these sounds to cheer myself on or even to spoil my mood. In the past I would sometimes say to myself, "Oh, Kohlhof, what have you done again?" With this I can bring myself down at the speed of light. "Oh"—or even better—"Oh, no, Kohlhof." Then I call myself by my last name. It immediately feels as if someone else is reprimanding me.

Michael: Why the hell do you do this? Why do you make yourself feel bad?

Christian: I sometimes use it when I want to eat or drink less of something, as a kind of self-discipline. Once I overdid it a bit. Whenever I passed the sausage counter in the supermarket, I quietly said "Ewww" to myself. After only a few times, I automatically gagged when I just smelled the sausages. And that's how I manage to live more vegan bit by bit. This works well with alcohol as well. It helps me to reach my goals. An inner *yesss* or *wow*, when I have achieved something, helps me enormously and confirms me in my actions.

Michael: Yeah, it's really great how haunting these sounds are, like emotional conditioning. When someone else makes a sound like that, I'm glad when I manage to detect my own behavioral pattern that is related to it and to fight against it. Whereby for me as a visual type, sounds have less impact than images, like these animated GIFs that every messenger service offers now. I immediately notice that I am back in my behavior pattern and can consciously decide to curb my typical behavior. Then I try out a different approach.

Christian: "Oh, no."

Michael: Great. That works well. I have two more gestures, especially for the visual types among us.

Christian: Okay, show them to us.

Michael: Dear readers, please imagine me standing in front of you, speaking to you, holding my hands in front of my chest with open palms.

The Guide

With this gesture I am showing a way into the future. It looks something like I am holding an imaginary shoe box loosely in my hands. [*laughs*] That feels good. I hold the shoebox in front of my body and now move my hands forward step by step, as if I were shaking the shoebox and move it forward a little with each shaking. I often observe this with politicians when they want to convince us of their *wonderful way into the future.* It is indeed one of the universal gestures that are understood in the same way all over the planet. One name for this gesture is *the guide.*

Calm Down

Calm Down is the gesture that looks like I am making a bed. I hold my hands out, about waist level with the palms down, and pat my imaginary bedspread at the foot of the bed down one more time after I've shaken it up. With this gesture I want to say, "Everything is fine. We have the situation under control and will now take the right steps." *Calm down* was the last of the universal gestures. The basic rule is that all asymmetrical gestures are less credible than symmetrical gestures or are even perceived as funny. All the gestures we have discussed so far were symmetrical gestures, except for the thinker pose. Two hands on the chin would look funny.

Asymmetrical = funny

An asymmetrical gesture is, for example, when I lift one hand up and the other hand down. It looks almost clownish. Turning one leg to the side is also an asymmetric gesture. Everything that is slant and does not appear symmetrical has less impact.

Now we have gone through all the relevant gestures and have also discussed some physical things.

Christian: Have we now completely covered the iceberg?

Michael: Well, not quite yet. Successful communication depends 70% on rapport. We are now through with that. So we'll still talk about the 25% that depends on the *how*, on the way I communicate. Then we'll talk about the remaining 5%, the *what*, the content of our communication.

Christian: So that was the easy part. The next one follows.

Michael: Yes, everything is under control [*pats the blanket down*]. The future will be wonderful [*shakes the shoebox*].

Everyone probably knows these gestures. From now on I will be more conscious of who uses them and when, and also in which situations I use them myself. It's good to know that all these subconscious and at the same time visible actions mean something. It's like a kind of secret language that is known all over the world and which I will learn to decode from now on.

IT'S HOW YOU SAY IT

"THE SOUND MAKES THE MUSIC" - GERMAN PROVERB

Christian: We are still busy with the iceberg of communication. So far, we have mainly talked about rapport. We'll talk about the content, the *what,* of my communication later. Now it's all about *how* I communicate successfully. How do I design my communication so that it reaches the customer, the employee and myself?

VAKOG PREFERENCE

Michael: Exactly. We have already processed 70% and understand that rapport makes up the largest share of successful communication. Methods to create rapport include smiling, shaking hands, eye contact, the correct use of gestures, body language, addressing my conversation partner by name, and taking into account the different sensory preferences. Now it is all about *how* we communicate. The *how* makes up 25% of successful communication. *Sensory preference* is a good keyword here. It is amazing how different we humans are. Each of us has our own model, our own perception of this world, which we interpret in our own way via the five senses and the additional, sixth channel. The five senses are the VAKOG channels: visual, auditory, kinesthetic, olfactory, and gustatory. The sixth channel is the stories we tell ourselves, the voice in our head. So it is important to consider all of these channels and the different preferences of my counterpart. Where is your preference again?

Christian: I don't even need to look for that, I just listen. My preference is the auditory channel, yours is the visual one.

Michael: Right, I have a visual preference. If I can't see it or write it, I can't understand it. That's why I like to use flip charts and notepads. I scribble everything down in front of me. This helps me to stay focused.

Christian: Yes, I have noticed that quite often. Even with auditory preference, I observe that you like to paint and always make sure that something looks good. I can even hear it when you speak. You like to use words that serve the visual sensory channel such as: "It looks as if...," "It's getting bright...," "It's becoming clear that...," "It's a transparent maneuver."

Michael: That's right. "I have the target in sight." You often say things like, "That sounds very good." I actually have a hard time finding descriptions that express how something sounds. I have a visual image in my mind rather than the sound of something in my ear. So the question is, how can I take advantage of that? How does this contribute to successful communication? Our goal is to influence through communication, because we want to lead successfully and leadership is my ability to influence. Influencing means communicating holistically, not only through my words, but through my entire existence. For example, how do I recognize my own preferences and those of others?

Christian: Well, we have already established that a certain amount of behavioral flexibility is helpful. If I can adapt my behavior, I have a greater chance of success in my communication. In this case, flexibility can mean using more visual terms to get a point across to my counterpart.

Michael: Okay, from now on, when I want your opinion, I'll ask you, "How does that sound to you?" That question will probably speak to you more than if I ask, "How do you see this?" or "How does it feel to you?"

Christian: Absolutely. You can also ask me, "Shall I draw it one more time for you?"

Michael: How about, "What are you thinking right now?"

Christian: Similar to, "Make me a sketch." It is not so easy for me to see through it. So if I adapt my language to the sensory preference of the other person, I communicate more forcefully and thus more successfully.

Michael: It can help to keep a certain order, especially in groups. It is difficult to consider the different preferences with several discussion partners in particular. In a one-on-one conversation, it is easier to address individual preferences. How do I proceed in groups?

Christian: Risk spreading. I distribute my choice of words to different senses.

$$\to K \to V \to A$$
$$10\% \quad 50\% \quad 40\%$$

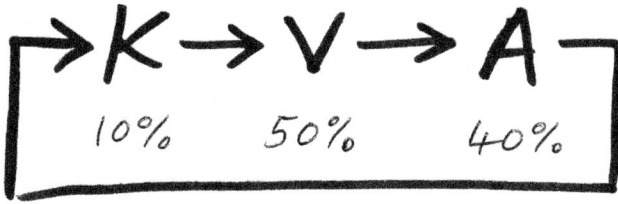

Illustration: KVA
To serve all preferences, I first address the kinesthetic sense, then the visual, and then the auditory.

Michael: So I try to address different preferences. I have learned that the order is important. I start with the kinesthetic channel. An example is the following question at the beginning of a group session: "Good morning, how are you feeling today?" With this, I have addressed the kinesthetic channel. Ten percent of the population has a kinesthetic preference. Why do I address them first? Because I most likely lose exactly this preference. They mentally leave the conversation the fastest if I do not pick them up continuously on the kinesthetic channel. Therefore, at the beginning, I ask, "How are you? How do you feel? What is your state of mind?" The group I address next is the visual group since it represents the majority, with about 50% of people having that preference. The auditory group is just behind with 40%, so they come next. For this order, I remember the abbreviation *KVA*: kinesthetic, visual, auditory. When I am done with all three channels, I start again from the beginning.

Christian: The good thing is that people with auditory preference hear you from the beginning anyway. So you can reach them on the soundtrack during the whole event.

Michael: Right. I cover all the preferences. Of course, shaking hands helps to break through to the kinesthetic people at the beginning. I worked in product management for a while, where we regularly had new devices in our product line. When we passed the new models around in a meeting, I was able to observe very closely who had a kinesthetic preference. They couldn't concentrate on anything until they had the product in their hands.

They didn't let it go so quickly and almost had difficulty passing it on. Only then did I have their full attention during my presentation. They were also fully involved in the group discussions. That is why we always have *kinesthetic toys* with us in our workshops. These are balls or blocks, for example, which we use to put in the hands of people with kinesthetic preferences. They can touch and feel it. In this way, we direct their attention and curiosity to our content. It works in a similar manner with the other preferences, even in an email. For example, I start with, "Hello, how are you? You may have noticed that the sales figures have not been particularly good in the last few weeks. When do we want to talk about how we handle this? Love, Michael." "How are you?" is kinesthetic. "You may have already seen," is appealing to the visual channel. "When do we want to talk about it?" is for the auditory. So I went through the three preferences. In the next paragraph, I start again from the beginning and try to spread my expressions as broadly as possible. Of course, this must not seem unnatural either. It is not absolutely necessary to always strictly follow this order. The important thing is that I don't lose anyone and trigger all preferences regularly.

Christian: Cool. There are certainly more methods I can use to optimize the way I communicate, aren't there?

Michael: Sure. There are still some tricks that contribute to the 25% of the iceberg under the surface. That 25% of the iceberg helps us to lead and influence successfully. Now the reader probably thinks to himself, "Gee, why is he saying this again?" I do that because that is exactly the trick. Chief Repeating Officer is what the Google founders called themselves. They recognized that a great deal of power lies in repetition. In the past, there were scratched or "broken" records that played the same thing over and over again. Repetition is one method. When 20 million bits are thrown at each of us and a result set of 7±2 comes out at the end, I increase my chance of being part of that result set by constantly repeating my message. I need three repetitions to convince my counterpart and six repetitions to make him or her remember my message. Three times to convince, six times to memorize. We have already repeated it a few times and we are happy to do it again. With twelve repetitions I am on the safe side and even more successful. How many repetitions to convince?

Christian: Nine times or six times? [*reconsiders*] Nine times.

Michael: And to memorize?

Christian: Yes, exactly. There are even more methods that can be used to improve the 25% of my communication that comes down to the *how.* What else can one do, apart from constantly repeating?

SPEAK "I"

Michael: *One can.* Did you notice what Christian just said? He's smart. What can *one* do?

Christian: We already had the example with the white shirts. You said to me, "Christian, you always wear this beautiful white shirt. But I notice that you always wear it."

Michael: Yes, I remember. I'm not sure which of us always wore the white shirt. It doesn't matter.

Christian: *But* is something that *one* must not do.

Michael: *But* ruins everything. I'm not allowed to do that, no one is allowed to do that, it should be deleted from the vocabulary.

Christian: I use *and* instead: "Christian, you are wearing a white shirt and I have noticed that you wear it often."

Michael: Right. Replacing *but* with *and* is already part of the advanced level. The pro level is to just shut up and put a point to it. NLP masters say, "Christian, you always wear such beautiful white shirts." Period. Now you expect something else to come. Nothing is coming. You will still notice that I tell you that you always wear these beautiful white shirts. I could perhaps say, "... and I look forward to the day when I see you in a Hawaiian shirt." Either way, I'll be able to give you my message. To simply end the sentence with a period after the first part is mastery. That's the hardest part for me. Just shutting up.

Christian: Just shut up. Apart from *but* there is also *one.* I did that intentionally wrong just now. *One can, one should* and *one might.* Who is this *one*? I just leave it out, speak for myself and I speak *I* instead of *one. I do this or that* or *please could you do that* or *let's do it together.* In any case, it's not just anyone.

Michael: May I share an anecdote?

Christian: Yes, gladly.

Michael: I was 18 years old. I had already told you the story about my mother. As a child, she and her family were expelled from Hungary during the Second World War. All this caused a lot of suffering in my family. So I always had a very pacifist attitude and I never wanted to get involved in any kind of war. It was clear to me at that time that I would refuse military service and not join the German Armed Forces. Back then, every man at 18 years of age had to choose between military service or civilian service. In order to refuse military service, I was required to give a written explanation. This was critically evaluated and then either approved or rejected. So I wrote down the history of my family in great detail and explained my attitude towards the use of weapons. At that time, there was a man in our circle of acquaintances (I unfortunately do not remember his name), who kindly helped me a lot, out of his own conviction. He had made it his business to help people like me to be recognized as conscientious objectors. I remember our meetings well. He read my letter in peace, smoked his pipe, and then said, "Scratch out *one* everywhere from your letter and replace it with *I*." I had formulated sentences like "one shouldn't harm other people," or, "if one does something, then..." I was 18 years old when he taught me that, and I will never forget it. It left a lasting impression on me. Since then, I've learned to erase *one* from my vocabulary. At school, in Germany, I was taught never to start a sentence with *I*. This often led me to formulations with *one*. The *I* at the beginning of a sentence may be a question of style. And, today I know that it also means taking responsibility when I speak in the *I* perspective. That's why when I speak or write in German, I do allow myself to start with an *I* at the beginning of a sentence and not the imaginary *one*, which doesn't even exist. With conscious language, I lead myself and others, and in doing so I take responsibility.

That was my anecdote about *one* and conscientious objection. By the way, I made it, was recognized as a conscientious objector, and was not forced to do military service.

Christian: Like at home: *one should tidy up the kitchen*. We've already introduced the modal operators: *must, may, can, shall*. Our readers will have noticed that we often use the modal operator *may* instead of *must*. As a boss, *you may,* or even, *you want*. It helps me when I say, "I want to clean up the kitchen" instead of, "I have to clean up the kitchen." I then approach things in a completely different way. *I may* and *I want* work much better than *I have to*. Because I don't want to *have to* do anything.

Michael: My wife will be thrilled when I come home tonight and say exactly that to myself. And also do it.

Christian: "I want to clean up the kitchen." Great, Michael. Thanks a lot. We may now stop with this chapter.

Michael: And we want to stop.

The effect is quite different when I speak of myself, instead of an anonymous someone. The anonymity of "one" can also be a sort of cover-up when I actually want to say something else, something more like, "I'm sorry... but I meant it anyway." Nevertheless, sometimes it is not easy to do away with these words.   Awareness helps a lot. Since reading this chapter, I always cringe when I say "one" or "but." So it seems to work better than I thought. I think it is quite simple ;-)

ADVICE IS A VICE
STORIES FROM THE ADVICE MONSTER

Michael: We have now reached the last part of the iceberg. It might be helpful if I made a short recap so that our readers can continue to have clear orientation. How does that sound to you?

Christian: Good idea. Explain the context of the iceberg again. We've talked about so many topics that readers can easily get lost in it.

RECAP

Michael: Okay, it was mainly about leadership. We ask ourselves what leadership actually is. We answered this question with our definition, *Leadership is my ability to influence.*

Christian: I like the way you say it.

Michael: *Leadership is my ability to influence.* The question we then asked ourselves was: *How do I influence?* We talked about *Star Wars* and *the Force*. We want to use our techniques and methods for the good like Luke Skywalker. We don't want to misuse them for something bad like Darth Vader. We want to influence ourselves and our employees to achieve our grand master plan, our Purpose, our Vision, and our goals in the company. I influence through my behavior, charisma, and communication. As a manager, I am faced with the challenge that what I communicate to my employees is also right for them so that I can have an influence on them. Every day, 11 million bits of information rain down on each one of us, of which only a handful of information actually remains, around 7±2. I want to get this result set of 7±2 through to my employees. To increase my chances of success, which is usually around 0.00001%, I use the iceberg of communication. Like any good iceberg, this one has only a small tip showing above the surface. What happens above the surface is the content of the message of our communication. *What* I communicate. The remaining 95%

takes place below the surface. Seventy percent of it is the rapport, i.e., the relationship I have with my conversation partner. A further 25% is the *how* of my communication. I create rapport by smiling, eye contact, shaking hands, gestures, body language, addressing them by name, and by considering different sensory preferences. Each person has a special preference for one of the five VAKOG channels. VAKOG stands for visual, auditory, kinesthetic, olfactory, and gustatory. We have also talked about sensory preferences of the 25% *how*. Especially in groups, it is important that I address the three senses in a balanced way. Ideally in the appropriate *KVA* order: kinesthetic, visual and auditory. It works just as well in digital communication like email or video calls. Another trick is to repeat my message. Three repetitions to convince, six repetitions to memorize. I think we have now repeated this enough times. Once more to remember: three times to convince, six times to memorize. As a manager, I automatically take on the role of Chief Repeating Officer. We have removed *but* and *one* from our vocabulary, because positive language is more effective. We have replaced the former with *and* or have simply finished the sentence. We replace the latter with a concrete, real person, for example, *I*. Now we can move on.

Christian: I think you should now tell us something about advice, especially about unsolicited advice.

Michael: Should I?

Christian: Yes, I think so.

Michael: You're probably noticing it right now. Christian just got me started by giving me unsolicited advice. That is our topic. *You should do that*. It's enough to make your toes curl. We have replaced *one* with *I* and now we have arrived at *you*. The you-form is the advice-monster. When I tell you or others what you should do, I am an advice monster.

Christian: From my experience, you should do that.

Michael: What would it sound like to get advice from you?

Christian: What?

Michael: What is the advice monster?

Christian: The advice monster is that reflex I have when someone tells me a story in which they describe a problem. Of course I have the solution immediately. I know what the person has to do to make herself feel better. Because I have read all the guides and the complete literature. Besides, I'm simply the greatest. Politicians are too, they simply always know the right solution and know exactly what to do.

Michael: Wait a minute. [*pause*] Bullshit!

Christian: Advice monsters lurk around every corner. They quickly jump out when they hear that someone has a problem or a challenge. An advice monster then says, "Oh, I know that one. Do this and that. Try it this way and that way. I have read this book, you should read it too. Think about it." This is a first-rate rapport killer. My counterpart will certainly become very quiet pretty quickly.

Michael: Language works. I'm still baffled by all the advice you gave me.

Christian: This also ends the conversation. The other person is baffled and prefers not to hear anything at all. I, on the other hand, feel super, because I was able to give great advice.

Michael: Yeah, great. I will implement all your advice immediately.

Christian: I am sure of it.

Michael: How can I make it better? Fun aside. I mean, I can tell from my reaction alone that it's not very helpful. When I tell you something and you come at me with, "You should do it this way and that way," I immediately think, "The hell I will." In our case, your reaction was even agreed upon beforehand and yet I still had this thought: How can I do this better as a manager?

Christian: You should first drink a glass of water and take a deep breath. [*pause*] It's easy to give good advice.

Michael: I'll follow your advice and drink a nice, cold glass of water. [*drinks*]

ASK, LISTEN, AND BE QUIET

Christian: What helps you when you have a problem? What helps you when you get to a place where you just can't move forward? What can your counterpart do to help you move forward?

Michael: Honestly? Sometimes, just listening. Often my own internal monologue, which I can share with someone, helps me. I often come up with the solution myself. In a conversation with someone else, it's kind of a different mindset. The moment I tell someone else, my problem becomes clear to me. The solution is then often obvious. Sometimes, I also ask for concrete advice or similar experiences. "Have you ever experienced a similar situation? How did you solve it?" or "May I ask you for advice?" This can be helpful, if it is indeed a comparable situation and the advice is valuable. When I need this kind of support, I ask for it specifically, so it is not unwanted or unsolicited advice.

Christian: What did I just do?

Michael: You asked me a question.

Christian: I asked you a question and then listened.

Michael: Right. And then I listed three options and realized which one was my preferred solution.

Christian: The mood is immediately a completely different one.

Michael: Yes, that's right. I'm busy trying to work out a solution instead of thinking about why I didn't like the advice from an advice monster.

Christian: So you can simply ask a question at the point where you are actually tempted to give unsolicited advice. In what other ways can I help you solve a problem?

Michael: I don't need any help right now.

Christian: Oh man, at least pretend you do. [*playfully offended*] Ask questions and listen!

Michael: Ask questions and listen. Do you know Columbo, I mean Inspector Columbo?

Christian: I thought you meant the capital of Sri Lanka.

Michael: Well, that is also beautiful and is called Colombo. I mean Inspector Columbo from the crime series in the 70s. He always wears those big beige trench coats and scurries around solving his cases. You know what he does all the time? He's asking questions. Throughout the episode, he asks all kinds of people all kinds of questions to solve the case. Probably, he has identified the killer after only five minutes, yet he keeps asking more and more questions. They needed to fill up the episode. "There, behind the hedge, the gardener stood at the window and looked out." Columbo responds, "Really? What was he looking at?" In his quirky way, he asks one question after another and listens to everything very carefully. Only at the very end, in the last two minutes, does he put all the puzzle pieces together and solve the case.

Christian: Columbo also uses another very casual technique. After each conversation, when he has pestered all the people with his questions, he slowly leaves the room. Before he disappears through the door, he always turns around again and says, "I noticed one more thing..." That's awesome. Everyone is already sure that it's over, the tension drops, and suddenly he notices something strange.

Michael: That is exactly what the Columbo method is. I can use it to lead. Ask questions and listen carefully. *God gave me two ears and one mouth and I should use them proportionally.*

Christian: Just ask and listen. How can I become an even better listener?

Michael: I use the thinker pose for this. I take my hand to my chin and consciously put myself in listening mode. This is how I influence and guide myself to make listening easier.

Christian: When someone tells me something, I quickly find myself thinking about what I can answer. According to the mantra, "I also know a story about that." This is the advice monster's little brother. So I try to listen consciously and wait patiently until my counterpart is finished. Then I can tell my story.

Michael: Am I listening to respond or listening to understand?

Christian: That's a great point. At first it can be tricky to distinguish between the two. It is well worth it to make the effort

Michael: What else can I do?

Christian: Sometimes it helps to keep quiet for a moment. When I ask someone a question and nothing happens because the person I'm asking takes the time to answer, something good usually comes out of it. I can stand this silence. Especially in coaching situations, I am sometimes tempted to break the silence and say something. I have found that it usually doesn't help. So I simply endure the silence.

Michael: So there are three elements: Ask questions, listen, and be silent.

Christian: Right. It is helpful to give your counterpart time to think.

Michael: As a group coach, I often experience that as well. When I ask a question, it often takes seven, eight, nine seconds until someone says something. It wasn't always easy to endure this silence. In the past, I often thought, "Oh, nobody's saying anything, maybe I should just move on." Now I have learned to endure it and I enjoy these moments. Almost always someone says something after all, and often this contribution is especially valuable.

Christian: Sometimes it feels like an eternity.

Michael: And all eyes are upon you. At first it's really uncomfortable.

Christian: Maybe readers still remember the *Happy Birthday* trick. I sing the Happy Birthday song in my head in those situations, it lasts exactly 15 seconds. I wait out the silence and give my counterpart time. This is a good amount of time and a great way to distract from the silence and the staring eyes.

Michael: Yeah, that's great. I'm just going to sing *Happy Birthday* in those moments.

Christian: Just sing in your head and do not tell the others. [*silence – 15 seconds*]

Michael: That was a long silence, let's get the energy back up.

Christian: Silence also works great on the phone. Just keeping your mouth shut is a great negotiation method, especially on the phone.

Michael: Time for a recap. What did you take away today?

Christian: Or rather: What have we left out? I left out the advice monster.

Michael: Right, we were talking about the advice monster.

Christian: And we talked about his little brother: "I only listen to you because I am thinking about what I am about to say." Therefore: ask questions, listen, and use the silence.

Michael: All right. I'm using that one now.

First of all, thank you for this recap. I understand what you are doing. You help me to keep your own content in my head by repeating it—great stuff. It works. I think I'm now convinced of your definition of leadership and I look forward to the next time you mention it as a reminder.

I know these advice monsters only too well and, quite frankly, I have often seen them in myself. I feel a little embarrassed. From now on, I will keep my advice to myself until someone asks me for it. At least I'll phrase it more cleverly with the help of your questioning technique. Because I am sure that my advice is clever. Often my counterpart does not even know how clever my advice is ... ;-)

KISS EINSTEIN!
FORMATTING COMMUNICATION

Christian: Today, we'll simply finish the iceberg. So please keep it simple. So simple that everyone understands.

Michael: Why is the saying, *Keep it simple, stupid*?

Christian: There is a comma before *stupid*, so it means *you're stupid*.

Michael: Okay. So if I don't keep it simple as a boss, I'm stupid.

Christian: Right. Or *please keep it simple for me, stupid*. I can also say *keep it simple and stupid*, in the sense of *keep it simple and easy to understand*.

Michael: Short and to the point.

Christian: Right on. Iceberg ready. Is anything missing?

Michael: Besides *Keep it simple, stupid* (we've already checked that off), there's a second technique. It's about the *how*, which contributes 25% to making communication successful. It is a formatting formula. In four steps and by following the right sequence, I can format my message so that it comes across in the best possible way.

WHY → WHAT → HOW → WHAT IF

(→ WHAT IF NOT)

Illustration: Format Frame
This is how I format my message effectively.

Christian: Let's give an example.

Michael: I had a coaching call this morning. A client told me about a problem. She is faced with the task of informing her team that two of her employees will leave the company due to the Corona crisis. The goal is to save costs. She was looking for the optimal way to deliver this message without the team spirit suffering and so that her employees understand for what Purpose this unfortunately has to happen now.

Christian: Why is this necessary?

Michael: This is the first step: Before the *what*, it's about the *why?* For what Purpose? "Because sales have collapsed by 70%, our company's existence is threatened, and if we don't act quickly and reduce our costs, we'll have to shut down the company by July."

Christian: Okay, this is the *why*. What happens now?

Michael: "Unfortunately, we have to part with two employees. They will leave the company on April 30 and will be released from their duties as of next Monday. Effective immediately, they will no longer be part of our team.

Christian: This is not only the *what*, it's almost the *how*, the third step, isn't it?

Michael: Almost. The *how* is the date in April and the release from work on Monday. *How* is also, "I would like to thank the two colleagues for their contribution over the past years and for bringing us forward as a team. I appreciate them for their expertise and competence that they have brought to the table and I hope that we will continue to be friends in the future, even if our paths are now parting."

Christian: What if?

Michael: The fourth step, *What if. What if* we do this now? "If we do it this way now, we will ensure that everyone else on the team is very secure and that we will get through this difficult year together so that we can continue to work on our common Vision in the future. This is the only way we can achieve our common goal in this community with all the committed employees who come here every day, even if, for the time being, only virtually."

Christian: And what if not?

Michael: *What would happen if we didn't do that?* is the fifth question that underscores the message. "If we don't do this now, it means that we'll probably all go home by the end of July and lose all our jobs. In which case, the company will close."

Christian: And then the communication is over?

Michael: Right. This *format frame* is the formatting formula: *Why, What, How, What if.* And if I want to give my message greater emphasis, I can add the *What if not.* Great method. I can also use it in a report or if I want to express an important thing in a different way. It doesn't matter if it is something positive or negative. I start with the *why* or the *wherefore*, then name the *what*, and then the *how*. At the end I phrase the sign-off with, *"If we do this now, this and that will happen."* That's how I create motivation.

Christian: That's how I manage to balance the connection between Vision and Purpose. It's about the survival of the company. The wording makes it clear that the decisions I make today are aligned with this.

Michael: Right. That's what leadership means. I have to make that decision. It's a baseball flying toward me that I may hit. And if I communicate this ball—despite the hit—in a clean and understandable way, I will be successful as a leader, as a company director, as the boss (of my life).

Christian: For what kind of communication can I use this method?

Michael: Face-to-face, in groups, in emails, on the phone, in a conference call. We humans are fundamentally wired a certain way. In the beginning, we all want to know: *Why? Wherefore? What is it actually important for?* When I have understood this, I am open to what follows. In the past, I often made the mistake of starting with the *what*: "Hello, I have to inform you that we are going to part with two colleagues."

Christian: Start with *why*.[32]

Michael: Someone might try to write a book about it. I won't do it. *Start with Why* is exactly the point of simple communication: *Why? Wherefore? For what*

---

32 In allusion to the book "Start with Why - How Great Leaders Inspire Everyone to Take Action" by Simon Sinek.

Purpose? And only then do I explain what it is, how it is, and what happens when we do it that way.

Christian: What does *KISS* have to do with Einstein?

Michael: *KISS* stands for *Keep it simple, stupid*. Einstein was more eloquent there. He said, "If I can't explain it simply, I haven't understood it well enough."

Christian: Not that stupid at all, Einstein.

Sounds convincing. I'll keep it in mind. KISS: Why, what, how, what if?

"WE'RE ALL INDIVIDUALS"

– GROUP OF JERUSALEMITES, 33 A.D.
SATURDAY, AROUND TEA TIME
MONTHY PYTHON'S LIFE OF BRIAN, 1979

VAKOG

EVERY HUMAN BEING LIVES IN HIS OWN UNIVERSE

Christian: It was the weekend. How do you feel?

Michael: Great, I feel wonderful.

Christian: What makes a great weekend for you?

Michael: What was great this weekend was the quality time I spent with my loved ones, my wife, and my two children. Yesterday, I rode with my daughters to our neighboring town on a bicycle. My little girl, she's two years old, sat behind me in the child seat. My five-year-old daughter was riding her own bike. Together we rode through the fields for half an hour. It was really nice to wander through nature with the two of them.

Christian: What did you see when you were driving through the fields?

Michael: It was very sunny yesterday. We drove past a yellow canola field, it looked really nice. I explained to the two girls that oil is extracted from it. We could even see the windmills on the horizon. There was a light breeze, with people occasionally passing us. It was great, the weather and the landscape were just fantastic. On the way back, the evening sun was a little lower and was already slightly orange. It was a picturesque setting, almost corny.

Christian: Did you hear anything?

Michael: From time to time I heard my daughter's bicycle bell. And of course my own voice when I looked around for her or talked to the two of them. Overall, it was relatively quiet.

Christian: Did you smell something?

Michael: I could smell the rapeseed field. And on the way there we drove through a small woodland, it was still a little cooler in the early afternoon. There I had a really fresh, spring-like forest smell in my nose. Very aromatic.

Christian: What did you say to yourself as you drove along there?

Michael: I felt really happy and content. I was thinking how nice it is to ride through these woods and fields with my two children and my bicycle. I was very aware of this moment and I felt very happy.

Christian: I can totally understand that, I also rode my bike yesterday.

Michael: How was it for you?

Christian: At this time of year there are a lot of beautiful birds out. Yesterday, I also heard some of them singing really loud. Even while we are recording our podcasts, I hear them sometimes. I wonder how it would sound if we amplified the birds' twittering with separate speakers in the garden. I find that totally fascinating.

Michael: What else was nice about your weekend?

Christian: Coincidentally, I also drove through a forest. I totally enjoyed feeling the sun through the trees and then the shade again in turns. The light's brightness changed constantly and there were many different smells in the forest. Sometimes it smelled like warm wood and sometimes like damp earth.

Michael: Are there any other impressions that stuck with you?

Christian: I noticed that in some places the forest still looked very wintery, very barren and brown, while in other places it was slowly turning green and the leaves and flowers were beginning to sprout. I enjoyed that very much. I also saw a wild boar.

Michael: How did you feel?

Christian: Light. Especially when I had a tail wind.

Michael: What was going through your mind?

Christian: *It is so beautiful*, I thought. It's nice that I can experience this.

Michael: If this day had been a taste, what taste would it be?

Christian: In the evening, it was asparagus with butter sauce.

Michael: It goes with spring, very nice.

Christian: Now we have gone through all *VAKOG* channels. Were you able to notice that we have different preferences?

Michael: I heard something.

Christian: I have seen different things with you than I have heard with me. Of course, we also asked each other about our overall impressions.

Michael: We know our preferences now. We are now in the middle of the topic of *people's otherness*. One way in which we as humans differ from one another is through our sensory preferences: visual, auditory, kinesthetic, olfactory, and gustatory. I even notice this while we talk about it in full consciousness and share our sensory impressions. And yet it is always the visual impressions that come to my mind first. I still have the pictures of the bicycle tour with my children very much present. When you asked me about the sounds, I couldn't think of much else except silence. On the other hand, I could remember the thoughts that were in my head very clearly. I felt happy. In terms of my taste, I think of the barbecue we had in between. If someone had spontaneously asked me about my weekend, I would have probably just described the images in my head and told them about my thoughts, because these are my preferences. My preferred channels are the visual and the digital-auditive channel, or what my thoughts and the images I myself have in my mind. I am not sure which of the two channels is number one. Both are quite distinct. The other sensory channels come after these two. How about you?

Christian: For me, the auditory channel is very strong. After that comes the visual. I perceive quite a lot about that one as well. Perhaps it has something to do with my joy of design. Of course, I know the inner voice inside me, it is just not as strongly developed. Meditation might help to calm the voice down a bit.

Michael: I could try that.

Christian: I am convinced of that. Currently, I also pay a lot of attention to smells.

Michael: That's interesting. The gustatory, the sense of taste, is one of those things. Sometimes, I feel like eating simply because I like the sense of taste so much. I also like to drink wine or whiskey because of the taste. Sometimes, although rarely, I also like to smoke a cigar. I enjoy the aroma, the smell, and all the taste impressions. In any case, these are also very prominent with me. Maybe this channel is the one I prefer. That would at least explain why I should lose a few pounds.

Christian: You can certainly activate your inner voice. What do we do with it now? We now know that there are the *VAKOG-channels:* visual, auditory, kinesthetic, olfactory, and gustatory. We also know that each person has different preferences regarding these channels. So how can I use this as a boss in leading my employees?

Michael: With this knowledge, I can build understanding and trust in other people and create a great team. That would be a short answer that comes to mind.

Christian: Very nice, and how do I do that specifically?

Michael: *Each fool is different.* Before I realized how much we humans are already different on this first level of perception, I always thought, "Anyone can see that," or, "That's obvious, we've all heard it." No, we did not. That only became clear to me with time. Everyone perceives things differently. There is a nice example of me at home. As I mentioned before, I am a very visual type. If there is a mess in the apartment, kitchen or living room I notice it immediately. Every little thing catches my eye. My wife has a different sensual preference, she doesn't notice all that. She has more of an auditory and a kinesthetic preference.

Christian: Well, I can see it too and I still don't care. [*laughs*]

Michael: That's your decision, then. Whether you care or not depends on your Values. You decide what you do with your perception. What I clearly observe is that we actually perceive different things. The perception of our environment is different for everyone. My wife is very sensitive to the feelings of other people, and she has a very precise antennae for this. This is not so pronounced with me. We complement each other very well. It is the *pot-and-lid principle.* We complement each other with our strengths and have a certain potential for conflict because of our differences. The way I just described it in the relationship with my wife, it's the same in teams. In a team, there are people with different preferences, even if they have known each other for quite some time. I recently had an exciting workshop with five founders who have known each other for over 10 years. They now have a joint company and we did a few workshops on leadership. It was an open round and we talked about leadership and communication. So we inevitably came to the VAKOG topic very quickly. There is a little test that I often do with the participants to quickly find out what their preferences are. It only takes 10 minutes and everyone fills out a small questionnaire. We talked through the results and worked out how this manifests itself in everyday life. The results were really very exciting. One of the five has a very strong visual preference, another one has a kinesthetic preference. They noticed this for the first time and understood why they were constantly bitching at each other. Both felt irritated because, in their eyes, their own preference was not taken into account sufficiently in the actions and communication of the other. It was a real aha-moment. The VAKOG topic, which sounds so loose and fluffy at the beginning, then became a two-hour, very profound exchange, during which it became clear to everyone what preferences they bring with them and what potential they have. It has contributed to a great deal of mutual understanding.

Christian: You just said they *felt irritated.* That is colloquial and a kinesthetic expression. How did that express itself? What might a conflict that arises from that look like, and how do the two of them manage to get their act together? How can I do it better?

Michael: The conversation between the two of them went something like this: "You're always painting these crazy things and you always want to visualize everything."

Christian: "I didn't realize it bothered you. Why does it?"

Michael: "I always have the feeling that you don't listen to me at all and only think of some charts." Different patterns in the communication between the two of them became apparent. It quickly became clear that there are people who would like to talk about a topic first, they prefer the auditory channel. Those who quickly jump up and run to a flipchart or pick up a paper would like to visualize it. The situation is completely different for people with kinesthetic preference. For them, it is vital to first get a feeling for the other person and for the situation they're in together. They ask themselves, for example, "Where do we actually stand with this topic?" It is often also reflected in their gestures. Gestures are often used or structures are pointed out in the room using the hand. People with a digital-auditory preference may say when dealing with a topic: "I would like to think about this in peace and quiet and sort my thoughts. I don't want to hear or see anything, I need a moment's rest first. I let my inner voice have its say." In this founding team really all preferences were represented, it had a great impact on their work roles. A visual preference is, of course, always great for tasks like creation, design, and so on. People with auditory preferences are good at interacting with other people. I think of the call center staff alone. It would be great if they all had an auditory preference. They are good listeners. If they are also very empathic, i.e., have another preference for the kinesthetic channel, it is super helpful to quickly build a relationship with the calling customers by empathizing with the problem. Under pressure, people with opposite preferences quickly fall behind in those situations. Therefore, the distribution of roles in consideration of the respective preferences is very important in the founding team.

Christian: I can now use this information in two ways. On the one hand, I can consciously pay attention when someone communicates with me to which senses they address. Especially when I notice that something doesn't fit. I can then mentally take a step back and pay attention to the channels of perception that she uses or addresses. In the past, for example, people with a pronounced digital-auditive preference sometimes annoyed me. I would stand next to them and listen to their inner monologue while thinking to myself, "That's obvious, what's taking her so long?" On the other hand, I can adapt my language to my counterpart when I know what preferences she has. I can adapt my choice of words, my descriptions, and so on to the senses that work better for her.

Michael: Ultimate behavioral flexibility.

Christian: Exactly. Here it works through the words I use, the sounds I make, and the pictures I draw.

Michael: The person with the most behavioral flexibility leads. By the way, there is a correlation between the preferred sensory channels and the color types from the Insights Model, i.e., the personality types. The two models seem to be related. I am a typical case. There is a strong correlation between the visual channel and the red energy. Doing, moving forward, and at the same time taking things in through the visual channel are often related. Opposite of this is green energy: people who attach great importance to harmony and togetherness and at the same time have a kinesthetic preference and react more to feelings. I have therefore consciously connected myself with the emotional level and expanded my vocabulary with fitting expressions such as, "How does it feel for you?" or "I feel with you," in order to build up a competence in it. Today, when I speak with someone who has a kinesthetic preference, I use this vocabulary much more emphatically and consciously. It feels more natural and more comfortable each time. You recently told me that you did an analysis of our podcast and examined which words from which area we use frequently. It was great feedback because the result was that we use a lot more auditory and kinesthetic words than visual ones. So I thought, "Yeah, I've finally reached my goal." Now I've practiced so much behavioral flexibility that I'm able to get by with a kinesthetic vocabulary.

Christian: There you could already see the finish line. [*grins*]

Michael: Yes, exactly. [*laughs*] You got me. Again, I'm in my red comfort zone.

Christian: When I talk to my team now and there are many different people sitting in front of me, how do I manage to take them all with me?

Michael: Up to about 10 people, that is 7±2, I try to fit in individually. When I sit in a meeting with people who have more of a kinesthetic preference, the first thing I do is use my appropriate vocabulary. Then I pay special attention to my body language and gestures. I may try to make light body contact, a handshake or a hug, depending on the situation. In workshops, I quickly find out if someone has an emotional preference. I lay out or share various toys. People with a kinesthetic preference always grab the toys first. At least, the probability is very high that they have that preference. I then pay close attention to the reaction when I shake hands with someone or adjust my vocabulary. This can also quickly go too far. If I notice that someone describes something very visually or expresses something in pictures, maybe paints something, because they have paper and pencil at hand, I try to respond to that again. Of course, this is only possible in a smaller group.

Christian: And in a larger group?

Michael: It's difficult, of course. When I give a speech in front of 20, 30, or maybe even 100 people or more, of course I can't manage that individually. So I rotate. I alternately use kinesthetic, visual, and then auditory language, images, and expressions. Sometimes I even try to incorporate a sense of smell or taste, if the context allows it. The three most important senses are KVA: kinesthetic, visual, and auditory. I have learned to start with the kinesthetic, because they are the first to switch off mentally. Therefore, I remember the KVA formula to build up rapport. In this way, I am effective and more successful in the *How* of communication.

Christian: Great, thank you very much. How does it all feel for you now?

Michael: My inner voice tells me, "That looked good."

That is fascinating. I'll have a look at what expressions people around me primarily use. Again, I have the feeling that I can suddenly decode a language that was previously unknown to me. Paying attention is probably also one of the strengths of a leader.

MENSCHENKENNTNIS
THE FOUR COLOR ENERGIES

Christian: Hello Michael, how are you?

Michael: Fantastic. We celebrated the birthday of a mutual friend this weekend. Today, I'm slowly feeling better.

Christian: [*laughs*] It was a great party, wasn't it?

Michael: Absolutely, I had a lot of fun. It was a nice, colorful evening.

Christian: Colorful is a good keyword. Let's talk about colors.

Michael: Gladly, life is so beautifully colorful. Above all, people are colorful. Human behavior is very diverse. The German word *Menschenkenntnis*, which is a very common and popular term, literally means *knowledge of people*. *Menschenkenntnis* is the skill to detect and understand the diversity in people and human behavior, the ability to judge character, and the discernment to predict how people might think, feel, and act.

Christian: That's right, that's what it's all about. Since people are very different, I want a technique to better classify and understand my employees, so that I can also adapt my communication and thus help them to understand me better. Ultimately, it's about management and corporate governance. It's about how I get employees to do what I want them to do.

Michael: There are several methods that can help. When I was in my first leadership role, I only brought people onto my team who had similar mindsets to my own. Of course, I created a fantastic monoculture that was not necessarily successful. It makes more sense to create diversity on the team. Different personality types are important and helpful to be successful. As a manager, this naturally presents me with special challenges. Dealing with this diversity is not necessarily easy as a leader. It is, of course, easier for me to communicate and work with people who function just like me.

Christian: What tools are there that I can use for this? It is certainly not a new problem in our history of mankind.

Michael: Phew... Our human history is 300,000 years old, or at least no older remains of Homo sapiens have been found. The oldest were found in Morocco a few years ago. So our species has been around for 300,000 years, and so have the challenges, or rather the opportunities, to make something out of our diversity. We can shape interpersonal interaction so that they flow really well. Hippocrates33 invented the first method for this. An ancient Greek, 500 years before Christ, thought of the first system of how to recognize and classify different types of people into *the four temperaments*: choleric, melancholic, sanguine, and one more.

Christian: The phlegmatic.

Michael: The phlegmatic, exactly.

Christian: None of this sounds particularly positive.

Michael: That's right. The terms he chose back then have rather negative connotations in today's language. They weren't that popular back then either. Today, nobody likes to call themselves *choleric*, even if it's true. Basically, he did a very cool thing, similar to other more recent models that implement psychological findings stemming from the 1900's. However, he was also quite wrong in some things. He attributed the differences in human behavior to medical properties such as passing bile. We have indeed learned a thing or two over the last 2,500 years.

Christian: What happened then?

Michael: Then came Brian, at the time of Christ. *The Life of Brian*. Anyone who knows Monty Python will smile now. Everyone else has now received a great film recommendation. The famous line, "You're all individuals" originates from this film.

Christian: "Not me." [*chuckles*]

---

33   https://de.wikipedia.org/wiki/Hippokrates_von_Kos about 500 B.C.

Michael: [*grins*] That's the point. When it comes to models and personality types, of course, we always talk about commonalities and a boxes, always in a positive sense. In the end, of course, the following applies: *everyone is an individual*. Nevertheless, there are a few things we can make use of in our communication.

Christian: What positive boxes are there that I can use? Are they scientifically proven?

Michael: The scientific basis goes back to C.G. Jung. "C.G." stands for Carl Gustav. At least, the basis for the Insights Model goes back to his work. Jung was a contemporary of Freud and Adler, two other big names in the world of psychology, at the beginning of the 20th century, around 1900. He analyzed human behavior in depth and identified some polar characteristics. Some of them are still common in everyday language today. Therefore, some terms are somewhat biased.

Christian: Give us an example.

Michael: *Introverted* and *extroverted* are two examples. We often have a somewhat misguided idea about these terms. The actual definition is the source of motivation. Whether I am an introverted or an extroverted person is determined by what motivates me. Extroverted people get their motivation from interacting with people and things when they are out in the world. Introverted people tend to be more introspective and like to think about themselves and their feelings, other people, and the world. Only after careful inner reflection do they take action. Each person has his or her own preference on the scale from introverted to extroverted. Some have a very extreme preference for one or the other, while others lie somewhere in between and are very balanced. Like much in nature, it is a normal distribution. This dimension is an example of Jung's insights. It still works very well today.

A second dimension is a scale, with those who are task-oriented on one side, and those who are more people-oriented on the other. This is about how I make decisions. Do I make a decision based on pure factual information or do I mainly consider the influence on other people in my decisions?

Which preference I have is also evident in my use of language. Again, I may have my personal inclination somewhere in between the two preferences, or I may lean toward one of the extremes. With Jung's two polar dimensions g, we have described the first basic framework to talk about the Insights Model. These dimensions result in a 2x2 matrix. It is a four-field matrix in which the four dimensions—introversion and extroversion, task and people oriented— are combined with each other. I can assign a color to each field in this matrix. I then associate each combination with a color. That is the magic of the Insights Model. There are many models of personality psychology. I have been using this one for many years and still find it most practical for my daily work. It is one of my absolute standard tools for everything that has to do with leadership and management.

Christian: So a 2x2 matrix, in which the individual quadrants are colored.

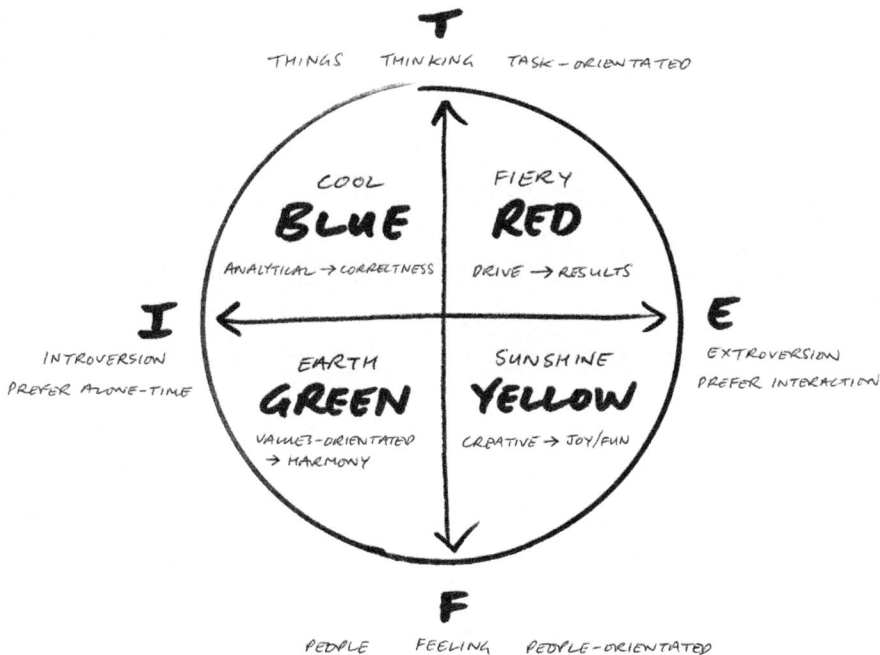

THINGS   THINKING   TASK - ORIENTATED

COOL
BLUE
ANALYTICAL → CORRECTNESS

FIERY
RED
DRIVE → RESULTS

I — INTROVERSION / PREFER ALONE-TIME

E — EXTROVERSION / PREFER INTERACTION

EARTH
GREEN
VALUES-ORIENTATED → HARMONY

SUNSHINE
YELLOW
CREATIVE → JOY/FUN

PEOPLE   FEELING   PEOPLE-ORIENTATED

Illustration: Insights Color Energies
In each of us, there is an individual mixture of preferences and color energies.

Michael: Right. The four colors are blue, green, yellow, and red. I often concretize the color designation to fiery red, sunshine yellow, earth green, and deep blue. I will show you why. What do you associate with the color blue? Imagine that I paint a blue spot in front of you. How does blue feel to you? What do you see?

Christian: Hmmm… [*thinks*] I associate something cool, analytical, profound with blue. Maybe also calm, deep water, something with water in any case. A certain energy level.

Michael: You see? Something deep. Hence deep blue. What do you think of green?

Christian: Trees, closeness to nature, Value orientation.

Michael: Nature, hence earth green. What about yellow?

Christian: With yellow I think of the sun, of energy, warmth, fun.

Michael: Sunshine yellow. That leaves red. What do you associate with the color red?

Christian: When I see red, I think caution, fire, heat, stop.

Michael: Yes, exactly. Fiery red, people often associate it with danger. Most people have these associations that you just had in your head and named so quickly. The answers to the questions I asked you are very similar for most people, there is at least a high correlation. Remarkably, this even works internationally in almost every culture. There are only a few exceptions where the colors are set differently. The Insights Model takes advantage of this and combines Jung's psychological principles with very comprehensible color associations. That's what makes it so pragmatic and is the reason why I'm such a fan of it. Let's go through the four colors once again. Blue represents the analyst. We are talking about human behavior. Someone with a lot of blue energy is very accurate and attaches importance to 100% results. Punctuality and order is very important to her. People with primary blue energy do things properly, they prioritize correctness over speed. The motto of the blue color is, *We do it correctly.* The green energy is the energy of Value orientation. Its motto is: *We do it in a Value-oriented way.* It is about harmony between people and about what connects people, what makes a community. Values are crucial for people with green energy. Yellow is the *sunshine* energy. I can recognize sunshine people very quickly. They are often very creative people who like to have fun and celebrate. Their motto is: *We do it together*. A few people are welcome to join in. For people with yellow energy it is not untypical to socialize with 20 or 30 people at a party. Finally, there is the red energy. That is the color of the *driver, the doer* . The motto is: *We do it now.* Sometimes also: *Why wasn't it done yesterday?* Or it could have been already completed by now. These are the four basic types in the Insights Model. Each person has an individual combination of these four preferences, like a fingerprint. Each person, therefore, has his or her own individual spectrum of preferences.

Christian: So how do I recognize which of these preferences someone has? How do I use this model?

Michael: I can tell by the various parameters. Often the language, the choice of words, indicates the individual's primary preferences. *Correct* = blue; *that's fun* = yellow; let's *go!* = red; and *thinking in peace* = green. The speed of speech is another distinguishing feature. The red energy speaks very fast.

Christian: Curious you yourself should say that, Michael.

Michael: You got me!, It certainly is true for me. The red energy likes to talk loud and clear (often in front), and rarely minces matters. I also like to shoot something out quickly. The yellow energy likes to talk a lot. Everybody knows a friend or colleague who, once the flow of speech has begun, hardly ever stops talking. This is probably someone with a lot of yellow energy. People with a lot of green energy are rather reserved in the speech part, the same applies to the speed of speech. The green energy is more of a calm consistency, the tone goes down, it is quieter than with the two extroverted red and yellow energies. I often recognize a green energy preference in people by the fact that they wait until the end to speak themselves. They like to let the others finish first and only then take over. However, they also expect to be allowed to speak at some point and to be given enough time to express their feelings in peace. People with a lot of blue energy tend to be quiet, sometimes seem a bit cold. Their speech can be somewhat louder and clearer than in green energy, and they express themselves with a lot of restraint in body language. Now we have gone through all color types. What is your preference, Christian?

Christian: I think I have a preference for yellow energy. I like it when the sun is shining.

Michael: I have to smile because since we've known each other, we've often talked about *fun.* You often say that it is important to you to have fun with all the things we do. You use the word *fun* very often. Each of these basic types typically has a preferred VAKOG sense channel. It is normally distributed as so often, so there are of course exceptions. In red energy, the visual channel is the preferred one. People with a lot of red energy like to see charts, graphics, and facts. They like to draw on paper or flip charts, just like me. People with a lot of yellow energy, like you, like to talk and listen. Mouth and ears play an important role. Your preferred channel is auditory. In green energy, the preferred sensory channel is feeling, kinesthetics. Therefore, people with a lot of green energy like to use related words, for example, "It feels like, ..." In blue energy, the sixth sense channel is the preferred one. So people with a lot of blue energy typically have a very distinct inner voice. It can also become loud and leak out. I can understand this well, because my inner voice is also very strong. It was an exciting experience to find that out. [*smiles*]

Christian: Thank you for the detailed description of the personality types. In the next chapter, I will discuss how I can use them in management and what potential conflict they can create.

Michael: That's right. Many colors can mean more conflicts and also better results. That's exactly the point.

Hmm... interesting. Some of the features you mentioned really resonate with me and make me think, "Yes, that could match. That applies to me." With others, not at all. Maybe it is not always obvious what type of person I am or what my preferences are. Perhaps there are different mixtures and combinations of color types and preferences. Or maybe I am also a chameleon. In any case, it explains the different behaviors on my team. I would like to find out more about which colleague has which preferences.

PSYCHOLOGY IN MULTICOLOR

DIVERSE TEAMS

Christian: We have already talked about the Insights Model color psychology and different personality types. It was about understanding other people and their preferences better. I would like to go a little deeper into the subject and answer the questions about how I can use this precisely as a manager. How can I adapt my behavior? How do I recognize conflicts that arise in a team due to different personality types?

Michael: With pleasure. Let me briefly repeat the four basic types based on C.G. Jung's psychology and the color associations. They are actually consistent worldwide, regardless of culture or nation. People with primary blue energy are what we call the analyst. They are very accurate, paying attention to correctness and precision. People with blue energy do things very correctly, they do things right. The earth green energy is the energy that is very Value-oriented. To people with green energy, harmony between people involved is very important. Then there are the creative ones, they have a lot of yellow energy, sunshine yellow. They are interested in options and different points of view. Being creative does not necessarily mean that someone paints or does anything artistic. It can also mean that creative, unconventional methods, ways of thinking and acting are applied to things that may not seem so creative. An accountant can also be a very creative type, who, for example, is constantly thinking up new, creative and clever methods. Then there is the red type. With red energy I am more driven to tackle things. That's why this type of person is called a *driver,* the one who goes first, without asking any questions until afterwards. These are the four basic energies: Blue, green, yellow, and red. The first step for me as a manager is to recognize the respective energy in my employees. We have already talked about this. I often recognize it in people's behavior and in their language, their body language, their expression, their choice of words, their basic attitude, even their facial features. There are some additional tools that I can use to recognize this. They are very easy and intuitive to use, so I quickly identify which color energy is predominantly present in someone. Before I talk about how I adapt my behavior to my counterpart — that's what it's all about in the end, adapting my behavior, my communication to someone who is different from me in order to achieve even better results—I want to know where I am at, because everything is relative.

Christian: Where do you stand?

Michael: My personal preference is the red energy. I like it crisp and to the point. I want things to run and get done. My secondary preference is the yellow energy, then comes the blue energy. The energy I prefer least is the green energy. If I want to adapt to another person, it is important to know what my own preferences are. Adjustment is relative to what I myself am like. When I was a child, I thought that the whole universe revolved around me, that I was ground zero, the reference point. At some point, I realized that I am just one of billions and that my position is relative to the universe. Only when I have understood my relative position can I begin to understand where other people stand, for example in the four-color spectrum. Then I also know how to adapt my behavior.

Christian: As a person with red energy, you are rather extroverted and task-oriented. Someone with green energy is more people-oriented and introverted, so she is in a completely different position than you. That has the potential to cause conflict.

Michael: Right, that's usually the case. *People like people who are like themselves.* That's why I tend to connect with people who also have a lot of red energy right away. Rapport is immediate. There is a basic understanding for each other from the beginning. If, on the other hand, I meet someone with opposite energy (in my case it's actually the green energy), then it takes a little more effort to develop rapport. In the past, in such cases I used to wonder and think, "What's wrong with her? Why doesn't she say anything? Why does everything take so long, yet she's so calm and quiet?" My thoughts immediately judged this person. Today, I know that it is just someone with a different energy preference and therefore I can detect this quickly; I have been working on it for several years and have improved myself. I understand now that it is perfectly okay that other people are the way they are. It is my responsibility to adjust to this and to adapt my behavior when I work with them, especially as a leader.

Christian: As a manager it is, of course, easiest to build a team where everyone has the same color preference. In your case, it would be easy if all the people on your team also had a red energy preference. You get along with them right away, you can work with them, and when you give clear direction, things just flow. So you build a team that consists only of people with red energy, right?

Michael: [*grins*] Too bad our readers don't see your mischievous grin. That is a provocative question. Unfortunately, this is exactly what happened to me many years ago. As marketing director, I built up a marketing team of 40 people. With this team I did my first *Insights* training as team building. Each individual was given a personal profile, which helped them to evolve very well. As a manager, I got an impression of how my team as a whole was positioned in the context of the four color energies. It was even more detailed, there are further differentiations of color preferences to 16 or 72 types. And lo and behold, I had successfully managed to hire mainly people who had a red-yellow preference just like me. *People like people who are like themselves and inexperienced managers hire people who are like themselves.* At the beginning it felt really good, because everybody got along well and was on the same page. In the end, it went catastrophically wrong because without a healthy combination of the other preferences, we were simply unable to deliver good results. For a good result, I also need the blue energy that makes sure that things are done right. I need the green energy so that the whole thing is Value-oriented and runs harmoniously, so that it makes sense and feels good for the team. I need the yellow energy to call up several options and to allow creativity to try out new things.

Christian: That means, since that experience you have built up a team in which all color preferences are represented?

MONO-CULTURE
→ WEAK

POLARIZED
→ CONFLICT

DIVERSE
→ HIGH POTENTIAL

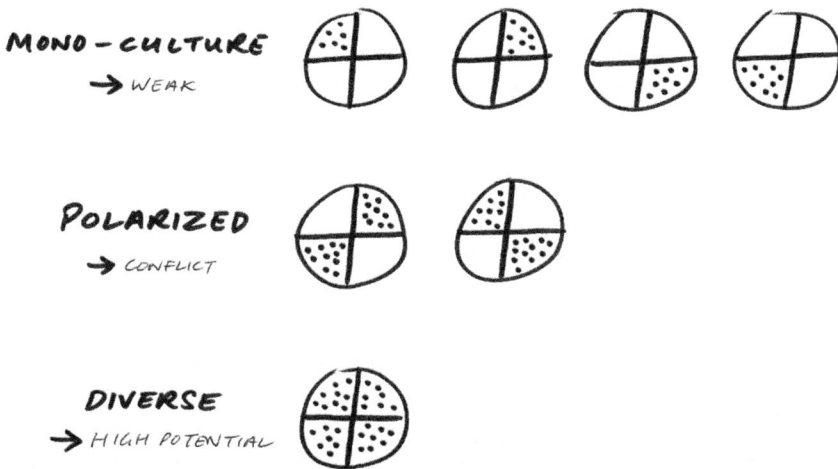

Illustration: Team Wheel
The more diverse the team, i.e., the more preferences are covered on the team, the better the results the team can achieve.

Michael: Since then, I've been paying close attention to it, yes. Even with this knowledge, I still find it helpful to use tools and instruments like *Insights* to make sure I'm doing it right. My goal since then has been to build teams that are very diverse in their preferences so that all color energies are represented. With a diverse team, I simply achieve better results. However, it does come with the responsibility of making sure that the people on the team get along as well. That's why I always do these trainings together with the team and create awareness for this kind of diversity, because it leads to a better result in the end, for everyone involved. It's great for everyone when we as a team create something that we would otherwise not have been able to do. It requires the ability to deal with conflict at the same time. Let's go through the typologies in concrete terms. Red and green energy are on the same axis, so they have rather opposite preferences. Conflicts can sometimes arise between people with red and people with green energy. As a manager, it is my job to build understanding for each other. On the other axis are the blue and the yellow energy. On one side is the analyst, on the other is the creative person. Here, too, understanding is needed so that these two types get along well with each other and appreciate each other.

So as a manager, I can make it clear that diversity means strength for the team. By the way, the same thing also works via the so-called main axis. Here, introverted people face the extroverted people. In this dimension too, conflicts and lack of understanding often occur, which can hinder the team's performance. The counterpart to this main axis is the axis between strong task orientation and people orientation. This is where conflicts occur most frequently. This is where understanding for each other and, if necessary, mediation between these preferences is needed most to make the whole thing a huge success instead of having a team that is bickering all the time.

Christian: How do I do that? For example, I have a yellow color energy and I like to try things out; I believe in speed, in fun, and am always looking for new options and ways to accomplish tasks. There is a person on the team who has mainly blue energy and is a pain in the ass because he wants to do everything super precisely, costing a lot of time. What can I do? Or in other words: on my team there are now all the conflicting combinations, red with yellow, yellow with red, and so on. They all have to deal with each other now. It is unfamiliar for everyone.

Michael: That's right. What can you do? What can I do? What can any of us do? We can all become more attuned to each other. The ideal situation is a team in which everyone is aware of the issues and makes an effort to adjust to each other. Let's stay with your example. You primarily have a yellow preference. One of your colleagues or your boss has a blue preference. Ideally, knowing this, you should react thinking, "All right, I'll allow the blue energy. I understand why these things are important to this person. I'll try to work more precisely, to be more accurate, to be more punctual, to listen more, and to rethink things." However, your colleague and your boss with a blue energy preference is thinking, "When I'm dealing with Christian, I allow more options, discuss a little more with him, make sure we have fun together, and have some leeway so that it is not a purely matter-of-fact, transactional affair." These would be the typical topics that people with yellow and blue energy have in their collaboration. In this way, it is very pleasant for both.

Christian: So I create awareness for the respective preferences and, in the best case, we meet somewhere in the middle. We have mutual understanding for each other and know where the bumps in communication are and what we can do wrong.

Michael: Right. Unfortunately, this ideal case is only the final state, the goal of a journey where I lead and accompany the team. It takes a lot of work and training to build up this awareness and knowledge. It is a competence that I acquire to deal with the different types. On the way there, it is my responsibility as a leader to set a good example and to adapt myself to the different preferences of my employees and colleagues.

Christian: Once again, in a nutshell. A management summary: What can I now take away from it for myself as a manager?

Michael: The most important thing is to adapt my behavior to the respective preferences of my counterparts. That sums things up and is of course easy to say. Many people now think to themselves, "All right, no problem. I'm just a little more introverted, a little more people oriented, a little more task oriented, depending on the situation." I've been dealing with this for 13 or 14 years now. It's not something I can implement overnight. It is a discipline, it requires practice. It's just like going to the gym. I'm allowed to train and exercise again and again to get better. Then at some point, the cycling effect comes, and everything clicks. In fact, it doesn't go away, I don't forget anymore. If I want to be really good, I may work and train again and again. I have one more tip. If I adjust to other people and notice that someone else thinks differently than I do and start to adjust my behavior and to accommodate her, then this person will only notice a change when I feel it in me, too. Only when I think, "Oh shit, now I'm really out of my comfort zone, I'm sure I'm exaggerating completely," will my counterpart notice a change in my behavior. This was an important insight for me. Only when I myself think, "Michael, now you're overdoing it a little bit," is exactly the point where my counterpart notices my adjustment in the first place. Before that, I am still in my comfort zone, in my preference. This exercise, this stretching of my own behavioral flexibility, is an ongoing task. The goal that I set myself is called *ultimate behavioral flexibility*. The reason for this is simple: the more flexible I am, the more successful I am in working together, in living together with other people.

Christian: And the more options you have, the better the decisions you can make. The more flexible one leads.

Michael: Exactly. The more flexible one leads.

Understanding my own preferences as well as those of my environment helps me not only in my professional context, but also in my private context. Living together, organizing the household, and dealing with friends, families, and children is much easier if I understand when my counterpart is in his comfort zone. For me, the true insight of this model also lies in the understanding that there is no judgement between the different personality types. There is no ranking, no better or worse. It is a neutral understanding of how I and my environment function. It is a good tolerance exercise. With the help of this model, I learn to appreciate the strengths and weaknesses of each individual, including my own, without judging them.

STRENGTHEN STRENGTHS
EVERYONE DOES WHAT THEY DO BEST

Michael: Hey Christian, I would like to ask you a question about my strengths. What strengths do you see in me?

Christian: You ask me about your strengths? Hmm... Let's see. [*thinks*] You are a maker. You just do things, that's one of your great strengths. You know what you want. Your second great strength is that you usually get what you want. You have excellent communication skills and are persuasive. Your communication skills help you to get what you want. In addition, you have a high level of competence, a lot of experience and a lot of know-how about leadership, even internationally. You can put yourself in people's shoes very well and are very empathetic.

Michael: Wow, thank you very much. Now I feel great. That's music to my ears. What does that mean now? For what reason are we talking about my strengths, other than making me feel better?

Christian: If I know what your strengths are, I can integrate you better in my company. I have different strengths than you, they are complementary to yours. That makes us much stronger as a team. I can fall back on your strengths. If I want to convince someone to do something ASAP, I send them to you. I use you, Michael, as a tool.

Michael: That is useful.

Christian: That is super useful.

Michael: It's nice to hear it that way. In the past, I was not aware of my strengths. All the things you just listed were not clear to me. I was much more aware of my weaknesses. I often received the feedback that I should listen better. Not in the sense of first listening and then speaking, but in the sense of being more attentive and empathic while listening. I have therefore tried over again to become better at this and to build up competence in listening. We have already talked about this. It was a particularly nice feeling for me that you mentioned empathy as one of my strengths. I have worked a lot on it.

Christian: For what Purpose did you work on it?

Michael: Very good question. I've been working on my weaknesses to make progress. I thought it would make me feel better. Crazy, I feel completely different now. Two minutes ago, when you said all the positive things, I felt better. Now I'm thinking about my weaknesses again, just like before. It totally pulls me down. My body is getting heavier, I'm kind of sitting deeper in my chair now, like I have lead in my feet. I would rather get out of here quickly.

Christian: I don't want you to listen better. If I need someone to listen, I'll use someone else.

Michael: Wonderful. I like that. Consequently, for me, if a person comes up to me and needs someone to listen, I just say, "That would certainly be a great conversation with XY. I'm not the right person for it."

Christian: Yeah, sure. Of course.

Michael: Now that you mention it, I once had a similar situation. A while ago, I asked a friend something about a certain topic. I can't remember what topic it was. He said to me, "You better talk to my wife about it, she has the right antennas for that." He was obviously aware of his strengths and perhaps thought, "Oh, I really have no idea about this topic. Listening to this is a waste of time. You should talk to someone who is better at it." Now I understand what actually happened. If I am aware of my weaknesses, I can simply delegate and distribute them within my team. It's better to have someone who is competent in this. If I am aware of my strengths, I put the pedal to the medal and stay on the ball.

Christian: Absolutely. It becomes even clearer when we turn the tables. Imagine a member of the team is a particularly good listener. He's more of a quiet type and prefers to hear other people talking rather than talking himself. He simply does not like to be in the spotlight. Now I need someone who motivates my team, puts himself in front of the employees, and convinces them to start a new project. Someone who rushes forward head-on and pushes the team. If I now ask the rather quiet type, my best listener, to take on this task, he will certainly not be happy about it and probably not very successful.

Michael: [*smiles*] I remember something one of my colleagues said 15 or 20 years ago. He said to me, "If you need somebody to kick in a door, call me. I'm gonna kick in that door. That is exactly my thing." That's not my thing. I was just shaking my head at the time and wondering why the hell someone likes to do that. Now, 20 years later, I think, "It's good to know that you can do that. If it's needed, I know I'll get back to you."

Christian: It can happen that you are standing in front of a closed door that you want to get through. I had a colleague at the HypoVereinsbank, whose specialty was to reject people and turn opportunities down . If it was in any way about rejecting someone or declining something, she did it with an incredible amount of joy and fun. "Nope, we are not working with you." I was quite inhibited in such situations. Not her. She even had a great competence in communicating the rejection eloquently and sympathetically, not like my example. She was the best rejectionist I have ever met.

Michael: Great. Turning people down or terminating is a difficult issue. It's not easy for everyone. In a situation like this, I think carefully about which of us on the team has the competence to deliver the message in a way that is best for the person and the company.

Christian: Does that mean that all day long I only do things that I enjoy and that I am good at or do I do other things as well?

Michael: From my point of view, the world would be a better place if everyone only does what they enjoy doing, what they're productive at and get results for. Don't you think so?

Christian: Well, I still have a very Protestant work ethic, although I am actually Catholic. I think there are definitely things that are easy for me to do, even if they are no fun: Tax returns, cleaning bathrooms, setting up an accounting department in my company when there is no one else who can do it. There are some things that I just have to get involved in, which might not be fun for anyone.

Michael: Digging into something is one of those things.

Christian: In the meantime, maybe I can hand it off to someone who does it better and even enjoys it. To start with, I'll just dig in and get it done.

Michael: You mean, because as a boss it can help me understand the tasks and issues that maybe later my employees will take on? Even though I may not necessarily be up to it, I can perform my role as a leader better. If I understand what happens and what the tasks mean, I can better delegate and manage them and choose the right expert. There is a very famous belief that fits well with your Protestant work ethic, as you so nicely called it. "If I work hard, I succeed." That is also a work ethic. Only hard work leads to success. That is a limiting belief. If I believe that I can only be successful if I work a lot, I will work very hard all my life and maybe be successful, too. I imagine my life differently. I imagine how it sounds, how it looks, and how it feels to be successful. For me, it doesn't feel like hard work at all. It feels easy and joyful.

Christian: I heard something similar the other day. It was about being happy. Many people believe that if they work hard, they earn a lot of money and are automatically happy. I think it is exactly the other way around. I make the decision to be happy, E + R = O. I decide on this response. Making money follows.

Michael: *Live your Purpose and the money will follow.*

Christian: Once I have made this decision, I work on the things I enjoy.

Michael: And you are strong in these things. You use your strengths.

Christian: I no longer believe all those sayings like, *I have to bow and scrape, Life is not as easy at the bottom, You can't teach an old dog new tricks.* Pick any one of them or many others.

Michael: It was a total relief for me to redefine my belief and realize that work does not have to feel like hard work to be successful. If something worked out seamlessly, it didn't really feel like success. I immediately thought, "Did I even deserve this?" Nobody can answer this question. Everybody has a different opinion about that. What does that even mean? How do I measure success? That is nonsense. I have the result that I wanted, so I'm happy. I have achieved something. Even though I find it easy and I achieved it in an easy way, it's still fantastic. Actually, this should be the ideal. I'm thinking about all the strengths and weaknesses in a company. Let's say a company has 1,000 employees. I build up two scenarios. In scenario A, all 1,000 employees exchange ideas about their strengths and weaknesses and start working on their weaknesses. All employees try to become better at their weaknesses.

Christian: They try to weaken their weaknesses.

Michael: *[laughs]* Right. Like me. I had a weakness in listening and I started taking courses, attending advanced training programs, and working hard on myself to be a better listener.

Christian: You are in customer happiness mode. You try to make others happy with it.

Michael: So in scenario A, all 1,000 employees work on their weaknesses. They try to improve their weaknesses by dealing with them extensively. In scenario B, all 1,000 employees are aware of their strengths and work on developing them further. I see you grinning and cheering. *[laughs]* It feels quite different, doesn't it? The employees are aware of their weaknesses in order to avoid rough mistakes, but only work on their strengths, on what they enjoy and what they find easy. The feeling that arises when 1,000 people are only working on building their strengths is incredibly motivating and inspiring. Scenario A feels rather grey and heavy like lead, very dull.

Christian: Absurd pictures often help me at this point. Imagine an orchestra with all these gifted musicians: A violinist, a violist, an oboist. They are all really good and have endless fun with their instruments. Now a new conductor comes along and says, "Alright friends, let us work on our weaknesses. You, dear violinist, play the oboe from now on. You are really bad at it. Dear viola player, from now on you will play the piano."

Michael: Fantastic. That's really a great picture.

Christian: This orchestra will probably not be successful. I'm thinking especially of this English woman who is a really bad singer and who has exclusively recorded LPs. Well, anyway.

Michael: We prefer not to mention her name.

Christian: Let us imagine a soccer team. There is a super striker who is a super bad goalkeeper. Now the coach says, "Dear striker, you will stand in the goal until you are good at it." The coach will probably get fired.

Michael: So, in conclusion, I am playing to my strengths and working to make them even stronger. I am only aware of my weaknesses. Done.

Christian: Exactly. My weaknesses are irrelevant. I can simply delegate them to someone who is better at it. For the violinist, it is irrelevant that he plays the oboe badly.

Michael: It would never occur to him to work on this weakness.

Christian: I certainly have many weaknesses that I don't know yet, because I may never have tried them before. I try out a lot and prefer to use my strengths.

Michael: Powerful topic, thank you very much. That was very easy.

The orchestra example is powerful and the idea that everyone in the company only does what they do best is wonderful. I would love to do only the things that come easy to me. In project work this can certainly be implemented well, roles could be redefined, and tasks could be better distributed. In everyday business, on the other hand, I imagine it to be more difficult to implement. Every job has its own tasks. All managers have to submit various reports, conduct performance reviews, or participate in meetings, whether he or she likes it and has a strength for it or not. New tools have to be mastered, and sometimes unpleasant tasks, which nobody likes to do, have to be done. If everyone picks out only what they are good at and like, it will surely end up in cherry picking. Some things would fall by the wayside. To solve the problem, work has to be completely redistributed throughout the company. I might also need completely different people on my teams. Basically, for every task in the company, I should find someone who is happy to do it. Not a bad idea actually...

SITUATIONAL LEADERSHIP
FROM MICROMANAGER TO COACH

Christian: I welcome you warmly on your first day with us as a barista. I am very happy that you have applied for the job, Michael. Let's start with an espresso. I'll be happy to show you how we make espresso here at *chicco di caffe.*

Michael: *[laughs]* That's a good idea.

Christian: You take this portafilter in your right hand and turn it to the left out of the winding. It falls down almost automatically into your hand. We tap out the coffee grounds that are still in it here, into this drawer. With this brush, you can remove the remains and clean the portafilter. Now you hold the whole thing under the grinder, and it will automatically start grinding fresh coffee until the carrier is full. Now press firmly with this tamper.

Michael: This thing that I use to press firmly on top of it is called a tamper?

Christian: Yes, exactly. Press it straight on until the freshly ground coffee is completely flat, with about 20 kilograms of pressure. Tap a little bit again so that the remaining ground coffee falls in, then tamp it again, turn it, and now hook it in the machine. Now press the button with the two little cups on it. Now you only have to put two espresso cups under it.

Michael: Great, very simple.

Christian: Frankly, I had hoped that you were already a bit further along and that I could easily delegate tasks to you. Even so, I really have to start with micromanagement and show and explain every move to you. We are now in the middle of the topic of management styles.

Michael: I didn't realize that I had applied to be your barista. Fortunately, I'm ultimately behavioral flexible, so let's go, no problem.

Christian: Which management style is the right one? I have just tried micromanagement. I literally took your hand and guided you, basically it was supervised work.

Michael: I thought it was great, otherwise I couldn't have done it. This espresso machine is definitely a little more complicated than others.

Christian: For other tasks, I would like to do it differently and not necessarily instruct you in such hair-splitting detail

Michael: Maybe you could say, "Just make some coffee."

Christian: Yes, or, "Create the website." If I took your hand and said to you, "Now click here on the right with the mouse," you would surely get a hair dryer.

Michael: Absolutely, I would freak out.

Christian: So which management style is the right one?

Michael: Good question. I've learned that it varies a lot from person to person. So it's again about different personality types. Another thing I learned is that it can be different not only from person to person, but also from situation to situation. In which situation is the person I would like to lead as a manager in right now? How can I best support them as a manager? What does he or she need from me at the moment?

Christian: Briefing a new employee in the coffee bar certainly requires detailed work. I'd better explain everything in detail and manage in very small steps. After I have explained this one, two, three, sometimes 10 times, I can move on to the next management style.

Michael: Which one is that?

Christian: I call it *teaching*. In our example, I ask the new employee to prepare 10 espressos in a row. I stand next to him and watch how it goes.

Michael: Micromanagement, the first leadership style you mentioned, has more of a negative ring to it. In non-judgmental terms, I can say that you are very involved as a leader, you go into great detail and get involved. Hands on... In *teaching,* as you called the second style, I teach someone something. What is the difference?

Christian: I can already fall back on competence in *teaching.* The employee is not yet fully trained, still he has done or seen it before. He will certainly ask some more questions and I also frequently ask questions and am close to him to give him feedback and to help if necessary. I reinforce the positive responses with statements like, "Hey, this is going really well," or "This cappuccino looks great, keep it up."

Michael: In micromanagement, you still lend a hand yourself. You collaborate, you help out, and say step by step, "Now you press this button," "Now you do that." You work on the result with four hands at the same time, while you may only be watching in teaching mode.

Christian: Right. I'm watching the whole time.

Michael: Similar to a piano teacher sitting next to the student the whole lesson. The student is allowed to play the piano himself, the teacher sits next to him and comments and gives tips for improvement.

Christian: Right, the teacher does not press any key himself.

Michael: Unless he's demonstrating something. Then we are back to micromanagement. I see. What is the next management style?

Christian: In the next phase, I can take one step back as a manager. For example, I say to my new barista, "The guests will be coming soon. When someone orders an espresso, you make an espresso. If someone says *cappuccino*, you make a cappuccino. Then you ring them up. If you have any questions, I'll be over there doing the bookkeeping."

Michael: So you're not standing next to him anymore. You're still present, just not involved yourself. The employee can do the job more or less alone.

Christian: Correct. He has the competence to do the job on his own and has already gained experience. So it's working. If a situation arises that he can't handle, I'm there to help him. If everything is going well, I leave the employee alone.

Michael: So we have already discussed three different management styles. One is micromanagement, where I get involved hands-on and demonstrate. The second is the teaching style, in which I teach a person something without becoming active myself. And lastly, the coaching style, where I am available to the person as a coach, especially in situations where the person is not getting anywhere. In this way, the person can become even better and develop further without me being in a teaching function or acting as a micro-manager. What other styles are there?

Christian: In the next stage, I can say to my employee, "Listen, you're running the store. You can do it. See you next week for our 1:1 interview." So I don't need to be present at all, discussing open questions and topics only in a regular staff meeting.

Michael: Then you get the result and that's it?

Christian: Right. That is delegating tasks.

Michael: The model we just discussed, in a slightly modified form, is a rather famous leadership model and was originally developed by Kenneth Blanchard.

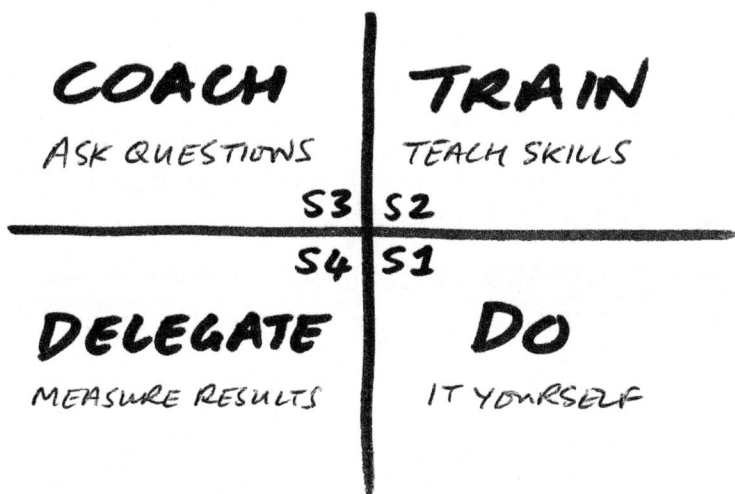

Illustration: Situational Leadership
My task is to adapt my leadership style to the competence of the person I am leading and to the situation we're in.

Christian: It shows that I can choose different leadership styles in different situations and with different competencies of the employees. If I choose the wrong or always the same style, regardless of the person and situation, it can be quite frustrating for both me as a manager and the employee. If she can already run the business on her own, she will look at me funny when I explain to her which button is the right one for espresso.

Michael: Then it would be micromanagement in the negative sense.

Christian: That's exactly why this style of leadership has a negative taste to it. If a person has a high level of competence in their tasks and I explain to them exactly what they have to do, I indirectly question their competence. Then I get reactions like, "I can do this, let me just do this," or, "Hey boss, please let me do my job. You do your job." I catch negative vibes directly.

Michael: How do I know which style is the right one? When do I switch from one style to another? It can be the other way around. For example, I notice that an employee does not yet know how to operate the machine, even though he or she actually wants to run the store on his or her own. How do I deal with this?

Christian: With new employees, new activities, or new skills, I start best with micromanagement in a positive sense. If necessary, I quickly switch to the teaching and coaching mode.

Michael: Similar to a gear shift. I start in first gear and then quickly shift into second, third, and then fourth gear.

Christian: When I hire an experienced barista for the coffee bar, I ask them to prepare an espresso on the spot. I see how she handles the machine and can decide on a management style accordingly. Either I show her again and go into micromanagement mode or I say goodbye, give her the key to the store, and leave her my phone number. So I can move very quickly through the different management styles and move towards delegation. Staying in micromanagement for a long time is suboptimal. It's just as bad if I start delegating instantly. "Michael, you applied for a job as a barista. I am very happy and I have no idea if you have what it takes. Here's the key to the bar, I'll talk to you next week."

Michael: "Have a nice day. I'll be back tonight to pick up the cash register."

Christian: It will surely be empty, because no customer got a single coffee. You scared them all away and are demotivated to the max yourself. The exciting thing about the model is that the leadership style depends on the person himself and the activities that the person does. For instance, let's take an employee who makes a great espresso and does not yet know how to froth the milk for a cappuccino. As a manager, I start with milk foam, in micromanagement mode, whereas I only coach on the espresso.

Michael: The same applies to the evening cash register accounting, which requires a completely different level of expertise.

Christian: Correct. I only coach a professional barista at the bar, if at all. During the billing, I show him step by step how to operate the laptop. "Come here, I'll show you. Every evening you take this laptop and open the following file…"

Michael: Do I discuss this with my employees? I'm sure she'll notice that I'm behaving differently. How do you deal with this?

Christian: I do not have the feeling that my employees are aware of this. Since I adapt my management style to both the employee and the situation, the employee often doesn't even notice. It is perceived rather positively by them. If I get feedback from my team that someone needs a little more help in one place and less help in another, they will get more or less help from me accordingly. That is great for the whole team. That is why it is called situational leadership. I adapt to every employee and every situation.

Michael: Okay, cool.

Christian: There are still a few traps I can fall into. We have already mentioned the first trap briefly. If I start with delegating and only see afterwards that the employee is not yet ready, it is usually too late. I transfer it to our example. So I give a new employee the key to the bar and say goodbye. After a week, I come back and find the bar in total chaos. Then I backpedal and say, "Okay, look. We'll start again with the espresso." A lot can break in the meantime and the new colleague is totally frustrated.

Michael: This is the classic situation. I hire a new employee and say to him, "Here is your new workplace. Just get started, we'll meet in a week and you'll present your results to me." The poor guy.

Christian: [*grins*] Yes, after a week I again go through every presentation with him and show him how to use Microsoft Word and PowerPoint. So I go from delegating back to micromanagement and back to delegating again.

Michael: There's an expression for that: *valley of despair*. That's all that's left. Both the managed and the manager are in despair, because something is missing. When I shift from first to fourth and back to first gear, the engine grinds. This is not a good idea.

Christian: What do I do when I shift into fourth gear and notice I've gone a little over the top?

Michael: In a car, I would probably shift back into third or second gear instead of straight into first.

Christian: I go back from delegating to coaching mode to see if it works. If not, I shift down a gear and try the teaching mode before explaining every single move to him.

Michael: So if I don't know how far an employee is, I start in micromanaging mode for safety. If I then find that she has understood what it's all about, I switch to teaching mode. The next step, if she can manage so far, is the coaching mode. If the employee herself no longer needs my coaching because everything is running smoothly and my help is hardly necessary, I switch to delegating mode and I can devote myself to other things.

Christian: Right. That's how I do it with this one employee and exactly this task. If the same employee is doing a new task, I go through the four styles again from the beginning.

Michael: So as a boss, I adapt all the time, non-stop.

Christian: Uninterrupted. I am attentive all the time.

Michael: I adapt myself and my management style to every situation and also to the different personality types. As a manager, I am therefore very busy with adapting.

Christian: Absolutely, it strengthens my communication skills. *Communication is what the listener does.*

Michael: *The receiver is always right.* Three repetitions to convince, six repetitions to memorize.

Christian: Great, then we are done here. I need a coffee first. I'm sure you'll make yourself one now, right?

Michael: How did that work again with this portafilter machine?

I like the model. It makes much of what I already do intuitively clear and understandable. It also helps me to reflect on the individual leadership situations and competencies of my employees. This is very much about training employees. Co-workers often take care of this among themselves. In addition, I also have learned that I myself don't need to be able to do all the tasks that I delegate to my team. Here, too, micromanagement only gets me so far. This model assumes that I am very close to my employees. Depending on how many employees I manage, micromanagement in particular is no longer manageable. So I need another solution that is either more efficient or entails smaller teams.

"ONE MORE QUESTION"

— INSPECTOR COLUMBO, 1971

COACHING AS A LEADERSHIP STYLE
THINKING OUTSIDE THE BOX

Christian: What's on your mind right now, Michael?

Michael: I am concerned with the topic of coaching. I'm trying to figure out what will bring our readers forward the fastest.

Christian: What else?

Michael: I am also concerned with the extent to which my experience with coaching can be relevant in this context.

Christian: What experiences do you have with coaching?

Michael: A few years ago, I didn't know anything about coaching. I was aware of it, however I had no idea how valuable it could be. I actually went through a coaching process myself, but as a coachee. At some point I understood how much it helped me and how much I could suddenly achieve through it. I still had no real idea how it works and I started to get interested in it.

Christian: What is coaching all about?

Michael: Coaching is about expanding your own solution space. Coaching gives me new perspectives that allow me to spot and consider more possibilities in my actions in order to achieve my goals, both professionally and privately. The role of the coach is to point out exactly these different ways and possibilities. It helps her coachees to think through, empathize with, and explore these possibilities. As the person being coached, I suddenly recognize new ways or consider options that I have previously excluded. It is precisely these paths that usually lead to success. Coaching removes stones from the path, mostly the stones that I have put in my way myself.

Christian: [*ironically*] Coaches usually have more experience and know exactly how it works. They can give the coachee the right tips and simply say, "If you want to go there, do the following...," "If I were you I would...," "You should definitely..."

Michael: "You have to do it this way and that way." [*laughs*] Unfortunately, you can't see the big grin on Christian's face when he said that. That's not the point, of course. As a coach it is my job to just ask questions without having an agenda of my own. Questions that expand the space for solutions and allow new possibilities without me as a coach having any idea where the journey is going. It is not about teasing certain answers out of the coachee in order to lead him to where I want him to go. The coach does not lead the coachee. The opposite is the case. The coachee explores possibilities and leads both the coach as a supporter and himself to his own personal solution that is right for him.

Christian: That makes it sound as if the coach is completely unnecessary.

Michael: Indeed it may. There's a world of difference between going around in circles in my own thoughts and having someone ask me questions in conversation that I've never asked myself before or that I'm cleverly avoiding to answer. In conversation with someone else, processes take place in the brain. Processes that help me to find answers to different questions and to receive suggestions. This is what the coach is there for. Once I know how it works, I can also coach myself in a monologue. If someone else asks me the questions, the coach is responsible for the process, so I don't have to worry about it myself and can concentrate on my answers and the solution space. Therefore, it always has a great added Value to hand this responsibility over to a professional outsider. This ensures that the process of the coaching session is guided and controlled from start to finish without controlling the content.

Christian: What do you know about coaching today that you were not aware of two or three years ago?

Michael: That coaching serves to constantly learn and develop myself further. It has a lot to do with self-development. The coach doesn't have to be an expert in topics that concern me. Coaching is primarily for self-reflection. It can, of course, help the coach to understand the context and vocabulary of the coachee. You and I work as business coaches with people in leadership roles, in executive positions, or with entrepreneurs. However, it is not useful to blurt out alleged solutions that pop into our heads and steer the coachee towards them or give them input on content. It is dangerous if the coachee ends up feeling that he has not developed his own solution. Before I share my own experiences on a topic with my clients, I always ask whether this is desired. I only do this if I believe that it really helps the coachee at this point. He or she can always decide this for himself or herself. "May I share my own experience with you? Maybe it will help you in your thinking process." Often, my client then looks at me in astonishment and says something like, "Uh, yeah, sure." It is not the classic task of a coach. In a purist approach, a coach does not bring in his own experience and thoughts. It is therefore important to make it clear that the coach is just leaving the actual coaching room and entering an exchange of experiences. This is a big difference.

Christian: And if the coachee explicitly asks for tips and tricks?

Michael: Then I say that as a coach that's not really my job. It's primarily about the thoughts and feelings of the client, the coachee, about exploring and questioning different possibilities. "Why do you think the way you think? Why does it feel the way it feels to you?" and, "Couldn't you make a different decision with regard to your thoughts and feelings?" It is important to clarify this first. When it is clarified and understood, depending on the situation, I decide to step out of my coaching room and enter the room of exchange of experiences. I always point out that these are only my own experiences and it does not mean that this is the right answer or solution for the client. "It is only one of many possible answers that you may consider in order to find the right solution for you."

Christian: The solutions sought are often decisions. I want to get from A to B as a coachee and for that I have to make decisions. "Do I take this step next or that step?" So it helps me to have an option. To be precise, *eight opossums* help me. [*grins*] There are always at least eight options or possibilities that I have. That's why I like to refer to them as eight opossums, if you will. Simple and easy. If I want to get from A to B, there are at least eight ways. Some of them seem absurd, some are obvious. It helps to realize that the obvious solution does not always have to be the right one. It can be the right one, and it can also be another solution.

Michael: Give me an example.

Christian: I had a conversation with a coachee the other day. It was about a new employee, or rather about her interest in working in his company. He had two options: either he hired her as a new employee or not.

Michael: So he saw it binary: To hire or not to hire?

Christian: At first, I also considered it binary. We discussed all pros and cons and did a reframing. Among other things, I asked him all these coaching questions like, "What do you think you know now that you will probably find out later?" Suddenly he surprised me with a new opportunity. He said, "I can also simply hire the employee later." Basically, he was coaching me with that, too. So we were already at the third option. What other possibilities would there be?

Michael: Now I'm your coachee and I'm going to give an answer to that. Do I hire someone or not? Do I hire them later? Another possibility would be to extend the application process further to make me more confident in my decision. I will have further interviews with the candidate, perhaps other colleagues in the company will also have an interview with her. This way I get a better, more detailed picture before I make my decision. Another option might be to hire her under different conditions. It might not have to be as a full-time employee from the start. I could hire her part-time or as a temp or even as a freelancer. So I can go through different scenarios, modalities. Maybe this is a suitable solution.

Christian: Another option would be to simply not do the tasks this person is supposed to do at all. Or I might consider switching jobs with someone else if the decision is a cost issue. Maybe there is someone in the company who doesn't fit in very well and is basically superfluous. I shouldn't necessarily officially justify it that way, it's still a possibility.

Michael: I could refer the person to a partner company where she might be better off and where she could add more Value as an employee. That way, I could also work with him or her indirectly. That is another option.

Christian: And we already have eight or nine possibilities. Some of them may not be possible for various reasons, others are worth thinking about.

Michael: Yes, exactly. And now?

Christian: Where does the name *coach* actually come from?

Michael: I found that out the other day, it's interesting. My mother is originally from Hungary, I mentioned that before. There is a small town there called Kocs. In the 16th century, a famous, revolutionary type of carriage was invented in Kocs. It was much more comfortable and pleasant and became a big hit. Within the following 50 to 100 years, this type of carriage became popular throughout Europe. This new carriage from Kocs coined the German word *Kutsche*. Later, in the 1700s, universities in England coined this term as we use it today. If students at that time had difficulties passing their exams, they would get a tutor, a helper. Colloquially they called him *coach*, i.e., carriage, because he was responsible for getting them from A to B.

Christian: On a path that was still predetermined at the time.

Michael: Right, on a path that was still predetermined at the time. The coach was the vehicle for the students to reach their goal. That's how the word *coach* came to be colloquially. It was not until the end of the 19th century that this word was transferred to the field of sports, also at universities. The sports teams of the universities adapted the term to their coach. Therefore, the term has been occupied by sport, especially in the 20th century. Only in the last 20 or 30 years has the term arrived in the business world, basically still with the same function. The task of a coach is to bring people from A to B. In doing so, I help people to recognize their A in order to understand where they stand and who they are. Then the coachee may define the B, such as determining the goal of the journey. With the help of the eight opossums and other techniques, I can explore the different possibilities from there. At the end of a coaching session, the question is always, "What are you planning to do now? What do you want to implement? And would you like me to ask you next time how it went?" That's how we create the feeling of commitment, through accountability. The obligation to work on the implementation.

Christian: Like a little homework.

Michael: Yes, exactly. If nothing happens, we were just talking about it. Then nothing changes.

Christian: If you are a coach, what are you not?

Michael: As a coach, I am not an advisor.

Christian: Okay. So that means no saying, "you should, you have to."

Michael: Right.

Christian: Instead, "From my experience you could try..." [*chuckles*]

Michael: "Why don't you do that, that's a great idea, don't you think?" [*laughs*] No, not at all. It's not a great idea, there's no way I'm playing the advisor. As a good coach, I'm a supporter of the person. My role is to help my client, the coachee, to develop so that she can achieve her goals.

Christian: For that you even agree to so-called coaching contracts, right? Coaching contracts. What is that exactly?

Michael: Right, a contract is important. Every coaching process, at least if it is conducted professionally, always includes a so-called contract at the beginning. It is not a comprehensive contract with rights and obligations for which I need lawyers. It is a simple, yet clear agreement between the client and the coach. It sets out the objectives to be pursued and the appropriate behavior. It includes simple things like being punctual for sessions, the length of each session, the starting time of the sessions, the overall range of these, over what period of time the coaching takes place and what the role of the coach is and is not. We have already discussed many of these things. The contract lays out what the client can expect from the coach and the coaching process as well as some ethical guidelines within which we operate in a coaching relationship.

Christian: What else is important?

Michael: Asking questions. Just like the questions you are asking right now. A good coach asks good questions and does almost nothing else. I have learned that asking good questions is a real art. There are many methods for this from the NLP world. It provides different models for different questions. I am immensely fascinated by how much good questions matter. I can tell you are about to ask me, "And what else?"

Christian: Of course I could ask that. We have now reached the end of our coaching session. What was especially helpful for you in this session?

Michael: Learning something new was especially helpful, as I do in every session. The reflection and the conversation about coaching always triggers a change in my mind that takes me further. One of the greatest insights for me is that in a good, professional coaching relationship, not only does the client learn and progress, but I as a coach do as well. I am very grateful to all my coachees for this.

Christian: What do you plan to do until our next chapter?

Michael: I intend to consider how we can help our readers with the topic of coaching in leadership styles. Because coaching is a tool from the repertoire of situational leadership. And we want to talk about this more intensively. Coaching is one of four distinctive leadership styles with a lot of potential. It has become my favorite topic.

Christian: Great, thanks Michael. I am curious.

Michael: Thank you, Christian for the great questions.

I am also curious about that. Maybe this could help me in managing employees whose tasks I do not understand or do not want to understand myself. So it could be the solution to the challenges following the last chapter. Coaching instead of micromanagement. I can learn the patience that is certainly helpful as a coach. I can simply learn to be a good coach.

One more thing: Are there really always eight opossums? Even if there aren't, I like trying to find all these options. It automatically forces me to see more solutions than the obvious ones. This allows me to train my own out-of-the-box thinking and that of my employees. "Hmm... What other possibilities are there?"

THE COACHING FISH

GET OUT OF THE SHOWER!

Christian: So, Michael. Get out of the shower now!

Michael: Are we starting our coaching session?

Christian: Yes. You like to say to your coachees, "Get out of the shower." Does that mean you don't like freshly showered clients or what do you mean by that?

Michael: *Get out of the shower* is a nice saying from my coach training. The picture has stuck with me. It is an analogy, because the coaching process is always a very personal matter.

Christian: Like taking a shower.

Michael: Yes, exactly. Most of the time it's about very personal issues that I don't necessarily want to bring up in public and I don't want to discuss them with everyone. So a coach is a strong confidant. The image of the shower is supposed to convey that the coachee is in a similar situation during the coaching process as when he is taking a shower. He is vulnerable, uncovered, without protection, and exposed to external influences. As a coach, I do not belong in the shower stall with the coachee.

Christian: So, "Get out of the shower."

Michael: Right. The coachee is in the shower with his problems and the topics he wants to work on. Only he belongs in there. As a coach, I merely accompany my coachee and support him or her from outside. I never go in the shower with them, I never insert myself in the problem. I may sympathize and show empathy. I never identify myself with the problem.

Christian: I tell him, so to speak, that he may now wash under his arms.

Michael: When I go into the subject with my coachee, I might say things like, "I'm totally sorry about that, how awful. This is really bad." The moment I say something like that, I'm standing in the shower stall. That's not good. Outside the shower I say something like, "What you're experiencing right now must feel pretty hard for you. I am with you in my heart. How can I support you?" I perceive what happens in the shower and I show empathy. I express my understanding of the situation and the feelings of the coachee. Nevertheless, I don't immerse myself in the actual feeling.

Christian: You don't go in and help with the showers either?

Michael: No. You mean in the sense of, "Raise your arm." That doesn't help. I ask typical coaching questions that help the coachee to come up with new ideas himself, maybe to try something different. I don't know whether we should stay with this image any longer.

Christian: Hold on. I actually would like to stay with the idea of the shower little longer. There is a lot of water in the shower and where there is water, there are often fish.

Michael: Wow, what an elegant bridge.

Christian: Right, because I would like to talk about the *Coaching Fish*.

Michael: The Coaching Fish is a great concept.

Christian: As a coach I get out of the shower and think directly about a fish.

Michael: What fish are you thinking about?

Christian: A fish with a pointed mouth, a fin at the end, and a thick middle.

Michael: Like a flounder or a plaice?

Christian: A surgeonfish, or something like that.

Michael: That's not a trumpet fish, is it? I'm sitting in a restaurant and a delicious fish is swimming on my plate in lemon juice. It is large, wide in the middle and thinner at the end, at the fin. What does this have to do with coaching?

FOR WHAT
PURPOSE?

START

ASK
QUESTIONS

WHAT
ELSE?

EXPLORE
OPTIONS

FINISH

HOW
EXACTLY?

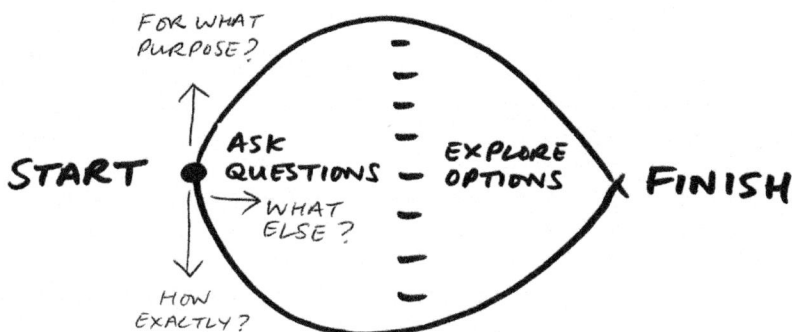

Illustration: Coaching Fish
Chunking up, down and sideways, we widen the set of potential solutions in a coaching conversation. As a coach, I ask questions that help the coachee to explore new options and to eventually make decisions on which actions to pursue.

Christian: Usually the coachee goes to a coach with a problem or challenge. She wants to have this problem solved. This challenge is something she has on her plate right now. Often times, the real issue is a completely different one.

Michael: The initial problem describes the pointed mouth of the fish?

Christian: Yes, I could see it that way. I can also put the cart before the horse, or better, the fish. In any case, it is a sharp topic at the beginning. My job as a coach is to make the initial theme a bit bigger. I try to tease out which possibilities, solution, options, points of view, and perspectives there might be beyond that.

Michael: I now imagine this point at the very front of a fish's mouth where it starts.

Christian: Then you work your way backwards and the fish gets thicker and thicker.

Michael: Like an x-axis along which time runs. It runs like a spear through the fish, a swordfish. Time runs through this fish, and in the conversation the subject is stretched out more and more. It becomes increasingly dramatic, worse, thicker and fatter, doesn't it?

Christian: Depending on your sensory preference, it can also become clearer and more distinct. Or simply wider. There are more possibilities. What are the possibilities, for example?

Michael: It's about exploring how I can approach the subject. You have a nice picture for that too.

Christian: You mean the eight opossums as an image for the options. Right, because eight opossums are better than less than eight opossums.

Michael: So we start in a coaching interview with a concrete topic that the coachee brings along. Often there is another topic underlying this to which we work our way through skillful coaching questions until the coachee has identified eight options for action that can be considered as a solution. In the end, the coachee chooses one of these alternatives and achieves the result he wanted, the goal he has not yet achieved.

Christian: Right. The first topic the coachee names at the beginning is right at the front of the fish's mouth. Often the coachee thinks to himself, "This will be an easy session. I'll just tell Michael what it's all about and then we'll be done pretty quickly." Often it turns out that these topics, which are mentioned at the beginning, or at the front of the fish's mouth, are not the most important ones.

Michael: During my training, I learned a statement about this: "The problem presented is never the real problem." Have you had the same experience? Do you have an example?

Christian: Sure. Let's take a simple, boss example…

Michael: I'm a boss and I have an endless amount of work with a million things to do, and I just don't know where my head is. I can't get all the work done. So that's my problem. Too much work.

Christian: Please give me a tool to solve this. [*grins*]

Michael: [*smiles*] Sure, gladly. Wait, I have a pill for that.

Christian: So you show him some tools, for example the 2x2 matrix, which is used for prioritization and recommend some books like *Getting Things Done*. Often, the underlying theme is not just the volume of work. What could be an underlying theme?

Michael: For example, that I can't say *no*.

Christian: Yes. Possibly.

Michael: What else?

Christian: Maybe I hired the wrong people. Or my business model is not the right one. Maybe I can't concentrate, I get distracted too easily and spend the whole day on Twitter, Facebook, or LinkedIn.

Michael: Maybe I have a problem giving up control. I think I do everything better than everyone else. [*pause*] This is a great example of a *presenting problem,* "I can't get the work done," and the *real problem,* "I want control over everything." All these issues may come up in the conversation. We then go into each option and make the fish thick in the middle. We put all eight opossums and more inside and discuss all the options. How does the fish get smaller again in the end?

Christian: Once I, as a coachee, have identified the various options for approaching my real problem, I can start to reduce my options again. I can decide which of the issues I want to tackle first.

Michael: After I have asked my coachees for the hundredth time, "How else can you solve this issue?" they often think I am pushing for a specific answer. I am not trying to do that, because I don't know the answer myself. Once we get to the point where all the options are on the table, I often observe that from there on it goes very quickly until the coachee feels which option is the right one for her. In our sessions, we repeat all the options once or twice so that we get a good overview and a feeling for the different paths. Afterwards, the coachee will quickly realize which solution is the best one for her.

Christian: Yes, that is amazing. I experience it mostly the same way.

Michael: It's this fish...

Christian: Sometimes it even happens when we are at version six or seven and have not yet found all eight opossums. But I keep asking, "What other options are there, what could an eighth version look like?" Then I often recognize the light bulb going on in my counterpart's head. "Oh yes, now I have it."

Michael: Let me summarize what we talked about. *Get out of the shower!* As a coach, I always stand outside the shower and don't identify with my coachee's problem. I sympathize and show understanding and empathy, yet do not empathize with the emotions myself. The second image is the coaching fish. A coaching session starts with a supposed topic or problem. Often other underlying issues are hidden behind it. Therefore, I expand the topic and ask specific coaching questions in order to increase the solution space. We go in search of at least eight opossums. We explore each of these 7±2 options to deal with the topic. So the fish becomes wider and bigger. At the very end, it comes together again in a pointed way. The coachee decides on his own on one of the possible paths he wants to take. As a coach, I am left with the polite question, "Would you like me to ask next time how it went or would you rather not?" Usually, the coachee answers, "Yes." In the next conversation, we then pick up where we left off. What else is important for successful coaching?

Christian: Maybe we should clarify the difference between coach, consultant, and mentor.

Michael: Consultant, coach, or mentor. [*ironic*] Isn't a coach all in one?

Christian: The coaching fish ultimately describes that I, as a coach, support my coachee in the thought process. Time to reflect is one of the great added Values of coaching. Time to look for solutions yourself in peace and quiet.

Michael: Of course we are talking about professional coaching in the true sense of the word. We're not talking about the soccer coach or a workshop presenter. The term is used nowadays for many things.

Christian: As a soccer coach, I am more of a trainer-coach.

Michael: In English it's the same word. So sometimes it is misunderstood. We are talking about a professional coaching process, the certified coaching, for which I have trained, am learning a lot and practicing a lot. In profession-al coaching, I support the thought process of the coachee, I would even say I challenge my coachee's thoughts by asking him questions. These questions lead to a new perspective on a known topic and help the coachee to find new answers. Of course, I challenge my coachee's thoughts only if I am allowed to do so. During the sessions, I ask quite frankly what my coachee expects and what not, what is allowed and what is not. Pure coaching supports the thought process, it is mainly mental work. How is that different from men-toring?

Christian: Didn't you recently write an extensive paper about this?

Michael: Yes, as a matter of fact, I did.

Christian: Well, as a coach I do not know the solution to the question of the coachee. It can even be a hindrance if I know it and give my coachee some advice. Advice does not usually lead to a good result in coaching. As a mentor, however, I know solutions because I am experienced, right? As a mentor, I tend to help more in the substantive topics in which I have a lot of experience.

Michael: Yes, at least that's what I expect from a mentor. I've had several mentors in my life who have helped me a lot. Most of them I only had contact with very sporadically, only a few times a year. The conversations were incredibly cool, super interesting, and always at eye level. Most of my mentors were 10, 15, 20 years or more ahead of me in life and career and simply had a different perspective. They shared very specific tips and told me how I could solve certain situations. A coach would never do that. I thought it was great. I wouldn't have wanted a classic coaching session with my mentors. It was helpful for me to benefit from their experience and to actually get desired advice. It's a completely different thing than coaching.

Christian: Imagine your mentor asks you, "Okay, that's seven choices, which others are there? Hello?! Are you alright?"

Michael: The term *mentor* originally comes from a Greek myth. A king's son had to take over his father's official duties on short notice because the king himself had to go away for a long time. He provided his son with a *mentor* for the period of his absence. Hence the name mentor. The funny thing about the story is that it would have gone wrong if there hadn't been a goddess involved to judge it. The mentor himself basically had no idea what to advise the king's son. It was only because of the goddess' intuition that it worked out well in the end. The mentor's own solutions were not suitable for his mentee. My conclusion from this saga is that as a mentee I cannot blindly rely on advice, instead I always question the intentions, the experiences my mentor has had in order to find the right solution for me. Coaching is a super valuable process that helps me to look at things differently and to come up with new, better solutions myself, or to find a solution in the first place. The solutions suggested by my mentor are not necessarily always the right ones for me. I can learn a lot from a mentor and critical questioning is definitely appropriate.

Christian: Often a mentor's solutions comes from decades ago. "Back in the 80s, I solved it like this…"

Michael: When I was 35 years-old, I had a mentor who was about 75 years-old. We had super nice conversations. In terms of business content, he was on a completely different level. Basically, it was all about whether or not the company was making money at the end of the day. "What else can we do to make money and increase returns?"

Christian: Mentor, coach, that leaves the consultant as the third fish. What distinguishes the consultant from a mentor? He comes in and says, "Here's how we do it."

Michael: The consultant comes with good advice, basically like the mentor. The difference with a mentor is that the consultant then puts it into practice. For example, I temporarily bring a consultant onboard with a project team. He works with me for a while, maybe he is part of the team temporarily. Sometimes it feels like an employee, except that he doesn't appear on my payroll. He's just there temporarily because I need a certain skill for a project for a short period of time. Often, these skills are not so common. They're more specific and therefore more expensive than the skills my other employees already have. That is what a consultant is for me. In a project I need a certain expertise and I buy this expertise selectively by hiring a consultant. A consultant implements. The mentor does nothing. The coach does nothing at all.

Christian: He asks, then keeps his mouth shut and listens.

Michael: Right, he doesn't do anything, he doesn't consult. What does he actually do? He actually has the best job of all. He opens up the psychological box in the top of the head. My problems are my problems, not the problems of the world. The solutions to them have almost always been inside myself.

Christian: What do you take from this session for yourself?

Michael: Clarity.

Christian: May I ask you about it again next time?

Michael: Yeah, sure. With pleasure.

Eight opossums inside the coaching fish; there really always seem to be eight. For me as an outsider, the solution is often immediately obvious, even if it is not yet visible to my counterpart. At the beginning it was not always easy for me to hold back with my advice. I thought it takes a lot of patience and time to come to a solution. But that was nonsense. Since I understood what it's all about, the coaching technique has become an integral part of my leadership toolbox. After all, the goal is to be there for my team as a mentor, coach or consultant, depending on the situation. It helps me to become clear about my situational role and the requirements of my counterpart, both privately and professionally.

WEEKLY ONE-ON-ONE
THE WEEKLY STAFF MEETING

Michael: You once said an interesting thing in one of our Chief Seminars. I remember it very well. You said, "The most important meeting I had as manager was the one-on-one-conversation," which is often abbreviated as 101, 1:1, 121, and 1-on-1.

Christian: Yes, right. This is true in the business context as a manager. In the private environment, it might be a different matter.

Michael: I'm just imagining it. In his whole life, Christian only has 1:1 conversations. [*laughs*]

Christian: For a while I actually managed to run my companies almost exclusively like this. I think I covered 70-80% of my management activities with the weekly 1:1 meetings. The rest are other meetings like weekly management meetings, Strategy meetings, and so on. Essentially, I achieve the most with the 1:1 meetings.

Michael: Before we talk about exactly how it works, how is it that these meetings have such a big effect?

Christian: Why do we do management? What is the ultimate goal of management? Management means achieving results and retaining employees. I either want to achieve the results that I set out to achieve as the founder of the company or that are given to me when I am an employed manager. On the one hand, there are KPIs that I want to achieve such as specific business goals, making money, and so on. On the other hand, I want to keep the employees on my team. I want them to enjoy working for me and to support me in achieving my goals. Of course, only those I really want to keep. I part with the employees that I don't want to keep relatively quickly. These are sometimes opposite poles. There are the goals that I want to achieve and there are the employees that I want to keep.

Michael: The two main functions of management come from Peter Drucker. The first is to achieve results and the second is to retain employees. Peter Drucker is one of the great management gurus. This focus has helped me enormously. As founder, managing director and as an executive, my first reaction to achieving results was, "Yes, sure. I understand." Then I thought about the second point, *retaining employees,* especially about this word "retaining." That got me thinking. Could you perhaps tell another anecdote about it and explain exactly what it means?

Christian: With pleasure. I'll try to explain how I can achieve these two goals, then it will become clearer. So the question is how I can simultaneously achieve results and retain employees. Peter Drucker has found that managers who are particularly successful at this have four things in common. They did the following four things particularly well. First, they have built up a good relationship with their employees. Second, good managers constantly talk about performance. They know their goals and they talk about them continuously with their employees. "Dear employee, this is where we want to go. The following pays for it, the following doesn't." They give constant feedback and always align themselves and their team with the goals they have set. Third, they develop their employees. I coach employees who may not yet be ready to help me achieve my goals in a great way, so that they can do so as soon as possible. Employees feel valued, they learn continuously and can develop themselves further. This helps me achieve my goals and retain employees. If I now have a good relationship with my employees, constantly talk to them about performance, and develop them further, then I can provide them with work. Peter Drucker calls it *push work down*, providing employees with work in such a way that they have enough to do and, above all, work on the right things.

Michael: That means you adjust the system so that the right work is distributed to the right people. With the four principles: build a good relationship, give feedback on performance, develop employees, and distribute the right tasks. This is the groundwork to get results and retain employees.

Christian: Right. That sounds quite simple now, of course. It takes me a while to achieve that. The order I just mentioned is important. So I first build up a good relationship before I *push work down* and distribute work. It is also helpful to talk about performance before I develop the employee. "If you do this, it's great. That pays less towards our goal. Let's think together about how you can get even better at it." The order is important.

Michael: Here comes the magic. You often talk about how to do all this with a weekly 1:1. I always listen to you carefully. What do you mean by that exactly?

Christian: The first question is how I can build a professional and trusting relationship with my employees. The bad news is that people often need time to build relationships. The good news is that if I give myself and my employees time and use it properly, it is relatively easy to build a good relationship. For example, I sit down with each employee for half an hour every week. I use this time qualitatively to establish a relationship. That means I have about 24 hours a year to build a relationship with the employee. That works well.

Michael: Doesn't it also depend on how many people I have on my team?

Christian: Of course, if I have 50 employees and spend half an hour a week having a 1:1 conversation with each of them, time will be tight. I recommend a team size of six to nine employees at most anyway. I once had nine direct employees, which was quite exhausting. I usually conducted all my 1:1 conversations in one day. At that time, I divided them into two days. Four and a half hours of 1:1 conversations in a row is pretty demanding. Each employee is an individual and I get involved with each one with her different preferences. I have therefore often divided the teams and brought in a management level. At some point I managed to have only two weekly 1:1 conversations. That was very convenient.

Michael: So 50 people on a team without another management level is difficult. I have a rule of thumb in the back of my mind that also applies here: 7±2 is an optimal team size.

Christian: Right. I consider six to nine employees to be optimal.

Michael: So you also had a phase where you only had two direct employees and successfully led them through 1:1 conversations. And that means you had a lot of time for other things. Many managers and coachees have the problem that they can't get anything done and are busy with an infinite number of things. How do these weekly 1:1 conversations solve this problem?

Christian: A major time killer is often those rushed-in-between talks. Suddenly, an employee stands at the door and says, "Boss, do you have five minutes?" "Yeah, sure," I usually say as a boss. For several reasons, these conversations are unfavorable. The first reason is that I actually don't have those five minutes right this moment. My head is somewhere else. The second reason is that the employee has usually been dealing with the topic for a very long time before she stands in my doorway and wants to push it through in just five minutes. This brings us straight to the next reason. It's usually not just five minutes. Often the employee has a problem that I am glad she has and not me. Of course, that doesn't work in favor of a good relationship. For example, if there is a regular 1:1 meeting every Thursday at 9:30 a.m., the employee can prepare herself, collect her topics, and prepare them properly. She can rely on me engaging with her and taking the time for her topics. That's the great thing about it from my point of view. My employee knows that I take half an hour for her every week like she does for me. We can discuss the topics in peace and quiet and I'm fully involved.

Michael: Every week, same time, same place, same employee, right?

Christian: Ideally, yes. The important thing is that it does not get cancelled. That shows reliability. It is also important that the appointment is in the calendar. Every Thursday at 9:30 am. It will also be on the calendar for November 2022.

Michael: So it's in my calendar as a recurring appointment, as a serial appointment. In Google or Outlook calendar, wherever. Every Thursday at 9:30 am.

Christian: Right. Of course, everyone gets sick at times or is on vacation. Then it can be cancelled. Another appointment or a business trip on that day should not be used as an excuse. If there is no other way, I postpone the 1:1 conversation in time. It will still take place in the same week. It is only postponed, it is not cancelled.

Michael: Can I do it by phone or on Zoom?

Christian: That's fine. Of course, it's better if I sit across from my colleague to really get to know each other. I therefore recommend that we meet in person at the beginning. Then, when things are going well and we get to know each other better, we'll also talk via Zoom. The telephone is also possible; for a while, I used to make 1:1 phone calls with my employees. It works, however, it's better via Zoom and personal meetings.

Michael: Once the rapport is built and relationships are established, phone calls are much easier.

Christian: Right. The most important thing is consistency. Another success factor is that I understand that the meeting is for the employee. That means that her topics have priority at first. Why? Because it is always easier for me as the boss to get a few minutes of time from my employees than the other way around. If I go to an employee and ask: "Do you have five minutes?" the answer will usually be, "Yes, sure, boss." For the employee, it is often a larger hurdle to come to me. I often respond to, "Boss, do you have five minutes?" with, "This is a bad time." So I always start 1:1 with the same question. "What's on your mind? What do you want to talk about today?"

Michael: It's a nice, open question.

Christian: Right. Open questions, where everything is allowed. If the employee wants to talk about soccer or the weather, we talk about soccer or the weather. If the employee still wants to talk exclusively about soccer six months later, we might have a different topic. Usually, my employees had very similar topics on their list as I did. I always had a list of five to ten topics myself. When we did get into the swing of things, the topics were usually very similar.

Michael: And what else?

Christian: Aside from never missing the meeting, it is helpful to ask the right questions.

Michael: What are the right questions?

Christian: A good introductory question is, "What is currently on your mind?" Open questions are important. If nothing more comes after that, I ask coaching questions like, "What else is there? What else is on your mind?" At some point, my employees came into the meeting with a broad grin on their faces and often said, "It's okay, I'll just tell you what's on my mind." It sure can be a bit playful.

Michael: And the meeting takes half an hour, right?

Christian: Right. Half an hour is a good time window.

Michael: Is that enough? Is it too much?

Christian: It is enough. There is also the possibility to agree on larger topics in a separate meeting if it is not enough. If we want to work out or discuss something in greater depth, such as, "Let's develop an offer for this," we do this in a separate meeting outside of the 1:1 format. Therefore, 30 minutes are perfectly sufficient. From time to time it may take 45 minutes, like after a vacation. In addition, the time restrictions mean that employees prepare themselves and use the time well to get their topics through. It is an efficient, on point, high-quality meeting for both participants. I often notice that those who are efficient in our 1:1 meeting also get to the point quickly in other meetings.

Michael: How are the thirty minutes typically structured? Are there fixed components of the meeting?

Christian: When we are in a steady state, we discuss the employee's topics in the beginning. She has a free choice of topics. Then, we talk about my topics and if there is time left we do some personal development. That is like a coaching session to develop the employee. For me, it is important that my employees are able to present, amongst other things. Together, we think about which books could help them, which Ted Talks are suitable, and how she can develop further. In addition, my employees are required to take turns running the weekly team meetings to develop their presentation and communication skills.

Michael: And you discuss that in a 1:1 meeting?

Christian: Yes, exactly. I give feedback and tips. For example, "Try it like this or use a communication starter." I give ideas and impulses. Then there is the challenge for my employees to manage projects.

Michael: Sure.

Christian: So additional, small projects that are not necessarily part of the regular line function.

Michael: You mean projects that don't necessarily have anything to do with the actual role of the employee, but come on top?

Christian: Yes. For example planning a team event or organizing the relocation of the headquarters, depending on the previous knowledge and skills of the employees.

Michael: I have one final question. You just described that beautiful expression *in the steady state*, when meetings find their rhythm. What are your experiences with it? If I start with the 1:1 meetings tomorrow, what is the relationship like at the beginning, how do these meetings develop, and when do I typically get into this steady state? How much patience do I need until things run smoothly?

Christian: In most cases, the employees are happy to have regular meetings. They think it's great when their boss makes time for them every week.

Michael: Do you also tell them how you usually structure it and how it works?

Christian: Yes, definitely. Just like I did now.

Michael: So you are completely transparent?

Christian: Completely transparent. "I want to build up a good relationship with you, that's why from now on I'll take time for you every week."

Michael: Completely transparent, just as we discussed. So the employee receives the recipe, the blueprint for the 1:1 meeting, knows the Purpose of the whole thing, and why you are having these conversations.

Christian: Of course. My employees are mostly managers themselves. So they can pass it on to their employees as well. It scales quickly for the whole company and is easy to learn.

Michael: Great.

Christian: I have also experienced objections from my direct reports. An employee once said to me, "Half an hour? I have to work." Another one once said, "What am I supposed to talk about for thirty minutes?" With a few "What else?" questions, it went quite well. One employee absolutely didn't want the 1:1 meeting. We stopped working together. After three to six months, things usually run smoothly.

Michael: Fantastic.

WEEKLY

30 MINS

WITH EACH DIRECT REPORT

FOR THE EMPLOYEE

SCHEDULED

NO CANCELLATIONS

10 / 10 / 10

| FOR THE EMPLOYEE | FOR ME (BOSS) | FOR THE FUTURE |

Illustration: Weekly 101

For me, the weekly employee meeting is one of the most effective management tools and an essential part of a successful management culture.

Especially for executives in the mid-level management, these discussions are often a particular time challenge. On the one hand, I want to take time for my employees, on the other hand, I want to get my own work done and at the same time prepare 1:1 with my boss. The tip to have an optimal team size is therefore very helpful. If there are too many employees, this is hardly manageable if I also want to complete projects of my own and pursue further development. It is important to limit meetings and preparation time, so we simply get through the topics faster. To do without 1:1 meetings is indeed fatal. It is a question of appreciation towards the employee and really an efficient and effective leadership tool, both for the manager and the employee.

"BETWEEN STIMULUS AND RESPONSE, THERE IS A SPACE.

IN THAT SPACE IS OUR POWER TO CHOOSE OUR RESPONSE.

IN OUR RESPONSE LIES OUR GROWTH AND OUR FREEDOM."

— VIKTOR E. FRANKL

SIX SITUATIONS OF FEEDBACK
...OF WHICH THREE ARE, AND THREE ARE NOT.

Christian: Michael, can I tell you something?

Michael: Yeah, sure.

Christian: It always gets me all worked up when you keep sending me voice messages. You have a new idea here and something else there. Can you please do it differently?

Michael: Can I be honest?

Christian: Sure.

Michael: Shut up.

Christian: Shut up? That's a good idea. You mean instead of giving you feedback, I can just shut up?

Michael: That's an option.

Christian: That's a good option. If I feel something is triggering me, maybe it's better to say nothing and guide myself first.

Michael: That's a wise insight.

Christian: Just shut up for once.

Michael: *Just shut up, man.*

Christian: That means giving someone feedback while something is triggering me is not a good idea, right?

Michael: Yes. As a leader, feedback is often a big issue. I ask myself, when did that ever work well for me? When have I ever gotten really good feedback that made a difference to me? I can probably count the times on one hand. And when I think about how often I've given feedback—and I used to give a lot of feedback, formally and directly—I'm not sure that I've really done any

THE ROOTS OF BEHAVIOUR

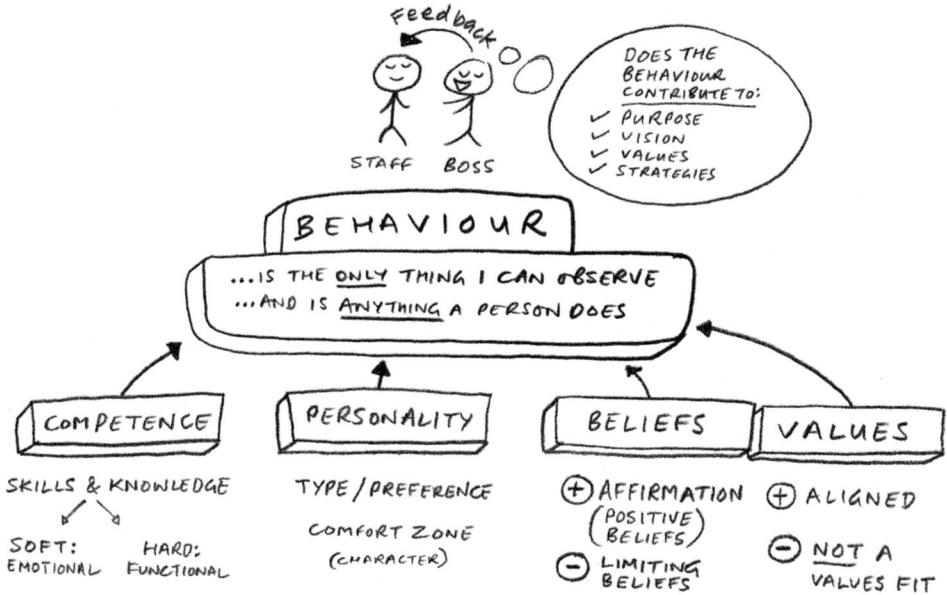

Feedback

STAFF   BOSS

DOES THE
BEHAVIOUR
CONTRIBUTE TO:
✓ PURPOSE
✓ VISION
✓ VALUES
✓ STRATEGIES

BEHAVIOUR

...IS THE ONLY THING I CAN OBSERVE
...AND IS ANYTHING A PERSON DOES

COMPETENCE

SKILLS & KNOWLEDGE

SOFT: HARD:
EMOTIONAL   FUNCTIONAL

PERSONALITY

TYPE / PREFERENCE

COMFORT ZONE
(CHARACTER)

BELIEFS

(+) AFFIRMATION
(POSITIVE
BELIEFS)

(−) LIMITING
BELIEFS

VALUES

(+) ALIGNED

(−) NOT A
VALUES FIT

Illustration: The Roots of Behaviour

good. In fact, I fear I've done rather the opposite. My feedback may even have had a negative effect at times. Feedback is a double-edged thing that I have long found very ambivalent.

Christian: I suppose this trigger feedback used to be the kind of feedback I gave most often. If something triggered me, I had a lot of energy to tell him or her to stop doing it. What really accomplishes something is positive feedback. You often talk about that one, key figure: 85 percent.

Michael: Exactly, and of the six situations of feedback.

Christian: Do you want to go through those?

Michael: I'd love to. Feedback means observing another person's behavior and then telling that person what they could change. That can be in a leadership role, or in another role. Sometimes I also think, "I'd like to tell that person right now that what just happened wasn't so great." That thought just comes up and I want to tell her what I noticed. That's where the whole story starts. Now, if I'm a leader, I get to ask myself first, "To what end do I even want to say something to the person about his behavior?" and also, "To what end am I allowed to say something, and to what end may I not?"

Christian: I have an idea for the Purpose: reaching goals, achieving results, and retaining employees.

Michael: Management's job is to achieve results and retain employees. I'd like to add to that: reaching goals in line with Values, the Purpose of the company and the Vision. Then we are already on the topic of retaining employees and implementing Strategies. Purpose, Vision, Values, Strategies. Achieving results and retaining employees. That's my lens as a leader. Now I look more sharply at the behavior of the other person, to whom I was about to say something, and ask myself whether their behavior has a positive or negative impact on our common goals.

Christian: Let's assume that I have basically hired the right people. That means that the probability that the team will also do the right things is already relatively high, right?

Michael: When things are going well, yes. I often think about a certain behavior of an employee and then realize, "Yes, it does contribute to the achievement of the goal and this behavior is not currently hurting anyone." I then accept the behavior. In this case, I may constantly and repeatedly give the person positive feedback and simply thank him or her—just as I do with everyone else. This is where the 85% comes into play. Eighty-five percent positive feedback. "Thank you for just doing it this way. It contributes to the outcome." That makes me feel good.

Christian: In the sense of, a pat on the back, "great, well done?"

Michael: Careful. There's another subtle difference. Of course, I am also doing this.

Christian: "Well done. Good dog!"

Michael: I'm the kind of guy who gets a funny feeling when someone tells me, "Well done." Then I wonder, "Who gives you the right to judge that I did something well?"

THE 3 TYPES OF FEEDBACK THAT ARE-

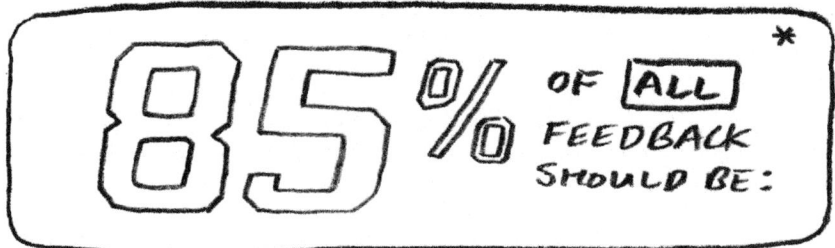

#1 POSITIVE AFFIRMATION

GIVE THIS TO:
EVERYBODY, EVERYDAY

ACTUALLY...

85% OF [ALL] FEEDBACK SHOULD BE: *

POSITIVE AFFIRMATION

☑ GIVING PRAISE IS GOOD

☑☑ GIVING GRATITUDE IS EVEN BETTER

Feedback

BEHAVIOUR

*— IT'S HUGE!
AND HARVARD AGREES!

Christian: You feel that the person then puts himself above you?!

Michael: Yes, exactly. Just like when someone says to me, "That wasn't so great now." I then think to myself, "Who are you?" I have learned to simply say thank you instead of praise or patting people on the back. I say thank you and associate it with the good feeling when I observe that this behavior has a positive effect on goal achievement and that we will definitely reach our goal. This is a beautiful way and is called positive affirmation. According to Harvard,34 this is something that we as leaders should actually be doing all the time and in reality, unfortunately implement it far too rarely. Consequently, I should give positive feedback six times as often as I give other feed-forward for a change that is actually needed.

Christian: We have already talked about this shit sandwich. I'm going to tell you one or two positive things and then I'm going to tell you what I actually want to tell you: Specifically, what's not going so well. And finally, I'll say something positive again so you don't feel so bad. Do I always build this 85% positive feedback into the shit sandwich or can it also be stand-alone feedforward sometimes?

Michael: It can also just be a stand-alone feedforward, sort of a stand-alone compliment. It's positive affirmation. "Thank you so much for what you just did, I think that's great." *I think* or *I feel* are often appropriate phrases, for example. In defense of the good ol' sandwich, I think that's still better than just addressing the meat without the buns around it.

Christian: So poorly conveyed feedback is still better than no feedback at all?

Michael: I am not sure about that. Connecting the positive with the suggestions for improvement is still a better technique than just mentioning suggestions for improvement. If all I do is grumble, I usually accomplish less than if I say the positive things and reinforce them. It works even better that way than with the shit sandwich. That's positive affirmation. Every day I give every employee at least one positive affirmation. This is the first of the six feedback situations. I apply this 85% of the time.

Christian: Thank you very much, Michael. Now I understand the 85%. How about the remaining 15%?

34   Jack Zenger, Joseph Folkman: https://hbr.org/2013/03/the-ideal-praise-to-criticism - HBR, 15 March 2013

THE 3 TYPES OF FEEDBACK THAT ARE—

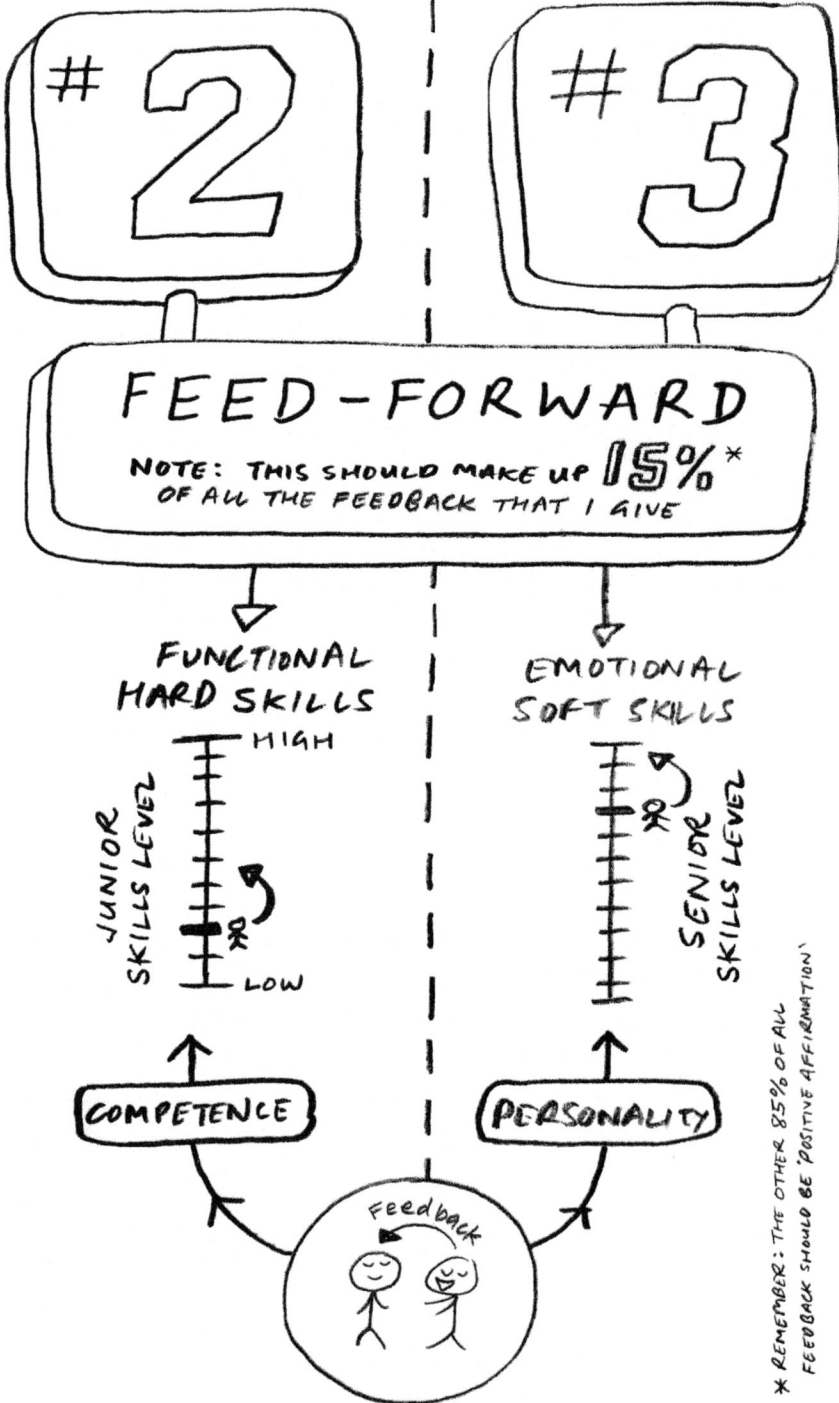

#2 #3

FEED - FORWARD

NOTE: THIS SHOULD MAKE UP 15%* OF ALL THE FEEDBACK THAT I GIVE

FUNCTIONAL HARD SKILLS

HIGH

JUNIOR SKILLS LEVEL

LOW

EMOTIONAL SOFT SKILLS

SENIOR SKILLS LEVEL

COMPETENCE

PERSONALITY

Feedback

* REMEMBER: THE OTHER 85% OF ALL FEEDBACK SHOULD BE POSITIVE AFFIRMATION'

Michael: Those are the cases where, when I'm observing someone's behavior, I notice that it's not playing into our goals, Purpose, and Vision, or it's not in alignment with the Values. She may be behaving in a way that makes it hard to achieve results and retain employees. There are two cases I distinguish here. The first is the simpler one. Here I observe that someone doesn't yet have the necessary skills or competencies to do certain things. In this case, I give feedforward in the sense of, "How can I support you to do this or that even better in the future? What are some options for gaining this competency? What type of training might help?" Maybe a coach, a buddy, or a development plan will help you to only learn through positive affirmation in the future.

Christian: So that would be instructing and coaching as a leadership style?

Michael: Yes, exactly. Further development. Personal development. As a leader, I help my employees grow into bigger roles, even with time and money. Maybe even with my own time and knowledge. I can go into training mode with an employee myself or make sure someone else teaches the person. So this is about hard skills, this is the second feedback situation, giving feedforward with the purpose of building hard skills. That leaves a few percentage points of the 15%. The third feedback situation has the purpose of developing soft skills, i.e., the EQ or emotional quotient. This also contributes significantly to achieving results. This situation is similar to the previous one. Again, I give feedforward to help the person build appropriate competencies, only this time it's about soft skills instead of hard skills. In the context of EQ, there are two recurring issues. One is the issue of awareness, which is how I come across to other people and how my behaviors affect others: self-awareness. The second big issue is behavioral flexibility. Behavioral flexibility means being able to adjust to others and approaching others in my own authentic way to make it easier for them.

Christian: You once shared a story in which someone told you that you achieve more with a smile. After the meeting, you got on a plane, deliberately smiled more, practiced your behavioral flexibility, and then got a bottle of wine as a gift. Would that be a feedforward for a soft skill?

Michael: Yes, absolutely. It's cool that you remember that. The funny thing was that the person actually initiated the conversation with, "Can I give you some feedback?" For me, that was a terrific day, a very successful and important day for my further career. He first said, "Yes, you're in. You made it, we are taking you on this journey." Then he said, "Can I give you feedback on what will help you on the journey?" That was a very positive shit sandwich. And then exactly the feedforward you mentioned followed, "If you smile more in the future, what just happened here will happen in the future. People will be joyful and laugh with each other." And that's exactly what happened afterwards. Now that was exemplary. I just realized it in this conversation, thank you.

Christian: You're welcome. So now we've talked about hard skills and soft skills. Now we're at 100%. Were those all feedback situations?

Michael: Yes, that's right. One-hundred percent. Strangely, we have only discussed three out of six feedback situations. So there's still more ahead.

Christian: I'd be curious if I didn't already have an idea of what direction this is going in already.

Michael: I get into one of these feedback situations because I observe someone's behavior and I have a feeling: I want to say something to that person. What we've described so far was positive affirmation, for one thing. Eighty-five percent. The other thing was about feed-forward to build both hard and soft skills. Now the interesting thing about human behavior is primarily what drives the behavior. That is, on the one hand, what a person can do. That's what we call competencies, skills, knowledge, etc. On the other hand, it is also our personality or character, that is, the type of person we are with our preferences, our comfort zone. All of that impacts how I behave. However, there is another category that has an influence on my behavior. What was that again?

Christian: These are the things that I believe. The things that I believe to be true. My beliefs can be positive, in the sense of, *I can do anything*, or negative, in the sense of, *I've always been bad at math*.

Michael: Exactly. For the positive beliefs, there's this notion of self-affirmation. It's like positive affirmation, only I give it to myself. The negative beliefs are the so-called limiting beliefs or limiting choices. Colloquially, I could say

I'm getting in my own way. So I could actually achieve results, retain employees, make a positive contribution, only for some reason I'm holding myself back from it. I might have something in my head, something that I believe that makes me decide not to do it. That's a situation where I can also get a feedforward. So if I observe an employee who is prevented from doing something by a limiting belief set, I'm more likely not to give her a positive affirmation about it. If there is a limiting belief set, it can be dangerous if I then mistakenly start giving a bunch of feedforward: "Build such and such skills and work on your mindset and so on." That's where I go wrong, unfortunately. I can only help someone with this if she recognizes her beliefs are limiting herself and is willing to work on it. Here I better call in a coach, at least if I haven't been trained as a coach myself or know something about NLP.

Christian: If I have a coaching education as a manager, I might be biased. So I ask myself if I am the appropriate coach. It is similar to the situation in my own family. That's why I'm banned from coaching at home. [*grins*] On top of that, of course, I can't coach myself either. So the distance that an external coach has really helps.

Michael: Yes, that's true. It feels like a conflict of interest to say, as a professional coach, "You may seek an external coach for this." However, my own experience is also that I've never been able to do it myself as a manager. I couldn't do it then either, and even now I feel much more comfortable when someone else does it. It's a funny feeling when I try to do it myself.

Christian: For example, Michael and Christian are good coaches that you can book. [*laughs*] There is another aspect that I find quite exciting. Someone once told me that there are things that I can manage, and then there are things that I can coach, or better, things that are coachable. And then there are behaviors that require therapy. At that point, I can admit to myself that this is a bit out of my scope. Because behaviors and beliefs can also become pathological. So that's the next decision that may have to be made.

Michael: Then it goes even deeper and coaching may not be enough. Here I might be in better hands with a psychologist or psychiatrist. Possibly there is something really wrong and it results in a certain behavior.

Christian: So actually maybe pathological.

THE 3 TYPES OF FEEDBACK THAT ARE ✦NOT✦

#4

COACH
BY A PROFESSIONAL

INDIVIDUAL MUST REALLY WANT TO GROW

⬆

IF MANAGER IS NOT QUALIFIED TO COACH IT SHOULD BE DELEGATED

⬆

THE PERSON HAS LIMITING BELIEFS

⬆

Feedback

#5

FIRE
(FAST)

DECIDE CAREFULLY, EXECUTE QUICKLY

⬆

MAKING THE HARD CHOICE

⬆

AMICABLE SEPARATION IN LINE WITH THE VALUES OF THE ORGANISATION

⬆

NO VALUES FIT

⬆

Feedback ✗*

* NOT DIRECTLY FEEDBACK BUT IT IS A TERMINATION CONVERSATION

Michael: There is another case, something that also strongly influences our behavior and that is our Values. We talk very often about the Values fit. This is a fit of the shared Values in the company and the Values of the individual. The greater this fit is and the more the Values match, the more we are aligning behaviors that lead to us achieving results together and retaining employees. So, if I am in a situation where I observe a behavior and by process of elimination I find that it is not a competency thing, nor is it related to personality type, nor is it a limiting belief set behind it, then it could be that something else is influencing the behavior. It might be the fact that the person does not fit the company Values. If I then approach the matter with feedforward, I will quickly find out that it doesn't work. This is where I really busted my chops a lot of times. I think anyone who has ever been in a leadership role can probably relate to that. It's that Sisyphus thing. I try to get someone else to change, or worse, I try to change them myself and then quickly realize that it doesn't work at all. I keep getting to the point of giving feedback and absolutely nothing changes. This could be a good indicator that there is a Values problem. The fit is missing.

Christian: Or if things are not going forward and you end up thinking, "I've brought this up so many times..."

Michael: Yes, exactly. We've talked about the TEV model and topgrading before. If the Values fit is missing, I don't have a feedback situation. Rather, I have a situation where I may decide as a manager to terminate the working relationship. It is then simply better to part ways. In the end, this usually leads to a better situation for both sides. Now we have already discussed five situations. Number one: Positive affirmation. Number two: Feedforward for hard skills. Number three: Feedforward for soft skills. Number four: Dissolve limiting beliefs through coaching. Number five: Separation due to lack of Values fit.

Christian: And now?! Now we are back to the beginning?

Michael: That was quite cleverly initiated. [*grins*]

Christian: Triggers. When something triggers me, the problem is not with the other person, but with me, deep inside me.

THE 3 TYPES OF FEEDBACK THAT ARE **NOT**

#6

SHUT UP AND DO NOTHING

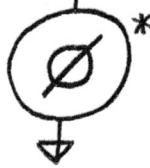

∅ *

LEAD MYSELF TOWARDS
PERSONAL SUPERIORITY
⬆
THE ABILITY NOT TO REACT
⬆
RISE ABOVE IT,
GIVE IT SPACE
⬆

Feedb...

THIS IS A
TRIGGER

* THIS IS THE SYMBOL FOR 'EMPTY SET'

Michael: That's the situation when I watch someone and think, "Whoa, what's that?"

Christian: "Just the way he's walking already bugs me!"

Michael: I can tell because it triggers something emotional in me. So when I'm annoyed or feel ticked off ,that's the trigger feeling. That goes from zero to 100 in a few seconds. Here it helps to evaluate the situation rationally and ask myself the crucial questions: *Does she get results with it?* "Yes, she does." *Can I keep the right people on the team with this behavior?* "Yes, the others all seem to be okay with it." *Does it pay into our Purpose, Vision, Values and Strategies?* "Yes, it does contribute." Then I get closer to the truth and realize that this is all about me right now. The problem is within me. I have a red button here and someone is pushing it right now.

Christian: Hella, my wife, says "It always takes two. One who pushes the button and one who allows the button to be pushed."

Michael: Yes, wonderful. You know what Patrizia recently said to me? "I have realized, my darling, you are my trigger companion in life."

Christian: Caregiver for the triggers?!

Michael: Whenever I realize, "There's a person triggering my trigger right now," that's a trap. The truth is, of course, that the other person is not triggering anything. She just does what she does. I myself trigger the trigger. That only takes place in my own head, in my mind. If I now start to consider these people, who supposedly trigger my trigger and don't really do it at all, as my trigger companions in life, then I suddenly discover a completely different relationship with these people. And here we are again at the beginning. Where we started the conversation so beautifully. Because in this case, in the sixth situation, in the supposed feedback situation, the right action for me is to just shut up and work on myself. There's a nice word for that: Superiority. Practicing superiority. And in this context what I mean by superiority is to stand above things. To stand above the situation and to accept others as they are.

Christian: That sounds very simple when you say that. In fact, it is for me, too. How do I do that? Just shut up!

Michael: It's a perpetual task. I find that it gets easier with time.

Christian: Great, thank you very much Michael. Let's shut up now.

Michael: Thank you. Feedback is a gift. Thank you.

Phew... For the first time, the feedback issue feels easy. Saying positive things is much easier for me, as the feedback sandwich hasn't seemed particularly helpful for a long time. Exposing limiting beliefs and triggers, combined with the six feedback situations, makes a lot of things clearer for me! Now I'm still asking myself: How can I help myself and other people recognize and overcome limiting beliefs and address the red trigger buttons? Perhaps I'll go back to the subject of beliefs. And again, I'm back to myself. Self-reflection. Awareness. Superiority. Ultimate behavioral flexibility for life.

FEEDFORWARD

FEEDBACK WAS YESTERDAY

Christian: Michael, may I give you feedback?

Michael: Absolutely, with pleasure.

Christian: You're going full steam ahead with our book. We're making great progress because you're constantly editing the table of contents and thinking up new chapters and content. If you continue like this, we will be finished with our book pretty quickly.

Michael: Thank you, my pleasure. Cool feedback. Now I'm curious what's coming.

Christian: What just happened?

Michael: You asked me if you could give me feedback.

Christian: So I asked for your permission first.

Michael: I said, "Yeah, sure." I had to smile a little bit because I thought, "Oh shit, what's going to happen now?" Then came all the positive things. Frankly, I've been waiting for the *but to* come and a list of things I'm not doing so well yet. They didn't come at all, so the feedback just felt good to me.

Christian: What are you doing with this feedback?

Michael: I'm proud that my red energy, with which I sometimes cause a stir, is appreciated. It was a valuable recognition for me that the way I drive things forward is appreciated by you and contributes to our results. I felt confirmed.

Christian: Will you put more energy into it now? Maybe you think, "Hey, what I'm doing is well received, so I'll do more of it."

Michael: Definitely. Although over the last few years of my life, I have learned to be a little careful with my gas pedal. In our collaboration, I now know that it's okay if I work like this and step on the gas. Christian thinks it's good, I feel confirmed and more secure in what I do. So I think, "All right, I'm allowed to be the way I am. So I'm going full throttle now."

Christian: Very good. I have focused my feedback on our common goal on Purpose. We want to write a book together. So I can actually get you to work even more and even better on our book if I give you positive reinforcement.

Michael: Yeah, right. In that context, if you had told me something that I could do better or where there might be more to get out of it, I would have liked to hear it. I've almost been waiting for it. That's an experience I've had with feedback, or better, *feedforward*. We call it feedforward in our workshop seminars, because the trick to good feedback is to encourage someone and bring about change in the future. Actually, it is only about the future and not about the past. When I relate it to the past, it sounds more like, "You are to blame." That doesn't help at all. Many people start with something good, then something bad follows, and in the end, for motivation, they say something good to close the feedback sandwich. If I know at the beginning that something bad is about to happen, it's still a shit sandwich, even if something nice is said afterwards to be polite. It remains a shit sandwich.

Christian: "It's great that you came to work on time today, but...," then comes the thing about going out for too much coffee.

Michael: [*grins*] Yeah, right. I have worked in large organizations and corporations in the past and have learned a lot there in terms of feedback, linguistic methodology, and positive language. All of this is super valuable. Looking back, I realize how much time I wasted with useless, ineffective, and time-consuming feedback processes. There was semi-annual feedback, annual meetings, formal feedback, quarterly meetings with the line manager. Both sit down and think about what they should say. First I do then the other spends hours thinking about what he can share with me. It has become an incredibly complicated thing. Sometimes we have written one or two pages of feedback and have forced out a jumble of crap, in which the essence was totally lost. In retrospect, I'm really baffled that I went along with it for years. Basically it's only about two things: One thing is what you just did with me, positive reinforcement in the things I'm really good at. If I have my way, we can do this much more often around the world. Then things would really progress everywhere and everyone would feel good, strengthen their strengths, and make a big contribution. Praise begins at home. I would have liked to have been praised more by my father. Praise from parents really brings a lot. The second thing that's important is that I get straight guidance for the things I often mess up. Tips on how I can do things differently in the future to make it work. Because the way I'm doing it right now doesn't seem to work. From my point of view, I don't need a feedback document that is pages long with 10 points, elaborately packed in a sandwich and with a little bow around it. Often I didn't have enough clarity about my actual strengths and weaknesses, which I would have been more aware of.

Christian: Speaking of praise. I initially tried to make my feedback as precise as possible. I referred to the table of contents and mentioned that the work according to it will bring us far forward. I could have simply said, "Great job you're doing. Thank you, keep up the good work."

Michael: That sounds more like a slap on the back. "Good man, great job."

Christian: Yes, exactly. And then quickly disappear again. The feedback may be concrete. If I remain vague and say, "Great job, Michael," you don't know what you did well and what exactly will pay off on our goal. Another issue is the frequency of feedback. You just mentioned annual or semi-annual feed-back processes. I am thinking directly of a car trip, for example from Munich to Ingolstadt. I hold the handlebars, step on the gas and think about steering after half a year, in this case maybe after 10 kilometers. Pretty sure I'd hit it somewhere, like right at the first bump or turn. What happens in reality when I drive from Munich to Ingolstadt? I steer continuously. Even when I'm driving straight ahead, I make small steering movements. From my point of view, feedback is really powerful when I steer a little bit, like when driving a car. "A little more of this, a little less of that." I don't think of feedback as good or bad, I see it as a steering movement. "A little more in this direction, now a little more in the other direction," just light steering movements. Then I can't hit anything. Then nobody is angry with me when I give feedback. Nobody expects something like, "Now he's steered to the right five times, now surely at some point the *but* has to come and he'll steer to the left." Just more and more of this, less of that.

Michael: So more *in the moment* instead of once a year.

Christian: Yes. All the time.

Michael: Does that mean I always have to give feedback?

Christian: As a boss?

Michael: Yes.

Christian: Do you have another task?

Michael: Okay, I see. The way you described it with the steering wheel, it sounded a lot like correction.

Christian: Yes, rather steering movements. My task as a manager is to achieve results and to retain employees. When the results are moving towards the goal, I say, "Great, you are going in the right direction." If the results are moving in a different direction, I say, "Better go more to the left or more to the right."

Michael: Let's say the car is going in the right direction and I don't need to take corrective action. How do I then encourage my employees? You encouraged me earlier and did not correct me. You didn't say, "More left, a little more right," but you simply said, "Great, run. Keep going like that."

Christian: It was already a correction. I encouraged you to edit the table of contents. I told you that it would get us to the goal and that you did a great job. If you continue to work on our book, you will think, "Ah yes, Christian said that the table of contents will help us, I am good at that. Then I'll continue with it and step on it even more." I'm guiding your behavior with my positive reinforcement.

Michael: Understood. Strengthening basically means, "You're already doing very well and you can do even better."

Christian: Encouragement is not a correction in the sense of taking countermeasures, rather in the sense of even more, even better. More left, more right would perhaps be more of a reduction of what you have done so far and a call to do more of something else.

Michael: In the car example it means, "He already steers to the left and drives to the left, he could turn in harder and go further left."

Christian: Yes of course, because the curve is now even tighter. I only see that when I turn into the curve. Sometimes there is a tree behind the curve that I couldn't see before.

Michael: Okay, good. Now I'm thinking about Christmas.

Christian: I'm glad to hear. What are we doing for Christmas?

Michael: Handing out gifts. This is how we have framed it: feedback is a gift. The picture totally helps me. It's a nice mindset to think of Christmas when I give feedback.

Christian: Give or take?

Michael: Both. Feedback is a gift. Feedback is always a gift. It works with give and take. When I give feedback, I always do it with the intention of giving the other person a gift. He should get something out of it. I do not give feedback because I want to make a point to someone. I want them to move forward. If I give feedback to someone, she does a better job and has a better career or a better life. Feedback always has a positive intention. That is one side of the gift. On the other side, I always accept feedback as a gift. I accept it. I am thinking about a situation with my mother. I don't know if she is listening to our podcast or reading this book. Anyway, I remember Christmas not too many years ago. She gave me a present, painstakingly wrapped, and we were immersed in the Christmas spirit with carols playing, and the smell of mulled wine brewing. It was in my parents' apartment and the atmosphere was super nice, very christmassy. We ate well. So I opened my present from her and found seven socks in seven different colors: orange, bright green, blue, purple and many more colors. One pair for each day of the week. I should say that I only wear dark blue and black socks. Very rarely do I wear white socks, when I play tennis, for example. And I never play tennis! Anyway. I'm sure my mother meant it very kindly and maybe she's also convinced that colorful socks look good on me. After all, I am a colorful guy. At that moment I thought: "Oh dear, I really don't need them. What am I supposed to do with it?"

Christian: *Feedback is a gift.* [*laughs*]

Michael: Right, it's a gift. What do I do when I receive a gift? From my mother, from my colleagues, from my supervisor? I accept it and say thank you. Then I take my time to think about what to do with it and how to implement it. In any case, I say, "Mom, thank you very much for this gift." Then I give her a hug and am happy that she has given me something. *Feedback is a gift and it works both ways.* I give feedback with the intention of giving a gift, and I accept feedback like a gift, no matter what is in it.

Christian: There is also the saying: *If someone gives me feedback, I learn more about the other person than about me.* I find that exciting. Let's stick to the example with your mother. You learn from her that she either likes colorful socks very much herself, that she thinks you should wear colorful socks more often, or that she doesn't think you can tell the fresh socks from the used ones. Therefore each pair has its own color.

Michael: I suspect the former.

Christian: In any case, you will learn something about your mother that is new for you. When I gave you feedback earlier, you also learned something about me. Namely, that I might not want to take care of the table of contents myself right now.

Michael: I already know that. [*laughs*]

Christian: Thanks. [*laughs*]

Michael: The older I get and the longer I deal with the topic of feedback—it's been haunting me for over 20 years now—the more I think about whether I should give feedback at all. I would like to take this opportunity to apologize to all those to whom I have given feedback in the past that was not as good as I would give it today. You might be happy to know that nowadays I actually decide to shut up more often instead of giving feedback. I try to accept that others do things differently than I would and that my feedback could only scratch the surface of motivation, no matter how good I deliver it. That's why I more often choose the version: period. Nothing more.

Christian: Just shut up.

Michael: Just shut up. The sandwich is just a good slice of bread, with no shit in between. The way you just did it, positive reinforcement, nothing more. "You did a great job with the table of contents. It's great that you're taking care of the structure." Period. Just a delicious slice of bread.

Christian: In the past, giving feedback was often all about being right. Then I stumbled upon a saying that gets to the point: "Do you want to be right or do you want to have a good marriage?"

Michael: "Yes, dear." [*laughs*] The smartest thing I can say to my spouse.

Christian: Being right is no longer the point for me, I'm now interested in other things, in a good relationship, a friendship, in making faster progress. Therefore, I often refrain from giving feedback.

Michael: There are often many ways to reach your goal. In the past, if I noticed that someone was taking a different path, I often took this as an opportunity to give feedback. Of course that was total nonsense. By doing things their way, they also reached their goal. Sometimes I just need more patience to recognize that. Today I know how to wrap my head around it: "Just let it happen, keep your mouth shut, and only intervene when necessary. And always encourage positively." It was a nice talk with you, Christian.

Christian: At this point, coaching can help unravel all kinds of possibilities. And now, get out of the shower.

It is good to read that there is an alternative to the feedback sandwich. I find that a bit trite by now. I think feedforward is great. It immediately lifts the mood and makes the conversation much more pleasant. Together, with the attitude to strengthen the strengths and concentrate on them more than on weakening the weaknesses, the feedforward conversation is much more valuable for all involved. The pragmatic approach compared to complex feedback processes also plays into my cards. A lot of time is often wasted here and more frustration is caused than motivation is created.

INTRINSIC MOTIVATION
INSTEAD OF EXTRINSIC DEMOTIVATION

Christian: Tell me, Michael. Are you as a human being intrinsically or extrinsically motivated?

Michael: What do you mean? Can you explain the difference?

Christian: May I tell you a story about it?

Michael: Sure, absolutely.

Christian: Some time ago a couple of guys were playing soccer outside on a garage driveway opposite my house. They were totally enthusiastic and wildly motivated. They had a lot of fun and made a hell of a lot of noise. It really annoyed me. So I offered them some money. I gave each of them one euro for every hour they played soccer there.

Michael: Hold on. [*confused*] The guys were bugging you, you wanted to get rid of them, and then you offered them money to stay?

Christian: Yes, right. They got money for playing soccer. So in the short term, they played much better. They enjoyed it and got money for it. The next day, I upped the ante and gave them two euro per person. I did that for as long as I wanted to afford it. Then, I suddenly stopped giving them money. "Thanks guys, you play great soccer. From now on, I'm not giving you any more money." What do you think happened? They left and said, "This is crazy, we don't play soccer here without money anymore." They ran away and I never saw them in the garage driveway again.

Michael: You reached your goal.

Christian: I transformed their intrinsic motivation, which they had when playing soccer, into extrinsic motivation. Suddenly, they liked to play soccer because they received money from me. I took that away from them and they left. It was no longer fun for them. I am intrinsically motivated when I do something because I want to do it, because I enjoy it, because it corresponds to my Purpose and my Vision. I am extrinsically motivated when I receive something for my actions, for example a goodie, money, candy, chocolate, recognition, a medal, or certification. So I ask you again my question, are you intrinsically or extrinsically motivated?

Michael: [*thinks*] I believe I'm intrinsically motivated. I'm just contemplating whether this has ever been different, whether my intrinsic motivation has shifted to an extrinsic motivation. I think I've experienced that. I'm thinking about bonuses right now. At some companies I worked for, I got a bonus at the end of the year when things went super well. That certainly motivated me, although I did not work for these companies because of the bonus. If the bonus wasn't that high one particular year, it did kind of bother me.

Christian: Why should you work for less money? Why should the boys suddenly play soccer without pay?

Michael: As the head of the company, I have some ideas about how to deal with this, since I naturally intervene in the motivation equation with a bonus payment.

Christian: Yes, right. It was of course a trick question whether you are intrinsically or extrinsically motivated. The question behind this is the question of wherefore. That can vary from task to task.

Michael: In the end, that's my decision, too.

Christian: Right. If I work for a company where I am exclusively motivated extrinsically, my Purpose, Vision, and Values would not fit the company either.

Michael: I myself and my life plan would not fit the company. In such a case, I don't even need to start working there, do I? They probably wouldn't even want me there.

Christian: In the best case, you would not want to work there.

Michael: I agree.

Christian: Let's think the whole thing through a little further. Employees that I hire as managers are basically intrinsically motivated, otherwise I wouldn't hire them. So it is my job as a manager to prevent them from being extrinsically demotivated.

Michael: Great. I'll remember that. I rely on intrinsic motivation when recruiting employees and making sure that they are in line with our Purpose, Vision, Values, and Strategies. Then I just mustn't mess up anything with any extrinsic elements.

Christian: Of course it is relatively easy to say, "My team is not particularly motivated right now, let's introduce a bonus plan."

Michael: I experience this often in coaching. Companies are really stepping on the gas and suddenly they reach the point where the motivation of the employees is at its lowest. How did you deal with that?

Christian: I would rather answer another question instead, for example, "How would I deal with it now?" Now I would ask myself, "How do I recognize that my employees are motivated? How do I recognize that motivation went down the toilet?"

Michael: For example, you notice people are in a bad mood. There is very little laughter, people are sick more often, they go home earlier, they do not work overtime, or only very unwillingly. The drive is gone, the fire has gone out.

Christian: I may have set up an extrinsic demotivation program. You say, "The employees do not smile." Do I smile as a boss? You also said: "The employees do not work overtime." Do they even have to work overtime?

Michael: We're back to the topic of *perception is projection*. What I radiate as a boss is what I get back. We reap what we sow. The example I set and the beliefs I convey influence those around me. So what can I focus on to make sure I succeed? It is exhausting to decide to go ahead as a boss, to smile more, to step on the gas, and have fun.

Christian: And finally, as a boss you are paid for having a not very exhausting job. [*grins*]

Michael: Yeah, I guess that's true. [*laughs*]

Christian: How did the saying go? *You are not paid just to have pleasant conversations.*

Michael: It may help me remember who I am and what motivates me. I can approach this through the different personality types, through the Insights Model types, and through the color energies. I have a preference for red. Results and performance are important for me. For yellow energy, having fun is important. So I can think about what is fun for each employee, for the whole team and the company culture. There are three basic motivators that arise from the need for performance, power, and belonging. For some people performance is something very motivating, for others it is power, and for others it is belonging to a group. So I try to understand where we stand as a company and as a team regarding these three points and where each individual stands. I look through the psychic glasses and consider how I can motivate the team and each individual employee.

Christian: When we discussed motivators, corporate events, celebrations, or bonus topics at *chicco di caffe*, we always had one thought in mind: "Happy employees are not more productive than unhappy employees. However, productive employees are happier." That's the first motivator, the performance aspect you mentioned. This is also about the so-called topgrading. We will come back to this in more detail later. Employees want to perform and achieve results. My job as the boss is to let them do that.

Michael: Performing is not necessarily hard work. It is about results. It's about relaxed productivity, easy going, "fluffy" performers.

Christian: It is even easier when I get rid of the productivity blockages. How can I make it even easier for my employees to be productive? What about power in the company? If someone is motivated by power, is it an extrinsic motivation?

Michael: That's another trick question, isn't it? I think motivation through power is also intrinsic. Some people have an intrinsic need for power, others don't. In this case, if I suddenly have no more power because something has changed, if there are suddenly different conditions due to external effects, then I am missing something. This is ultimately about fulfilling needs. Every person has needs that have to be fulfilled in order to be motivated.

Christian: So I can very easily demotivate extrinsically on the matter of power as well?

Michael: Absolutely, good question. I can withdraw power.

Christian: I can also withdraw belonging.

Michael: Right, I can exclude someone from a group. That leads directly to demotivation. "From now on you are no longer part of this group, this team. Thank you for your help." Boom, motivation gone. If someone is motivated by belonging, I can motivate them by belonging to a group, by working on common subjects. Belonging, power, and performance. It all depends on what motivates each individual in the particular situation.

Christian: So for me as a manager, it's all about finding and hiring intrinsically motivated employees and then not extrinsically demotivating them.

Michael: What do you think about celebrating success? How does that help me to motivate employees? Or is it rather just a reinforcement?

Christian: Some of my employees actually once said that they would rather have a higher salary or a bonus instead of the Christmas party. I don't believe that such events motivate, they are simply fun. The question is, what is the goal of a Christmas party? Are we doing it because we've always done it this way or because that's the way it's done? Or do I have a Christmas party because I like to celebrate with my employees?

Michael: My theme was yes, *celebrate success*. It's all about recognizing what has been achieved. We were just talking about the situation when motivation and the mood is rather low. How do I get out of it? I often wondered how I could recognize that motivation was down. I reflected again on our Purpose, our Vision, our Values, and our Strategies and asked myself what we have achieved in the last three, six and twelve months. What achievements can we be proud of? We have achieved these successes together as a team and have thus also made a difference in the world. When I think about it, I quickly realize that it is quite a lot that we have achieved. Now we can all take a deep breath and enjoy it. Often we think ahead and plan the future. The focus is on "more, more, and even more." I take great pleasure in occasionally looking back on the successes and acknowledging them. From time to time I do this for myself, more often with my team. It has to do with appreciation. *Smell the roses*. Just pause, have a coffee in peace, and enjoy the sun.

Christian: Yes, you are right. There is a big difference between acknowledging the performance and successes that were achieved together in the company and saying, "It wasn't that bad."

Michael: "It wasn't that bad." Look what we have achieved, we can be proud of it. Now we're taking big steps forward. In some situations, it is helpful to look back and be happy about how far we have come, how high we have already gotten on our way to the summit of Mount Everest and where we once started. Half a year ago we thought all this was impossible. There is absolutely no reason to be demotivated. We can still manage the rest.

Christian: From now on I will give you one euro for every podcast we do. [*thinks about it*] Better not.

Michael: That doesn't get us anywhere. In a few months, we can go out for ice cream together. My treat.

Christian: We remain intrinsically motivated to do the podcasts.

Michael: Absolutely, I'm getting up early again tomorrow for the next podcast, with a smile on my face.

Christian: I am happy. It is amazing what we have already achieved. This is actually already podcast recording number 44.

Michael: That's awesome. Celebrate success.

Christian: Incredible.

I prefer to work with intrinsically motivated employees. They usually like to go the extra mile because they enjoy their work and find fulfillment in it. Alignment with Purpose, Vision and Values is a good way to select the right team members during the recruiting process. However, it is a fine line to extrinsically demotivate these employees, because of course intrinsically motivated employees also want to be adequately rewarded. So where is the border between the two? At what point is a bonus or a salary increase an extrinsic demotivation and at what point is it an appropriate appreciation? So it's my job to continuously ensure that my employees' "wherefore" is always their contribution to fulfilling the Purpose. As soon as the money alone is the answer to the wherefore, the mood tips. Then it only feels like compensation for pain.

3.

LEADING

TEAMS

WORLD-CLASS-HIGH-PERFORMANCE-VIRTUOSO-KICK-ASS TEAMS

CONFLICT ABILITY

DIVERSITY LEADS TO CONFLICTS AND FROM THESE ARISE BETTER RESULTS

Christian: We talked about the fact that, as a manager, I hire employees who are intrinsically motivated, fit the company Values, Purpose, and Vision. We also discussed that each employee has individual preferences. So how do I turn a number of individual employees, who all fit me in their individuality, into a *high-performance-kick-ass team*?

Michael: That is a very good question. At the beginning, we start with each employee in their individuality, as you just said. At what point is a team really a team? Which step turns a group of people into a team?

Christian: Worst case, I'm a team myself.

Michael: Team of one. I'm not sure if that meets the definition. What brings a team together and makes a group of people an awesome team that does great things? There are various terms for that: *world-class-team, kick-ass team, functional team* and *high-performance-team* are often used in the literature. Then there is the term *virtuoso teams.* There is a good book with the same title.35 Personally, I can think of a whole lot of things about this topic.

Christian: Let's start with the first component.

Michael: The first component is already familiar to our readers. *This is how we are gonna run this company.* Our joint master plan consists of Purpose, Vision, Values, and Strategies.

Christian: The team knows why we are a team, what is expected of us, and why we do all this. A team has a common master plan.

Michael: Exactly. The team knows that we are doing all this for a common Purpose. Everyone gets up in the morning for the same Vision, goes to work for the same reason, shares the same core Values, and has the same

---

35   *Virtuoso Teams: Lessons from Teams that Changed Their Worlds*, Pearson Education, 2005.

understanding of how we want to work together and what we're working on. We all want to achieve the same goals.

Christian: Basically, the tools and techniques I use to move a team in a certain direction are the same ones I use for my company and for myself. *This is how we are gonna run this company:* Purpose, Vision, Values, Strategies. It is not a big difference.

Michael: That's right, the essential ingredients are there. Depending on the size of the company, we go one level deeper at team level, for example, using the Stop-Start Continuity Model. We have often used the master plan with Purpose, Vision, Values, and Strategies at the team level in a similar or even the same way as it was formulated at the company level. In a team, however, a few things are added at the human level. We are currently still very functional in the description of what makes a team and what binds it together. Another component for a successful team is the handling of conflicts. This insight was surprising for me at the time. Because conflicts are actually necessary to achieve better results as a team.

Christian: Aha. Does that mean it's good if the employees argue all the time?

Michael: Let's call it healthy conflicts. It's about the ability of the team to deal with healthy conflicts in a certain way. It is important to allow a variety of opinions and positions that will lead to a better outcome in the end than without a conflict situation. The Insights Model is a good example to explain this. A colorful team with different personality types is always more successful in the end than a monotonous team in which all members have a similar character and the same color energy. The more colorful the team, the better.

Christian: How do I create this kind of conflict in the team?

Michael: By building a colorful team. It's similar to building a soccer team. I analyze which personality types, characters, and skills are already present in my team to represent everyone. I pay special attention to the characters that are still missing when hiring new employees. In the past, I would not have done this. Back then I was rather afraid of too many conflicts that can arise from the diversity of people when they are supposed to come together, work together, and achieve results. Today, I do this very consciously and make sure that we are as different as possible. I also communicate this quite openly to the team. Everyone knows about it and there is a high appreciation for the differences between colleagues. Each one makes a contribution in their own way, which leads to us creating something in the team that goes beyond the abilities of each individual. We create more than what each of us could have achieved alone or in a group consisting of the same types.

Christian: So I find employees who are as different and confrontational as possible, put them together in an office and say, "You are now a team." My feeling tells me that this could lead to difficulties. Isn't there something else missing?

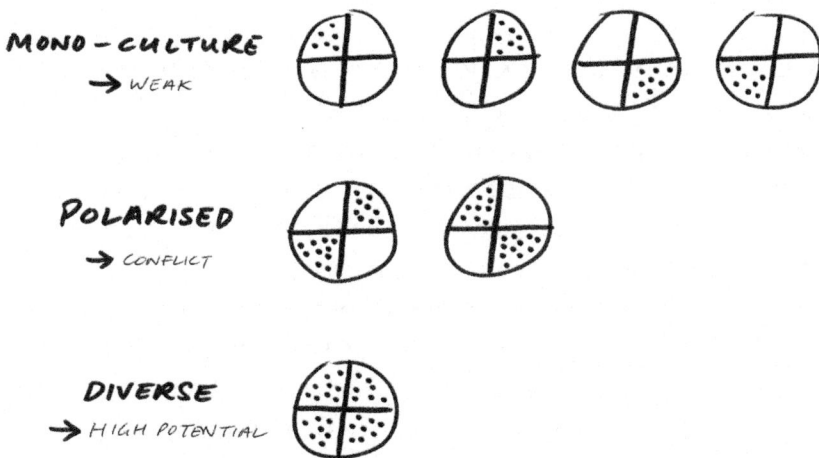

Illustration: Diverse teams
The highest performance is achieved by a diverse team if we succeed in appreciatively transforming the conflicts arising from greater diversity into even better results.

Michael: Yes, there are still a few components. A common Purpose, a Vision, and a common understanding of Values. This point really bears repeating over and over again. Common Values are especially crucial. Different personality types are not the same as different Values. As boss, I make sure that everyone on the team is aware of this difference. All team members show appreciation for the diversity of each individual and, at the same time, understanding for the similarity in terms of the code of Values. We all believe in the same Values and may live them out in different ways. This combination leads to a better result. The trick to ensure that the members of such a diverse team aren't at each other's throats is that everyone knows how it works. There are great diversity training programs that are based on personality types like *Insights* or similar models. Such approaches that keep the Values at the center of a team's efforts do a lot for the success of the team.

Christian: What do you think about trust? I just imagine what it would be like to be part of such a team. We have the same Values and share a common Purpose. Now I also need trust in the team, in my colleagues, that they are really working in the same direction and contributing to our Purpose. I think trust is an important component of a high-performance team. How do I achieve this?

Michael: Yeah, you're right. In fact, trust may be the first, most important component. Everyone on the team can trust each other. Of course, team building is key. We go somewhere for a day, go on a scavenger hunt in the forest, one is blind, the other is mute, and so on. It's also really fun for half a day. There are other ways to build trust, such as the Lifeline Method. We have already discussed this and we both use it very often. Everyone on the team takes turns telling their personal story to get to know each other better. For five to ten minutes, each person talks about who they are, what makes them special, what they have experienced, and what has shaped them. The others listen carefully. Everyone can truly unwrap everything: Where do I come from? Where am I going? What do I actually want to achieve in life? What is important to me? What have I learned? When in my past have I ever had bad luck? Which special moments have remained in my memory? I am a big fan of lifelines. I learn an enormous amount about the person and about myself.

Christian: Trust means that I can show myself to be vulnerable. I also share the things that didn't go so well in life. That way the others understand that even though I am the boss, things don't always run smoothly, it's not always sunny. Usually, when I need to show someone my resume, I tend to only include all the things that are top-notch: I was top of my class, studied the most difficult things, etc. Basically, I really show off my skills to make myself look good. And to build trust and really get to know each other, it is important to show that not everything is shiny.

Michael: I agree with that. As the boss, I also have the responsibility to set a good example and provide an authentic figure for a meaningful cause. The moment I share something from my life, I take a leap of faith. I tell them things that I wouldn't actually talk about in public. I open up to my team and give them an insight into my history and my personality, including my weaknesses. Of course, I hope that the individual people in the group will acknowledge this accordingly. If someone introduces himself to me bragging and telling me about all the great things he has done, my trust will decrease rather than increase. The five percent of topics that I don't usually want to tell or only tell my best buddy are often the ones that build up team trust.

Christian: To build trust in the team, are you doing this lifeline exercise, the one where everybody shares what went well and what didn't go so well in life?

Michael: Yes. Maybe I'll briefly explain later how the exercise works exactly. A fixed time window is important. All participants have time to prepare their lifelines in peace. Some need a little more time, others want to start right away. Those who are rather fast will start. This provides a framework for each preference and personality type. Then it goes round in turns. Each participant has the same amount of time to tell her lifeline, about five to ten minutes. Seven minutes plus one minute for questions is best. With a team of seven people, it is 7 x 7 minutes = 49 minutes + 7 minutes for questions. So after about an hour, everyone has heard from everyone else how their lives have been. It is super exciting and a lot of fun. When I do this exercise, I often go first to make sure everyone understands how it works from the start. The others are then often very surprised about how in depth I go and think, "Wow, is he really telling us this?" So they all feel just as free and also go very deep into their lifeline.

Christian: I also always come out of this exercise very overwhelmed, because it is impressive how quickly and deeply I can get to know and understand people through it.

Michael: I get to know a person just by what they decide to share. Each person consciously decides what he or she will talk about in the round. This choice alone says a lot about that person. At the same time, I learn a lot about myself through the choices I make. I reflect on what I am talking about to demonstrate vulnerability and openness, to build trust. It is a beautiful exercise in self-reflection.

Christian: Let me come back to the beginning. We now have the right employees, a diverse team, confidence, and a clear direction moving forward. What else do I need for a successful team?

Michael: I can think of another important point about conflict ability. It's important to be able to give each other feedback, to be able to discuss things openly. It makes sense to introduce an appropriate mechanism for this. This could be a 360-degree feedforward, for example, in which everyone tells what strengths the person has and which things are not among their strengths, so that everyone is aware of them. Another possibility is 1:1 conversations to create a feedforward culture and to be able to say things openly in a safe environment. We both often talk about the fact that it is much more important to encourage each other and speak in a positive language than to talk about weaknesses or areas of improvement. It may well be part of our principles to give feedforward and to constantly encourage each other. "You're doing a really great job, you're really good at it..." If I notice that someone is perhaps standing in their own way at some point, I can say, for example, "If you pay more attention to this, in the future you will go further." Just this whole communication box that we've been talking about.

Christian: What is also important is how decisions are made within the team. Do I make the decisions alone? Do we decide together? Do you decide? These are the famous questions that are often not clear. It is important that the decisions made are supported and accepted by the team, even though they may not correspond to my own opinions or I may have voted against them. The others can rely on me to support every decision made by the team.

Michael: Absolutely, that's super important. I can think of one more aspect of all the methods and models. As the boss, it is my responsibility to bring all these models, methods, and techniques into the team and to encourage them. And so, little by little, the team brings in its own ideas and methods that help us work well together. As the boss, I am responsible for the way we work together. I am accountable. I may encourage it so that this way of working becomes established in the team. I have learned another great saying and have painstakingly learned how to put it into practice: *Get out of the way*.

As the boss, I may get out of my people's way and trust that they will get it done without me always being involved and believing that I can do it better. One of my superiors once gave me a really good feedforward that made an impression on me. He said, "Michael, you have a really awesome team there, you do incredibly good things, you use all these methods, and even develop your people further. That is really great. One thing that you can do more is get out of the fucking way." Let people do their own thing and pull yourself out a little bit. *Get your hands off*. That was hard for me back then.

Christian: Just don't interrupt work.

Michael: Exactly: *Let them do their job*.

Christian: I am thinking about: *Get out of the shower* when it comes to coaching. Now it is: *Get out of the way*. It seems to go on like this.

Michael: *Get out*.

Christian: Just let it get done. That is also trust, to have confidence in the team and show them: "You'll do it." Maybe they do it differently than I expected. So what?

Michael: In the end, management is all about getting results and retaining employees.

Christian: What else do we need for a *kick-ass team*?

Michael: Advancement. That is also my task as boss. To grow myself, and above all, to ensure that there are enough opportunities for my employees to develop themselves and learn new things. It is my job to stimulate curiosity, to encourage curiosity in the team, and to try out new methods. This means I'm constantly learning and developing myself. This is something I really like and have fun with in our partnership, Christian, because you enjoy these things as well. These opportunities ensure that I feel comfortable in a team when I realize that I can move forward, develop, and grow personally, even as a boss. The spirit of being able to develop as a person in a team, to exchange new ideas and be open for new things is what makes a great team.

Christian: Great. I'm really excited about what I can learn from you in the next chapter.

One thing is becoming increasingly clear to me: how much the behavior of the team, the performance, the trust and motivation of each individual depends on me as the boss. No wonder that so many employees repeatedly state in studies that they leave a company not because of the job, but because of their boss. It's obviously not my job to always lead with good performance, to show the best results, and to have an answer to every question. I become an excellent role model due to my personality, my humanity, and how I shape the team. Showing weaknesses, having confidence, listening, self-reflection and ongoing education, responding to different personalities, valuing differences, as well as dealing with conflict – all these are not only core competencies of a manager, but also useful for any human being. With these skills I contribute to a better world.

TRUST FROM UNDERSTANDING

THE TEAM AS A YOKE

Christian: In this chapter we talk about teams. TEAM is the abbreviation for *together everyone achieves more*. That is why teamwork is so popular. After all, as a team we are responsible for the result together. So if I don't feel like it, I can hide in a team and let the others work. That's what you always say in your workshops.

Michael: Is that it? Well, then we're done.

Christian: Why do I work on teams at all? I could do it all alone.

Michael: Your question reminds me of a situation many years ago. At that time, I explained to my boss that I would like to take on leadership responsibility. He then asked me, "How come?"

Christian: For my resume.

Michael: That would actually have been the honest answer. My gut feeling at the time told me that I wanted to lead a team. I wanted to develop in that direction and learn to lead a team. When he asked me this question, I answered, "I want to do something that is bigger than what I can do alone." In retrospect, I think the answer was not so bad. At the time, it felt unspectacular, but it was true. I was able to achieve goals with my team that I would never have achieved on my own. At that time, I wanted to learn how it worked.

Christian: That is the point at which I developed, for example, from a freelancer or a self-employed person to an entrepreneur. I hire more employees, expand my business, and can therefore do more things and achieve greater goals than I can on my own. My company is growing, and tasks and projects are developing in a way that I can no longer manage alone. I build teams that can implement these projects and that become more and more specialized as the company develops.

Michael: Yes, they are also becoming more human. People are fundamentally more group oriented. I can't really survive on my own. It would be boring. We can do more as a group than we can alone. Only in this way has mankind come so far in the first place, thanks to collaboration among groups and teams.

Christian: On a team, there are other people besides myself who are good at other things. They have a different personality type than I do, along with different strengths. All these different strengths, energies, and power can be bundled in a team. I can think of a nice story about this. May I tell it?

Michael: Please.

Christian: I was at a wedding a while ago. When the priest started to preach, most people automatically went into a kind of snooze mode. Then the priest stood up on top of his pulpit and said very loudly, "Marriage is a yoke." All the wedding guests were suddenly wide awake and alert again. All thought, "A yoke? Like a yoke?" That sounded very negative at first. He explained that a yoke is a tool with which two animals—oxen or donkeys—can combine their strength and plough better together than alone. The yoke makes them stronger together than each of them separately. Marriage is a yoke through which two people combine their strengths to get through life together better than alone. In this sense, a team is also a yoke. Through a team, I can also manage to combine the energy and power of different personalities, competencies, and strengths, thus "plowing" to achieve the company mission better.

Michael: Thanks for the mental picture, I will order a yoke for my wife and me from Amazon later! I'm just imagining what it would look like on a team if we all were to use such a yoke and plow through the office. A beautiful picture. Of course, this also requires trust. Both my wife and the people on a team can trust that we are all plowing in the same direction with the yoke holding us together.

Christian: If this is not true, it does not work.

Michael: Then the yoke becomes a pretty sucky experience.

Christian: I don't even dare say it. I do it anyway. How do I "subjugate" my employees in the sense of working in tandem like the oxen do with a yoke?

How do I bundle all my energy on a team? There is an infinite amount of literature on this topic, and things can go wrong.

Michael: For me, trust is the most important thing. It's key to have confidence that the yoke has a Purpose and that we can achieve something positive with it, because I put my work, my energy, and my strength at the service of the common enterprise. We have put together a team and have already agreed on the big issues. We have a common Purpose, we fight for the same Vision, we have a fundamentally consistent set of Values, and have defined Strategies that we want to achieve. Now the question arises how to deal with interpersonal issues. A trainer once said, "Where there are people, there is *peopling*." People are different and people are imperfect. This causes friction and conflict which is what the trainer used the term *peopling* for. I like that sentiment, it's true. So we are again talking about the diversity of people. How do I now deal with *peopling*, with human differences, imperfections and the resulting friction? How do I humanize as a leader?

Christian: I'll come back to the topic of trust. When we talked about Values, we realized that it is important that everyone has the same understanding of Values, including trust. Nevertheless, everyone has a different picture of trust. When I think of trust, I think of a climbing harness.

Michael: I think of a handshake where I look someone in the eye.

Christian: Yes, exactly. We can agree that trust is good. Yet we still have different images in our minds. How can I recognize that there is enough trust within a team to work well together?

Michael: I was just thinking about a story you once told in a workshop about a boss. You said that he not only knows all his people by name, but he also knows exactly where they are in life, what their children's names are, and so on. He is in total contrast to another boss who just talks about how awesome his team is and what results he has achieved and basically doesn't know much more than that about his team members. It's a sign of trust when the team members really know each other and get involved with each other. It is a sign of recognition. Knowing each other is a good prerequisite for working well together. When I know someone, it is easier for me to recognize their role in the team. It is easier for me to accept and appreciate what they bring to the team in terms of content and expertise and as a person.

Christian: To *humanize* ultimately means to acknowledge one's counterpart as human.

Michael: Yeah, the people on my team aren't like batteries that I put in somewhere. They're all valuable, interesting, unique people. I want to get to know them. Everyone has their preferences and decides how much they want to reveal. The lifeline exercise is great for introducing yourself to a new team. I like doing this exercise when I join a new team as a coach. This way, everyone gets to know each other a little better. Even when I do it with teams that have known each other for ten years, the pennies still drop and everyone learns even more about the others. I once did the lifeline exercise with a team that has known each other for over 20 years. It was amazing. Even after 20 years, they still learned new things about their colleagues and have seen themselves in a new light ever since. Everyone was very surprised how much it helped to strengthen and build trust even more. The first step in a team is to reveal something about yourself in order to get to know each other and build trust. As the boss, I always go ahead in such rounds and start with my own lifeline. I'm practically the first to let my guard down to signal, "I'm ready to open up. I am also vulnerable."

Christian: That's what building trust is all about, showing vulnerability and letting your guard down. That's why it's important to mention in the lifeline story where things didn't go so well in life. It is also significant to share weaknesses or difficult times in one's life. In the business environment, we often tell people how great everything is going and how terrific we are, especially in a job interview. Well, in a job interview, I wouldn't show myself vulnerable, of course, unless it is specifically asked about difficult situations in life. Later down the road, it helps to be vulnerable in order to build trust. The employees realize, "The boss is also just an ordinary person."

Michael: When the boss presents and reveals these things about himself and becomes vulnerable, it is a sign for me as an employee that I can do it, too.. Implicitly, it's a permission. If the boss does it that way, it is also permitted for me. In the past, during the lifeline exercise, I often asked the question about the highlights and the lowlights, i.e., the difficult situations in life. Today, I ask what I have learned from different situations. Of course, this is mostly related to the highs and lows, because I often learn the most from dramatic situations, from particularly positive and particularly negative experiences. Therefore, today I pose the question, "What have I learned that will help me for the future?" As a team, we want to achieve something together in the future and not chat about the past, about old stories. It's about creating a basis for achieving our goals together.

Christian: Let's come back to my original question. How do I recognize that there is enough trust in the team? We have not yet answered this question. We have talked about how I can build trust in the team. What makes a team in which the members trust each other more successful compared to a team where there isn't such a dynamic?

Michael: Relaxed productivity. The team with enough trust achieves more with less conflict. They find it easier to achieve their goals.

Christian: We have said that healthy conflicts are helpful.

Michael: Right, absolutely. They are even necessary. Healthy conflicts are great. At least conflicts over content, where we can still go out together in the evening and eat and drink something together. Healthy, content-related conflicts, not human ones.

Christian: And for that I need trust?

Michael: Yes, and understanding.

Christian: I can more easily resolve a conflict on the factual level if I know that the other person means well and that we have the same goal. Confidence in pursuing the same goal and wanting to run in the same direction is important.

Michael: Also, understanding and appreciation for otherness. This is also a part of trust. I used to have a hard time trusting people who are completely different than I am. I learned over time that otherness is useful and contributes to my own goals. Now I have confidence that *different* is a positive attribute. Now I appreciate discussions in which someone takes a completely different position than I do, because it gives us strength actually have a discussion, to find a compromise that is perhaps a better solution than my own way of doing things. It's about understanding that being different is enriching for a team. That was a great learning experience for me.

Christian: Because of this trust, I can lead conflicts on the factual level and then make a decision to solve the conflict. I can trust that we all go in one direction, even if I alone would have preferred a different solution. I carry this decision with me because I know that we all pursue the same goal.

Michael: That brings us to the topic of decision-making processes. Everyone is involved. I trust you completely.

Christian: I'll buy us a yoke now.

Michael: I fully understand that.

Christian: Then there is no conflict anymore.

Everybody is familiar with these team-building events that you mentioned in this chapter: Walking around in the forest and letting yourself fall backwards, hoping that someone from the team will catch you. Surely one or the other can get something out of it and it is meaningful to spend time together outside the office, to experience something together. However, I am just realizing how wasted this time is when I do nothing to actively build up honest trust. I am beginning to understand the importance of methods such as the Lifeline Exercise, the Insights Model, mutual reflection, and the expression of individual strengths. Maybe that's why these team events have such a bad reputation: they are rarely structured properly.

HIRE SLOW

IT'S ALL ABOUT ATTITUDE

Christian: *Hire slow and fire fast*. This saying means that I should think carefully about who I hire and take my time. If I find that someone doesn't fit into the company and I want to fire them, I should react quickly. We will talk about the second point in more detail later.

Michael: What do I do when my reality looks exactly the other way around? Often, I desperately need someone. At the same time, I realize that a certain employee does not fit into the company, yet I cannot bring myself to dismiss her. I often observe behavior based on the principle of *hire fast and fire slow*. [*smiles*] It's not so easy to put it that way.

Christian: What is the reason why you want to fill a position as soon as possible? Do you think the work will be done faster then?

Michael: Well, I have a lot of red energy and I like to make decisions quickly. I am also willing to take risks. *Hire slow* has really stuck in my craw. I have become much more careful when hiring new employees.

Christian: At *chicco di caffe* we have hired a lot of new employees in a short time. Unfortunately, we made a few mistakes at the beginning. We saw someone we liked because she looked as if we had seen her before or perhaps she went to the same university as me or worked at Starbucks before.

Michael: What's the part of our brain called again that makes these super-fast decisions? Amygdala?

Christian: The reptilian brain?

Michael: Yes, it is a primeval behavior to make a decision in a blink of an eye. I need something right now, really urgently. *Fight or flight*, run away or fight. The decision must be made now. In such cases, a part of our brain takes control that sometimes would have been better left at home that day.

Christian: This approach can work for a while. At *chicco di caffe,* Ralf and I did all the interviews ourselves at the beginning. At that time, we had a pretty good feeling about who would fit and who would not. As we grew and had more and more employees, they also did some of the hiring. This made things much worse, which is why we quickly started to set up a strict process. First of all, a telephone interview was conducted with each applicant to find out if she wanted to work for us at all, whether the working hours and locations were suitable, and whether the salary was roughly the desired amount. We have had many crazy experiences. One of our employees was already pretty much hired. When we then talked about where he would be deployed, he said, "Well, in Ulm." We replied in bewilderment, "Ulm? No, Munich." That's why we clarify such essential aspects right at the beginning in the first phone call. This is followed by a personal conversation, which includes a visit to the coffee bar. In the basement of our headquarters, we had a really nice test bar. Here we held training days to see what the applicants could and couldn't do at the bar. For those who applied at the headquarters, we also arranged a "get-to-know-you" meeting where they got to know the respective colleagues personally and introduced themselves. Each colleague from the head office had a right of veto.

Michael: So you filtered very thoroughly to see if the basic things like work location, availability, and so on, fit. At that point it was still possible to find ourselves in the situation where the potential hire had a six-month notice period required at their place of employment and couldn't even start on time.

Christian: Right. We first clarified basic things like, "Do you even drink coffee?"

Michael: Was the first interview a telephone or video interview?

Christian: A telephone interview.

Michael: Then was the applicant allowed to come by and make coffee for you to see if she was even suitable for a coffee bar? After that, she had a chance to meet all the other employees who also got an impression of her, right?

Christian: Meeting the colleagues was only something we did for the applicants in the head office, like product management, marketing, and so on. The applicants were allowed to introduce themselves to them personally. There was a rule that every employee was allowed to veto. In a few cases, we bypassed the veto right and hired the applicant anyway. These were often wrong decisions, indeed. In these cases, we in management turned a blind eye and thought, "Oh come on, we've been through such a long process, it'll be fine." The employees had an inkling about whether or not the person would be a good fit. If we overrode them, it was always bad.

Michael: So it's a systemic approach, where several people contribute to the decision-making process and it's not just the boss making the decision.

Christian: Right. It was important to me that we have a process that is not depending on me and, above all, not depending on my daily mood, on my emotional state. If I go into a job interview with the thought that I absolutely need someone, I'm more likely to hire someone, even if he or she doesn't fit perfectly.

Michael: I like that. We did it similarly. In addition, we had a very comprehensive job description for each role. It was very annoying at the beginning and cost me a lot of time. It was a very analytical and extensive task. At that time, I first had to think about a structure for my team, along with which roles and competences I actually needed for my marketing team. Then I formulated a one- or two-page role description for each position. The shorter I tried to make the job description, the harder it was. I tried to put it in a nutshell so that I could validly query and test it later in the selection process. It cost me several hours of time. It was good preparation for the interviews because I knew exactly who I was looking for, what skills I was looking for, and what I wanted to ask in the interviews. Then, a similar process followed as you described. The applicants were pre-selected and filtered through telephone interviews. They were then invited to an full-day recruiting event where they met seven, eight, nine, or even ten people from the company. In this way, both the candidate and the ten colleagues were able to gain a good impression of each other. Each of the ten colleagues then assessed how well the candidate fit in with our company, our culture, and our Values. We will talk about this later when we talk about TEV. It's good if not only one person evaluates the talent, experience, and Value fit, but if several people make an estimation. It is especially important to hear several opinions about the V, the Values fit. I have had an experience similar to the one you are describing. Whenever I disregarded the estimation of my colleagues, especially with regard to Values, I regretted it.

Christian: This job description you mentioned is called a *scorecard* in some systems. In the end, it is about making the implicit knowledge about a role in the company explicit. The implicit knowledge about which skills help to achieve the goals. The goal of such a scorecard is to make the decision about hiring an employee regardless of my personal daily condition and presence. For example, our scorecards state the mission of the position, and the difference and/or contribution the position makes to our Vision and Purpose. For me, the best part of the scorecard is the goals. We have included them in very concrete terms. What goals does the new employee receive from day one for the next three to six months? Of course, we have formulated these as SMART Goals. Once I had this scorecard in my interview, I could ask about exactly these requirements and decide whether or not I believed this person would achieve these goals in the first three months.

Michael: It helps a lot if the goals are clear and the metrics are defined to measure it. The candidate can also see her own success as an employee from this later. I just remembered something about the application process that has often worked well. From time to time, we put candidates in unusual situations and observed how they behaved. Values express themselves primarily through behavior. My Values determine my behavior. The classic example is a restaurant visit with the entire team. We observe how the candidate behaves in the team, at the table, towards the waiter and the staff. We have created another, somewhat more unusual situation, by inviting her to our coffee bar. We had a small café on our campus. Walter, one of our baristas, engaged the candidates in a chat and invited them for a coffee. The candidates thought they would just have a cappuccino and see how things were going here. Of course we didn't tell them anything about the actual Purpose of the action. Walter later gave us his feedback. We wanted to know what he thought of this person, because it happened again and again that applicants behaved differently towards their colleagues at the coffee bar than towards the board of directors in the executive floors. That says a lot about a person's Value system. When it came to filling a management position, there was also an additional interview with my boss, our CEO. I was CMO in this company at the time. This conversation didn't just take place at a desk in an office, they were always somewhat unusual situations. For example, the interview usually took place on the weekend. Many candidates were flown in and were accordingly on location for a few days. On a day off, we then scheduled the interview with the CEO, for example, in the pool of some five-star hotel.

Christian: In swimming trunks?

Michael: Yes. Culturally, it was not always possible to carry it out, and that's the most extreme example. Every applicant for an executive position had one and a half hours to talk to the CEO. Sometimes there was a pool bar and they would have a drink at the bar. Depending on the situation, the candidates also received an invitation to an extraordinary dinner, a private party, or a trip to the desert. The exciting thing is that many candidates already felt safe when they talked to the CEO of the company in such an environment, they were quite euphoric. In these circumstances, occasionally different behaviors come to light than under normal circumstances. It shows how well someone is in control of himself, can regulate his behavior, and can cope with the situation. Even if it is a conversation in a relaxed atmosphere, it is the CEO of the company who is sitting at the bar. It was cool and made an impression. It also helped our culture and showed how seriously we take the hiring process and that it is different at our company than in other companies. We were pretty colorful, so it fit in well with our employer brand.

Christian: You mentioned that applicants sometimes play pretend and act differently towards the CEO than towards the barista, for example.

Michael: Yes, consciously or unconsciously.

Christian: I think it is a good approach to extend the time span of the hiring process. For example, I see the probationary period as a kind of extension of the period to conduct interviews and get to know each other better. The candidates get to know the company and the colleagues get to know the new employee. Hopefully, most people find it difficult to pretend for six months.

Michael: My boss taught me a rule of thumb back then. He said, "You can assume that two thirds of all the people you hire are hiring mistakes." Two thirds are mistakes. At the time, I thought that I was sure that I was making the right decision 80%-90% of the time. I was good at it. Even after that, I was still convinced that despite the rule of thumb I would achieve a higher success rate, 50% at least. In retrospect, I can say that it takes years to fill a position optimally without making hiring mistakes. Reality caught up with me and our mantra was, as you also say, that I only really find out during the probationary period whether the person belongs to these two thirds or not. Our goal was to identify and say goodbye to 100% of these two thirds during the probationary period if possible. I apologized for the misjudgment and took responsibility. It is important to recognize the mistake and draw a line under it during the probationary period and to not cause any drama that drags on for years. That doesn't help anyone.

Christian: Either *yes, super,* or *no*. Whether before or after the probationary period, I only hire the person when I think, "Yes, super." The person will totally rock, "We absolutely want her." If it's more of a, "Well, it will do. Maybe she can still develop here and there," then, in my experience, it was always a hiring mistake. At the end of the probationary period I always ask myself the question, "Would I enthusiastically rehire this employee again or not?"

Michael: This is going towards topgrading. Actually, I only want A-players, only superstars on the team. After six months, I know if the employee is a superstar, or at least if the potential is there to become one. In most cases, during this time I have given feedback here and there to see how the person is handling it and gets going. Here's a nice analogy: When driving a car, I also know when it's time to pull over.

Christian: Absolutely. Number one is, I may be absolutely and mercilessly honest with myself at this point. Number two is to establish a system that allows me to ask these questions in order to get an honest answer from one round to the next.

Michael: So after six months, I have sufficient control over my amygdala (which wanted to make a decision within two seconds right at the beginning), and I'm ready to go. After six months, I have taken enough time for my cerebrum to make a mature decision. After six months of probation and the decisions made, do I have only top stars on the team? Have I made 100% correct decisions? Exceptions confirm the rule.

Christian: Obviously.

The more choices I have, the easier it is, of course, to let people go or not hire the candidates I'm not 100% sure about. However, if I only have a small selection of candidates and an urgent need for support, I am more willing to turn a blind eye. It's exactly in situations such as these when, from here on out, I'll need to remember your words: Hire slow and never out of desperation. Because the consequences are usually more painful for everyone involved. Besides, I always have a choice, eight to be exact.

THE RIGHT PEOPLE ON THE BUS
TALENT, EXPERIENCE, VALUES

Christian: Hello Michael, how are you?

Michael: Fantastic, thanks to the wonderful coffee you made me.

Christian: Yes, it is delicious. Life is just too short to drink bad coffee.

Michael: Absolutely. So thank you very much for this one.

Christian: You are very welcome. Speaking of coffee, how do I actually choose the right employees?

Michael: This is an exciting topic. Employee selection is a big issue, especially for companies in the growth phase. In fact it is true for all companies, no matter how fast or slow they grow. It's so crucial because the people I hire usually stay and it's easier to hire than to fire. So it can be quite expensive to make the wrong choice when selecting employees. I like to use the TEV model. It has proven itself over the years and I continue to use it very successfully. The three decisive parameters when hiring an employee are T (talent), E (experience), and V (Values).

Christian: I like these three-letter things: PPP, TEV, ...

Michael: The T stands for talent. What is talent for you?

Christian: A talent is innate. I either have a talent or I don't. I recognize it by "That's how I am" or "That's how I've always been" sentences. Things like, "I've always been bad at math." So, therefore, I have no talent for math.

Michael: So you're talking about things that are naturally easy for me. "Little Michael has a talent for playing the piano. It's just easy for him." For that reason it's worthwhile to keep sending him to piano lessons. Exactly. The T is the talent, a gift. Of course, I can learn anything without talent. Even without a talent for playing the piano, I can learn to play the piano very well. Without talent, it might be a bit harder for me, it takes longer and maybe I'm not quite as good as someone who is more talented than I and practices just as much.

So when selecting employees, I look to see if the candidate has talent. Talent also means to me, what kind of development can the person make in my company? What potential does this person have to assume other roles and more responsibility in the future? What role can the person grow into with the company? The second parameter is the E, which stands for experience. The question here is what the person has already done in the past and whether these experiences are useful for the role I am currently recruiting for in my team. For example, if someone has been programming Java for five years, he or she will have a capital E. They already have five years of experience. If I am looking for a Java programmer, this parameter is met.

Christian: Even though he may not have any talent for Java programming at all, he has experience. He may have a preference and the competence.

Michael: Absolutely. What we call preference and competence in psychological types correlates with what we understand as talent and experience in the TEV model. That's the E. If someone brings talent and experience, it's obviously a perfect combination. The third parameter is the V for Values-fit. The decisive factor here is not which Values the candidate has in detail, but whether the Values of this person fit with our corporate Values.

Christian: As we know, corporate Values tell us what makes our company. Based on the Values of employees and potential employees, I can see whether or not the candidate will be a good fit or not.

Michael: Values-fit is the keyword. A perfect fit with the company. How well do the Values of the individual fit with the Values of the company? If they fit well together, it indicates that the collaboration will work and good results can be achieved. If the Values do not fit together ideally, the collaboration tends to be more difficult. I use these three parameters to select new employees for my company. I evaluate the candidates in the interview and throughout the application process based on TEV: Talent, Experience, and Values-fit.

Christian: And how do you do that specifically when someone is sitting opposite you?

Michael: I ask questions to tap into the issues. I can't ask the applicant directly, "What are your Values?" I can certainly present the company Values and ask what the person thinks about them, in which situations he or she has lived these Values before. For example, I can ask how he or she makes decisions or whether further career steps are planned. Often decisions and motives reflect their own Values. It often shows where one or another preference lies, as well as revealing talents and experiences.

Christian: So you only hire people who have talent, experience, and a Value-fit?

Michael: Right. Ideally, yes. During the hiring process, I gather evidence of the *T, E,* and *V.* Depending on whether he has a lot or little talent, experience, or Values-fit, I write a big or small *T, E,* or *V* in my notebook. So if I notice during the conversation that someone has a lot of experience, I draw a capital *E* in my book. Of course, only if the experience matches the role for which I'm hiring. Ten years of experience in Java programming will only lead to a capital *E* if I am also looking for a Java programmer. The same goes for talent. If the talent is useful and I already have in mind where I see the person in perspective and where they can develop with this talent, I draw a big *T.* If it doesn't fit the roles I need, it's just a small *t.* It's the same with Values-fit, the *V.* When the person tells me about their motives and decisions in life, I get an impression of their set of Values. If my feeling tells me that it fits the company, I note a big *V.* At the end, I have three letter combinations in front of me in upper and lower case letters. I then draw my conclusions from this and make my decision.

Christian: What does the best rating look like?

Michael: The best thing that can happen to me is, of course, if the candidate brings a capital *T,* a capital *E,* and a capital *V.* Someone who is talented, has a lot of experience in relevant areas, and also fits in with our corporate Values; I hire this person immediately.

Christian: Sure, that's easy. So the worst combination is if you only wrote down small letters: little talent, little experience, and does not fit into the company.

Michael: This is where the crux starts. Of course, if someone has little talent, little experience, and is not a Value-fit, the decision is easy. Under no circumstances do I hire that person. There is one case that is worse. Maybe we will go through the other cases first. I'll leave this as a cliffhanger for a few minutes.

Christian: The worst case in the TEV model... coming soon! And not yet...

Michael: Right. What is the second best case? All the letters are capitalized, which is easy. This is the best case: TEV. The second best case is when someone has a lot of talent, rather less experience and fits well into the company, so a capital *T*, small *e* and capital *V*, TeV. Why is this the second best case? I can promote and enlarge the *e* through further education, development measures, coaching, training and so on. I can develop a small *e* into a big *E* relatively easily. It may take a little time and a little effort. It is absolutely feasible. Therefore TeV is the second best-case scenario.

Christian: Especially if the Value fit is right, it is feasible. Because then the person fits well into the company, I myself get along well with her in terms of Values and can manage and develop her well.

Michael: Exactly, and if talent is there, the person learns quickly and is eager to learn. It's easy for the person and they are motivated to acquire new skills. Skills is another word, by the way, that is often used today. Skills are competencies and competencies are experiences. The terms are therefore very close together. Another combination is tEV – little talent for other things, lots of experience in the role I'm looking for, and a Value fit for our company.

Christian: That means that she simply does what she has been doing so far, this time for our company. She also fits in with us.

Michael: Right. He fits into the company and does a great job in his role. I just can't expect that person to do anything else in a few months or to be flexible enough to adjust to different roles and move from marketing to IT and then to accounting. In the TEV model, this person is typically called a specialist. She is good at what she does and delivers brilliantly and is a good fit for the company. As long as I'm happy with that as a manager, she will probably be happy with it as well. The collaboration works. These were basically the most important combination options that work well: The specialist, the one who learns quickly and a lot, and the performer with all three capital letters. Let's come to the most difficult case. This occurs as soon as the *v* is small. Imagine talking to a candidate and thinking, "Wow, this is an absolute super talent with an impressive amount of experience. He could take on an incredible amount of work and really get us ahead. He's basically been doing this job for so many years. I could really use his talent and experience. I'm not so sure whether he fits into our company or not. Values-fit is difficult. It could be that he might clash with some team colleagues."

Christian: Well, if she really has that much experience and talent, I would hire her, wouldn't I?

Michael: I could think that. Experience shows that TEv is a dangerous time bomb. At least, the risk is very high. The company Values reflect all employees and our strengths. If someone doesn't fit in and doesn't get along well with their colleagues, things will go wrong at some point. They may be pursuing their own goals that don't fit in with those of the company and the team. Experience shows that it often goes wrong and leads to frustration and many conflicts.

In the TEV model we call this type the terrorist. Because other Values lead to other targets at the end of the day and an explosion occurs. Tev is a very dangerous case, which unfortunately is also not easy to detect. If I have a strange feeling about Values-fit, I don't hire the candidate.

Christian: That means you would never hire a little *v*?

Michael: No, never.

Christian: The other two parameters don't really matter, because I can gain experience and I can make up for talent with experience, right?

Michael: Basically, yes. However, a capital letter in addition to the capital *V* is necessary. Because without talent and without experience, it will be a long, arduous journey. Without talent, it's a specialist who may not necessarily grow with the company, but who still performs well and does a good job. Especially with talent I can quickly build up experience. That all fits quite well.

T = TALENT E = EXPERIENCE V = VALUES

$TEV \longrightarrow$ HIRE + KEEP   ✓ SUPERSTAR

$T\hat{e}V \longrightarrow$ HIRE + DEVELOP   ✓ APPRENTICE

$tEV \longrightarrow$ HIRE SPECIALIST   ✓ SPECIALIST

$TEv \longrightarrow$ FIRE FAST   ✗ ♂* TERRORIST (TIME BOMB)

$tev \longrightarrow$ FIRE   ✗ PARASITE

Illustration: TEV
These three simple criteria make the hiring process much easier for me: talent, experience, Values-fit.

Christian: *People like people who are like themselves*, we talked about it. If you do a Value check now, you are probably biased, aren't you? How do you approach it?

Michael: Yes, absolutely. Many years ago I was allowed to build up a marketing team with 40 people. I made the mistake of hiring mostly people who were similar to me. I liked these people and I didn't know all the psychological methods and leadership models yet. It was a total disaster. Today I am much more systemic. Systemic means for me that I am not the only one who interviews the applicants. On the contrary, I am thinking of a system that interviews the candidates. I ask a number of colleagues, employees, or co-partners to get to know the candidate. Maybe I even ask outside experts. I ask at least six or seven people who talk to the candidate and whose valuation I take into account. "Please tell me your estimation of *T, E,* and *V*." I then listen carefully and we discuss together, especially when it comes to the *V*. Some people use scales for their estimation, for example a score from one to ten. Anyone can do this as they please. My experience shows that when it comes to the Values-fit, it is more of a binary thing. Either zero or one.

Christian: Yes, super or no.

Michael: Right. And even if there is a two out of three match with the company Values, I'd rather leave it. Even with only one misfit of three Values, there's a high risk that it'll go bang sometime.

Christian: Great. After this interview, I will give you a big *T* for talent, a big *E* for experience in management, and a big *V*, because the Values-fit is also there: TEV.

I know of several rating systems that work in a similar way. However, most of them are very complex and try to objectify the candidate evaluation as much as possible. Regardless, this is not completely feasible; y there is always some gut feeling involved in the evaluation, no matter how many metrics and criteria I use. I like this very simple, pragmatic, and at the same time focused, approach. Before I start the selection process, I make it clear to myself which skills and personality I am looking for so that I can make the assessment as accurate as possible.

PEOPLE REVIEW
EMPLOYEE EVALUATION WITH TOPGRADING

Christian: We have already stated that we take our time when hiring new employees, *hire slow*. For example, I select new employees with great care using the TEV method. I don't want to hire someone just to have someone new; I want to build a world-class team. The team members should fit together with each other and with the company, be able to trust each other to work well together, and deliver better results than each individual could on his or her own. Now that I have found and hired these people, how can I evaluate them in our day-to-day business to help them develop?

Michael: There is the so-called HR cycle: hiring, developing, and firing. The topic you are describing right now is about the middle part, the advancement of employees.

Christian: Retain employees.

Michael: Right. Retaining the right employees. "Employee development" are the two keywords. How do I promote the team as a whole and how do I encourage each individual employee so that he or she can be an optimal player in our Virtuoso Team?

Christian: We wouldn't be bosses if there wasn't a 2x2 matrix for this.

Michael: Absolutely. Each model from the business school can be mapped as a 2x2 matrix. This model is called topgrading and was originally developed by General Electric. It has been circulating in management literature for 30 or 40 years and has proven to work really well in practice. We have been using it very successfully for many years, so it has become an absolute standard. Has this also been the case for you?

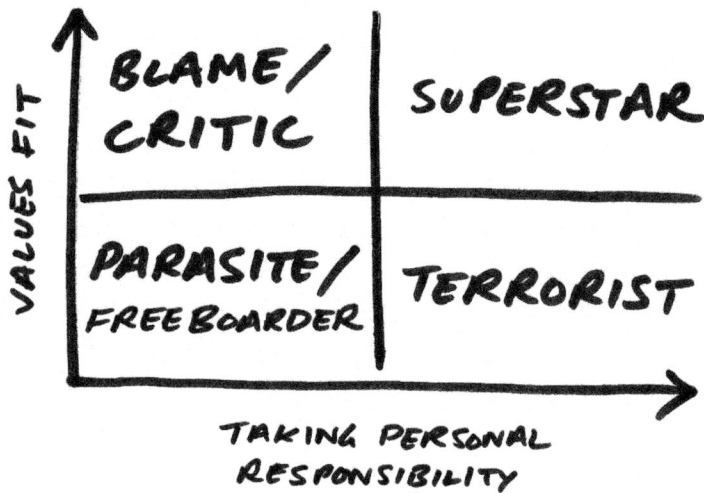

A hand-drawn 2x2 matrix. The vertical axis is labeled "VALUES FIT" and the horizontal axis is labeled "TAKING PERSONAL RESPONSIBILITY". The four quadrants are: top-left "BLAME/CRITIC", top-right "SUPERSTAR", bottom-left "PARASITE/FREE BOARDER", bottom-right "TERRORIST".

Illustration: Topgrading
With the topgrading model, I identify who fits my team, who I promote and who I better part with.

Christian: Yes, sure. The model divides employees into ABCD employees. We have also applied it very successfully at *chicco*. Every three months, we evaluate our employees in this system.

Michael: Wow, every three months. We did it only every six months. We showed it to the candidates when they were hired. We explained to them exactly how we manage our company and develop each employee. Then we explained to them the model with all four quadrants. However, we didn't call them A, B, C, and D as we originally did at General Electric, but we gave them more meaningful names. The A players were the *superstars* for us, the B players were labeled as *development cases*, so they still need some development. And we also had descriptive terms for C and D players.

Christian: Basically, only the A-players are really positive, right?

Michael: Yes, actually I only want A-players in my company. When I put together a soccer team, for example, a national team with which I absolutely want to win, I naturally need top people.

Christian: We often use the image of an orchestra. In an orchestra I need an A-player on the violin, an A-player on the oboe and I don't accept a D-player on the cello just because I might not hear it anyway. [*pause*] I apologize at this point to all cello players. I only want A-players in my orchestra and only A-players on my team.

Michael: So my job as a manager is to make sure that everyone becomes an A-player, and that way the whole team consists of A-players only.

Christian: What is an A-player anyway?

Michael: Good question. Let's introduce the axes of the model, then it becomes clear. As in any 2x2 matrix, there is an x-axis and a y-axis. The y-axis shows the Value fit, i.e., how well the person fits into the Values of our company. We talked about Values-fit and TEV in detail. There are various definitions on the x-axis. Which ones did you use?

Christian: I have always considered the model in the context of the goal of management. What is the task of management? To retain employees and to achieve results. That's why we have deduced on the y-axis, which runs upwards, how much the employee helps me to keep the team together. On the x-axis, which runs upwards, we evaluated how good the results she delivers are.

Michael: Cool.

Christian: You did it a bit differently, didn't you?

Michael: Yeah, just a little bit modified. Basically it comes down to the same thing. When you ask, "How much does the employee help to keep the team together?," you are referring to the company culture. And an essential mechanism for corporate culture is working with Values. So it is very similar to our version. On the x-axis you said you evaluate the results. I know another label for the performance of an employee. In the HR language, we often talk about performance management. On the x-axis, we evaluated how much someone takes personal responsibility. That worked best for us. Someone who takes matters into their own hands, takes responsibility for their actions and results. There is a particular reason why we did it this way. We'll come to that in a moment when we talk about the C and D quadrants.

Christian: In the sense of, "Did the person do their best to achieve this result?" That's what responsibility means at this point, right?

Michael: Then the x-axis would be something like *Effort*, i.e. how hard the employee tries. It definitely has something to do with the result, with performance, with responsibility. That describes the x-axis. Maybe we'll leave it at that for now and take a closer look later. Basically, everyone can decide what they want to write on the axes.

Christian: So there are the superstars, stars or A-players. In the matrix they are in the upper right quadrant. There I have a high Value fit, the employee fits very well into the company, and helps to retain other employees. At the same time, she puts the pedal to the metal, is good at what she does, and delivers great results responsibly.

Michael: A-players are allowed to do anything, as long as they stay in their A-quadrant and are superstars.

Christian: What do I do with them?

Michael: Hold, *keep them sweet*. Keep them sweet so that they can be cozy, not in the sense of relaxed, rather in the sense of: they feel at home and would like to stay at the company. That also means developing them further, giving them opportunities to take on other roles, perhaps promoting them. A promotion may also mean that they are allowed to leave the A-quadrant and work their way into their new role. Benefits such as a company car, public transport ticket, and so on can also help to keep someone sweet. *Keep them sweet.*

Christian: Removing obstacles also helps make your work easier. There is a great saying: *Happy employees are more productive and productive employees are happier.*

Michael: Very nice. I'll remember that.

Christian: That means I give A-players the chance to be productive by asking them, "How can I help you?"

Michael: Great, good mindset.

Christian: Absolutely, I can assume that A-players are most likely to constantly be on the lookout.

Michael: Sure, everybody wants A-players. Whether they perform as well elsewhere as they do here depends on the culture, on the manager, and on the company's leadership model with its Purpose, Vision, Values, and Strategies.

Christian: Correct. An A-player in my company can be evaluated and perform completely differently in another company.

Michael: Yeah, when I'm working as an A-player on something I don't believe in and I think it sucks, I'm probably only an A-player for a short time. At some point, my motivation suffers and so does my performance.

Christian: It can also happen the other way around. I don't get along at all in a company and am only a B or C player. If I then change the company, I suddenly become an A-player.

Michael: That is exactly the point. Imagine the case of you interviewing someone and finding out that they were fired from their last job. It just didn't work out there. Already a *self-fulfilling prophecy* sneaks in and there is the danger that I am imagining things, that I have prejudices, and that I let those prejudices become reality. This can have a positive outcome, because he may have had a good reason why he left. Maybe he is a superstar with us because our company works differently and our culture and Values are different.

Christian: Let's go to the next quadrant.

Michael: To the upper left quadrant. We also have a high Values-fit there, it fits our culture and helps us retain other employees. At the same time, performance, results, and the assumption of responsibility don't really work. How do we deal with B-players?

Christian: These are possibly employees who have not been with the company for that long and have not yet learned how we are productive and achieve results in the company. They may not know the structures yet.

Michael: You might not really trust them to be working to the best or most confident of their abilities *yet*, that could be the case. I can't necessarily expect someone who's new to the company to be an A-player right away, can I?

Christian: That depends on the task.

Michael: It's possible that the person may still learn something, maybe needs training for the new job first. Maybe the person still lacks a skill, maybe they lack a competence that is necessary to become an A-player. For instance, they aren't sufficiently networked yet or haven't made friends with other people quite yet. The heading of this quadrant is *Development*. In this case, I invest in the employee to quickly develop her into an A-player.

Christian: So I invest in her skills, abilities, training, and development. If that doesn't work out and she is still a B-player afterwards, maybe there is another issue.

Michael: It can also be a question of attitude. Another nice label for this quadrant is *blame-critic*. It is someone who constantly blames others or the world for their own failures, their own mistakes. This person is not *at cause* of their life, rather in the role of the victim. She constantly criticizes others or complains about the circumstances. Such people are good at assigning blame and criticizing others. They aren't very good at taking responsibility themselves and doing things better.

Christian: So someone can be a high Values-fit and still be *blame-critic* at the same time.

Michael: Yes, basically the person fits the company and just doesn't have the right attitude. As the boss, I can help by giving feedback, pushing and pointing out, "You know, I see you more in the *blame-critic quadrant, at effect* and not *at cause*. You do have the potential to be an A-player." People who consider themselves A-players are then very surprised and accelerate at full-throttle speed to quickly land back in the upper right quadrant.

Christian: Yes, they are usually grateful for the feedback and start running immediately. That's why these small steering movements to constantly counter steer are so valuable. What about the next quadrant?

Michael: The next quadrant is at the bottom left. There is no Value-fit here, nor is the performance suitable. People in this quadrant do not seem to fit culturally into the company and therefore have no positive impact on the team. They do not deliver good results and do not take responsibility.

Christian: Why would I want someone like that on my team?

Michael: It's obvious: he gets a salary and does nothing in return. [*grins*]

Christian: Isn't that just great. [*laughs*]

Michael: The title for this quadrant is *Freeloader* or *Parasite.*

Christian: He has a warm workplace, gets a fine salary, and wastes a lot of time with small talk. Since he doesn't do much, he doesn't do much damage either. He just rides along.

Michael: Freeloaders don't like working overtime either. They tend to come in around 10 a.m., go home at 5 p.m. and have a long, extended lunch break. It's perfectly okay to go home on time. Only if the performance is lacking, it is a symptom of little motivation and little effort.

Christian: How do we deal with this?

Michael: The model recommends *fire. Adiós.*

Christian: You mean a separation talk?

Michael: Yes, we let the employee go. She might fit in very well somewhere else and perform phenomenally. He just doesn't fit in with us.

Christian: It's rather tricky to develop the employee into an A-employee. There is a need for action in two dimensions, both in terms of Value-fit and productivity.

Michael: What this model makes very clear is that developing a Value-fit is not feasible. The only options are through brainwashing or through significant personality development. Neither are realistic options.

Christian: I'm making a note to produce another chapter on brainwashing.

Michael: Absolutely. Especially about the military implementation. [*laughs*] All kidding aside. Of course, there is the case of someone who has just fallen into a hole. She might be going through a divorce, someone has died, or something in life has just gone wrong. It happens to everyone at some point and can upset your own Value system. The compass is then simply missing for a while. Have you ever had such a case on your team?

Christian: Yes, definitely. The important thing is not to fire someone immediately just because I placed him in the C-quadrant during my first evaluation. I should at least observe and evaluate it regularly. There can also be mistakes in the classification. I have experienced that as well. On one team, a team leader rated all the employees as A-players and said, "I simply have a great team." Another team leader was a bit stricter or more realistic, and more often said, "Well, it's kind of okay..."

Michael: Assessing the Value-fit is a real art.

Christian: So it's better to do two or three reviews before I say goodbye to someone. Unless the person is still in the probationary period. In that case, I would rather part more quickly. Now the last quadrant is still missing.

Michael: Is it now the B- or D-quadrant that is still missing? I never know which way it goes.

Christian: I can't remember it either. In any case, it's the ones that are super productive and don't fit into the company.

Michael: Yeah, right. And what do I do with them?

Christian: Opinions differ on that. I am of the opinion *fire fast*.

Michael: Often, someone in our workshops is taken by complete surprise at this exact point and says something like, "I knew it, I have a colleague who falls exactly into this category." I sometimes ask the provocative question, "Have you ever fired someone too soon?" Often the answer is, "I've been thinking about firing this person for a year or two. But we need her. I can't find anyone new that fast who can do that."

Christian: Let's unravel this case in more detail. How can I actually fire someone who is productive and delivers great results?

Michael: Does he really deliver results for the company? I have experienced these cases many times. A person doesn't fit culturally into the company because they have different Values. He or she takes on a lot of responsibility, is a real doer, and implements things quickly. After two months, she presents me with results from a project that we never discussed and that doesn't fit our Strategies and goals. It ate up time and resources, it didn't fit our Values, and there was no sign of team play. When I asked: "What did you do this for?," the answer was, "I thought it was important." Everyone else just shook their heads. That is dangerous. That's why we labeled the D Quadrant as *terrorists.*

Christian: Since this person doesn't fit in with the team, possibly even has a bad influence on the team, and is often not liked by the other employees, they might be glad if I quickly part with him. *Fire fast.*

Michael: I have also had some interesting experiences with that. The first time I fired such a person from the *terrorist quadrant*, it took me a year to get myself through it. I hesitated for a year. When I communicated it to the team, a staff member came up to me afterwards and said quite forcefully, "Michael, it was about time!" It was way overdue, and the team had expected me to take care of it. I was totally relieved and really happy when she said that.

I have also had valuable experiences with people on my team where I've had to fire someone's friend. The employee can sometimes even distinguish between friendship and corporate goals better than I anticipate. Most of the time, they have understood that the friendship can continue outside of the work sphere, accepting their colleague leaving the team. They see that it doesn't work properly and understand the decision. I have often been surprised by people who didn't see it as black and white. They were not upset with me as boss, instead they could understand the decision.

Christian: The work is usually pretty well distributed afterwards. Often, concerns arise like, "Who is doing all the work?" We discussed it openly with our colleagues and jointly considered who could take over what. In the end—if divided among all— it is not that much.

Michael: On the contrary. I have also experienced that the team has really blossomed again and the overall performance has increased rapidly after a short time. The role was quickly taken care of. The fear never came true for me.

Christian: Great method, 2x2 matrix, ABCD players, Virtuoso Teams.

So as soon as there is a conflict of Values between employees and the company, the situation is in most cases hopeless—good performance or not. Values become critical when they make a difference in the company. A lack of Value fit is an absolute deal breaker, I have understood that. Topgrading is one way to identify this. Even if, consequently, a position remains vacant for a longer period of time, employees with the right attitude towards the company will understand. While the exact placement in the matrix is not entirely possible without my own judgment and gut feeling, it helps me to compare team members and ask the right questions. With the help of topgrading, I can ultimately make faster and better decisions to build a high-performance-kick-ass team.

FIRE FAST

GOODBYE, FREELOADERS, AND TERRORISTS!

Christian: Bye, Michael.

Michael: Ciao, Christian.

Christian: Goodbye, it was nice with you. Bye, take care. Okay, usually it's not that fast when I fire somebody.

Michael: Not quite. I wish it were.

Christian: It is not a nice experience to kick someone out.

Michael: Absolutely not. I found that very, very, very, very difficult the first time. I always put it off for a long time. Hiring people, I liked. Actively separating myself from someone was hard.

Christian: And we like to say, *fire fast*. It has two aspects for me. One is, if I let someone go, I let him go fast. Two is the termination interview. That should also go quickly. Not a never-ending horror show, but a quick, compact conversation in which I get straight to the point. "Unfortunately, it's over at this point."

Michael: Keyword is *leadership*, show leadership.

Christian: Correct. Don't get into the conversation and rumble around. "Let's see, maybe we'll still get it right." No. When I make the decision to fire somebody, it's over.

Michael: So it is important to make a decision. Once it is made, it stays. And then?

Christian: Then I communicate my decision.

Michael: Okay and in between?

Christian: I allow as little time as possible to pass in between.

Michael: I have learned to check beforehand whether everything is clean in terms of labor law. So I make the decision and get some advice from a lawyer on how I can best carry out the decision without getting into legal trouble. The third step is the implementation. I quickly convey the termination in a compact conversation.

Christian: Right, it is very important to separate these decisions. I first make the decision to separate from someone. Then, I decide how to go through with the termination. However, sometimes it is not so easy, for example if the employee has a permanent contract. I might also have to pay severance.

Michael: A year later, I'm still brooding over the same decision.

Christian: Right. Most of the time it costs me even more money because of the missing productivity and the negative side effects. These costs are just not that obvious, so for the moment it might feel better not to terminate the employee. Why do I fire someone in the first place?

Michael: Good question. You always say that the goal of management is to achieve results and retain employees.

Christian: Things get difficult when someone doesn't achieve the results we agreed upon or when someone doesn't help keep the team together.

Michael: Either the person doesn't perform, or he doesn't fit the culture. In the worst case, both are true. Like General Electric's 2x2 matrix, the topgrading.

Christian: Uh-huh, now we've come full circle. So if I consistently place someone in the lower quadrant of topgrading, it's a clear indication that we're going to split up. It doesn't matter whether she delivers results or not, as soon as the person is bad for the team and doesn't fit into the company, it's advisable to end the collaboration.

Michael: We basically have three quadrants in the topgrading model from which cases can arise where separation makes sense. In the lower two quadrants, the Values are not correct. This is a case that will never go well in the long run. If the chemistry is not right, the Values and the culture do not match, or the person simply does not fit into the team, things will go wrong.

If the person is in the lower right-hand quadrant, he or she is a ticking time bomb or a so-called *terrorist* who may be working against the company's goals. In the lower left quadrant, the person is a *freeloader* who does not perform, just swims along and scores without making a contribution of his own. Then there is the case of the B-player, the *critic*. It is not necessarily an urgent case from which I am forced to part immediately. If someone stays in the B-quadrant for a long time, they fit into the team yet don't perform, don't take responsibility and don't develop, then at some point I'll have to make a decision. Right?

Christian: Yes, otherwise he's just a nice guy.

Michael: I can try to give him different roles. "Try this one or try this one." Maybe it's because of the role that she hasn't unfolded into an A-player yet. At some point, I have to be honest with myself. Maybe it's just a nice guy.

Christian: Yes, maybe she's just not sitting at the right desk yet. As a B-player, she at least fits into the company. The Value-fit is there.

Michael: Maybe through training and development she will be able to better fulfill her role.

Christian: The Value-fit is not given in the lower two quadrants.

Michael: And I can't change that, not through training and not through development.

Christian: C-employees and D-employees therefore mean *separation talk*. I prefer to make this decision quickly instead of putting it off.

Michael: It behaves contrary to performance. I'm even quicker to part with people who are supposedly high achievers and don't fit in with the company's Values. This is the classic *fire fast* case. At first, it's often against one's gut instinct, because this person is doing a lot. The freeloader, on the other hand, does not perform at all, so it doesn't hurt so much to let him go.

Christian: B-employees and C-employees without a Values-fit are just expensive in different ways. They are expensive because A- employees may quit due to the difficulty of working with them. "I don't want to work there, the team doesn't fit." Or they might say, "Look, they are kept and tolerated here in the company, although they don't really fit in here."

Michael: The freeloader doesn't hurt, he just stands and rides along. The train runs anyway.

Christian: The freeloader can at least still take part in the Christmas party and ensure a good atmosphere. So if I have decided to part with an employee, there are still the legal aspects.

Michael: We'd better not give advice here, but leave that to the professionals.

Christian: That is also my experience. It helps to have a good employment law expert who makes sure that the contracts are airtight and, if necessary, also goes to court.

Michael: For this I'd rather spend a few euros more per hour than less. Good lawyers have always been very worthwhile for me. I have also had a chance to learn that.

Christian: They cannot be expensive enough.

Michael: During a lecture someone once said, "When we started our company, we discussed whether we should really spend 350 euros per hour on a lawyer. Today, we would never spend so little again, because now we know to spend 600 euros per hour for a good lawyer." In the end, one hour for 600 euros is cheaper than ten hours for 200 euros.

Christian: Of course I can also hire a lawyer. In this case, it would be the more expensive option. If I have now decided to give someone notice and have also clarified the employment law requirements, a separation interview will be held. Ideally, this happens quickly. I prefer to go through it within five minutes and say quite openly that it was my decision. The employee can pin the decision on me. I give him the chance to say, "Okay, so it was you."

Michael: It's basically just the official communication of the decision that was made. It is not a discussion on the subject. I don't want to get into a dialogue and talk at length about why and how all this happened. It's just the communication of the decision. "At this point, things are just not working anymore. I have made the decision to go separate ways."

Christian: My experience is that the employee understands what's going on immediately, even before I start talking. My body language and my posture tend to be different than in other types of interactions. Employees quickly realize this and in these moments their thoughts are already elsewhere. They immediately think about what this means for them. "How long will I still get my money? How do I tell my friends and family?" and so on.

Michael: Mentally they have already left the room, understandably.

Christian: So it is best if the conversation is over quickly and if I try to be nice. I have also tried to have long conversations, which have dragged on for hours and even days. It does not help. Quick conversations are better for all parties involved.

Michael: Reminds me of the German proverb *Better an end with horror than horror without end.*

Christian: Then we are already done, aren't we?

Michael: What happens after the interview? We have informed the employee that we are separating from him. "We are terminating the work relationship at the earliest possible date." Then the employee leaves the room and sits down in her office for another three months.

Christian: Here, too, *fire fast is* better than slow. I once had an employee who quit her job herself. She had a three-month notice period and continued to work for us during this period. It became a total chaos. All she did was keep the others from working, hardly contributed anything, and would spread bad vibes. It became a disaster and I released her.

Michael: At some point it was clear.

Christian: That's why I now tend to release people immediately in such cases.

Michael: Let me summarize our conversation again. On the one hand, *fire fast* means making a decision quickly. When I have made a decision, it sticks. Then I check the labor law situation and clarify how I will implement this decision and what I have to take into account. The third step is the interview. I announce the termination to the employee: short, sharp, and to the point. Five minutes are sufficient for this. The fourth step in the *fire fast* approach is to release the employee immediately. I let them go, pack their things, and say goodbye. So it can be really easy.

Christian: Great. Then I'll pack my things now.

Michael: Okay, we're going to end without the horror at this point. Bye.

Certainly, the motives and the circumstances that lead to termination always play a role, whether I release someone immediately or use the person's work performance for the remaining time, even if on a low flame. It is a valuable tip to quickly go through these often unpleasant situations and above all to make the decision quickly. The longer the uncertainty lasts, the higher the risk that it will end in a complete disaster. Hire slow and fire fast. Not the other way around!

VALUES ELICITATION
FINDING TRUE VALUES FOR STRENGTH

Michael: Tell me, Christian, why do you always say that you don't care about anything?

Christian: That's what's important to me.

Michael: It's important to you that you don't care about anything?

Christian: Exactly. It's important that you know that I don't care about anything. [*pause*] We're in the middle of the topic of Values now. For example, I don't care that we are most likely going out of business today.

Michael: Yeah, I think so, too [*grins*]. Because we're talking about a topic today and sharing a method that we usually make quite a bit of money with.

Christian: Yep. We're about to leak the recipe of our "secret sauce," disclose everything so that you can apply the method yourself.

Michael: Exactly. What is important to you? Why are we doing what we're about to do? Wherefore are we doing it?

Christian: Wherefore? What's important to me along the way?

Michael: Wherefore.

Christian: I want the world to be a kinder place. I'm making a contribution to that.

Michael: Exactly. I want people to live easier lives. I'm making a contribution to that.

Christian: Having fun at work is also important to me. That doesn't mean that it always has to be fun, but that a certain lightness resonates as often as possible. That's how relaxed productivity comes about. Of course, freedom is important to me. And fellowship with people.

Michael: It's important to me that things are done quickly and results are achieved while in the midst of relaxed productivity. [*pause*] So. What do we want to talk about today?

Christian: We're already talking about Values. These were our personal Values, our personal Purpose. We have already mentioned many times that Values are also very important to the company. What we haven't discussed, however, is how I can discover what my employees' Values are in the first place. Have we ever mentioned the trip to Mars in this context? We all go to Mars together, get out of the capsule, and then see the *how:* how we act.

Michael: Who exactly is going to Mars? Only our best, our fairest, and our dearest?

Christian: Exactly. That's *one* method. Of course, there's a much cooler method called "full disclosure."

Michael: Now I'm kind of out of business. Soon, I won't be giving any more workshops, because everybody can apply the method themselves. Cool! So we're going to do a little workshop on Values. As a reminder, wherefore do I need this again? That's actually stuff for softies, right?

Christian: Values are "softy" stuff?

Michael: Yes.

Christian: Then I would call it pretty hard softy stuff. Because it's pretty hard-softy stuff that I need for everyday life, like when hiring employees. I use the Values, both company and personal, to check whether someone fits into the company. To be more precise, I look at how my counterpart thinks and behaves, for example, when I give feedback. I may also simply not give feedback if I have hired someone who does not fit into the company, right? Instead, I say, "This person is simply not a good fit." The TEV model, on the other hand, which we described, says that feedback is especially important in leadership positions.

Michael: So Values are a pretty tough topic. I use Values to decide who to hire, who to develop, and who to promote. So the Values should fit together. If the Values don't fit, then I part with the employee.

Christian: If the Values don't fit, that's one of the two reasons why I should fire someone.

Michael: Yes, exactly.

Christian: Not only should, actually *will* fire.

Michael: Well, it is not always so easy to tell whether someone fits the company's Values or not. There are several factors that have an influence on people's behavior. Even as a boss, I can only observe people's behavior, which may give me clues about a person's Values. Unfortunately, I cannot look into their heads and see the Values written there. To put it simply, I learned that there are three main factors that help in determining someone's behavior. The first factor is competencies, or what someone is capable of. The second influencing factor is personality type, often called character. And the third is Values, which have a very strong influence on behavior. The biggest challenge for me is still to separate these three influencing factors from each other. That is, to distinguish between the influence stemming from Values and the influence that the personality type has on the the person's behavior. Just observing the behavior is sometimes not enough to decide whether the Values match or not. I must be clear about what the essential Values of my company are in the first place. I need to begin by defining them very explicitly. After all, I want to be precise and make the right decisions based on Values. So let's talk about how I can define these Values for my company accurately so that I can use them to make the right decisions about who to hire, who to promote, and who to part with.

Christian: I would like to clarify one thing. You said I can observe behavior. Here, of course, we are fully in the topic of VAKOG. I observe through my sensory organs. Observing means I see what my counterpart does, how he moves, how he looks, and maybe how he smells. Everything else I cannot observe. That would be mindreading or pigeonhole thinking.

Michael: That's exactly right.

Christian: So the only thing left for me to do is just observe the behavior. Insane.

Michael: Are you now ready to share the recipe and go out of business?

Christian: Yes. Here we go.

Michael: So, step one is the topic of *how I'm going to bring everyone along*. My key takeaway was that defining the Values of a business is not a democratic event. And yet, I just said, it's about *bringing everybody along*.

Christian: Who decides which Values apply in the company?

Michael: Where do they actually come from? What do you think about that?

Christian: So far, I've built companies from the ground up. The Values just kind of evolved, mostly based on the behavior and personality of the founders. At some point we shoveled them free, so to speak, and pinpointed what they were: we discovered them, made them explicit.

Michael: I think that's the standard situation in a young company, although it can also be different. Once, we built *Values by Design*. I think that's more the exception. Let's stay with the case where the Values are brought in by the founders and somehow implicitly embedded in the company. They continue to grow, unconsciously, until somehow they are a bit fuzzy. Suddenly there are 20, 25, 30 employees, and out of the blue they don't all fit together anymore. Then the very process that you have just described so beautifully starts. The Values are simply *shoveled free*. This process is called *elicitation, Values elicitation*. This is the process we are about to describe.

Christian: Values elicitation. We're shoveling free.

Michael: I'm bringing everybody along. I've done this process that I'm describing now hundreds of times. Going out of business. Here we go. It starts with me asking all the employees, "Tell me, when you're at home, what do you say about the company? , What are you describing?" Imagine describing to your partner, your parents, or a good friend *what* the people in your company *are like*. The answers are collected in the company, no matter how many employees, whether you have 20 or 2,000. Everyone is asked this question, and everyone is allowed to give input. Everyone asks themselves these questions: What are we actually like? How do we or our colleagues behave? Which behaviors are okay and which behaviors are undesirable? Collecting responses from all employees is a preliminary stage. All this input is then given to the workshop participants in a relatively unstructured way.

In preparation, they read through it. It is best if the workshop participants review the raw data—i.e., the O-tones—and the input is not processed or interpreted. How does that sound to you so far?

Christian: Sounds like a process that can be done anywhere for any company without incurring huge costs.

Michael: Yes, it's a simple process that takes maybe about an hour. Some make flip charts out of it or share photos. Others brainstorm with Post-it notes plastered on the wall and take pictures of them. Still others write up a few keywords in a shared document, such as a *Google Docs*. Some also create an online survey. There are many methods. The important thing is making sure everyone was surveyed and allowed to give their input. Then the workshop follows. Of course, it's important who takes part in it. Usually the founders and the leadership team, if there is one. So ideally those who represent how the company works and whose Values already fit together. If there are a few people who don't quite fit, that's okay, too. The process smooths that out. Then the group workshop takes place. The most awesome method I know is quite different from what most have probably experienced. That's because it's based on... [*Michael's voice rises*] [*pause*]

Christian: I can't bear the suspense.

Michael: I know. It's unbearable. [*laughs*] The most awesome method is based on an NLP script, so it's sort of a psychological method. Because when it comes to Values, it's very, very important that we don't think about who we would like to be, but rather we focus on who we really are. The Values we then define are only the Values that make us strong. The Values that help us achieve our great goals, our Vision. Part of really good Value-based management is that I identify strengths that help us get to the goal. Participants are asked a series of questions in the workshop, which I like to read out loud right away. They start writing them down.

Christian: Should we pretend we're in a workshop?

Michael: Okay, sure. Please take out a piece of paper and a pencil. That's all you need. As always, it's all very simple in coaching. Now I'm going to ask you a series of questions. Please just write a few adjectives on the piece of paper.

If there is a noun in between, that's okay, too. Adjectives are preferred. Feel free to ask questions during the process. We'll go through it in order. Ready?

Christian: Ready.

Michael: Okay. Now think of one person who has impacted your company in a particularly positive way. Don't write anything down yet. Just think about who that person is. See, hear, feel the person in front of you. Do you have someone?

Christian: Not yet. Can it be someone who is in the company?

Michael: Of course. I don't want to know the answer. What Values and attributes do you see in this person that have a positive impact on the company? Now please write down the attributes and qualities that are important to you. Adjectives. Two, three, four adjectives. In a workshop like this, there are ideally eight to ten people, maybe even twelve. We have also done this with 25 people. That's plenty. Everyone writes down adjectives, like you just did. [*pause*] The second question: If everyone in the company had the qualities of this one person you just imagined and if they permanently radiated and lived these qualities, how would the company be different? If possible, write down only adjectives. Twelve people in the room are writing adjectives on their paper right now. The following questions will feel a little different now. Go with the flow. Just take what your subconscious mind feeds you. Here we go: If your company were a song or a song with lyrics —or maybe just a sound—what music, what sound, would your company make? What qualities do these sounds, this music, convey? Adjectives, please.

Christian: Okay.

Michael: Now think of poems, quotes, or books that your company brings to mind or would be fitting. If your company was a written word, what book would it be or what famous quote or poem? What are the characteristics in it? What are they like? What is this written word like?

[...*pause for thought...*]

If your company were a picture, maybe a painting, a beautiful view, or a statue—anything visual—what image comes to mind? What Values and feelings does it evoke for you? Please write down adjectives.

Christian: Only the positive ones?

Michael: As you like. Trust the process.

[…pause for thought…]

Michael: Now please think of some particularly positive moments that you have experienced in your company. What feelings did you experience? What Values did you express in those positive moments, which ones struck a chord with you? How did you feel at that time?

Christian: Okay.

Michael: What Values influenced you? [*pause*] Write them down.

[…pause for thought…]

Michael: Now please think about what you enjoy most about your work at your company. What do you Value about the moments you're remembering right now?

[…pause for thought…]

Christian: Yes.

Michael: That's about it. If I didn't tell you the rest right now, we wouldn't go out of business. Can you show me what you wrote down? What do your notes look like? Describe that, please.

Christian: I came up with 20 to 30 adjectives. A couple of them surprised me. Some I mentioned earlier and a few are new. *Powerful*, for example, just came up as a new one for me.

Michael: Perfect! We'll get to the positive and negative things in a minute. There are 10, 12, 14 people sitting in the workshop and now they all have a piece of paper. So there's quite a bit of input and we're starting to consolidate that now. We're looking for common features. This is actually surprisingly easy. First, everyone goes through their words again by themselves and looks at how they are related. Everyone tries to group them in their own way, for example, with highlighters or lines or underlining, bold painting, repainting, etc. Now everyone looks for the three or four words that more or less sum everything up. Two things are very important here. At this point in the workshop, I always say, "Please listen very carefully," because it's the step that matters. Please choose only words that really speak to how your company is, or how you as a company would like to be. This is crucial. And secondly, they should be adjectives, attributes that give you strength as a company so that you will achieve your grand Vision. Now, with the 20, 30 words and these two filters, you can start putting together the vocabulary for the Value definition. This could be 10 or 12 words in total. Of those, please pick the top three, no more than four. Three to four is pragmatic. Cool. Now let's stop for a second. If we were eight to twelve people right now, we would go into a brainstorming process where everyone writes their top three or four words on a Post-it note and sticks it on the wall. These days, we do it online via digital workshop tools. It's even better and faster. At that point, we usually find that there is a lot of overlap and duplication. Duplicates are expressly desired. They show which words resonate with the most people, where the whole team stands behind. So we look for exactly these oscillation fields. Then we create word clouds on the wall with Post-its or just on the digital wall. Now we imagine this intermediate step and act as if we had already done that. Then comes the next step. Everyone now receives points and votes. So we vote. Everyone awards three points for the most important and most significant word. The second most important word gets two points. The third word gets one point. Each participant assign their points to the Post It on the wall. We count out the points and identify the words with the most. Even while voting, I keep asking the two filter questions: "Are we really like this? Is this really how we behave as a company?" and "Do these characteristics give us strength to achieve greatness?" Positive and negative don't matter, it's all about being *Purposeful*. Values serve a Purpose, that is, the Purpose of the organization, the Purpose of existence, and the Purpose of giving the team strength to achieve a big, fat Vision. This phrasing as a strength basically replaces the evaluation of whether the adjective is positive or negative. It is solely about the thing, the strengths. Because there are only two of us today, we'll skip this step and just simulate the workshop. Christian, take your list again and pick your top three words. Now, which of the remaining words match these? So the top word plus two or three other words that match it. Now, the simple step. Write the first top word on a sheet of paper. Make sure you write it in large and bold letters, with a thick marker. Then you take the second top word and write it three or four centimeters below it, so that there is still space in between. Then you take the third top word and write it again two or three centimeters below it. Under the first top word, write the following with a slightly thinner pen: *We are...* Now take the next adjective you like best from the list and write it behind the three dots. Then put a comma and the next word that goes with it. If you have a third word, put a period after it. If you have only two words, write, *We are x and y.* Now you do the same with the second top word and also with the third word. Sometimes I need verbs as linking words to make it round. That's the detailed work. In fact, in a group of eight, ten, twelve people, this process quickly leads to a precise result, especially when these people have grown with the company and fit together well. Now I'm totally curious to hear from you what you wrote down. I'll read out the words as follows: "Our Values are top word one, top word two, top word three." Then I go through all three words again and complete each one with the sentence, "To us this means.... Top word two to us means ... we are..." And then top word three the same way. Go for it. Now it's your turn.

Christian: Quick spoiler: I got to two words.

Michael: Ok, also good.

Christian: I was keeping an eye on the technology. And yet, even though I was doing two things at once, podcasting and this process, I came out with these two Values "We are powerful, we are fast and energetic." The second Value, "We are positive, we are in the flow and having fun."

Michael: Cool, "We are powerful, we are fast and energetic." "We are positive, we are in the flow and having fun." Awesome! That really gives me goosebumps because we're talking about our own company, COA Academy. To me, it fits very well with how we really are.

Christian: Yes, we've already phrased our Values, too. We've been working on them for a while. They're worded a little bit differently. Essentially, they are the same Values.

Michael: We should do it again together with Leonie and the others in the team and see what results form from it. It's been a while since we formulated that.

Christian: Definitely.

Michael: To all who are listening or reading right now, I wish you much joy and much success. This is how we filter and decide who will join us on our journey and who better to drop off again. Have I forgotten anything?

Christian: Maybe one small thing. This also works for my personal Values. The questions work for a company just as they do for me personally. I can ask "What am I like?" and shovel my Values free, pin them down, myself.

Michael: It's really great. I've only seen it happen two or three times in the last 12 years, when companies give every employee the opportunity to participate in such a Values workshop. Ideally, along with the Values, everyone then defines their personal Purpose and personal Vision and strategies to achieve the Vision. We call such a life workshop IT'S MY LIFE. Afterwards, it is much easier for employees and managers to identify whether the shared Values and goals fit together and are aligned, i.e., have the same orientation. That is the beautiful utopia of John Strelecky's bestseller.

Christian: You mean, *The Big Five for Life.*

Michael: Exactly. Where it describes exactly what great things can happen when the Values and the Purpose of the company are congruent with those of all the employees. I actually witnessed that once. To this day, it is the most impressive business setup and the most successful corporate culture I have experienced. I wish that for everyone listening and reading.

Christian: Amazing.

Michael: Now we're out of business. What are we going to do now?

Christian: I don't care.

Michael: As long as it's relaxed and productive and the world becomes a little bit better.

Christian: Exactly. Powerful, positive, energetic, and having fun.

Defining my own Values and those of the company in this way is actually incredibly easy. That wasn't always the case in the past when I often experienced disastrous results. The questions posed here are brilliant. Of course, it also requires a certain willingness on the part of the employees and myself to face these personal questions and share the answers. So it really isn't "softy" stuff, but rather pretty hard stuff. And at the same time, I feel what it means to be in tune with my Values and live them out on the job. That's what we call self-realization: where success starts feel like something completely independent of money, but that somehow often still leads you to it in the end. I love it.

CHALLENGE & SUPPORT

ACHIEVING GOALS

WHO DOES WHAT BY WHEN?

Christian: So now we know how to set up a kick-ass team.

Michael: Now we have reached our goal.

Christian: Right. Now there is nothing more to do. We know where we want to go and we know how to get there. Now it is a matter of moving towards this goal step by step.

Michael: We know what Purpose we serve, we know our grand Vision, and our Values that hold us together are clear. What do we do now?

Christian: How do we even realize that we have reached our goal? When I go up Mount Everest, at some point it becomes clear that I can't go any higher. I have reached the highest point.

Michael: I touch the summit cross and take a selfie.

Christian: As a company, I am aiming for a market share of 30%. I can then look at any statistic and say, "Alright, 30% market share." It is important to know when I have arrived. How do I know that I have reached my goal?

Michael: I define my goal precisely.

Christian: We have already talked about the topic *VAKOG*. I perceive my goal through all senses; I can feel, "Now I am here."

Michael: Do I do that for company goals and team goals as well as for my personal goals?

Christian: Yes, basically. In the end, these are my goals. With my company I want to achieve a goal, both for myself and for the company.

Michael: For example, we sit together with the entire team in a Strategy workshop and think about what we want to do to achieve our grand Vision. What is the difference between goals and Vision? Is there a difference at all?

Christian: On the way to the Vision I will achieve a lot of goals. In order to realize my Vision, I need intermediate goals so that I get closer to the grand Vision step by step. I use methods to clearly formulate these intermediate goals so that my employees know what they have to do and that they are on the right path to the Vision.

Michael: We defined the grand Vision as what we achieve when everything goes perfectly, three, four, or five years down the road. *This is where we will get, when everything goes ridiculously perfectly.* There is quality in it. I'm probably a bit unsure whether we will make it; as long as everything really goes well, then it will work. Just like with the Mount Everest climb. I have no guarantee that I will really reach the summit. There are a few factors that I cannot calculate, influence, or guarantee. It's a little different with my goals, isn't it? With my goals, I am much more realistic. I'm sure I can do it, and I'm taking it on very seriously. "This is where I want to get to in the next step."

Christian: Yes, I set goals for myself that I can realistically achieve. It's safe to assume that I have a high probability of reaching them. Of course, I can also set myself a goal, which means, "First of all, I'll find out if it's even feasible."

Michael: If the summit of Mount Everest is my Vision, my next goal is the first base camp. Everybody can do that. Nevertheless, I am allowed to set it as a goal and work on its realization. I know it will be exhausting and I will reach the base camp.

Christian: A goal in a previous stage would be to first look at my bank account and contemplate whether I can afford to climb Mount Everest at all. To save money for that is also a goal that I can achieve. And I know directly how to go on afterwards.

Michael: So, when I set the goals for my company and individual teams, I think very specifically about which ones I want to achieve along the way, depending on my grand Vision. So there are several goals.

Christian: Right. I have a Vision and on the way there are several small and big steps. At the same time, there are several team members who join in and make a contribution. They want to get things done. Then we are already at our SMART Goals, aren't we?

S.M.A.R.T

SPECIFIC MEASURABLE ACHIEVABLE RELEVANT TIME-BOUND

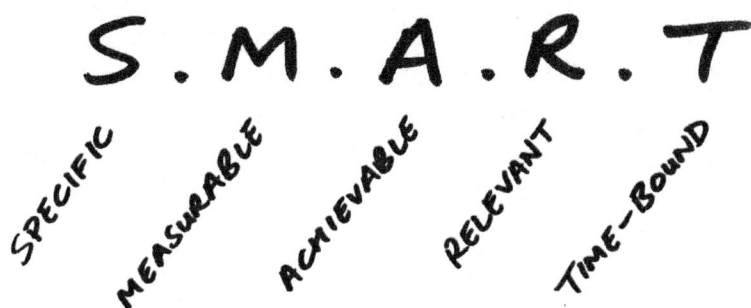

Illustration: SMART-Goals
I determine how I make the small and big steps on the way to my Vision measurable.

Michael: The word "Strategy" just pops up in my head. I used to think of Strategy as something very complicated, something nebulous that requires special cleverness. Today I see the term "Strategy" in a completely different light. Strategy is what we definitely want to do in the next six to twelve months to come a few steps closer to the grand Vision. These things that we want to tackle concretely are my milestones, my intermediate steps that I want to achieve on the way to the Vision.

Christian: Right. There are also small steps towards the milestones, which I will be completing in the coming weeks and months. And for that there are again small goals that I'll be completing today and in the next few days.

Michael: So Strategies are small goals. I can say that, right?

Christian: Yes. When we talk about it like this, it sounds totally simple.

Michael: In order to actually achieve the Vision, the whole team may make these goals and Strategies become reality.

Christian: Exactly, goals may be achieved and results delivered. That is what management is all about.

Michael: How did you do that? How did you develop the goals?

Christian: *SMART goals* were always too complicated. Nobody knew what the S, the A, and the R actually stood for.

Michael: There are actually several versions of this.

Christian: We have always assumed that the goals are reasonably realistic and, of course, meaningful for our overall goal, our Vision. Therefore, we have paid particular attention to set *measurable* and *scheduled* goals. Especially with short-term issues, the question was: *who does what by when?* It is a 3-X matrix on a flipchart. Who does what by when? There is a name, a result, and a time.

WHO	WHAT	WHEN
MP	WEBSITE CONTENT	23/08/20
CK	HIRE COPYWRITER	1/09/20

Illustration: WHO-WHAT-WHEN
Especially for short-term measures, the crucial question for me is: Who does what by when?

Michael: That's how we did it. Every year, we defined our annual Strategies. There were usually four, five, or six major fields of action. Of course, each field had a lot of things that needed to be done, and there was a lot of stuff associated with each of these actions. All in all, it was clear what we as a company wanted to achieve in the next six to twelve months. Four, five, six big things, which we also made measurable. We linked them to key figures so that we could see when we had arrived and achieved them.

Christian: Yes, Strategies are simply the small steps I take every day. So suddenly, there is nothing complicated about them. I have a Vision, I have goals, and in between are the things I do to run in the same direction.

Michael: With a goal, I link a time and a metric that tells me that I have reached the goal. You mentioned *SMART* earlier. I know the following definition. To make a goal achievable, it must first be *specific*, i.e. formulated in a very concrete way. It also has to be *measurable*. I define how I can detect that I have arrived there. The next *a* stands for *achievable,* the goal is possible. If my goal is to get to Mars, under current circumstances it is not really achievable in the next few months. Then, the *r follows* for *relevant*. So the goal plays into our Purpose, our Vision, and our Values. It is relevant and important that we achieve this goal. The *t* stands for *timebound*. When I have memorized these five aspects for my goals, my goal is *SMART*. In reality, our goals were a combination of, "This is what we want to do now" and "from the two or three measurements we can see that we have made it."

Christian: A Vision is not *SMART*. It is not necessarily realistic. With a BHAG, for example, I can certainly think, "Wow, maybe that's a bit exaggerated, a bit unrealistic."

Michael: Hmm, I would say the Vision is a SMART stretch goal.

Christian: Let's take the moon landing as an example again. The moment Kennedy announced it, it wasn't realistic either.

Michael: "We will put a man on the moon in this decade." He probably already had a hunch that it could work, he just didn't know for sure.

Christian: That is perhaps the point. At the time I formulate the Vision, it is perhaps 60% to 80% achievable. The shorter the time horizon, the *more achievable* the intermediate goals become. In the very short term, it would be, "You write this email in two minutes, you can do it." That is *very achievable*.

Michael: There is another issue that currently has become very modern in corporate management. *OKRs: Objectives and Key Results.* Google has made this method famous. It's basically very similar to the SMART methodology. I define an objective, a goal, and then I come up with some key results that show that I've achieved that goal.

Christian: Furthermore, there are also timeframes in this method. They make it easier to implement the goals in the company. It is a complete methodology. Ultimately, it's about exactly the same thing.

Michael: So the whole issue of goal setting is always about the same fundamentals: I think about what I actually want to achieve and determine how I measure that I have achieved these goals. Then the implementation is to constantly check that we are all aligned and focused and that no part of the team is suddenly thinking about doing something else. Staying on course, that's what it's all about.

Christian: The short-term goals can also change. It is no longer like a few years or decades ago, when there was a Russian five-year plan in which everything was fixed and implemented exactly as planned. It is possible to review it again after a week or after three months and determine, "This medium-term goal no longer makes sense."

Michael: I had a hard time with that for a while.

Christian: With five-year plans?

Michael: No, that goals can be flexible. That the Vision may be flexible. In my workshops, I like to set up a five-year Vision. It is an ongoing discipline and not a one-time event. I don't create a five-year Vision and work on it for five years, but I check every year whether the five-year Vision still fits my company. I develop the five-year Vision further every year. This makes it a North Star. When I look back after many years, I often find that the five-year Vision has actually come true, sometimes earlier, sometimes later than the five years originally planned. It has mostly come true. I was a bit stubborn about the flexible handling of the Vision at the beginning. "That's our fixed goal," I had thought. Then I learned that it's in flux. Goals and Visions are allowed to be in a flow.

Christian: Yes, it is like feedback and counter-steering. Framework conditions can change. The shape of the road changes, the environment changes, the crisis comes, the crisis goes, the market environment changes. Short-term and medium-term goals can change. The danger, however, is that employees may not take goals seriously. I have also had this experience. An employee once said to me, "I'm not doing this SMART Goal thing; everything will change again anyway."

Michael: We can then decide together.

Christian: Right. Things may already get done.

Michael: A SMART goal, a yearly Strategy, a six-month Strategy, and the whole world is changing pretty damn fast. The question is whether the world is changing so fast that, within six months, my Strategy changes. In exceptional situations, maybe it does. The Corona pandemic has shown that. That has rarely happened in my past. I can well imagine that a competitor surprisingly launches a new product or something similar and that this changes a lot for us and our company. That can happen.

Christian: How do we know that we have talked enough about the topic of goals?

Michael: Our goal was to talk about setting goals and what we are aiming for. It's always about metrics, about SMART Goals, and about OKRs. These are all basic principles, partly borrowed from psychology and the NLP model. It's about visualizing goals, making them measurable with the help of metrics, and being very specific. What else serves as a metric?

Christian: The small steps on the way to the Vision and "Who does what by when?"

Michael: I still have one topic as bonus material. The RACI model is practically the big brother of "Who does what by when?" Who from the team takes over which role and takes care of which topic? Now we have even provided bonus content.

Christian: Awesome. So we have overperformed.

Michael: World-class-kick-ass team.

That sounds almost too simple to be true. At the core, of course, it's all about who does what by when and how do we measure the result. The latter is often exactly the point at which discussions start. How do we measure that? And how much is achievable? The differentiation of Vision and goal helps me to do this. If I break down the Vision into individual steps, I can more easily define what I am measuring to get there and how long my stride needs to be.

RESPONSIBLE AND ACCOUNTABLE

RACI FOR REAL

Christian: Let's talk about who is responsible.

Michael: With pleasure. Fire away.

Christian: In German there is only one word for it. Someone is *responsible*. In English there are two words that make a big difference: *accountable* and *responsible*. There is a nice story about a butcher and a pig. Or wasn't there a chicken involved too?

Michael: I don't know the chicken yet, so I'm curious.

Christian: When I eat ham and eggs for breakfast, a chicken is involved.

Michael: Oh, I see. [*laughs*] The chicken was *responsible for* producing the egg.

Christian: Right. Responsibility.

Michael: It's an important issue when we talk about building a world-class-kick-ass team that delivers great results and goes beyond itself. People in a high-performance team are responsible, committed, and accountable. The story behind the terms you just mentioned —*accountable* and *responsible*— is as follows: *The butcher is responsible for the bacon and the pig is accountable.* It is actually a rather crude saying. The butcher is responsible for the bacon. The pig is also responsible, just differently.

Christian: Does that mean I can have several butchers?

Michael: Exactly.

Christian: Several butchers working together and all responsible, however, there is only one pig.

Michael: Okay, let's turn these images off. Accountability is always just one person, the one giving the account. Accountability only involves one person, while responsibility can include several. It's a good instrument for defining responsibilities in the team and distributing tasks. I can give responsibility to several people on a project. Only one person is accountable. Only one person.

Christian: Let's assume we have a kick-ass team and something needs to be done.

Michael: For example, a new website is to be launched.

Christian: So when the tasks are distributed in the team, I consider who is responsible, who is accountable, and who else is involved.

Michael: I can be even more specific and state that by June 30th we will launch our new website in line with our new corporate design and with a clear product offering for consumers and corporations.

R = RESPONSIBLE
A = ACCOUNTABLE
C = CONSULTED
I = INFORMED

WHAT S.M.A.R.T GOAL	R	A	C	I
LAUNCH NEW SITE BY 25/08/20	MP AH LR	MP	CK AM NRM	ALL

Illustration: RACI
This modified version of the RACI matrix is easier to apply.

Christian: That is a SMART goal.

Michael: It could also be formulated as OKR, as Objective with Key Results. It becomes very clear what needs to be delivered. Ideally, I communicate this in a round where everyone is involved. They can agree whether they accept the responsibilities. Then we decide who is specifically responsible for ensuring that the new website is up and running by June 30. That will be a number of people. There will probably be a designer, a programmer, and maybe a project manager who also collaborates with external people. Then comes the crucial step. Who is accountable for this project? Who makes sure that we stay on track and keep the ball rolling until June 30th? I used to think that it should be the one who knows the most about it. Today I see that quite differently. It's just someone who keeps the ball rolling and works with the people to get the project done. She regularly gives a status update and escalates if necessary. "It's not working, we need help."

Christian: What happens if she does not deliver? What happens if the new website is not up and running by June 30?

Michael: That can't happen. As the boss, I make sure that I am informed ahead of time through regular updates, as a kind of early warning system to signal if something is not working so that I can intervene. I spot the risks early on and help the team to find a solution and stay on track. In a very strict approach, it would have an impact on who is accountable. I can link the success of the project implementation to remuneration, a bonus, or something similar. If the project is not successfully implemented by June 30, this bonus will not be paid or will only be paid in part.

Christian: Someone who is accountable feels the consequences.

Michael: Right. Then it really gets to her. Not to the others, at least not as hard. That's the job of the person who is accountable. It's their job to keep the project running.

Christian: The one who is accountable can assign smaller subtasks, for example to the web designer or to the programmer, who in turn are accountable for their subtask.

Michael: The project team can conduct them in many ways. The team can organize itself or it can distribute the tasks itself. The most important thing is our goal: To get the website up and running with the following requirements by June 30th.

Christian: Let's come back to the chicken. When I make myself breakfast with bacon and eggs, the chicken is also involved as a supplier, so to speak. So there can be other people involved who support the project or someone I just ask for advice.

Michael: Right, *responsible* and *accountable* becomes the *RACI model*. I am a big fan of it. RACI stands for *responsible, accountable, consulted,* and *informed*. The person who is consulted is actually just giving input as a kind of consultant. He is not responsible for ensuring that his input is implemented. *Informed* is the weakest form of participation. Here it is a matter of clarifying who is to be informed about the result that is ultimately delivered. For them, it may be important to know how far the project has progressed or what the result will look like in the end.

Christian: Yes, good point. When distributing tasks, it is also part of the process to communicate when they are finished. What good is the bacon if it's just lying around somewhere? Someone else wants to do something with it. In the butcher's shop, the bacon is put on display or on my plate when it is ready.

Michael: Especially with larger projects, the end result is often different from what was planned at the beginning of the project. I can think of a great saying about this, too. *Planning is everything, plans are shit.* It's important to plan the project at the beginning and set a Vision: *Where do we actually want to go?* On the way there, a lot of things change and after three, four, or five months what has come out of the project is usually a different result than what was originally planned. It is still a good result, maybe even a better result. So I inform the people for whom the final result is relevant.

Christian: I plan what I want to do and still react flexibly to what happens.

Michael: Right. We plan to climb the summit of Mount Everest. We're planning the day and the date we're going to reach the top. Then we'll start with going to the first base camp. We might find that we have to take a different route due to the weather, which will take longer. It is important that we have a plan and at the same time enough flexibility to make decisions on the spot. That way, I make sure that I actually reach the summit, even if the route was a little different than I had planned.

Christian: The plan also helps to do a reality check. If my plan says that I want to reach Everest within two days, I realize at the latest when I fly to Nepal, walk up and down again, that the plan was not quite ready.

Michael: That's right. Plans don't work, only planning.

Christian: Right. My planning enables me to do a kind of reality check, whether what I have planned makes sense and is realistic at all. I collect information and compare my plan. I look at how others have done it, think about the best height for a stopover, and what material I still need. The goals and my Vision remain the same. I climb Mount Everest in a certain time frame, a SMART Goal. Only the path can be different.

Michael: The way is toward the goal. Good luck.

The RACI model is an old-school classic. In this modified version it actually makes more sense. It is simpler. Perhaps this is the reason why the classic version, although known everywhere, is rarely used in practice. It is a wonderful, completely underestimated instrument, both in small and large teams and projects. It unfolds its full effect in combination with a short project profile or a concise status update on which the most important project information and responsibilities are noted. Used correctly, it is immediately clear to everyone involved what their own role is. What I find most important is to arrange it pragmatically and not to write dogmatic, page-long documents.

I GET WHAT I MEASURE

SMART OKR

Christian: *Where awareness goes, energy flows.* My energy flows to where my attention is directed. The things I put energy into happen. They are realized. When I want things to happen in my company, projects to be implemented, tasks to be completed, I direct my attention to exactly these issues. I measure them. When I measure them and make them transparent, attention is focused on them and energy flows towards them. So I am to choose very carefully what I measure in my company, because as these things are accomplished, my employees spend time and energy on what is measured.

Michael: Simply doing the measuring is a good start. *You get what you measure* is a great saying that I have memorized.

Christian: There are two main questions I would like to ask. On the one hand, I ask myself what I am measuring. What is important enough in the company to be measured? The other question is: How can I tell we are doing something successfully or are getting better at it?

Michael: The questions sounds similar to our goal. How do I recognize that I have reached my goal, how do I measure that?

Christian: There are several methods for this.

Michael: Quite a few, actually.

Christian: So tell me about it. You surely know some of them from your call center days, don't you?

Michael: Yes, that's right. *We get what we measure;* I really internalized this message during that time in my career. The call center story goes like this: I was working for a company, a group, and suddenly I was responsible for customer care. I helped manage the call center. The entire company division had a very bad reputation and customers were constantly complaining about very poor service. So at the beginning, we didn't deliver good results to the customer at all. That was a big challenge.

Christian: So before you ran this department, they measured how often a customer called to complain?

Michael: Unfortunately not. It would have been nice if they had done that and we had this information before. In fact, all that was measured was how many emails, how many escalations, how many calls to the CEO landed on the desk. Because, it often happened that inquiries via informal channels found their own way to the CEO. "Hey, your store is down, can you please help me out and fix this?" Suddenly the request is on his desk. The CEO becomes the Chief Customer Agent, which of course he shouldn't be. That's basically when it started. So we started by defining a service level, a criterion that is often used in a call center. It was quite simple. We measured how long it took for a service agent to answer the phone. A customer would call the service hotline and we measured things like how often it rang until someone answered the call, and how long the music on hold ran until the customer talked to an agent.

Christian: That was already automatically possible, wasn't it?

Michael: Absolutely, that's the good thing about call centers. I can measure most things automatically, much more today than I could back in the 2000s. Today everything is completely digitally managed, routed, and allocated. I can now measure just about anything I want to measure, at any point.

Christian: So you could measure everything and you measured everything?

Michael: Not in the beginning. In the beginning, we only measured whether or not we were meeting this service level. If 80% of all calls were answered within 20 seconds, then we had achieved our goal. That was our first target.

Christian: That sounds a little bit like the Deutsche Bahn, the German Railroads Provider.

Michael: Yeah, right. Their goal was, or is, that less than 80% of all trains should not be more than five minutes late.

Christian: That is also a nice positive wording. It's actually a terrible goal.

Michael: I always have to think about this goal three times to understand what it means. Our goal was to have the customer connected to an agent within 20 seconds if he hadn't already found a solution via the automated menu of options by then. We did not achieve this at the beginning. In fact, at that time we were at a proud six percent. We were only able to answer six percent of all calls within 30 seconds. That was a really bad result. We hired many more people and optimized processes to achieve a better result at the outset. What helped us most was to break down the total number to individual areas, because this one goal applied to thousands of employees. To make it easier, we defined a service level for each individual area, each product, and were able to compare and benchmark them. This led to a real wave of success. There were teams of 10 to 12 people. We made the service level transparent and measured it for each team and then even for each employee. To ensure that we could also take into account different framework conditions and the respective possibilities on the team, additional criteria were also added, such as how long a call lasts, how the call is evaluated by the customer, and so on. We measured all of this on each team and were able to determine exactly where the problems lay. This gave us the opportunity to work very specifically on optimizations. We displayed the results on huge television monitors for everyone to see. So every employee could follow the improvements live at any time and also see when things were getting worse. This meant that colleagues could come back from their coffee break a little earlier, or didn't even take a break at all because they saw that someone was needed at that moment. It was a really valuable innovation to have everyone see the dashboard from everywhere. The results improved by themselves.

Christian: So the teams had different tasks and also differed in the achievement of objectives?

Michael: Right. In the beginning, everybody did everything. Part of the new Strategy was to distribute the calls among the employees according to issue, knowledge, and skills. That way, the agents were able to help the customer much better and faster. Having everyone do everything was part of the problem. We first had to find out and learn from our measurements. Only then could we find a better solution and route the right questions to the right employee.

Christian: There are certainly a lot of criteria. I'm guessing you measured the performance, response times, and the number of complaints, and the latter probably decreased. This is a classic quality indicator. What other indicators are there that I can measure?

Michael: You're talking about the big parameters that are important for us as *Chief of Anything*, as company leaders, team leaders, or even as the leader of my life to achieve my goals. We are talking about our Purpose, our Vision, our Values, and our Strategies. So we want to find out how much we live our Purpose, how close we have already come to our Vision, our goals. We have stated that these goals are SMART, as are the criteria that I can measure. I can only measure my Values indirectly. When it comes to Strategies, we are at a very operational level. Here I have very concrete KPIs, which I have formulated as Strategy, as Smart-Goal or OKR, depending on which method I use. All successful methods have in common that very clear KPIs are defined and are constantly measured, monitored, and reviewed. If one of my goals is "We improve our customer satisfaction by 10%," then I know exactly how to measure it.

Christian: How do I measure customer satisfaction? Through the number of complaint emails?

Michael: Yes, possibly. That would be an indirect measurement. The standard method for measuring customer satisfaction is the so-called NPS: Net Promoter Score. Here, I ask the customer the question, "On a scale of one to ten, how likely is it that you will recommend us to friends or relatives?" The customer then gives a number from one to ten. Most of the time, this is done digitally and the customer simply clicks on a number on the scale. A number of nine or ten is considered a positive recommendation; seven and eight are neutral; anything under six is considered a non-recommendation. Then I can present the evaluation of all answers as percentages that I balance against each other. In the end, I have a score between -100 and +100. Currently, this method is the most common method worldwide for measuring customer satisfaction, the recommendation rate.

Christian: What kind of range are we talking about here? Are there companies that reach a value of +100?

Michael: Yes, they do exist. If a company has a very small customer base and everyone clicks on nine or ten, then I quickly reach a score of 100. If however, a single customer clicks on another number, this becomes immediately apparent in the final result and is less than 100. Mathematically, I reduce the percentage of those who gave one to six from the percentage of those who gave nine and ten. I simply ignore information from seven and eight. A score of +100 is extremely rare. A world-class result, even from larger organizations with 50, 100, or even more employees, is a score of 70 and up. Twenty through fifty is considered good, under 20 is satisfactory, and once the score is negative, it is very bad.

Christian: So the score can also be negative.

Michael: Yes. If no customer gives a nine or ten and many choose a rate between one and six, the result is a negative value.

Christian: That means I basically have no fans at all, only enemies?

Michael: Right. Customers might think, "This is the only store with this product, so there's no way around it. Still, I can't recommend it to you."

Christian: As soon as the product or service is offered by someone else, I am gone.

Michael: Yeah, then I'll be gone and buy somewhere else. Such a company can only survive in the long run if it actually offers an unbeatable price that makes up for everything else or has a monopoly. It is not a sustainable business model.

Christian: In the case of the call center, a lot of criteria can be measured automatically. With every incoming call, I know immediately what is happening and I also ask for the score. At *chicco,* one of our challenges was that it is a relatively slow business. Not much changes every day. We have therefore introduced a so-called Prosecco limit. Every coffee bar that achieved a new sales record at the bar sends a text message with the new record number and receives a bottle of Prosecco in return. The nice thing about it was that everyone noticed when there was a new sales increase. We also sent an email to let everyone know who had received the bottle of Prosecco. Another method was a large glass cylinder that we had set up. Whenever a new coffee bar opened, we threw a small styrofoam ball inside. It was marked with the year's target.

Michael: It is very helpful to make progress transparent and visible to everyone. All employees are engaged and it's not just the boss sitting somewhere alone looking at the numbers. When everyone has progress and the goal in front of their eyes in the truest sense of the word, many things automatically move in the right direction. In the call center, we ended up hanging screens everywhere and making all the results per team visible with actual percentages for everyone, the entire organization, in real time and for the day, week, and month. We also communicated our annual target. We wanted to go from 6% to 80%. Everyone could see the progress every day. After just a few months, things got much better and we actually reached 80%. There was a huge celebration and great praise from the CEO. He addressed all employees and thanked them explicitly. The customers also noticed it and told us. In less than a year we have improved the entire service model from underground to world class. This would not have been possible without transparent measurement, quite the opposite in fact. It is unfair for employees to constantly tell them that the service they deliver is poor without giving them the tools and opportunities to improve. It's like me giving you a car without a speedometer and telling you that you're much too slow, please drive at least X kilometers per hour.

Christian: Difficult.

Michael: Impossible.

Christian: As a boss, I can use measured results and, for example, discuss them with my employee: "I looked at your figures from last week, how can I support you to get better?" Process improvements and structural improvements are much easier if I know the right figures.

Michael: As an employee, when I measure results I can work in a much more self-determined way, see my results, and can specifically think about how I can improve them. As a boss, I only have a support function—as it should be—and I am not forced to find solutions through micromanagement that I don't know anyway. I just had another thought. We just talked about service levels, NPS, and the customer perspective. Even as a boss, I can of course ask my employees about their satisfaction. "How well do you like it here in the company on a scale of one to ten?" "How highly would you recommend good friends or relatives to work for our company?" This is called eNPS—the Employee Net Promoter Score. It covers the internal perspective and allows me to get great feedback. "What can we improve so that you are still working here in two years?" That is the internal, the employee perspective. The customer perspective is the external perspective. Here I define what I want to measure in order to make our success visible. It can be customer satisfaction or, for example, the brand that I can measure. Internally, I measure the processes in the company and the satisfaction of my employees. Because the goal of management is...

Christian: ...to achieve results and retain employees. What I measure is what will happen. Therefore it is important to measure the right things and to focus my attention on them.

Michael: I learned one more thing. Ideally, I don't just measure one metric, rather pairs of criteria that complement each other. That way I create a balanced behavior.

Christian: For example, if I only measure how fast someone answers the phone, I know that they will answer the customer call faster and faster. But he may not be able to solve the customer's problem.

Michael: Right. Then the employee answers the phone in a flash and hangs up again in a flash. The result is corrupted. I get a sensational service level and the customers are still dissatisfied. I need an evaluation of the customer solution as a supplement and compensation to create balance. Financial figures are another good example. When I measure sales figures, it causes the sales team to turbo boost and generate high revenues. If I don't measure profitability at the same time and spend horrendous amounts on advertising so that the sales are not profitable, it doesn't help the company. So I need two measurements: sales increase and profitability. One of the two figures is not informative enough. Two variables are more than one.

Christian: That's what it looks like.

I think the ideas for visualizing success and the achievement of goals are great. It creates healthy competition and at the same time a WE feeling and motivation. In fact, what I measure is crucial. Because I also experience that we have far too many key figures that no one can sort through anymore and activities quickly run in different directions. This can also lead to a corrupted result. I can already hear your comment on this: Purpose, Vision, Values, and Strategies help with the alignment and bring the necessary focus. I got it.

LIFELONG LEARNING
KINESTHETIC LEARNS THE LONGEST

Michael: Tell me, how do you actually do that on such a world-class-high-performance-kick-ass team? An essential ingredient for such a virtuoso team is to constantly develop, learn, and educate oneself, both for you as the boss and for each individual on the team. How do you do that? How do you make sure that everyone continues to improve?

Christian: First of all, I will try to explain it using an example from my own experience. It has always been very important to me to educate myself further and to always learn something new. Having options and being flexible means a lot to me. I like to try out different things and ways and adapt very quickly. For some things, I remain committed, for others I don't. A good example of something I have taught myself is my sports sailing license. Basically, this is like professional skipper training. I first attended a course and quickly realized that even without any previous knowledge I could lead the course better than the trainer. He really struggled. So I thought to myself, "I can teach myself the material," and thus simply registered for the exam without attending the course. Mentally, I saw the cost of the exam, which I had already paid for. Even though it wasn't particularly high, it served as a kind of incentive for me. I really wanted to pass the exam, so suddenly I got really diligent, sat down and taught myself everything.

Michael: So you set yourself a concrete goal that you can measure and have already paid for. It triggers an obligation on your part, regardless of how large or small the amount is. You want to achieve the goal at all costs and not just throw the money out the window. And then you just do it, yes?

Christian: Yes, I want to go through with it and just do it. At least when I am convinced that this goal will bring me something and that I can learn, something useful.

Michael: What does studying look like for you? How do you prepare for an exam and for the goal you want to achieve?

Christian: I approach it with different measures. The things I know will be hard to remember, I write on index cards. Very old school. I read everything else, memorize it and then practice it again and again. I repeat it. For example, I practiced a lot of tide navigation for my sports sailing license. For this I had a large map, a compass, an oversized set square and tables. With this set of tools you can navigate. I practiced this very often. I enjoyed it so much that I could have done it for hours. I simply wanted to learn and understand it.

Michael: This is an example of something that you enjoy, that you like to learn, and that keeps you motivated.

Christian: Yes, exactly. The variety is especially important for me. For example, I am currently learning Italian. Sometimes I study with a teacher, sometimes by reading books, watching movies, or using an app to practice vocabulary. The different formats help me to keep up. I use one until I get bored, then I change the format.

Michael: Cool, I see.

Christian: How do you do it?

Michael: Looking back, I've actually learned the most from applying things myself and even teaching others. All of the topics we're discussing here I used to hear in a training session, read in a book, or observe from others. I was so enthusiastic about them that I simply tried things out for myself. All the NLP tricks, the language techniques, and the content from the executive coaching sessions, which I myself have taken part in, I have passed on and applied to my team. I have adopted all these methods and started to teach them to others, to discuss and listen to what others have experienced. I regularly organized training sessions and continuing education days with my team, something we took very seriously. Each time, we focused on different topics. I was always totally in the mood for it. In retrospect, after about 15 years, I realized that the thing I learned most was how to teach the topics to others. Explaining to others what I have learned myself, repeatedly coming up with other examples and questions, discussing them even controversially and dealing with the topics again and again, seeing new perspectives... That's how I eventually master the content. Even though I didn't feel so confident about some topics from the very beginning, the most effective training method was to pass on what I already knew and try out new things together, even as a trainer. This was the fastest way for me to progress and I also learned more and more during my own training sessions. Together with the participants, I was able to dig even deeper into the content.

The method that I like the least for my style of learning is the traditional teacher lecturing in front of the classroom. I never manage to stay awake and listen for more than five minutes. If it's a mixture and there's a lot of discussion or something happens in the room (group work, for example), then it's okay. Then I manage to stay motivated and retain something from the session. That, too, is a realization of how I learn best. I have learned to take time to study. For example, I dedicate a whole week to focus on my Italian course. I devote this week only to this course or topic and concentrate on the content. Not because someone stands in front of me for five days and explains something to me, but because I can actively devote myself to the topic, try it out, and experiment with others. This was an important insight on my journey: learning takes time.

Christian: I can absolutely understand that. I also spend a lot of time with the topics I want to learn. In different ways, with different media, through reading and speaking. What you just described is the Feynman method. Richard Feynman, winner of the Nobel Prize in Physics, said, "When I want to learn something, I read it through and then try to explain it to someone." Then I know whether I have understood something or not.

Michael: Right. Einstein, also a physicist, had a saying about it. "If I can't explain something easily, I haven't understood it well enough yet." Awesome.

Christian: What does that mean for me and my employees? Should my employees now explain to me everything that I already know, just so that they learn it?

Michael: Why not? Maybe they explain it to their colleagues.

Christian: For me, there are a few skills and abilities that I consider essential in the company. These include the ability to manage a project, to moderate employee meetings efficiently, and to present eloquently. I always support my employees to learn these skills themselves.

Michael: This is about behavioral flexibility, right? It's not a professional know-how transfer in the sense of: *How do I get even more aroma out of this coffee bean?* It's about being able to fill your role better.

Christian: Right. My approach is, if it can be done by one employee, it may be done by one employee. For example, if I was asked to give a presentation at a conference, I agreed and at the same time insisted on bringing a colleague to give the second part of the presentation. The nice thing was that from that moment on I didn't have to give a single lecture, because by then she was stepping up to do it and took the lead from there on out.

Michael: And she was certainly turbo-motivated.

Christian: Well, hello, I did the same with staff meetings. Hosting these meetings is always the task of the employees. I have often received feedback that meetings with customers are much easier and more effective since the employees have presented internal meetings for a few months.

Michael: Yeah, sure. You had the chance to build and train these skills. Funny you mention that. I also had an important experience in that regard. I have always enjoyed hosting and conducting workshops. That's why I have led most of the team workshops and meetings myself. I no longer do that today. At that time, someone from my team came to me and said on his own initiative, "Michael, we would love to host ourselves and would like to have you as a resource. It would be great if we could decide and lead the process and the structure ourselves and you would be there as a participant." This feedback has totally changed my perspective, my mindset, and I was super grateful for it. Until then, I always thought that, as the boss, I had to lead through the process myself. That was when I realized that I too could simply be a participant while someone else led the process and took over the leadership. Suddenly it became much easier for me because I only needed to give input and I could rely on my team.

Christian: For you it has become easier, for the employee it was motivating and maybe even the meetings have improved. I have also experienced this. I used to just stick to doing things my way and as soon as someone else took over, there was suddenly improvement.

Michael: I have learned that if I am good at something, I can still delegate it to someone else. I was still able to delegate what I considered one of my core competencies. That was great.

Christian: The core competence becomes a different one. Your core competence is then to hand over.

Michael: Absolutely right. Delegating and handing over tasks is a competence that I built up. That was not easy for me. I was more of a control freak about some things and wanted to be involved myself. Over the years, I have learned that it is much easier and better to delegate tasks completely and to trust others.

Christian: We just talked about adult learning. How can I now implement and ensure this for every employee in the company on an ongoing basis? Are workshops the right way? Is it a part of it? Does e-learning help?

Michael: I would always put it back to the three elements that work well in adult learning and which we have basically just described in our stories. Interestingly, these are all elements that are more kinesthetic in nature. The learner has a physical experience. When I teach content myself as a trainer, I have a physical experience. I don't just hear something, I don't just see something; I experience this role with my entire being. When I try something out, it is also an experience. I take responsibility for it, I discuss—perhaps even controversially—and I take a stance. I am also involved emotionally, so to speak. On the other hand, when I read a book, sit in a classroom, or just watch a video tutorial, I perceive it in a purely visual or auditory way. It is not a kinesthetic moment, not a physical experience. What I pay attention to in advanced training is that the formats are diverse and the experiences are balanced. Books are still a useful thing, classical training can also help, video tutorials, for example on YouTube, are often a great way to get started. There is a gigantic pool of content from which I can take a crazy amount. The greatest learning success is when I combine all this with experiments and discussion. And it is very important to make it easy and to teach it directly yourself. If someone wants to learn a new topic, it's probably a good idea to do this with YouTube tutorials or to attend a seminar. Afterwards, I would ask them to share the content with the team. I can link this directly and organize a meeting in which the team can also benefit from the content in an hour or two. In this way, what has been learned is reinforced, perhaps even extended by the employee's own preparation. The team gets something out of it and I also learn something. It is a win-win situation for everyone.

AUDITORY   LECTURE

                  READING

                  AUDIO-VISUAL

VISUAL   DEMONSTRATION

                  DISCUSSION

                  PRACTISE DOING

KINAESTHETIC   TEACH OTHERS

Illustration: Effective learning
Only when I teach something to others do I recognize if I have really understood it. For me it's the most effective way to learn. All senses are activated.

Christian: When you just mentioned the kinesthetic experiences, I was thinking again about my sports sailing license. There, too, I instantly experienced and associated what I had learned with all my senses. The easiest part to learn was navigating, because I experienced formulas and content using the map, the compass, and so on. I kinesthetically experienced the theory I had read before. If something really interests me, I imagined it with all my senses. That way I can memorize it well. It probably only works when I get really enthusiastic about something.

Michael: It reminds me of the story of a captain in the US Army in captivity. I think it was during the Vietnam War. Anyway, the story goes like this. The captain was a golfer and a prisoner of war for many years, locked up in a small cell. In order not to go crazy, he imagined every day with all his senses that he was playing golf on his favorite golf course. He played all the shots down to the last detail and imagined them mentally.[36] After many years of captivity he came back home. When he actually stood and played on the golf course, he had a much better handicap than before captivity. All because he felt his way into every shot with all his senses and played through every movement. Even his physical condition, his muscles, actually built up accordingly. He had better reflexes than before. *Mind over matter.*

Christian: You hear that about race car drivers, too. I once attended a lecture by Walter Röhrl, the rally driver. He did it the same way. While the others were partying in the evening, he sat in his room and went through the course curve by curve in his head. He associated it kinesthetically. He felt everything, probably even smelled the inside of his car.

Michael: I know this myself from playing the piano. When I learn a new piece and I really want to be able to do it, I eventually reach a point where I begin to be obsessed with it. No matter where I am, I begin to imagine how I play that piece, where the tricky parts are, where I pay special attention to making sure my fingers hit the right keys. The game goes on mentally. There is also a book about it by a famous coach. It is called *The Inner Game of Tennis*. The author describes how to win a tennis match not only physically, but first mentally.

Christian: Now it would be exciting to know if I can learn tennis only by using my imagination.

Michael: Here we go.

Christian: I'll try it out. See you next year in Wimbledon.

Michael: I'll warm up.

---

36 https://espygolfapp.com/blog/col-hall-p-o-w-veteran-hanoi-hilton/

Presenting content from projects, training, or further education to the team yourself is really a good idea. It's worth institutionalizing and rotating it so that everyone can pass on to their colleagues what they have learned or what they are really good at. This way, everyone gets an even better understanding of the topics his colleagues are working on and expands his own competence. Learning methods and the use of media can also be exchanged and tried out in a protected atmosphere. The better the whole thing works, the more these sessions can be expanded and also take place across teams, so that the entire company benefits.

DECISIONS AND PRIORITIES
ME, YOU, WE OR EISENHOWER?

Christian: It is 2020 and the Corona crisis has us in its control. Many entrepreneurs are freaking out. What can we do? How can we help them?

Michael: From a little crisis situation in my past, I memorized the baseball analogy. I know it from the United States and I think it is a good help especially in these times. My mentor in those days, Terry, taught it to me. At that time, he was strategy director of an international corporation. Today he is a professor at Stanford University. I was lucky to have him as my mentor. We used to see each other once or twice a year and only had half an hour together. For me, each of those 30 minutes was super powerful. At our very first meeting I told him about my new role. Back then I had over 100 people on my team and quite a lot of responsibility. It was very operational and super hectic. There was little time for planning. As an American, Terry knows baseball pretty well. When I explained my situation to him, he asked me, "Do you know what a batting average is?" I answered, "No, I don't." He explained it to me. "We use it in baseball to measure how often a player hits a ball." The baseball bat is the wooden bat that a player holds in his hand in baseball. The player stepping up to the plate to take his turn hitting the ball is called the *batter*. The batting average rates the player by measuring how many balls out of 100 the batter hits with his bat. The batting average is therefore a KPI expressed as a number between zero and one, with three decimal places. The best players in the world have a batting average of over 0.300 and very few have ever gone above 0.400. So the best of the best players miss over six out of ten hits.

Christian: That is quite a lot.

Michael: Yes, and yet it is world class. Terry then said with regard to my situation, "If you are in a leadership position like this, it comes down to your batting average as a leader." He compared the situation as a leader to baseball, basically saying that in hectic situations, it is important to make decisions quickly. I try to hit the ball as soon as it comes flying at me. If I wait and do nothing or delay the decision, the ball is lost. It is a miscount.

Christian: And the ball might land in your face.

Michael: Probably. Anyway, almost certainly nothing good will happen. So waiting is not an option. He said I should realize that as a manager I will not get every decision right. So, especially in crisis situations, it's much more important to make decisions quickly so that things can move forward. This baseball analogy helps me a lot, especially now in Corona times. I often think back to it. It helps me to relax and also to forgive myself if I make a wrong decision. It is important that I hit the balls when they come flying at me.

Christian: Another exciting aspect of this analogy is that the professional players have already tried out and practiced their hits beforehand. By practicing and repeating, they have achieved a hit rate of over 30%. The things I learned and the habits I've acquired outside of the crisis can be applied in the crisis. If I have practiced it before, I can fall back on it in the crisis and apply these things even more consistently.

Michael: Right. In this situation, I have to trust myself. We're standing on the field now and we're playing. I hit the ball when it comes flying. I am who I am and I perform what I perform. And that is a good thing.

Christian: Right, because it's just like you said, not making a decision is the worst way I can go. If I make a wrong decision, I can quickly undo it and learn from it. "Okay, I hit, it didn't work. Now we'll do it differently."

Michael: We are seeing the same thing happening right now in connection with the Corona pandemic in politics. Decisions are currently being made off the cuff every day. And decisions that have been made are revised after a day or two. It's a nice example of the baseball analogy. I would even say that we can observe very well which players on the political stage have particularly high batting averages and which do not. These are very tense times.

Christian: Yes, we can literally see who has already practiced making decisions quickly and who has not. Let's extend the picture a little bit more. Let's imagine that I'm standing on the field as a batter, a ball is flying at me and at the same time the coach calls to me. So the moment I hit the ball, I may also prioritize.

Michael: Prioritizing is very important. The Eisenhower Matrix helps me in this context. It helps me to distinguish between urgent and important things. I use this matrix very often. I paint a 2x2 matrix. On one axis I write *urgent* and on the other axis I write *important*. As so often I get four quadrants. In the quadrant in which both the importance and the urgency is high, there seems to be a lot piling up in crisis situations. There is also the quadrant with important things that are not yet urgent. These things I can do later. That leaves two quadrants with unimportant things. Unimportant and not urgent I just ignore. Urgent things, which are not so important, I try to delegate. I myself, as a manager, deal exclusively with the two quadrants that contain the important things.

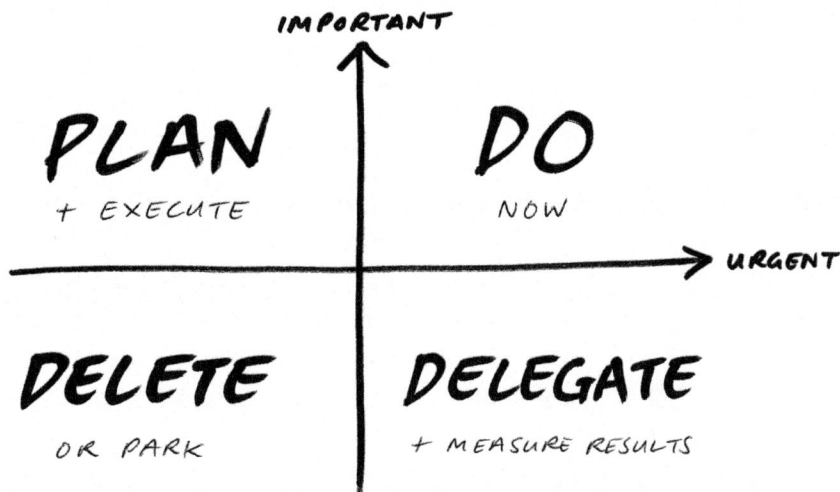

IMPORTANT

PLAN
+ EXECUTE

DO
NOW

URGENT

DELETE
OR PARK

DELEGATE
+ MEASURE RESULTS

Illustration: Eisenhower Matrix
As a boss, I only take care of important things. If I plan well, I have almost nothing urgent. I delegate or delete less important things.

Christian: What are the criteria for *important* and *urgent*? I still remember this from my company. Back then, everything was always important and urgent. Nobody really wanted to admit to themselves that a few things belong in another quadrant. So almost everything was squeezed into one. What is really important?

Michael: Good question. I usually draw this matrix in the morning and think about what is absolutely urgent for today and what should be done in any case. Right now in the midst of a crisis there are things that are like the ball in baseball. They come flying at me. If I don't do them immediately, I have lost. I can't afford that right now. On the other hand, when I plan strategically, I consider an annual basis or a three-year basis to be "urgent." In a crisis, I look at each day and maybe even look over the coming week. What may be done at this time is urgent. Whether or not something is important, I determine according to the impact of the task. What happens as a result if I complete or do not complete the task? Maybe it's just a small thing that doesn't have big, negative consequences for the company or me if it goes wrong or is not done. I can afford it if it is part of the 40% of the hits that miss. Then maybe it is urgent and not necessarily important.

Christian: *Urgent* has more to do with time, with the time of day and with what is written in my calendar. *Important* is surely related to my Purpose, my Vision and my goals, isn't it?

Michael: Yes, exactly. How important something is describes the effects on my Purpose, my Vision, my Values, and my Strategies. Especially in times of crisis, I look at it every day. What are we doing all of this for anyway? What is our Purpose and Vision? Where do we even want to go and what are we allowed to do— especially in times of crisis—to get closer to our Vision? If we have even fallen behind as a result of the crisis, I reconsider what we can do to make up for it. Values are particularly important in a crisis. They are the decisive guidelines for functioning as a team, even under pressure. When I say to my team, "Guys, go as fast as you can," "Baseball batting average," and so on, the Values tell me whether the ball that is just coming towards me is still on the field or already out. My Values help me to decide how and when I hit the ball, especially in stressful situations.

Christian: Originally, the Eisenhower matrix was a 2x1 matrix. Eisenhower apparently believed that things that are urgent are never important and things that are important cannot be urgent at the same time. I also find the idea interesting. I use it to review my decisions of what I have categorized as urgent and important. I ask myself, "Does this seem important to me just because it is urgent? Or is it really important?" Does it really correspond to my Purpose, my Vision, and my Values?

Michael: Good challenge. Especially now, in times of lockdown due to the Coronavirus, I often think about cash flow. The urgent issues are to maintain liquidity and manage cash flow. I make decisions now to keep the company in business. It is similar to our definition of Purpose. *Purpose is why we do what we do beyond making money*. We experience this with many of our clients. Money and liquidity are currently the main focus; these are urgent issues and that is perfectly fine. Because if I don't get the money managed, I can forget about my Purpose and my Vision and Values. Without money, we may not be able to continue with our plans.

Christian: So there are things that are urgent and at the same time really important.

Michael: Perhaps a crisis is the occasion when urgent issues become important. In many cases, Eisenhower was certainly right when he said that urgent issues cannot be important at the same time. The matrix may have been expanded to a 2x2 matrix without his knowledge. Maybe he also meant by this that he himself only cares about important things and hands over everything that is not important to others or simply ignores it.

Christian: What is also important in a crisis, apart from prioritizing, is communication with the employees. Currently, many employees are working from home and are very uncertain about their personal future, maybe even about the future of the company, about their job, and about their income. Therefore, communication with employees is both urgent and important.

Michael: That's right. Communication is the number one priority in a crisis. Remote work is also a big issue right now. Just yesterday we talked about it in a coaching session. It's important to use the digital channels and orchestrate them in such a way that feels good for the team and so that the employees work closely together and are close to each other despite the physical distance.

Christian: Let's come back to the decisions that need to be made. How do I make sure that all these decisions are made in the company? Do I make them as an entrepreneur, as a managing director alone, or can I delegate some of them?

Michael: Good question. I use a matrix for that as well. It's a little tool I discovered through one of my other mentors. The Decision Matrix. This mentor thing is really great.

Christian: Get a mentor!

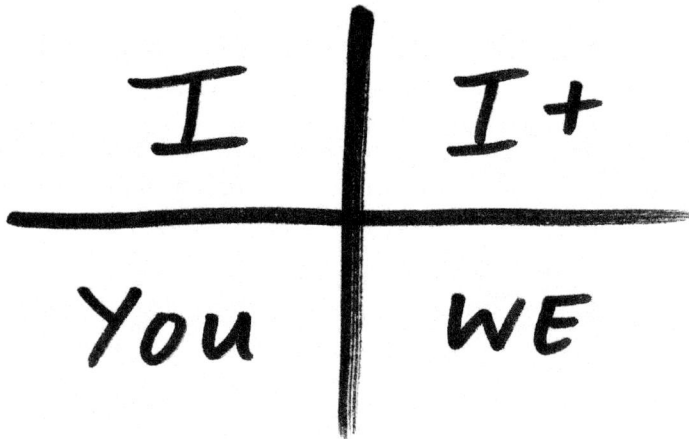

$$I \quad | \quad I+$$
$$\overline{}$$
$$You \quad | \quad WE$$

Illustration: Decision Matrix
We determine who makes which decision and how.

Michael: Yes, I can only recommend that. The decision matrix is also a 2x2 matrix. There are four decision modes. The first decision mode is *I*. Here I make the decision myself. The second mode is the *I+ mode*. Here, too, I make decisions as the boss. I get input from the team first and only then do I make the decision. The third mode is the *You mode*. In this mode I delegate the decision to someone else. I pass the responsibility for making this decision to someone else. She is accountable and does not have to ask me before. Of course, she can ask me for advice if she wants to. The decision is made by someone I choose, not myself. "I trust in your decision and will stand up for it. I stand behind you and we'll make it together." The fourth mode is *We*. Here we make the decision together. This mode often feels very harmonious, very democratic. However, it has a small flaw. It is important to determine from the beginning how we get to this decision. Do we decide by majority vote? Do we need a two-thirds majority? Do we need an absolute majority or is a simple majority sufficient? Do we decide by rolling the dice or by voting? All these things have to be determined in advance.

In all four modes, it is important that I plan who will decide what in advance with all people involved.

Christian: Another important decision: Do I have a veto?

Michael: Then it's no longer *us* who decide. Then it will be *me* again who decides. Classic. The important thing with these four modes – *I, I+, you, we* – is to agree beforehand which is the decision mode for the respective topic.

Christian: I decide on every issue and every decision that comes up, who makes that decision, right?

Michael: We decide. We agree which mode we will follow together.

Christian: Then the decisions are distributed. These apply to everyone, don't they?

Michael: Right. Everyone stands by the decisions that were made by whomever according to the decision matrix. That is very important. Everyone accepts each of these decisions. Everyone commits to it, no matter what decision mode was used. We do it together as a team. We can combine this wonderfully with the Eisenhower matrix—*urgent and important*—and the baseball analogy. In my opinion, these are really helpful and cool tools that allow me to steer through a crisis at a very high speed.

Christian: Great. Is there anything else important about it?

Michael: No, that's it.

Christian: Super. Then I decide that we are now finished with the topic.

Beautiful analogies! Actually, none of this is new. When I read your words, I realize how much of it still often goes wrong in reality. The world is becoming more and more complex and change is happening faster and faster, in large part, thanks to technological progress. Therefore, it is not only in times of crisis that we have to hit more and more balls and faster and faster. I will increasingly master this in my normal, everyday business. This cannot be accomplished through control and micromanagement without trust. Clear Vision, clear goals, and clear Values that define the framework conditions enable my employees to make these decisions themselves to together hit more balls and faster. Thank you very much for this great mental picture I now have to think about decision and priorities.

I GOT RHYTHM

— GEORGE GERSHWIN, 1930

THE RHYTHM OF THE BUSINESS
LAYOUT AND ORDER OF COLLABORATION OVER TIME

Christian: Hey Michael, you are a musician, right? The image of a drum set just comes to my mind. For a really good groove, my drum set consists of a bass drum, a snare, a hi-hat, and maybe in between my groove you can still hear the cymbal and every few bars a fill. This way a nice melodic rhythm is created in the song. The drum set provides the structure and every single component of the set is important for the rhythm. I like to use this image for the meeting rhythm in an organization, so to speak, the drumbeat in a company. Others call it the cycle, the heartbeat. I like the bass drum. I like to think of the team meeting as the bass drum and the daily huddle as the hi-hat.

Michael: And then there are the tom-toms and whatever they're all called.

Christian: There is always a filler every now and then. We do something special as a team every three months, for example. What kind of meetings are there in the day-to-day business? Which ones are important?

Michael: Let's stay with the music analogy. On the one hand, there is the entire song and on the other hand, there are individual sections consisting of bars and notes: whole notes, half notes, quarter notes, and eighth notes. It's the same with the company rhythm. There is the annual, quarterly, monthly, weekly, and daily rhythm. These are at least the rhythms that I have come to know and appreciate. Some meetings take place every two weeks. I have experienced this before.

Christian: There may also be companies with varying degrees of nervousness. Some work more like the Funk Style, they are very fast on the hi-hat. Others operate more in a laid-back rhythm. The differences also have to do with the industry.

Michael: I suddenly hear a bit of free jazz in my ear or 12-tone music.

Christian: That works when everyone has the same taste in music.

Michael: Rhythm to me is something that connects everyone. If we all play the same rhythm, the same song at the same tempo, we end up with a great groove. If everyone plays a different song or mixes in free jazz with different-ly tuned or even untuned instruments, none of us can last long. So we will certainly not sell many tickets.

Christian: What does that mean? What is really important in a company? With drums it seems to be obvious. What is it like in the everyday life of the company? Weekly team meetings are important, right?

Michael: At least we've always done it this way. That worked out well. We had the management meeting every two weeks for a while. However something was missing. That wasn't so good. We changed it back to weekly, restruc-tured and shortened it a bit. It was previously scheduled for three hours, which we always made full use of. That was just too long.

Christian: If you schedule three hours, it takes three hours.

Michael: Right. That's why I've become a big fan of very sharp formats. That's also my personality type. Every morning, a 10-minute daily huddle with ev-eryone together. Everything is just briefly touched upon and the day is struc-tured. So everyone knows about the most important things and is sorted for the day. It's totally beneficial and only takes 10 minutes of everyone's time. It works like a booster for the day. Everyone is totally focused.

Christian: We will talk about how a daily huddle works at another point. The goal is that each one gives a very short update on what happened the day before and what they are doing today. So everyone knows what is going on.

Michael: It's like a little rhythm. The next bar is the weekly team meeting. It is a valuable structure that helps to keep things focused. Even if I improvise and try things out myself from time to time, it helps to make the meeting efficient so that it doesn't become just an opportunity to chit-chat.

Christian: You mean the meeting structure? An agenda to structure the meeting helps.

Michael: Yes, exactly, the structure. I don't mean the content of the meeting, but the framework. Why are we here today? For what Purpose is this meeting taking place? Who is present and what do we want to achieve today? It has been a good meeting when after half an hour everyone leaves the meeting and has a clear action list. Who does what by when? This way I make sure that something happens after the meeting and that it wasn't just empty words.

Christian: The external structure is also important from my point of view. If we agree to meet once a week in a team meeting, then the meeting will take place. It will not be cancelled because of flimsy excuses. Like, "This week is bad for me." It is binding and obligatory for everyone.

Michael: Absolutely. It's basically the most important time the team has together. Everyone needs to be committed.

Christian: The topics of the meetings are different. In the daily huddle we discuss very operational, short-term things. In the weekly meeting we look at the whole week. In the monthly or three-monthly Strategy meeting, we take a somewhat long-term perspective. This is how we ensure that nothing is forgotten.

Michael: We're talking again about rocks, pebbles, and sand, the big chunks and the little grains, remember? All three things can be addressed in the right context through this meeting structure. We discuss the sand in the daily huddle. "I have a problem here and I'm not getting anywhere right now. Can anyone help me today?" The pebbles are more likely to be addressed in the weekly meeting. The big rocks might need an hour or two of your time. I put them on the agenda of the Strategy meeting. We can go deeper into them together in the group and take our time accordingly.

Christian: Imagine someone saying in the daily huddle, "Hey guys, I'd like to redefine the Purpose."

Michael: [*laughs*] "Sure, no problem. We have three minutes left. Let's do it."

Christian: "You two sit together later and do that please."

Michael: Or the other way around: I'm sitting in the Annual Strategy Retreat dealing with a system error that occurred with one of my 10,000 customers because the phone number was in the field where the email address should be.

Christian: Oh yes, I'm sure all managers can get upset about that for 15 minutes. [*laughs*]

Michael: Definitely.

Christian: The weekly check-ins with my direct employees are also important for me. Every week, half an hour with each employee. We have already talked about this in the context of management tools. These meetings help me enormously in managing employees.

Michael: You mean the 1:1 talks?

Christian: Yes, exactly. These meetings have raised my leadership style and my managerial skills to the next level. The meetings are great, I find them very important and helpful.

Michael: It's a great discipline to take half an hour of my time each week for my employees.

Christian: The employee always takes time for me as a manager when I want her to. If I ask, "Hey, do you have five minutes for me," she will usually say "yes." In the other direction, it's an inhibition threshold. "Boss, do you have five minutes for me?"

Michael: If the inhibition threshold is not there and you have seven or eight employees, who all need five minutes of your time in between, your day will be constantly disrupted. Your focus is no longer on the things that are important.

Christian: Then there are the quarterly meetings.

Michael: Yeah, they're great. I really like them. They're a lot of work, though. In the beginning, we did an offside with all people, the whole company, every quarter of the year. It was a whole day. Then, at some point, we reduced it to half a day because we couldn't just operationally take out the entire company for a whole day. We restructured it. About a month before the quarterly All-Hands, we prepared the top management team meeting. We thought about the goal and what we wanted to achieve in the upcoming All-Hands. Then, about two weeks before the quarterly All-Hands, we finalized with the next management level, the leadership team. This was a group of about 30 people with whom we did a two-day offside to plan everything very specifically, content-wise. In the actual All-Hands we then put on a really cool show with the entire leadership team of about 30 people in front of all 400 employees. In small groups, we worked out with everyone what we wanted to achieve in the next quarter, what our plan was, and what was relevant for the entire company. We had a clear process for this.

I owe it to our then CEO to have structured and prepared All-Hands this way. It would never have occurred to me to invest so much time to conduct this meeting. It was really elaborate. First, the preparation on the executive team, then the two days offside with the leadership team, and then half a day with everyone together. And that happened every quarter. It really does add incredible Value. We took the whole company with us, everyone knew what it was all about, where the company stands, what we are all doing this for. The Purpose, our Vision, and so on have become a bit more solid each time and the employees identify with it. The preparation time has definitely paid off. In retrospect, it is totally clear to me that it is our responsibility as a management team to organize such things. This way I can lead many people at once in a very meaningful and goal-oriented way.

Christian: I tried that, too. Before we had a reasonable meeting structure at *chicco*, we thought we could handle everything in one meeting. We drifted so far into operational topics that it was no longer useful. All employees wanted to bring up their own individual topics because there was no other opportunity. We simply didn't lead properly before. Over time, we revised this meeting structure and it went much, much better. Employees could bring up their topics in the daily huddles, team meetings, or 1:1 discussions. In doing so, our monthly or quarterly meetings have become much more goal-oriented and efficient. We were able to concentrate on the important, big issues again and no longer drift into minor, smaller issues. It is important to change perspective from meeting to meeting and to differentiate between the topics that are discussed in each format.

Michael: Then the hi-hat doesn't have to try acting like the bass drum.

Christian: Right, she will break through much better then.

Michael: I'm really looking forward to the groove.

Christian: I would like to mention one more thing. Seth Godin[37] once said, "There are three types of meetings and it is important not to mix them up." The first type of meeting is for exchanging information. Information moves from A to B. The second type of meeting is for forming an opinion, discussing, and brainstorming. The third type is exclusively for making decisions. Decisions are made here. I think this distinction is great. It makes it clear that there are different objectives of meetings and it doesn't make sense to put everything in one place. First, information is exchanged in a meeting, then discussions take place, an opinion is formed, and finally, I make a decision.

Michael: I think that's great, too. It reminds me of the model I use to structure my notes. I've explained that before. An *i* as a marginal note in my notes stands for information that is important to me. *A* stands for an action or a to-do that I take with me. A *d* I note next to the actual note when a decision has been made.

I think it's great to always make it clear what the Purpose of the meeting is right then. A board meeting, for example, is a typical decision meeting. We have had different experiences with this as well. When a board meeting takes place in a large company that is listed on the stock exchange, people are sometimes flown in specially. A week before the board meeting, they receive a document, a pre-read with around 100 pages, which they are supposed to have read and understood before the board meeting. Questions are also clarified in advance so that a decision can really be made in the board meeting. The pre-read already contains recommendations for action. When the board meeting comes together, everyone looks each other in the eye, makes a decision, and then commits to it.

Christian: Also, there are surely informational and opinion-forming meetings before, in which a few things are discussed in a somewhat smaller circle. In the actual board meeting, only the decision is made and that's it.

Michael: Another thing I've learned to appreciate about meeting structure is to always check in and look at the big picture, whether it's a tactical, short-term meeting or a strategic, long-term meeting. "What does this meeting, this decision, have to do with our Purpose, our Vision, the Values, and the

---

37   https://seths.blog/2009/03/three-kinds-of-meetings/.

Strategies?," "Where are we at the moment?," "How does it bring us closer to our big goal?," "How can the meeting be conducted so that it is in line with our Values?," "What Strategy does it pay for?" For example, I ask, "Is this still in line with Strategy number three and our Purpose?" That's how I always remind everyone of our grand master plan, our Purpose, the Vision, the Values, and the Strategies. I am the Chief Repeating Officer.

Christian: We often did a *start-stop-keep* at the end of a meeting. Thus, we decided to start with project X next time, project Y went well, and we better leave out project Z. With our master plan always in mind, where do we actually want to go?

Michael: Cool, I know it the same way. We called it the *start-stop-continue.* It's the same. We make very conscious decisions about what we do and what we don't do. At one point, we even called it a *stop-start-continue.* We started with the *stop* topics and the very first thing we thought about was what we didn't want to do in the future, especially in strategic planning. "What do we stop doing immediately to free up more time and resources for new, meaningful things?" Then we thought about what is already running very successfully in order to stick to it. To actively plan the stop topics was a great learning with a huge effect.

Christian: Strategy is also what we don't do.

Michael: Right. That's something I can definitely think about when I'm planning.

Christian: Exactly, we make a stop first. Then another fill and then we go on the ride.

Michael: Great. It was very successful and fun. To be continued.

Meeting culture is really an endless topic. It often seems like the search for the Holy Grail. I like your rhythm and especially the structure. It is really crucial that all meetings are well prepared, presented in a structured way, and that it is clear who is leading the meeting. I have often considered hanging a clock in our meeting rooms, with a digital display counting the money in real time, which is just burned by unnecessary discussions, inattention, or waiting for other participants. Unfortunately, various projects or topic-related meetings are often added to the regular rhythm meetings. The tip to question whether the meeting really makes sense and plays into our Purpose, Vision, Values, and goals before setting up the meeting in the first place is a good Strategy.

DAILY HUDDLES
PROGRESS - PLAN - PROBLEMS

Michael: The Purpose for our joint venture, for the CoA Academy, is to help people be productive in a relaxed way, right? How are you doing in that regard? Where are you at right now?

Christian: Well, we have completed two more podcast episodes in the last 24 hours. I also found someone to help us convert our podcast into chapters for our book, which we plan to publish soon. This is a big step for us. So much for *progress*, the first *P* of the *PPP-update*. The second *P* stands for *problem*. I have the following problem: You sent me the table of contents for our book. I noticed that it is really a lot of material. So I'm unsure how to deal with it and how to continue working on it. I will think about that again. My *plan*— what the third *P* stands for—is now to record more podcast episodes and start with the first chapters of the book.

Michael: Great. Now I have a good picture of where you stand. Do you need help with your table of contents problem? Should we change something together or do something to solve the problem?

Christian: Not at the moment. I will think about it again and if necessary I will get back to you tomorrow.

Michael: Okay, cool. All right.

Christian: What about your PPP update?

Michael: About my progress: I have created the table of contents for our book. It was fun and I am very pleased with the way it has turned out, especially with the way our book is slowly taking shape. I also talked to Andi about our next coaching session, which we will offer next week via Zoom. We have discussed how we are going to organize the session, so it's going well. I also reviewed the first section of our book that we are working on. My problem is that I need a bit more time for myself. Also due to the Corona pandemic, I have a lot going on, with several private projects that I'm working on right now. I feel how important it is to keep the balance, and right now it threatens to tip over a little bit. My *plan* is to work on the video nuggets in the next 24 hours, which we want to offer as another format. These are short videos with one theme each. We want to test this format. I'm mainly working on our company's branding, also for the book. I'd like to have a realistic picture of our book already, the book cover, and the pages inside right now, so I basically just get to write the contents in. That was my PPP update.

Christian: Okay, great. Thank you. Can I support you with your problem? Can we change something about our collaboration so that it is easier for you to stay in balance?

Michael: No, not really. I think it's great how our collaboration works. I wouldn't want to change that. It's just important to me that you're aware of my situation. If anything changes with me, I'll let you know.

Christian: Okay, great.

Michael: How do you feel now? Describe it in one word.

Christian: Energetic. And how do you feel?

Michael: Satisfied.

Christian: Great, that was our daily huddle.

Michael: And now?

Christian: We just had our daily huddle and presented our PPP update to each other, everyone gave their *progress-problem-plan* update. We shared what we've accomplished in the last 24 hours and how this pays off on our common goals. Our Purpose is to help people become more relaxed and productive. A short-term goal is to publish podcasts on various meaningful topics. In the mid-term, we want to publish a book. So we have made progress to achieve these goals and fulfill our Purpose. At the same time, each of us may have problems that prevent us from moving forward faster. We have also talked about this and considered whether and how we can help each other. Finally, each of us presented our plan, what we will do in the next 24 hours to achieve the goals. This way, we both got a good insight into each other's progress. You even shared something very personal: that you stumble, that you get out of balance. This helps me to understand you and your situation. If I know your situation, it is easier for me to work with you.

PPP

PROGRESS   PLANS   PROBLEMS

DAILY HUDDLE WITH 1 MIN ON EACH

Illustration: PPP Update
Everything that is important for me to know from my colleagues: what have I achieved, what am I doing today, and where I need help.

Michael: Yes, exactly. I'm looking at the clock right now. It took us about three and a half or four minutes for the PPP update. So it's a maximum of two minutes per person. If I now do this with my team of 10 people, we need about 15 minutes, maybe 20 minutes at the most. After that, everyone knows what's going on and how it's going. After 20 minutes, everyone is informed and up to date, assuming we pull it off just as smoothly.

Christian: Experience shows that it often takes even a little less time. We have just done it very thoroughly and explicitly. We often did it in 30 seconds per person. With 10 people, we are done after five minutes.

Michael: I've added another rule to the PPP update. I call it the *Top 3 rule*. I only allow three issues per *P*. In Progress, I also just mentioned three issues. A single one somehow seemed insufficient to me. I often feel the need to name three items. No more, because more than three is too many. Of course, it also works with only one big issue per *P*. Then it goes faster. One progress, one problem, one plan. Next.

Christian: When we do a daily huddle every day, sometimes there is not much to say about progress or problems. With the plans I expect something.

Michael: The daily huddle is a daily, very short team meeting to synchronize, share, and support each other.

Christian: Who participates?

Michael: Well the team. So you with yours, I with mine.

Christian: How long does a daily huddle last?

Michael: If it stays within 10 minutes, experience shows that it is most effective and even fun. It's really just a huddle—put our heads together quickly, briefly exchange, and then proceed. Under no circumstances do we sit down or stretch our legs. We also don't quickly get a coffee or something like that. Huddle, quick exchange and off we go.

Christian: And the PPP updates help to structure the exchange?

Michael: Right.

Christian: And what if a discussion topic does arise? Then I discuss it afterwards?

Michael: Exactly. Definitely not in a huddle. Discussion topics are only discussed by the people the topic concerns. Otherwise, the others just sit there bored and twiddle their thumbs. One more thing is important. We always did a check-in at the beginning and a check-out at the end. We asked ourselves how we felt at the moment. It's all about the emotional level. I myself tend to neglect this a bit sometimes. I learned that it is very valuable to hear from everyone how they are feeling right now. Every employee formulates this at the beginning at check-in and at the end at check-out. That's how I can tell if there is something wrong. If there is, then I approach the employee afterwards and work it out separately, outside the huddle.

Christian: That was once again a smart and snappy daily huddle with the two of us. Thank you, Michael.

Michael: We are heading towards our goal. Everything is in balance.

Stand up, do not sit down. Ten minutes maximum. Progress, problem, plan, and a short balance update per person. Everything else comes later. I will remember that. In most cases, we tend to turn a daily huddle into a 45-minute chat meeting. Not anymore. The time is over now. This will certainly lower the frustration level and increase the number of participants.

4.

"THIS IS HOW WE'RE GOING TO RUN THIS COMPANY"

— GRAHAME MAHER, 2008

IT'S ALL ABOUT THE PEOPLE!

WE ARE ALL IN THE EMPLOYEE BUSINESS

Christian: Hey Michael, you like to say: *It's all about the people*. What makes you say that?

Michael: Yeah, exactly. I've come across this saying in two places in the past that I remember. One time, someone said it to me in a somewhat cynical tone. At that time, a new CEO for our company was announced. He was said to be very popular. I was talking to a colleague at the time, and he said that the new CEO was a good guy that people liked. Then he brought up this saying and observed, "He's just a people person, you know? It's all about the people, man." He said it pretty snootily. I would have loved to respond, but I was just grinning and thinking about the story when I first heard it. In South Africa I learned: *It's really all about people*. Two years earlier I had arrived there and was asked to manage a call center. In the beginning, I only had a small team, then it grew bigger and bigger. It quickly grew to 220 people and by the end there were more than 2,500 people on the team. For me it really was *all about the people*. It was a pure people business. At that time, I handled more HR tasks than anything else. I came across this saying again when I met Moneeb, one of my employees at the time. It was my first day in South Africa, I came there as a greenhorn. On the one hand, I came from a different country and a different culture, and on the other hand, I had no idea at all about call centers. Moneeb, on the other hand, had been in call center management for well over 10 years and knew everything from top to bottom. He took me to task back then, in a nice way. I was practically his new boss. He looked me in the eye, blinked and then did something that we don't teach our coachees. He pointed his index finger at me and had a very serious, almost threatening expression on his face. He said, "Michael, the people can make you or they can break you." I remember it very well, I could still find the spot in the building where we were standing. It was on the 12th floor, Pier Place, Downtown Cape Town. I had totally mixed feelings. I found it kind of amusing, thinking, "Man, why is he making such a show out of this?!" At the same time, I realized that maybe I should take him seriously and listen to him. He obviously wants to tell me something. Many years later I called him and thanked him. He laughed and could actually still remember the situation —after more than 10 years! It was really a very beautiful moment. I took a lot with me from that exchange. Although I was his boss, he led me upwards. He said it so straight to my face and looked me deep in the eye that I really took it seriously. *It is all about the people.* He really lived and breathed it. He chose the form of communication with which he definitely got through to me. I was lucky enough to work in this environment for two years and had this slogan in my head from the very beginning: *It is all about the people.* It was a great success, perhaps the biggest of my professional career, at least in terms of people management and culture. We got along very well and really managed to put something together that moved mountains. I am very grateful for this mega experience.

Christian: *It is all about the people.* I am also thinking of the story attributed to Howard Schultz of Starbucks. He once said, "We're not in the coffee business and we employ people. We are in the employee business and we sell coffee." I was very impressed by that, because at *chicco di caffe* that was exactly the point. Eighty or ninety percent of what we did every day was about people management and customer care; it's also a people business. I claim only five to ten percent of what we did was actually about the coffee we served. Our customers don't just come for the coffee, they also come for the people behind the counter. I've never really found out how big the percentage of guests who come to us primarily for a chat is. I guess it's over 60% or 70%. Drinking coffee is just one part of the experience at *chicco.*

Michael: Well, actually it's also an iceberg.

Christian: Yes, that's right. We always thought we were in the coffee business. That was also the story we told ourselves, as well as the label, which was on top of it. In the end we were in the employee business.

Michael: The situation is similar for automotive companies. They are also beginning to understand that they are no longer in the car business, but in the mobility business.

Christian: At least that's what they tell us. That said, if you drive to one of the big car manufacturers and try to get a parking space at 10am, it's almost impossible. At least, before the crisis.

Michael: [*laughs*] Yeah, that's right. [*pause*] Later, when I moved to Qatar from South Africa, I met the new CEO I mentioned at the beginning. He was not only my boss, he also became my friend and mentor. Grahame was his name. His motto was said to be: *It's all about people,* and it really was. He really lived it with every fiber. For him, everything revolved around people. At the beginning, I found that difficult. We were always told we were a technology company, we had a cool product, we were building a data center, we were defining a pricing Strategy, and who knows what else. Then I realized that all this is still done by people and that it is also people who consume all this. The game I'm in as a boss, as a managing director, as a CEO, or as a senior executive is always the game of people. Everything revolves around people. I have come to realize that there are two sides to the coin, and this is exactly what I like about business. One side is the culture, the behavior, Values, customs, and rituals of a company, just what the company is like. On the other side is the brand, what the company radiates to the outside world, how it is perceived. I don't mean marketing and branding, but really what it stands for. For me, these two sides of the coin are directly connected. Only through a certain type of culture that comes from within can I convey or radiate a certain brand to the outside world. If the culture and the brand are not congruent, it will not lead to success. Pain and effort are therefore a sure bet in this situation and relaxed productivity is basically not possible at all.

Christian: Right. Both the people inside the company and the people outside feel that something is wrong. It is not authentic.

Michael: *It is all about the people:* brand, trademark, and the culture in any case.

Christian: In the B2B business, I always notice this. I have never sold anything to a company before. I always sell to a person who is part of the company. Of course, this person is connected to the company, the culture, and the brand in a certain way and is authorized to do or not to do certain things. Nevertheless, I have always convinced a person, not the company. It goes from person to person.

Michael: Yes, that's right. People to people. From human to human, whether B2B or B2C or B2B2C. This insight is super powerful for the sales team. When

I want to optimize the sales area, I think about who the people are that are involved. How do I approach them and how can I convince, influence, and lead them?

Christian: Again, behavioral flexibility helps.

Michael: I guess that's true. When I deal with many people—inside and outside of the organization—it helps me to be empathetic to each individual. I accept that each of them is different and try to understand the different types and their behavior. In the Rhineland, we say this: *Jeder Jeck ist anders,* which means *each fool is different*. And that is a good thing. I have come to understand this to be so true; different is always better. I really enjoy getting to know people who are totally different from me. It's always enriching to meet characters I've never seen before. I try to be open for everyone. I always take something new with me from my encounters. Diversity is a crucial ingredient for success. Diversity contributes to a better overall result. To achieve this, I naturally first try to understand the essence of people and how I can best communicate with them. Because I need communication in order to lead.

Christian: In this respect, I learned a lot from Ralf, my business partner at *chicco.* At the beginning, we liked going to the customer in pairs and seeing on the spot who managed to establish a better relationship with the customer or the contact person. That person was also the one who took the lead. One of us always managed to build up rapport and establish a relationship. Only once did it happen to us that neither of us actually managed to get through to the client. Nothing came of that.

Michael: *People like people who are like themselves.* Many sales people have a special stereotype in mind When someone talks about a really good sales guy, it immediately rings a bell, right? *This is a typical sales guy*. The question is: For whom is it a typical sales type? *People like people who are like themselves.* The way you did it, chapeau. Because the best sales guy is the one who builds the best relationship with someone. This is rarely the same sales guy, quite the opposite. That is a decisive insight. Maybe that's why it doesn't work out with that one customer because the salesperson does not yet have the necessary behavioral flexibility. She may not have been able to adapt to the customer. One solution is to send someone to this customer who doesn't have to adapt at all because she may have the same or similar preferences as the customer. She would have it much easier in sales.

Christian: *It is all about the people.* Now what do I do with it as the boss?

Michael: I embrace this and link it directly to my Purpose. There are two particularly important things. The first is people, the second is my Purpose. "Why are we all here?," "Why do we do this and not something else?," "Why do I feel like jumping out of bed in the morning and going to work?" Because that is exactly what I want to do. *It is all about the people and then getting the right people on the bus*, those who believe in the Purpose. Those who get up in the morning for exactly that, are motivated and want to fight for the grand Vision. At least, that's what I would do with it. [*grins*]

Christian: Then, when the right people are on the bus, I keep them there and deliver great results together with them.

Michael: Exactly. We achieve our goals and retain our employees.

Christian: It is all about the people, man.

Michael: And women.

That's right. People, needs, motives, ultimate behavioral flexibility. Do women have an advantage in this now? Or is this just a prejudice?

LEFT BRAIN, RIGHT BRAIN
RATIO AND EMOTION IN HARMONY

Christian: I would like to talk to you about our right and left brain hemispheres and what forms of disease this can result in for me personally and in the company. You like to use the example of van Gogh,[38] the artist who is said to have cut off his own ear.

Michael: Yes, that's right. I wonder how he managed to do that.

Christian: Pretty crazy to cut off your own ear.

Michael: For sure, he was probably a little bit one-dimensional.

Christian: When we talk about our right and left brain hemisphere in the company, what is it all about?

Michael: There is a general understanding that the right and left hemispheres of the brain have different functions. The left half is responsible for this ability, the right half for the other. The auditory center is more on one side, the visual center is more on the other, logical cognition tends to take place here, and so on. Currently, science is constantly coming up with new findings about which side of our brain does what exactly. We use this more as an example. Our readers will hopefully forgive that we mean what we say rather as a model.

Christian: I'm glad you said that. Everything we discuss on this topic is rather figurative and not necessarily medically correct.

Michael: We don't look at it scientifically.

Christian: It is more about the holistic approach. About the big picture.

Michael: In this context, you like to talk about *yin* and *yang*. I think that's great, because it's a 1,000-year-old image of diversity. Each one has a little bit of the other in it, and it's combined into one circle. It is a really beautiful

---

38   Vincent van Gogh (1853-1890) was a Dutch painter and draftsman.

portrait. Both parts make up a whole. This is what makes an organization, a company, or a team successful. It is important to bring both sides together; the yin and the yang coexist and together they deliver a great result.

Christian: What does this have to do with a company?

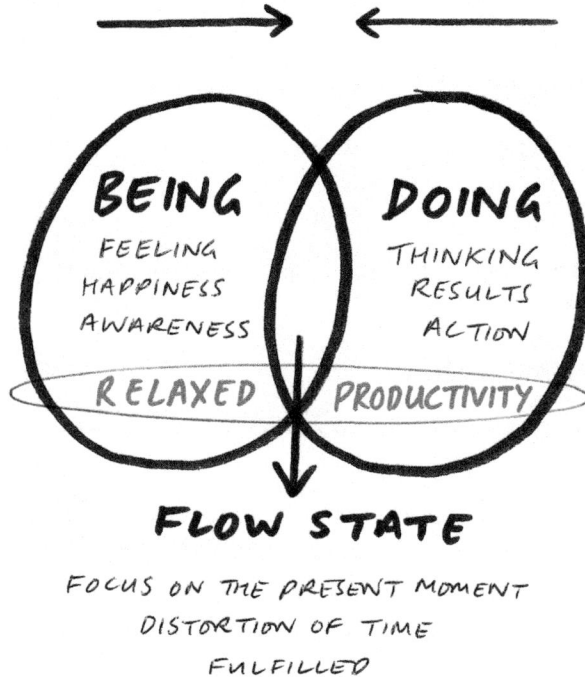

Illustration: Human Dynamic with Being and Doing.
Relaxed productivity results from the balance between doing and being, reason and emotion, relaxation and productivity. Vision and Purpose bring being and doing together into the flow state.

Michael: If we look again at the model of our master plan—the heart with the three circles—we see that in the middle, at the very center, is the circle with our Purpose. Above it is a circle with the Vision, and next to it the heart is painted. On the left and right below the Purpose there are two more circles. Bottom left are the Values and bottom right the Strategies.

Basically, I can compare the left side with our left brain hemisphere. This is about our being, our interpersonal behavior, our Values, feelings, the so called soft or emotional side. It represents the yin of a company, or whatever you want to call it. It is one side of our dynamics. On the other side, bottom right, are the hard facts, our Strategies and goals, our actions. This is what we call the right hemisphere of the brain, or the yang. In Jung's language, it is the task-orientation, while the left side corresponds to the emotional or people-orientation. So again, we recognize parallels to our *Insights* types and the color energies. There are organizations that are more on the right side, on the side of doing. They are more task-oriented. Others, however, have more of a feeling bent. Which companies can you think of that you would classify either on one side or the other?

Christian: First of all, I think that the companies that balance both are the ones that are most successful. In my opinion, companies that are only on one side will maneuver out of the market quite quickly.

Michael: I agree with that. Let's start with a few stereotypes for the sake of simplicity. Which companies come to your mind that are more task-oriented?

Christian: Especially very fact-based industries come to my mind: banks, IT companies, aerospace companies.

Michael: Yes. Companies that deal with very factual topics. Like you say, maybe a company that programs software, a tech company. What would be companies that are more on the left side of the brain, the emotional side?

Christian: Off the top of my head, I think of the NGOs,[39] i.e. non-governmental organizations that are very Purpose-driven.

Michael: The WHO,[40] for example.

Christian: Or environmental protection, everything that is good for the world and has a strong Purpose.

Michael: Let's look at individual roles instead of the corporate level. What are the typical roles in a company that are more right or left brain, more doing or more being?

---

39   NGO, English abbreviation for Non-Governmental Organization, German: Nichtregierungsorganisation.
40   WHO, English abbreviation for World Health Organization, German: Weltgesundheitsorganisation

Christian: A CFO, accounting, or sales department is probably on the right-hand side. Marketing managers are perhaps more likely to orient themselves towards the middle. A Chief Happiness Officer is definitely on the left side.

Michael: I think of social care, someone in the hospital, a doctor, a nurse. It feels like the left side of the brain. Psychologists also deal a lot with the feelings of people and their mental state.

Christian: Yes, it feels that way. Although I think it is not like that. As a doctor in a hospital, for example, I am very much involved in the technical side of things. At least I hope so.

Michael: That's right, everything can be 100% factual and factually correct there.

Christian: I would at least like to have a doctor who is also capable on the factual level.

Michael: That brings us to the essential point. What we're basically doing right now is very similar to the Insights Model types, just very one-dimensional. We're talking about preferences and attitudes. People are very different and that's good, because diversity means that we have different strengths. One uses the left side of the brain, the other the right side. One has more yin, the other more yang. One is more into being while another is more into doing. Whatever I call these two dimensions, it is important that a company covers both to get back to your point from before. You are right, of course. Because strength evolves from diversity, and this strength helps us to achieve our goals. Remember your example with the yoke? You saw marriage as a yoke.

Christian: At this point, I would like to make it clear once again that it was not my comparison, but the quotation of a priest. He said it at a wedding ceremony. And yes, it is true. When one of two oxen is stronger than the other, they plough in circles unless they use a yoke.

Michael: They don't move towards the target, they run in circles, that's true. The two holes look similar to the two circles I drew on a piece of paper in front of me for reference. If I can use both the emotional and the factual side profitably and align them to the same goal, I get the maximum strength to reach the goal quickly. And that is what it is all about. I need both sides of the brain, the soft side and the hard side. As a manager, essentially as a human being, I need soft skills and hard skills.

Christian: Our iceberg of communication, which we talked about for a long time, is also about the two halves of the brain. The rapport, which is most important for successful communication, takes place on the left side, on the emotional level. At the same time, I need the factual level for what I communicate. Both sides can be brought into harmony, both in 1:1 communication and holistically within the company. The rapport in the company and the factual level may be coherent.

Michael: So the two circles do not float anywhere next to each other, but overlap. There is an overlap between the two circles, an intersection. That's where the music plays, that's where I'm *in the zone*. There, our two cerebral hemispheres and those of the company are combined to ensure that we move toward our goals with maximum power. There I have satisfied and served all the different preferences of the people involved. Because, to be in the zone, every employee needs something different, of course. The one who needs more results is more likely to be strong on the right half, while someone else who needs more interpersonal contact probably tends to use the left half. It's my job as the boss to make sure that happens. I make sure that both sides are used and brought to bear so that all employees are happy, we achieve our goals, and fulfill our Purpose.

Christian: So far, so good. How do I do that?

Michael: You mean, how do I deal with the yin and yang thing? Well, the first step is for everyone to realize that it's important to me as the boss, and therefore to the company. We want people with a strong right brain and people with a strong left brain; we need people in being and people in doing. We want to position ourselves holistically because it has a Purpose. Only in this way can we fulfill our Purpose and achieve our Vision. So I speak openly with my employees about this model. I discuss it and reflect on it with each individual person: "Where do you see yourself more? On the left or right half? Are you more yin or more yang?" Whatever I call it, the important thing is that I create the feeling that both are desired in our company and that everyone here is at home, just as they are. Then I bring the whole thing in line with the business model and our master plan. *This is how we're gonna run this company.* So when we talk about Purpose, Vision, Values, and Strategy, we show that our Values in particular are the guarantee that we use both the left and the right side of the brain and Value both sides. I can't repeat it often enough in the company, at some point it is embedded in the culture. On the right side of our master plan are the Strategies and goals, what we want to do and achieve. On the left side are our Values, behaviors, our heart. We bring these two sides into harmony. "This is what we are doing this year. These are our behavioral guidelines. This is how we will achieve our grand Vision."

Christian: So I speak openly about what I want to achieve. I also talk about the left and right hemisphere of the company's brain.

Michael: Chief Repeating Officer.

Christian: Exactly, over and over again. "I want a burger. I want us to take this holistic approach. I want us to take the left and right hemisphere of the brain with us." I repeat it over and over again.

Michael: Purpose, Vision, Values, Strategies. Left brain, right brain. Yin and yang. Everything belongs to us. Everything belongs together. Holistic.

Christian: If I manage to do this and bring both sides into harmony, my company is healthy. I don't need to bite my ear off.

Michael: Everything is relaxed and productive. Relaxed left, productive right.

It's like the Insights types. I communicate that this diversity exists, that it is free of judgment, that we consciously want to develop balanced teams and create understanding for the respective preferences. I learn to deal with the resulting conflicts and make sure that no one on the team is condemned or "labeled" for their preference. Ideally, the top management is already equipped with different preferences and also communicates this openly within the company and proclaims this as a strength.

COLLABORACY

A COMPROMISE BETWEEN HIERARCHY AND HOLACRACY

Christian: *Trust and respect!* or *Trust and support*! We are in the middle of the topic of organizational structures. Have you noticed that?

Michael: Yes? How do we want to organize ourselves?

Christian: I am a fan of hierarchical structures.

Michael: Tell me about it.

Christian: I am a fan of hierarchy because I see some advantages. For example, I like clear structures. I think it's good when a few things are clearly defined. Who is my boss? Who is allowed to promote or dismiss me? Who decides about my vacation and my salary? I also think it's good for my employees to know who their boss is. It is always good for every employee to know who the boss is. Therefore, I find hierarchical structures good in principle.

Michael: That's interesting. At the moment, there's more of an opposite trend. Free forms of organization, home offices, and self-organized teams are becoming more and more popular. There are many examples of successful companies that work with forms of organization other than classical hierarchy. Do you see any advantages in this?

Christian: Yes. I think that a company can potentially be both more power-ful and more flexible this way. With a more consensus-oriented, democratic attitude, every member of the organization is more likely to feel that he or she has a say and can participate in decision-making. This has something to do with appreciation.

Michael: The key word is *agility*. It is possible to act faster, more powerfully, and more flexibly in a world that is changing more quickly and more radically.

Christian: Correct. I think that there is a suitable organizational structure for every company. At *chicco di caffe,* for example, everything was very standardized. In principle, one coffee bar works like the other. It is important that the same hygiene standards apply everywhere, that the quality is consistent everywhere, and that the billing processes are uniform. I find the classic organizational structure, in which a lot is specified from above, very suitable for *chicco*. In this way we were able to ensure that we offer our customers the same high standard everywhere. Not much changes from one day to the next.

Michael: What disadvantages have you experienced?

Christian: We have thought very carefully about what we have specified from above. Because if it was pointless or not equally feasible for everyone, it quickly blew up in our faces.

Michael: So when I specify crap, I end up with crap.

Christian: Exactly: *garbage in, garbage out*. So it's all up to the executive floor, to these omniscient entrepreneurial types who can do everything and do everything right. That is where the risk lies.

Michael: When I first joined the call center, several thousand people were working there in a very hierarchical structure. It was like a factory. It was always the same business, the same things were done day in and day out, over and over again. The bad thing was that basically every decision was passed on to the top. The standard answer of every employee was, "I have to ask my boss about this." This would even occur during minor customer inquiries. On the phone, the call center agent said to the customer: "I understand you, dear customer. I'll have to ask my boss about that." Then this agent asked his team leader. He answered, "Unfortunately, I can't decide that either, I'll pass it on to my boss." Then came the supervisor, who in turn said, "That has something to do with the product, I'm not allowed to decide that either." It was then passed on to some other manager, then to the executive, and at some point the case landed on the CEO's desk, who was then called upon to decide on a 50 euro credit for one of millions of customers. It crippled the entire company. That is the disadvantage of a hierarchically managed organization, because if things aren't clear, many decisions end up escalating upwards.

Christian: At *chicco di caffe,* the barista on site was allowed to make his own decisions. We made sure that the espresso tastes the same everywhere and that the milk froths the same everywhere. However, if a customer in the bar had something to criticize about the coffee or did not like the sandwich, it was up to the barista to decide whether to make the customer a new coffee or give the customer back the money for the sandwich.

Michael: So even in a hierarchical structure, there is trust in the employees to make their own decisions and room for maneuver in which they can act, even though this may not be the norm. I don't want to make a new coffee for every customer.

Christian: True. However, decisions are also made at the top as to who is allowed to decide what, so that there really is equal room for decision-making in all coffee bars.

Michael: I often know it from such hierarchical companies in which fixed roles that are specifically defined. These roles have a very clear role description. Everything is in writing, outlining precisely who is responsible for what, what specific actions are authorized and for what, and what it is not authorized, etc. In many companies, this is called *Policies and Procedures*. It is a document consisting of hundreds of pages. I'm sure that of the 70,000 corporate employees, there is no one who has actually read it, except those who have written it. The Purpose of this document is merely to provide the corporation with a set of rules, after which misconduct can be punished. With the help of this set of rules, I can then quickly get rid of people who have violated a paragraph of these *Policies and Procedures,* which of course they have never read.

Christian: This is the same trick as with the small print in insurance companies. I take out household insurance and as soon as I have a claim, it is written somewhere that exactly this case is not covered.

Michael: It's no longer pragmatic at all.

Christian: It costs trust and fun at work.

Michael: Right. Like with insurances. In the end, I make the decision based on trust. Even if I read the fine print, I am forced to google everything I don't understand and need to deal with it intensively. This can take weeks, so I seek advice that I trust.

Christian: Now we have talked about hierarchy. What about a contrary form of organization? For example, our collaboration has nothing to do with hierarchy.

Michael: That's right. We do not work in hierarchical structures at all. Although I also have a slight need for control and clear structure, freedom in my own way of working is very important to me. While I welcome some elements of a hierarchical organization and I understand some of its advantages, I prefer to decide for myself how I design and organize my work and how I proceed. This in turn does not fit at all into a hierarchical organization. I can understand very well why many high-growth companies and founders today have ambitions to shape their business differently than the generations before them. They strive for a higher degree of freedom. *Collaboration*, working together collectively, is the main focus. There are no simple work instructions like in a classical hierarchical structure. I have had a similar experience. We were a real team, a community of people on a journey together. All employees and even external companies worked together in a community towards a common goal and had a greater degree of freedom to organize their work than would ever have been possible in Rockefeller's time, for example, in a stale, conservative, and hierarchical structure.

Christian: That works best in a very flexible environment. You and I also operate in a very flexible environment with our company. We decide almost continuously how we work together and with whom. It is a relatively loose union in which we find ourselves.

Michael: Right. We've created a few cornerstones that guide us and give us a certain structure. This structure feels much more free, more flexible, and more loose than an old-school, hardcore hierarchical structure.

Christian: Let me guess: By the cornerstones you are referring to, do you mean our Purpose, our Vision, our Values, and our Strategies?

Michael: Exactly. The big master plan describes what we do, why we do it, where we want to go, and how we behave. It also defines the major strategic goals for the coming months. This master plan provides the framework for each employee. When everyone has this plan available, it is easy to decide whether what they want to do fits in with the plan or not. Does this count towards our goals and our Vision or not? The great master plan determines the cornerstones between which everyone can move freely.

Christian: Yet, we are moving in a 2x2 matrix again. We really can't help it. This matrix is spanned by the two axes *trust* and *support*.

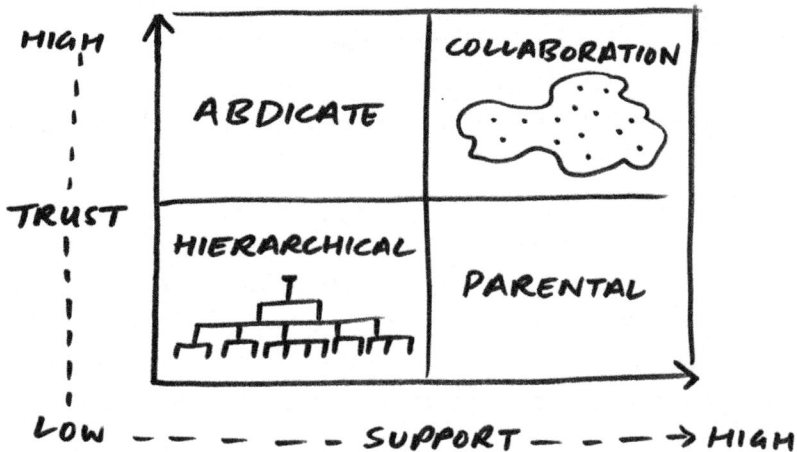

Illustration: Trust & Support
High-performance collaboration is based on trust and mutual support.

Michael: Right, there are once again four quadrants in this 2x2 matrix. Let's start with the lower left quadrant. There is little trust and little support. This quadrant describes the classic hierarchical form of organization. Here, too, is a certain amount of trust and support, only little of it is needed because everything is very clearly regulated and defined. The more rules there are, the less trust is needed. At the same time, the employees need less support, since basically everyone knows what needs to be done and what resources are available to them.

Christian: And if someone makes a mistake, you take the big rulebook, the 100-page document, lift your finger and say, "Here it says, you made a mistake. You were not authorized."

Michael: The opposite quadrant in the matrix describes what I mean by *collaboration*. A lot of trust and a lot of support is needed here to make it work. It describes a collaborative working environment. Everyone can decide for themselves how they organize their work, how they work together, and how they proceed. Here the different personality types and color energies come very much into play. One person likes to work in peace and quiet, the other prefers to have lots of people around him or her. One is more concerned with the cause, the other with the people. In this system I can develop myself much more strongly, move in my comfort zone, and pursue my strengths and preferences. I bring out the best in everyone. However, I need a high level of trust and support from the community to make it all work.

Christian: There are two more quadrants. One describes a high level of trust and little support. he other expresses a low level of trust and a lot of support. I can't think of any really meaningful organizational structure where this combination predominates.

Michael: Yes, that's right. It therefore describes the mistakes I can make when I strive for a collaborative model and fail to provide enough of the necessary components. In such situations, either trust in the employees is lacking, or the team receives too little support. In the second scenario, in which I put a lot of trust in the team yet it doesn't receive enough support, I let people down. "I trust you completely, you'll do fine." However, they need more resources, material, time, or know-how to be successful. If I don't take that into account and simply say, "You guys can do it, show me in six months what you've done," it won't work.

Christian: "You can do it."

Michael: It doesn't feel good to hear that. The team feels abandoned. That's why we call this quadrant *Abdicate*, in the sense of: *evading responsibility*. The other potential pitfall is lack of trust in the team. If I support the team members sufficiently and at the same time my trust is missing, collaboration in the team will not work either. In this case, I constantly have doubts. I start to control the employees, for example through micromanagement, and I am constantly overly cautious. This is similar to a parent-child role. I don't act at eye level with my people, but I am in parental mode. I have the feeling that the responsibility is too great for my child and I don't trust him or her to manage it. Even if I fully support it, without trust I cannot let go, and the team, consciously or unconsciously, starts to doubt itself. In that case, my company will not be successful.

Christian: It reminds me of when my daughter got her driver's license and we drove together for the first time. I had the urge to grab the steering wheel every so often.

Michael: "Here you have my support, you can still earn my trust." [*laughs*]

Christian: That is super demotivating. However, it can take a while to build up trust among each other. So it is possibly a transitional phase until the target structure is reached.

Michael: These are basic considerations about the form of organization. The question is, how do we want to be as a company? How do we want to organize ourselves? Should there be someone who determines everything and we dictate decisions top-down, or do we want to organize ourselves in a more modern way, allow more freedom, and benefit from different opinions and perspectives? There are also a lot of emotions in this topic. For me personally, it is important to find the balance that leads to the end goal. So the question is, with which form of organization do I best achieve my goals and my Vision? Which structure fits our Values and our Purpose? What culture do I want to create so that my employees are happy, are Valued and stay with the company? How do I best support my employees to be successful?

Christian: So it is not black or white, not either one way or the other. There are a lot of transition phases and opportunities to organize my company. I wonder if it isn't always a bit hierarchical in a certain way. Ideally, a Vision is always given. In collaboration, there is a hierarchically predefined Vision, which is then broken down into individual activities. In a classic hierarchical structure, there is also an organizational hierarchy.

Michael: Well, there's an important thought that comes to mind: structure is not the same as hierarchy. A structure is always necessary. The question is, how are we organized within the structure? Who is allowed to make which decisions? How do we work together? How many strict rules are there? There is a structure in every organizational model. You just described that you are very hierarchically structured, so your organization chart looks very classical like a pyramid. At the top is the CEO, below him the department heads, then the team leaders, and so on. Nevertheless, every coffee bar, every barista, every employee has their own room for maneuver. So there are predefined standards, and at the same time, not every employee is given strict work instructions, or allowed to make his own decisions.

Christian: Yes, right. It is often the case that employees know each other and exchange information. For example, the CEO might talk directly with a clerk, bypassing multiple hierarchical layers. Employees from different locations, who are not on the same org chart, know each other from a training they attended and might exchange experiences. The administrator in one department is married to the head of another department. These are all examples of the many, different ways in which information flows and how relationships and exchange of knowledge develop. In the past, this was called bypassing the official channel.

Michael: [*smirks*] So the bypassing of official channels is part of the collaborative model. That also only works with guard rails and a few basic rules.

Christian: What ultimately underlies the structure of a company are relationships between people.

Michael: It is all about the people.

Christian: Trust and respect!

An intriguing perspective. So my organization does not necessarily follow a scripted model. I am not forced to choose between hierarchy and holacracy, I can take the best of all forms of organization. It is important that I clearly define decision-making powers and the structure, and that everyone has the same understanding of the organization in our company. No matter which form I choose, Purpose, Vision, Values, and Strategies help employees and managers to make their own quick decisions in the interest of the company and the fulfillment of each individual.

THE GREATEST STRATEGY MODEL OF ALL TIME...

PURPOSE, VISION, VALUES, STRATEGIES

Christian: Tell me, how do you actually manage a company? How do you do that?

Michael: That is my favorite question. Can I tell you a story about it?

Christian: Please do!

Michael: I had already mentioned that I was in Qatar in the Middle East for a while on business. I was extraordinarily lucky to establish a start-up there for the company I was working for. At the beginning, we were a very small team, with just four of us. Then we grew relatively quickly and were 20 people. We simply started being a new company. I somehow had a very strange feeling about it. We didn't have a clever plan and I had the feeling that we didn't really know what we were doing.

Christian: You had an operative frenzy?

Michael: Yes, absolutely. We were just bluffing. We were running around like headless chickens. It's a pretty brutal picture, but that's how it was.

Christian: My father always says, "Operative frenzy replaces mental calm."

Michael: [*smiles*] Yeah, that's exactly what happened. I became more and more aware every day that we had to change something. We didn't have a CEO back then. It wasn't clear exactly what my role in the start-up would be. All I knew was that I was part of the top team and had commercial responsibility. We were under totally insane time pressure to get something up and running and get our product to market. At some point it was like, "We found a CEO. Next week, we'll have a first workshop together with him." The workshop was held in a huge meeting room in the Sheraton Hotel overlooking the Persian Gulf. It was a really impressive location. Then there was this moment that I will never forget. Grahame, the new CEO, got up and stood next to a flipchart. He drew three circles on it. First one, then two more circles underneath and next to it a heart. Then he drew a horizontal line from the bottom of the heart into the intersection of the three circles and said, "This is how we are going to run this company."

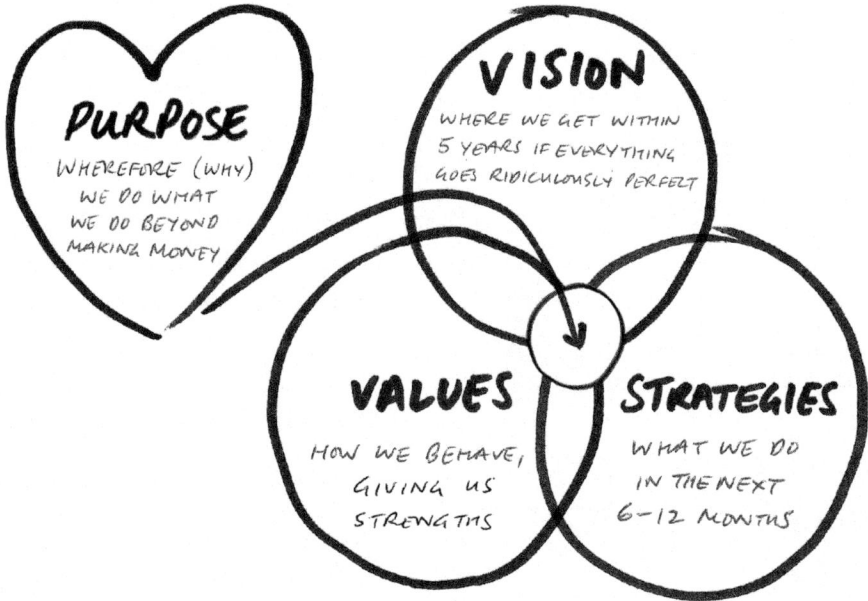

Illustration: The Greatest Strategy Model of all Times
Works for individuals, couples, teams and organizations.

Christian: There was first of all silence, right?

Michael: It was dead silent. The whole room was looking at him. I looked up into the sky gratefully and thought, "Dear God, dear universe, thank you so much for sending us this guy. I think he knows what he's doing and how to run a company." Grahame wrote the word *Purpose* over the heart and said, "Purpose is why we do what we do beyond making money."

Christian: We have already talked about that. We have adopted this as our definition of Purpose.

Michael: Right. In the upper circle, he wrote *Vision* in big letters. A little smaller, in the same circle he wrote *BHAG*—Big, Hairy, Audacious Goal—and the word *where*. And he said, "This is where we will get in five years." In the circle in the bottom left corner, he wrote *Values,*, "This is how we will behave." In the last circle, bottom right, he wrote *"Strategies."* He said, "This is what we will do in the next twelve months." Beside the word *Purpose* and the word *Values,* he painted an infinity-sign and declared, "This will always be our Purpose and our Values will remain. It is our DNA." He wrote the year 2013 in the *Vision* circle. It was 2008 back then and he said, "That is our five-year Vision." Next to *Strategy* he wrote "2009." These are the concrete actions we will be taking over the next twelve months. And then he concluded by saying, "This is my model, my framework, my belief. This is how we are going to run this company."

Christian: So there was no choice anymore?

Michael: No, that was his model and that's it. It was good that way. As CEO, of course, he has the ability to make such a stipulation. From my point of view, he came at exactly the right time, because we were in a complete vacuum regarding leadership.

Christian: It is basically not rocket science. It's the W-questions that we also learn when we call for help: Wherefore? Where to? Who? How? What?

Michael: The big questions of life.

Christian: Right. The big questions that are answered. It is striking. So how did he actually incorporate it into the company? Was everyone able to recite it by heart after a certain period of time?

Michael: Good point. It was a good start and some of us must have thought, "It's great to have a model. I'm sure it will be available later as a PowerPoint slide and maybe as a brochure."

Christian: [*grins*] "We'll print them out and make them disappear into the desk."

Michael: Yeah, right. Or we can hang it on the wall. Fortunately, it wasn't like that. It was followed by a process that took seven or eight months. Together with eight people on the leadership team, we defined our Purpose, Vision, Values, and Strategies. The Values took the longest. At the same time, we continued to build the company, it was going at full speed. We grew very fast. In the first year we were already at 100 people. We completed the model and included all employees. Grahame made it clear very quickly that this is not a grassroots-democratic event, that we need to get input from all employees, get all employees involved, and that the responsibility lies with us. It is our management task, also in the interest of the shareholders, to determine what the DNA of our company is. That is how we have done it. We have held many workshops where we gathered the thoughts, input from employees on our Purpose, Vision, Values, and Strategies. After eight months we organized an All-Hands. We pulled all employees out of the company for a day and took time for a full day meeting; all hands, all employees, were there. We started the day by presenting our plan. It was like a show, in a positive sense. We thought very carefully about who said what and that each of us would say something. It was important for us to get our plan to the point and let the exact words of our plan speak for themselves without explaining much. Our master plan got through to all 90 people sitting in the room with us. Coaches provided support and moderated us through this process. We did group work to review and understand each component of the plan in mixed groups. In the afternoon, the functional teams went out and developed their own plan for the department based on the master plan and shared it with the other departments.

Christian: What exactly did they work on in the teams? The Strategies? On what needs to be done next year to achieve the Vision? Because Purpose, Values, and Vision are fixed, right? There is no more discussion about that.

Michael: Right. We no longer discussed our Purpose, Vision, and Values. That was exactly the point. We sought input on that beforehand, which was very valuable. The intention of the day was to communicate, clarify, and align. We communicated our plan, the model, clarified questions that might have arisen, and aligned ourselves with it together. The goal was that we all move in the same direction with what we do and that everything pays off in terms of our Vision. That's why we set out the four or five major Strategies. So it was clear to everyone what are the big things that we want to accomplish in the next six to twelve months in order to move forward, to achieve our

Vision. What we didn't specify was what the individual departments, i.e., every employee, would do to contribute to this. That's what the teams worked on that day themselves. So, at the beginning, we presented the five things we wanted to have achieved by the end of the twelve months and then gave the teams the opportunity to decide for themselves what contribution they wanted to make. "What do you want to do? What can happen in your department so that we can achieve these five things?" We also used a great method for this, which we have already talked about. *Stop-Start-Continue*. In strategic planning, it's super important to take into account what we won't be doing anymore. Which tasks or projects do we stop? What do we stop with immediate effect? Until then, I had never thought about that. There were always more things that we wanted to do. At some point it was no longer feasible within the time frame. That's why we first asked what we will stop doing from now on. Then we thought about what we would continue to do because it proved to be sensible. Only at the end did we ask ourselves what we wanted to do additionally. What do we want to do that we have not yet done to achieve our goals?

Christian: I'll take the example of the Mount Everest ascent again, which we used for the Vision. I think about which steps lead me in the right direction and which do not. I simply leave the latter out because they don't take me to the summit. For example, I stop selling umbrellas at the base camp because it' s raining. Maybe I better leave that out.

Michael: I may have already brought equipment or thought about tools and tactics to help me climb Everest. On site at another planning meeting, I have new insights, additional information, and I realize, "Okay, good. That was a good idea at the time, now we need something else. We'd better not drag that up with us." So I decided to leave this part of the equipment at the base camp, because otherwise I would unnecessarily use up power and oxygen.

Christian: When you implemented this process, you had already been working operationally for two or three years, right? The company had been running for a while before the new CEO came in.

Michael: No, no. Grahame came after only two months. That was where we were really lucky. That someone with such clarity took on this leadership role, I have only experienced this one time in my professional life. It was like a gift from heaven. I have learned very, very much during this time. I was there for four years in total and experienced how we really lived this model. We used this model to run this company all the time. I admit, sometimes this consistency got on my nerves a little bit. "Can't we do something different or try something new?," "No, we'll stay on course. That is our plan. This is how we are going to run this company. If you don't like it, you can leave."

Christian: How did he manage to maintain this consistency?

Michael: Repeat, repeat, repeat. We had already introduced the *Chief Repeating Officer.* I learned that from Grahame. His expression or analogy he used was a scratched record. He was a bit older. I had barely caught vinyl records, so I knew what he meant: constant repeating, over and over again. We repeated our master plan in all forms and also encouraged people to repeat it, to think it through. That is the big success factor, the big difference. I understood it then for the first time. Having a Strategy developed by a few smart people is only five percent of the secret. Ninety-five percent of the job is to get it into the heads and hearts of all employees. After all, they are the ones who ultimately implement these Strategies.

Christian: How did he do that in concrete terms? Did he repeat it in every meeting, or were there special meetings for it? Was there a newsletter? What did these repetitions look like specifically?

Michael: Rhythm was a big issue. We held the All-Staff or All-Hands meetings I just mentioned every quarter. Once a year, we took a whole day for this. In the other quarters, the meeting lasted half a day. In each of these meetings, we repeated the big master plan, explained what it was all about, what we intended to do. We then developed this together with the employees over and over again in the small groups. Also in all the other regular meetings— top team meetings or regular team meetings— our Purpose, Vision, Values, and Strategies were constantly brought up. In everything we did, we always asked ourselves the question of whether this really paid off in terms of our Vision, our goals, our Purpose, and our Values. This discussion was omni-present. It almost had something religious about it. After a few years, there were 400 of us and everyone got it, in every conversation, in every meeting it was the topic. You could have asked any of the 400 people, anybody could have recited our Purpose, Vision, and Values. Nobody needed to read it. Some of them could list every single Value and the precise definition by heart. We did not force them to learn it. They just thought it was cool and identified with it. All our processes led to everyone constantly repeating and reflecting on it, which of course encouraged it. In annual interviews, in employee reviews, feedback interviews, job interviews, it was always a topic. Do you fit our Purpose, our Vision, our Values? The Strategies came at the end. The exciting thing is that once the Purpose, Vision, and Values have been defined, establishing the annual Strategy is totally easy.

Christian: Were you successful with it?

Michael: Yes. Our Vision was to become the best known and most popular brand in the country within five years— the #1 brand. We measured that with the NPS and brand awareness scores. We actually achieved that and even sooner than we thought. The whole country was talking about us, we were the benchmark. "We want to do it the way they do it." Our Purpose was *to make a world of difference for all people in Qatar*. This was often confirmed to us in many places. And we really did make a difference for all. It was a really nice feeling to make a difference both for the lower class workers, the poor who came from many distant countries, and the super-rich Qatari people who are native there. It was a huge success. We went public with a 2.2 billion dollar valuation and within four years we had a turnover of 500 million dollars. Of course, there were many other things that played a role in making this happen. I would not go so far as to say that the model was the only reason for our success. We were lucky in many ways and were in the right place at the right time. It felt quite remarkable to achieve this with such clarity and at such a pace.

Christian: Cool.

Okay, so slowly we are getting closer to the whole thing. You have talked so much about Purpose, Vision, Strategies, and Values that I was already convinced that this is a clever method. However, you have merely whetted my appetite and I'm eager to learn even more about how you actually implement this operationally in a large company. I have the feeling that there is still more to come. I like this guy Grahame.

...AND HOW WE TAKE EVERYONE ALONG
THE STRATEGY KICK-OFF

Christian: We have already talked about the great Strategy model: Purpose, Vision, Values, Strategy. Now I would like to know specifically how I manage to implement this in my company. How do I communicate it most skillfully? How do I take all employees with me? A lot of *how* questions.

Michael: If you'd like, I'd be happy to share some of my experiences.

Christian: That was my hope. I know that you have a lot of experience on the topic and offer special workshops on it.

Michael: The model you just described—Purpose, Vision, Values, Strategies—I call it *the greatest Strategy model of all times*. It has always worked, so I am absolutely convinced of it. I have been using it for about 12 years. We have already clarified how we will achieve our Purpose and our Vision. We have also discussed how I identify the common Values in my company that reflect our strengths and help us to achieve our goals. After that, I define the Strategies for the next six to twelve months that will lead to the goals being achieved and bring us a step closer to our Vision. When this has been done by top management or by the leadership team (depending on what I want to call it), the question arises, as you rightly say, how I now integrate this Strategy model throughout the entire company. How do I ensure that my 10, 50, 100, 500, 2,000 employees understand and implement the model? I do this in a collaborative way. Once or twice a year, all employees come together to create exactly this alignment. Alignment for the common direction, the common goal, and the necessary Strategies and actions to achieve the goal. For example, the process looks like this: We all meet together in a beautiful location, ideally outdoors in the countryside where we have a wide view. For strategic topics it helps to be in a different, free environment where I can let my gaze wander into the distance. It has an inspiring and liberating effect. I have a better perspective and can stand above things and see them from a new angle. For the first 10 minutes, we look back at the successes of the past and celebrate ourselves for it. We celebrate success. Surely you've done that too, right? When you have achieved an important corporate goal, it's great to celebrate it together and maybe give a short speech.

Christian: We always went to a Mexican restaurant and ate there. Unfortunately, celebrating often falls short. It's a good thing to remember and celebrate the small and big successes from time to time. That lifts the mood. It often happens that you quickly get lost in the problems of everyday life and you don't even see the success anymore.

Michael: Yes, it is important to acknowledge and appreciate that. We sometimes put together a little slideshow with photos of the teams and the milestones reached. This could be a trade fair stand, a brand launch, or a new product. I think it's nice when the people who have contributed to the success are shown or named. It's a small thank you that says to them, "This is how we are going to run this company. Thanks for your help; you have made an important contribution to our Vision and Purpose in the last weeks and months." Then we explain that we have also worked on our Values, our Vision, and our Purpose during this time and present them the result. "In order to do this together, we now present to you the four, five, six most important Strategies and goals that we want to implement together with you in the coming six to twelve months." Then it's a bit like a little show.

Christian: The presenter as show master.

Michael: It's good to have someone who leads eloquently through the program. I always think of Apple and their product shows. When Steve Jobs, was up on stage, and now Tim Cook, and introduced the next revolutionizing product, there's always a huge show and a real celebration that there's something new now. All the important people are there. It's good when the whole leadership team is up front and presents the Purpose, Vision, Values and Strategies together. In our company, the first person reads out the Purpose statement, which takes about 20 seconds. Then the second one goes a little further and says, for example, "Our grand Vision is... By the year, XY we will achieve... We measure this with the following criteria..." We just read it out, there is no interpretation or further words. Then the next one comes forward and adds, "Our Values, which give us strength on the way to our goals, are A, B, C." Then the next one says, "The Value A means [*Definition of the Value A],*" then someone follows with, "The Value B means [*Definition of the Value B].*" The next person says, "The Value C means [*Definition of the Value C].*" Now the Purpose, Vision, and Values have been presented and, depending on the leadership team, everyone has said something. In the second-to-last step, someone presents the Strategies for the next few months. "The following is what we will implement together over the next six to twelve months: number one, number two, number three…" Typically, the CEO takes the last step. He shows the entire leadership model with the three circles and the heart once again on a single slide: Purpose, Vision, Values, and Strategies.

Then everyone will have heard it for sure. I strongly recommend practicing the show together before the meeting. Starting at that moment, the charisma of each individual in top management is transferred to all employees and is multiplied, as our iceberg describes it. How much is happening at that moment in terms of interpersonal relationships should never be underestimated. Either the management team manages to produce rapport in these minutes and become part of the 7±2 result set, or not. Investing sufficient preparation time in order to deliver decently is really key.

Christian: Because, of course, everyone sitting there has very fine-tuned antennas. They keep a close eye on how the top management presents and works.

Michael: Absolutely. If I'm not sure of my actions up there, I can be sure that this insecurity will multiply. This is where I, as a manager, am really expected to deliver. I don't want to build up pressure. Here it is important to be confident about what the plan is.

Christian: Is that something I can really practice?

Michael: Absolutely. I have to do one thing for 10,000 hours until I get it down and get really good at it.

Christian: If I want to be really good at presenting something in front of people, I should practice it for 10,000 hours.

Michael: Well, if it looks like it's a piece of cake for me, then I've been prepared well enough. It's like being a good magician. He makes every trick look like it's child's play, although he's worked on every single trick for years.

Now that the CEO has repeated all this a second time, a number of questions often arise that need to be clarified. Questions may be asked at this point. However, the mindset in which we are now involved as a leadership team is not to be debated. We have sought input from everyone in the process. Today, it is a matter of generating a common understanding. Now clarity is being created. Now group work is taking place. The room is divided into cross-functional groups. About seven to ten people from different teams in different ages with different experiences and roles are now sitting at one table. Round tables are best suited for this. This is about diversity. If the people do not know each other yet then all the better. For example, I roll the dice beforehand or put the teams together randomly. We then start with the first aspect of the model. I show the Purpose statement on a large screen and say, "The Purpose of our company, the reason why we do all this—beyond making money—is .... [*Purpose Statement*]." In the next seven to ten minutes everyone in turn answers the question "What does this Purpose mean to me in my role?" Each person has one minute to answer this question. The point is that everyone in the group listens for seven minutes and speaks for one minute. With 10 people, each listens nine times. And that's when the magic begins to happen. Every employee now associates himself with the company's Purpose. "If that is our Purpose, then for me, in my role, that means that I..." Everyone now reflects for himself, listens to the opinions of others, and exchanges ideas with each other. Understanding evolves, different perspectives are considered, and in the end everyone grasps the big picture and has their minds on other things besides their own work. Then the moderator asks each table what has been discussed in the last eight minutes and what has come up on the subject of Purpose. I go to each table, for example, and pick up an answer. One person at each table gives feedback for about 30 seconds.

Christian: So you get an opinion from each table, which is then incorporated into the Purpose statement?

Michael: No, the Purpose statement is not changed anymore. It's more a matter of generating a uniform understanding of it, which is also consolidated in the mind.

Christian: I was asked this question once before in a workshop. The Purpose statement is fixed and will not be changed after such a discussion.

Michael: The discussion only serves the Purpose of uniform understanding. In the end, that is the most important thing. It is not necessary that the words be chosen appropriately for everyone, but that everyone knows what is meant. That was step one. Step two is the Vision. I also project this onto the wall, visible to everyone. For all employees at the table, there are again the same tasks, only this time with reference to the Vision. "What does this Vision mean for me in my role?" This exercise also takes eight minutes. Sometimes, I mix up the groups again, not necessarily after each exercise or it will be too hectic. Once or twice is enough. Here, too, one person from each table will report on the results.

Christian: Afterwards, the same exercise is done for the Values. Is each Value discussed separately or all together?

Michael: Individually, that is very important. Usually the Values are complementary to each other, so I set up a good corridor of Values and really make sure that everybody understands and internalizes every Value. We do another eight-minute round for each Value. This time, I ask the questions a bit more concretely. They are: "What does Value A mean for me and my role?" and "What behavior have I already observed in my team that can serve as a good example for this Value?" This way, we reinforce positive examples of behavior and make it clear how we want to act within the company. This is another reason why it is important to take time for each individual Value. For each Value, there is a round, and after each round there is also a short feedback from each table to the plenum. For three Values we have three rounds, for four Values there are four rounds. I would not recommend more than four Values. The three to four crucial Values that give us strength as a company. Then, we go through our Purpose, our Vision, and the Values and deepen them, now an hour has already passed. Finally the Strategies are presented again. For those we use a different process a bit later. By now it's usually time for lunch where everyone exchanges ideas in a relaxed at-mosphere, before continuing in a slightly different mode after the break. In the second part of the day, we often start after lunch with a short energizer, something funny or even a little dance to get loose. This lifts the mood and boosts motivation. Afterwards, all employees split up into their functional teams and start with the so-called *pitch and coach*. This works as follows: Each team receives a printout of our master plan— Purpose, Vision, Values, Strategies—then retreats into different rooms. The teams now have 20 min-utes to think about exactly what this means for their team. They think about what they want to do as a team in the next six to twelve months, which tasks and projects they want to stop, and which they want to continue. This is the *Stop-Start-Continue model*. I have tried different models and tasks. This has proven to be the best method at this point. It focuses on stopping projects and prioritizing them correctly. So the employees do not see our master plan as additional goals, rather as an aid to prioritization and as a focus for their activities. They have 20 minutes to make their own plan about the proj-ects they want to pursue, stop, and restart. Now comes the actual *pitch and coach*. Two teams come together in one room and pitch their projects to the other team. They have exactly 10 minutes to do this. Not a minute longer. Afterwards, the other team gives five minutes of feedback. This means they give suggestions on how the team can make their pitch and also their plan even better. After 15 minutes, it's time to change sides. The second team presents their *start-stop-continue* projects. Team one listens carefully and gives five minutes of feedback. With four teams in the company, I need two rooms in which two teams can pitch and coach each other. With six teams, I need three rooms, and so on. If there is an uneven number of teams, I divide a group up again so that it works out. After all teams have pitched once and coached once, there is a second round. In this iteration, the teams refine their plan and pitch within another 20 minutes. In the next pitch round, the teams are redistributed once more. This means that team one now pitches to team three and vice versa. Team two is in the same room with team four. After that there is a third iteration. Team one and team four are in one room and teams two and three pitch to each other. At the end of the day, each team has refined its plan in three iterations, coached three times, and knows the plan of all teams. After that, everybody is usually pretty exhausted. We let the day end with a beer and dinner together and then we all fall into bed satisfied. We did all this in just one day.

Christian: You said that feedback is given in the coaching mode. How do you moderate this?

Michael: That's a good question. The role of the leadership team is very important on this day. They are on stage in the morning and act as coaches in the afternoon. They walk through the rooms, answer open questions, see if the teams need support, and help if necessary. They do not actually sit at the tables. Although this is entirely possible, depending on how the company, the culture, and the leadership works. In the afternoon, the team leaders often take the lead. They moderate in the respective rooms or have thought about who to accept as co-moderator. When it comes to feedback, the team leaders set a good example as managers. They formulate their feedback positively and also make sure that this is adhered to throughout the feedback process. It is their task to assert themselves as leaders and ensure that their team is in the right mindset. The idea is more like, "My feedback is a gift, and it serves to help you make your plan and pitch even better." It's not about rattling off wild ideas or positioning yourself.

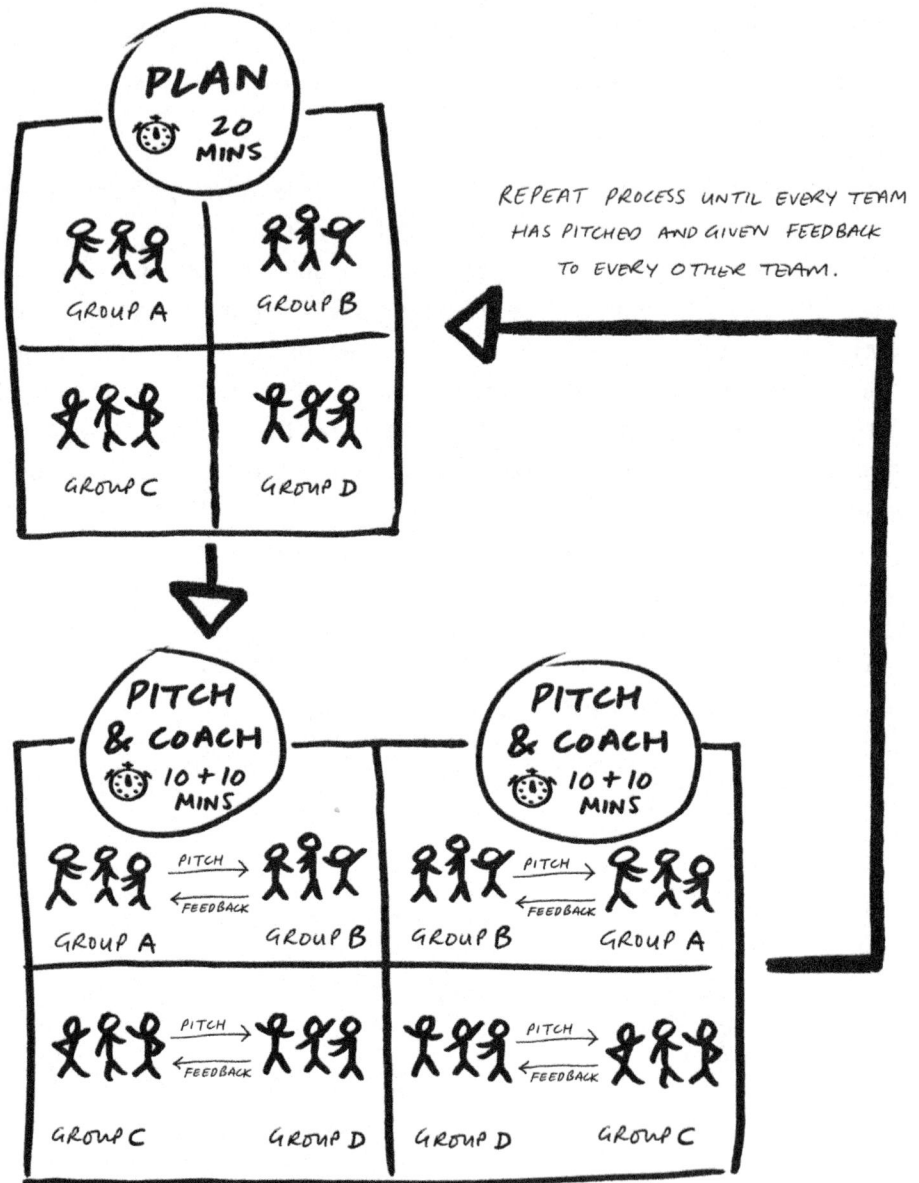

Illustration: PLAN-PITCH-COACH
This is an effective method of taking all employees along in a workshop format.

Christian: The participants are usually still in a positive mindset from the morning, when they internalized the company's Values, goals and, above all, its Purpose. This was also about the question of how we want to work together.

Michael: Right. The whole day is spent planning the future. *What will I do in the future?* It's not about pointing out problems or discussing why something won't work. It's about finding solutions.

Christian: One single day and everyone is there. I took them all along with me on just one day.

Michael: Great. Everyone is thrilled that they now know the big master plan and have been able to work on it. They have understood what contribution they themselves and others can make. They are happy that the management team has included them and feel Valued. The grand Vision and Strategies often have a mysterious aura. Now they can participate in it themselves and plan their own contribution within the team. I, as a CEO or leadership team, am happy that the implementation works virtually on its own.

Here we go. Here we have something that we can sink our teeth into. This is what I have been waiting for. That's the difference true leaders make: living a Vision, a Purpose as well as the Values within the company rather than just placing a fancy statement on the website. That's how all of this really makes a difference. It's actually quite simple when everyone on the top team is convinced and goes along with it. Then the master plan works, then I have high-performance-kick-ass teams and I am ready for the challenges of the future. This is how great things can be achieved. A great example!

CULTURE AND BRAND

CONGRUENCE BUILDS TRUST

Christian: Michael, we've talked a lot about how to achieve relaxed productivity in my company. We've talked about communication and culture. What we haven't talked about so far is how I can communicate the corporate culture to the outside world to win new customers. We have talked about Purpose and why we do what we do beyond just making money and creating jobs. We haven't talked much about making money and the necessary external communication. So how do I transport everything we have discussed in the previous chapters to my potential customers? How do I get my customers' attention so that they might think, "Hey, they have a great corporate culture. They stand for something and do what they do for a very specific reason."

Michael: Let's take a look at the big picture. Ever since we humans have existed, every single one of us has learned to build relationships with other humans. We have learned to recognize who is similar and who is different from ourselves. Through our behavior, we have developed a relatedness, a rapport with each other. This has been deeply ingrained in our behavior for 300,000 years. At the same time, the concept of brand has existed for about 150 years. Since then, the term has evolved into what it stands for today. Nowadays, it leads to a high valuation on the stock market. Up to 30% of the Value of a successful company is made up of the brand, and thus the name of the company. The question I ask myself is, to whom does this brand actually belong, and above all, *where* does it actually exist, and why is it worth so much money? Does it exist only in my head? If I say "Coca Cola" or "Disney," where do these brands exist? In your and my head! We shape them in our minds in the same way we shape and connect with other people. A brand can become like a human being for us. A brand has something very emotional and humane attached to it.

Christian: I judge a person by how I get to know him, by how he behaves towards me. I don't know what this person is really like. I can only assume how this person is according to what I feel. And it is the same with companies. Even with a company, as an outsider, I do not know what it is really like. I can only evaluate how it behaves towards me and what I feel. I only experience the brand from the outside.

Michael: So it's all about charisma and communication again. In interpersonal relationships, we always say how important it is as a manager to be flexible and to adapt one's own communication to different types. With a brand, I see it somewhat differently.

Christian: If I imagine a brand that always responds flexibly to everyone, I can't establish what it actually stands for. There is no uniform or clear message.

Michael: Right! Keyword differentiation. Differentiation is very important for a brand. For a manager, it is rather difficult. If I differentiate myself strongly as an executive, I may provoke results that I don't want to have. For a brand, however, I find it very important. When it comes to brand communication, I always think of the old *Blues Brothers* movie.41 The two brothers are named Jake and Elwood and have each other's names tattooed on the knuckles of their fingers. And that reminds me of an even older movie42 where the bad guy also has the words *LOVE* and *HATE* tattooed on the knuckles of his fingers. When his hands are clenched into a fist, one fist has the words *LOVE* and the other *HATE* written on it. The characteristic of a strong brand is that it is both loved and hated. Strong brands polarize. Some people love them, some hate them, and few have no connection to them at all. McDonald's is a good example. Some love it. They say they like it, they think it's great and the kids have fun. Others hate McDonald's. They say it's not healthy, makes you fat, is not sustainable, and so on. There are very few people who have no opinion about McDonald's. McDonald's is a powerful brand. Let's get back to the topic of brand and psychology. *People like people who are like themselves.* That also applies to brands. *People like brands that are like themselves.* I like brands that I can identify with because they fit me.

Christian: Unless you are a mismatcher.

Michael: That's right. Then maybe I'm into brands that are completely different to create a contrast or make a statement, well observed. Mismatchers

---

41 US-American film comedy from the year 1980.
42 https://en.wikipedia.org/wiki/The_Night_of_the_Hunter_(film).

actually deal with brands differently. They don't like the mainstream, but may choose a brand in protest to make a difference. They do not want to follow the masses. It is, so to speak, the differentiation from the differentiation. I mismatch with what actually fits me because I don't like it when something fits me. Let's talk again about the vast majority of matchmakers.

Christian: The Values of a company also polarize. In the best case, employees love the company Values. Those who have no use for them are better off going elsewhere. So how do I transfer these Values to my brand and communicate them to the outside world?

Michael: I think of it as a two-sided coin. On one side are the company Values, our core Values. Each of them has its own definition and there is a common understanding within the company. We have already talked about this a lot. On the other side of the coin is the personality of the brand. The Values within the company and the personality of a brand are not the same thing. I prefer to use the word congruent. Values and brand have to be congruent if I want it to work well.

CULTURE + BRAND
TWO SIDES OF ONE COIN

Illustration: Two Sides of a Coin
Culture and brand are inextricable from each other. They are two sides of the same coin and not necessarily the same.

Christian: How can I tell that the two are congruent? Or, put another way, how can I tell that it is not congruent?

Michael: By authenticity. If someone says about a company, "That's not authentic at all, I don't buy it. It doesn't fit them at all," then the two sides of the coin are not congruent. The company will have a hard time in the market. To project something to the outside that does not exist on the inside is rarely successful. Let me give you an example: Imagine the following message of a brand. "We care about you. We care about you and your family. You are in good hands here. For us, people are the center of attention. Happy Harmony."

Christian: Sounds like an insurance company.

Michael: At the same time, the culture of this company embodies core Values like, "We step on the gas, we deliver results, we make rational decisions, and are numbers-driven." These Values don't really fit into the family-like, harmonious atmosphere I have just described. Employees in the company will find it difficult to convey a brand to the outside world that is the opposite of the inner structure.

Christian: Let's assume it to actually be an insurance company, then I would probably sense this as a customer. If I have a claim, they might not get approved or costs might not be reimbursed. I either get cut off on the phone in seconds or don't get through to anyone. I may feel ripped off and like I'm not being treated as a human being. As a customer, I sense that what they communicate to the outside world is not true.

Michael: Right. In this case, brand and culture are two different sides of the same coin, but they are not congruent. And such a coin is worth nothing. Companies in their start-up or growth phases find it easier to build a strong brand. This is an opportunity to cultivate a strong culture with Purpose, Vision, and Values right from the start. These are the cornerstones of a company. When it comes to culture, the Strategies are not important yet. When I know where I want to go, how we behave, and why we do it, I take the second step. In the second step, I look at the market to see who the other players are, and how they operate and perform. Based on this, I look for a gap in which I can position myself and differentiate with my culture, my behavior, my strengths and my Vision. In the best case I radiate something from inside and outside that no competitor radiates.

Christian: When it comes to shaping the corporate culture, my efficiency is somewhat limited because the culture of a company depends very much on the founders and the first employees who shape the company. Both result in the DNA of the company, which is the basis of the culture. Basically, I first discover the culture of my company and then pass it on to new employees. With the brand, I have more creative freedom from the beginning, or am I wrong?

Michael: Yes and no. You're absolutely right about the first part of your statement. As a founder, I automatically bring my personality and set of Values to the table. Both flow into the culture I develop in a company. If I am aware of this, I can manage the corporate culture much more effectively and make it strong.

Christian: I don't really have much of a choice, do I? I can only formulate and communicate it well.

Michael: You mean the internal Values?

Christian: Yes.

Michael: Yes, that's right. It is difficult and not necessarily advisable to integrate a code of Values into my company as a founder that differs greatly from my own. At some point, I would no longer feel comfortable in my own company. Maybe it would be possible if I planned my personal exit from the beginning and therefore considered it very dissociated. As a start-up founder, I can of course say, "I will build it up like this for a year or two and then hand it over to someone else." That could work. Still, I think it is much more successful and above all, it is much more fun and easier to build a company that suits me.

Christian: It's different when I have a large, long-established company and want to change the culture. That is a long change process. Such projects are usually really big, take a long time, and only work sometimes.

Michael: Oh yes. In my opinion, changing the culture of a company is the biggest challenge in a business context. There are many stories of companies that wanted to change at the core. It worked for a few, not for many.

Christian: Let's get back to the external perception, to the brand. Here I have a lot more creative freedom. It is important to make sure that it is congruent with the culture.

Michael: The word congruent limits my creative freedom, of course. My Purpose, Vision, and Values determine the direction in the positioning of a brand. I can then freely arrange the detailed positioning. But there is also competition in the market. Ideally, I differentiate myself from the other play-ers with my brand and do not position myself in the same field as my com-petitors. Only in a cut-throat competition could it make sense to position myself in the same or similar field. Here I convince customers with other arguments, with product quality or the price, not with the brand. In the tele-communications sector, for example, there is cut-throat competition. The brands look very similar and hardly differentiate themselves from each oth-er. At least, that was the case years ago when this industry was consolidat-ing. Many telecommunications companies were red, magenta, or white with a plain font. They were gladly bought out by competitors who looked similar. It is a tactic to dress the bride to match the potential groom and make her look pretty for him.

Christian: The products on this market are simply interchangeable. I get internet access, bandwidth, and a telephone line. What else is important when it comes to brand and culture?

Michael: Well, the important thing is to understand who I am, what my preferences are as a founder or CEO, and what my brand should stand for. It is crucial to keep the two things apart and not to confuse myself with the brand. I actually once accompanied someone who did this very successfully. He himself was very results-oriented and people-oriented in our personality model. An extroverted type. He had a lot of yellow and red energy, orange probably describes him best. He succeeded in building a company that functioned very analytically. He even took on a rather introverted role, where accuracy and logic were very important. He did a lot of data-based analysis. He quickly became aware of the difference. Together, we developed a brand that was modern, youthful, and had analytical traits at the same time. It was always a balancing act between these two facets. Especially when we were discussing strategic topics, there were always situations where his creative thinking kicked in. At some point, he became more aware of this and was quicker to come around: "That's a great idea and I would really enjoy this personally. And it's not the right thing for our brand." He was fully aware that he had a different personality type than the brand he had built. He stood above that and could handle it well.

Christian: So he has managed to keep the brand and culture congruent despite his own, different personality type.

Michael: Yes, as far as I can tell. And I imagine it was very exhausting for him and the people around him.

I find that comprehensible. What I communicate to the outside world is only credible if I am convinced of it myself on the inside. This applies to me as much as it does to a company. If what I say and what I do, as an individual and as a company, are not the same, something is amiss. If on the contrary, what I say is congruent with what I do, then, both I and the company are authentic.

MAKE MONEY

MONEY IS A MEANS TO A PURPOSE

Christian: For us, a lot revolves around our Purpose. Purpose is what we do all this for, apart from making money. Now I want to talk about making money.

Michael: Rightly so. This, too, is important. Basically, it's about how I lead: how I lead myself, how I lead people, and how I lead a company. Management means responsibility, including the financial state of the company. Without money, there is little I can do to fulfill my Purpose and achieve the Vision. Without money, I cannot maintain employees who live our Values and act according to them. Without money, I go bankrupt and my employees leave the company. Values or not. Unfortunately, it doesn't work without money.

Christian: To keep the company stable, to achieve the Vision and fulfill my Purpose, I earn money. In doing so, I can weather any storm, such as losing a large customer or persevering during an economic crisis.

Michael: Exactly. The bottom line is that if I lead in a relaxed, productive way and fulfill my Purpose, I may make a lot of money.

Illustration: Earning money
Only if the money-making works can we as a company fulfill our Purpose and achieve our Vision through Strategies in line with our Values—for the benefit of all people involved, both inside and outside the company. It will not work without money.

That's it—relaxed and productive.

BIBLIOGRAPHY

CHAPTER 1 - LEADING ME

Favorite Books

Achor, Shawn. *The Happiness Advantage: The Seven Principles of Positive Psychology That Fuel Success and Performance at Work.*

Byrn, Rhonda. *The Secret.*

Covey, Stephen. *7 Habits of Highly Effective People.*

Dweck, Carol. *Mindset: Changing The Way You Think To Fulfil Your Potential.*

Kahneman, Daniel. *Thinking, Fast and Slow.*

Kishimi, Ichiro and Koga, Fumitake. *The Courage To be Disliked: How to Free Yourself, Change Your Life And Achieve Real Happiness.*

Plato. *Allegory of the Cave.*

Strelecky, John. *The Big Five for Life: What Really Matters in Life.*

Great Books

Albom, Mitch. *Tuesdays with Morrie: An Old Man, a Young Man, and Life's Greatest Lesson.*

Ariely, Dan. *Predictably Irrational, Revised: The Hidden Forces That Shape Our Decisions.*

Brafman, Ori. *Sway: The Irresistible Pull Of Irrational Behavior.*

Clear, James. *Atomic Habits: Tiny Changes, Remarkable Results.*

Csikszentmihaly, Mihaly. *Flow: The Psychology of Optimal Experience.*

Deida, David. *The Way of the Superior Man: A Spiritual Guide to Mastering the Challenges of Women, Work, and Sexual Desire.*

Duhigg, Charles. *The Power of Habit: Why We Do What We Do, and How to Change*.

Emmons, Robert A. *Gratitude Works!: A 21-Day Program for Creating Emotional Prosperity*.

Frankel, Lois P. *Nice Girls Don't Get the Corner Office: Unconscious Mistakes Women Make That Sabotage Their Careers (A NICE GIRLS Book)*.

Goldsmith, Marshall und Reiter, Mark. *Triggers: Creating Behavior That Lasts – Becoming the Person You Want to Be*.

Goldsmith, Marshall und Reiter, Mark. *What Got You Here Won't Get You There: How Successful People Become Even More Successful*.

Harris, Dan. *Meditation for Fidgety Skeptics: A 10% Happier How-to Book*.

Hicks, Esther and Hicks, Jerry. *The Law of Attraction: The Cosmic Law Behind THE SECRET*.

Hodgkinson, Tom. *How to Be Idle: A Loafer's Manifesto*.

Lama, Dalai and Tutu, Desmond. *The Book of Joy*.

Levitin, Daniel J. *The Organized Mind: Thinking Straight in the Age of Information Overload*.

Merath, Stefan. *Der Weg zum erfolgreichen Unternehmer: Wie Sie und Ihr Unternehmen neue Dynamik gewinnen (Dein Business)*.

O'Connor, Joseph und Seymour, John. *Introducing NLP: Psychological Skills For Understanding And Influencing People*.

Pletzer, Marc A. *Die Cappuccino-Strategie: Besser Ziele erreichen*.

Rendall, David. *Pink Goldfish: Defy Normal, Exploit Imperfection and Captivate Your Customers*.

Stankiewicz, Piotr. *Does Happiness Write Blank Pages? On Stoicism and Artistic Creativity*.

Tan, Chade-Meng. *Search Inside Yourself: The Unexpected Path to Achieving Success, Happiness (and World Peace)*.

Vanderkam, Laura. *168 Hours: You Have More Time Than You Think*.

Vanderkam, Laura. *What the Most Successful People Do Before Breakfast: How to Achieve More at Work and at Home*.

Watzlawick, Paul. *The Situation is Hopeless, But Not Serious: The Pursuit of Unhappiness*.

Watzlawick, Paul.*Ultra-Solutions: How to Fail Most Successfully*.

Williams, Caroline. *My Plastic Brain: One Woman's Year Long Journey to Discover If Science Can Improve Her Mind*.

CHAPTER 2 - LEADING OTHERS

Favorite Books

Blanchard, Ken and Cigarmi, Patricia. *The Minute Manager: Leadership Styles: Situational Leadership (Completely revised edition for today's managers)*.

Bungay Stanier, Michael. *The Coaching Habit: Say Less, Ask More & Change the Way You Lead Forever*.

Landsberg, Max. T*he Tao of Coaching: Boost Your Effectiveness at Work by Inspiring and Developing Those Around You*.

Rosenberg, Marshall B. und Chopra, Deepak. *Nonviolent Communication: A Language of Life: Life-Changing Tools for Healthy Relationships*.

Great Books

Carnegie, Dale. *How to Win Friends and Influence People*.

Chapman, Gary. *The 5 Languages of Love: How to Communicate in a Relationship*.

Charvet, Shelle Rose. *Words That Change Minds: The 14 Patterns for Mastering the Language of Influence (English Edition)*.

Dörner, Dietrich. *The Logic of Failure: Strategic Thinking in Complex Situations*.

Grinder, John and Bandler, Richard. *The Structure of Magic a Book about Language and Therapy.*

Heen, Sheila und Stone, Douglas. *Thanks for the Feedback: The Science and Art of Receiving Feedback Well.*

Kline, Nancy. *Time to Think: Listening to Ignite the Human Mind.*

Krogerus, Mikael and Tschäppeler, Roman. *The Communication Book: 44 Ideas for Better Conversations Every Day.*

Nasher, Jack. *Convinced!: How to Prove Your Competence & Win People Over.*

Rosenzweig, Phil. *The Halo Effect: ... and the Eight Other Business Delusions That Deceive Managers.*

Schulz von Thun, Friedemann. *Miteinander reden 1-4 (Faltschachtel): Störungen und Klärungen / Stile, Werte und Persönlichkeitsentwicklung / Das "Innere Team" und situationsgerechte Kommunikation / Fragen und Antworten.*

CHAPTER 3 - LEADING TEAMS

Favorite Books

Allen, David. *Getting Things Done: The Art of Stress-free Productivity.*

Boynton, Andy und Fischer, Bill. *Virtuoso Teams: Lessons from Teams That Changed Their Worlds.*

Collins, Jim und Hansen, Morten T. *Great by Choice: Uncertainty, Chaos, and Luck – Why Some Thrive Despite Them All.*

Gawande, Atul. *The Checklist Manifesto: How to Get Things Right.*

Lencioni, Patrick. *The Five Dysfunctions of a Team.*

Schmidt, Eric et al. *Trillion Dollar Coach: The Leadership Handbook of Silicon Valley's Bill Campbell.*

Smart, Geoff et al. *Who: The A Method for Hiring.*

Wiseman, Liz. *Multipliers, Revised and Updated: How the Best Leaders Make Everyone Smarter.*

Great Books

Bossidy, Larry et al. *Execution: The Discipline of Getting Things Done.*

DeMarco, Tom. *The deadline: A Novel About Project Management.*

Fried, Jason and Heinemeier Hansson, David. *ReWork: Change the Way You Work Forever.*

Gladwell, Malcolm. *The Tipping Point: How Little Things Can Make a Big Difference.*

McChrystal, Stanley et al. *Team of Teams: New Rules of Engagement for a Complex World.*

Pritchett, Bob. *Fire Someone Today: And Other Surprising Tactics for Making Your Business a Success.*

Rath, Tom. *Develop your strengths: with the StrengthsFinder 2.0.*

Rogelberg, Steven. *The Surprising Science of Meetings: How You Can Lead your Team to Peak Performance.*

Scott, Kim. *Radical Candor: Fully Revised and Updated Edition: How to Get What You Want by Saying What You Mean.*

CHAPTER 4 - LEADING ORGANIZATIONS

Favorite Books

Collins, Jim. *Good to Great: Why Some Companies Make the Leap...And Others Don't.*

Drucker, Peter F. *The Effective Executive: The Definitive Guide to Getting the Right Things Done.*

Ferriss, Timothy. *The four-hour work week: more time, more money, more life.*

Sinek, Simon. *Start with Why: How Great Leaders Inspire Everyone to Take Action.*

Great Books

Amoruso, Sofia. *#GIRLBOSS.*

Bessau, Hubertus et al. *Das Startup-Buch der mymuesli-Gründer.*

Bogusky, Alex und Winsor, John. *Baked In: Creating Products and Businesses That Market Themselves.*

Clason, George. *The Richest Man in Babylon: Secrets of Success in Antiquity - The First Step to Financial Freedom.*

Daly, Jack. *Hyper Sales Growth: Street-Proven Systems & Processes. How to Grow Quickly & Profitably.*

Doerr, John. *Measure What Matters: OKRs: The Simple Idea that Drives 10x Growth.*

Drucker, Peter F. *Daily Drucker: Business Knowledge for Daily Use.*

Ferrazzi, Keith. *Never Go To Dinner Alone! And Other Secrets Around Networking and Success.*

Godin, Seth. *This is Marketing: You Can't Be Seen Until You Learn To See.*

Goldratt, Eliyahu M. and Cox, Jeff *The Goal: A Novel on Process Optimization.*

Goldsborough, Ridgely et al. *The Why Engine CEO Edition.*

Harmon, Colin. *What I Know About Running Coffee Shops.*

Harnish, Verne and Ladanyi, Nikolai. *Scaling Up. Scale Up Too! Why Some Companies Can Do It... and Why Others Get Stranded.*

Harnish, Verne. *Scaling Up.*

King, Will. *The King of Shaves Story: How I Built a Great Business in Tough Times.*

Knight, Phil. *Shoe Dog: The Official Biography of the NIKE Founder.*

Lafley, A.G. und Martin, Roger L. *Playing to Win: How Strategy Really Works.*

LeBoeuf, Michael. *The Greatest Management Principle in the World.*

Monocle Series. *The Monocle Guide to Good Business.*

Robertson, Brian J. *Holacracy: A Revolutionary Management System for a Volatile World.*

Sandberg, Sheryl. *Lean In: Women, Work, and the Will to Lead.*

Semler, Ricardo. *Maverick: The Success Story Behind the World's Most Unusual Workplace.*

Sincero, Jen. *You Are a Badass at Making Money: Master the Mindset of Wealth.*

Taleb, Nassim Nicholas. *Antifragility: Guidance for a world we do not understand.*

Taleb, Nassim Nicholas. *The Black Swan: The Power of Highly Improbable Events.*

Taylor, William C. und LaBarre, Polly G. *Mavericks at Work: Why the Most Original Minds in Business Win.*

Thiel, Peter. *Zero to One.*

Walsh, Bill et al. *The Score Takes Care of Itself: My Philosophy of Leadership.*

ILLUSTRATIONS

LEADING MYSELF

LEADING OTHERS

LEADING TEAMS

LEADING ORGANIZATIONS

ABOUT THE AUTHORS

Christian Kohlhof studied particle physics, cosmology, and economics and is a passionate sailor and coffee drinker. After a professional excursion into aviation and banking, he recognized his real talents and preferences, started his own business, and successfully founded a coffee bar chain and a coffee roasting company. Together with his business partner, he led the startup to market leadership with more than 160 coffee bars. He made a successful exit and is now following his true Purpose: helping people achieve relaxed productivity. As co-founder of the CoA Academy, he works as a trained NLP coach and shares his experience as a true leader.

Christian has been happily married for almost 20 years and is the proud father of two wonderful daughters. They live together in Munich.

Michael Portz was successfully born in the Rhineland in 1970. For more than 20 years, he has worked as a manager with big brands, he has founded companies as an entrepreneur and business angel, and he has lived on almost every continent. He draws on extraordinarily colorful experiences in building and leading teams and companies. Michael has managed up to 2,500 employees and was responsible for several hundred million dollars in sales.

He learned a lot about people, cultures, leadership, and himself, which he incorporates into his work today. As co-founder of the CoA Academy and as an executive coach, he now helps people and teams to make their lives easier and achieve their goals.

Michael's passion is music. Where there is a piano and good humored people, he loves to create special moments with his music. Michael is currently living with his three-generation family back in his home country.

Leonie Schulze Bölling has been in the digital industry for over 12 years. For much of this time she accompanied well-known brands on their way into e-commerce at Amazon, and later specialized as a digital and innovation consultant in building and empowering innovation teams, especially in the German SME sector. She always follows her very personal mission: to make people enjoy their work and motivate them to achieve better results. Since 2021, she has combined her personal purpose with her duties as Chief Executive Officer of the CoA Academy. Her cheerfulness and her openness help her to inspire and captivate the people around her. She is also a passionate author, snowboarder, and mountain climber.

AHH, YOU'VE REACHED

THE END

OR HAVE YOU?

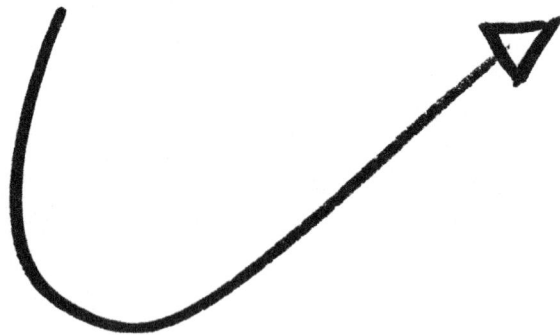

LEARN EVEN MORE
FROM TRUE LEADERS...

Would you like the opportunity to experience all these proven leadership tools and more LIVE with Michael and Christian?

Then join our **Chief of the Year** Remote Leadership Program.

After all, leadership (and life too) is always changing and challenging, faster now, than ever before. And, if you sometimes feel isolated or stressed when making decisions in your business, then our 6-12 month Chief of the Year program is just for you. We will help you to build a high-performing-kick-ass team to achieve your goals with ease.

If you've got an open mind and are interested in participating in workshops dealing with real business scenarios (including your own) in a confidential, peer-to-peer group environment facilitated by one of our professionally trained coaches, then I'd love you to come on board.

We keep our groups to a maximum of eight leaders because once you've experienced this intimate, "deep trust" within your group you'll wonder how you ever operated without this level of support at your fingertips.

At the end you'll graduate with your License to Lead Certificate and continue on with hundreds of other leaders in our leadership sharing network, the CoA Community.

Apply and schedule a first free call directly with me here and let's start your journey to become the greatest leader you can be.

Talk soon,

Leonie Schulze Bölling,
CEO, CoA Academy

Printed in Great Britain
by Amazon